AN OBSTETRICIAN ANSWERS YOUR MOST INTIMATE QUESTIONS ABOUT PREGNANCY AND CHILDBIRTH

OTHER BOOKS
BY NIELS H. LAUERSEN, M.D., PH.D.

It's Your Body: A Woman's Guide to Gynecology
Childbirth with Love

BY NIELS H. LAUERSEN, M.D., PH.D., AND EILEEN STUKANE
Listen to Your Body
PMS: Premenstrual Syndrome and You

It's Your PREGNANCY

Niels H. Lauersen,
M.D., Ph.D.

A FIRESIDE BOOK
PUBLISHED BY SIMON & SCHUSTER, INC.
NEW YORK

DESIGNED BY BARBARA MARKS

MANUFACTURED IN THE UNITED STATES OF AMERICA
10 9 8 7 6 5 4 3
LIBRARY OF CONGRESS CATALOGING IN
PUBLICATION DATA
LAUERSEN, NIELS H.
    IT'S YOUR PREGNANCY.

    "A FIRESIDE BOOK."
    INCLUDES INDEX.
    1. PREGNANCY—MISCELLANEA.   2.
CHILDBIRTH—MISCELLANEA.   I. TITLE.
    [DNLM: 1. LABOR—POPULAR WORKS. 2.
PREGNANCY—POPULAR WORKS. WQ 150 L372I]
RG525.L296 1987   618.2   87-4627
ISBN: 0-671-50211-5

TO THE LOVE AND

CARE OF ALL UNBORN

CHILDREN—HELP THEM

TO BECOME A HEALTHY

NEW GENERATION . . .

Acknowledgments

It's Your Pregnancy grew from the questions asked by my own patients and by expectant mothers who phoned or wrote from long distances. This book belongs to them, to you, and to future mothers- and fathers-to-be. Here is a guide to enhance your pregnancy by eliminating confusion over such matters as which is the most nutritious diet, what is a high-risk complication, is an episiotomy necessary, and many other issues. Thank you all for raising my consciousness about your concerns.

My most sincere gratitude also goes to each and every person who assisted in the research and preparation of this book, which was produced during long days and nights of work. All the latest research has been scrutinized and analyzed. My most sincere thanks goes to Eileen Stukane for her help in editing and perfecting *It's Your Pregnancy*. Her knowledge, judgment, and perceptions are profoundly appreciated.

My deepest appreciation also goes to Sue Janssen, who analyzed and focused the book, and added the finishing touches. Additional thanks to Judy Hendra for her initial editing and research, which created the framework for the book.

A special acknowledgment goes to Lori Leeds, my secretary, assistant, critic, researcher, and loyal friend, who has helped organize, refine, and complete the manuscript. My gratitude also goes to Donna Almodovar for her assistance in typing part of the manuscript in collaboration with Lori Leeds.

The research material was collected by Joan Affigne, Donna Almodovar, Dr. Yanni Antonopoulos, Carolyn Curtin, Carolyn Dittmar, Paula Freedman, Fidelina Gastel, Ubaldo Gastel, Rachelle Goldman, Margola Gross, Judy Hendra, Sue Janssen, Fern Kazlow, Lori Leeds, Pat Reichel, Maxine Siegler, Scott Siegler, Eileen Stukane, Allison Wardrop, and Kathy Wilson, who also helped assess and criticize some of the manuscript. My appreciation goes to each of them.

The original artwork was done by Laurel Purington Rand, Pauline Thomas, Ellen Felten, and Lynne Cooper. I wish to thank Adrian Rothenberg for her photographic and artistic advice on artwork. Heartfelt thanks also go to Lisa Kristal, Marie Lepore, and Ann Marie Ciafardini for their willingness to pose for the book jacket.

Special acknowledgments go to my agents, Diana Price and Joyce Frommer, for their support during the preparation of this manuscript.

I also wish to extend thanks to my legal adviser, Richard Allen, for his interest and advice in the project.

So many others have helped in countless ways that it is impossible to name them all, but I sincerely appreciate the effort of each and every one of them.

I again want to extend my thanks to all my patients and their partners, especially Angela and Richard Cohen, Barbara Fila, Madeline and Russell Kirk, Channie Tolchinsky, and Linda Velazco, as well as to all the women who have contacted me for advice. I appreciate their patience during the preparation of It's Your Pregnancy.

Finally my gratitude goes to Charles Woods, Eugene Brissie, and Barbara Gess—particularly Barbara Gess, senior editor on this project—for their criticism, understanding, and professional talent. They worked hand-in-hand with me to make this book clear and comprehensive.

I would finally like to extend my gratitude to the staff of Simon & Schuster for their valuable assistance in the preparation of this book.

—NIELS H. LAUERSEN, M.D., PH.D.
New York, New York

Contents

Author's Note

For the purpose of simplicity, when referring to an obstetrician in this book, I have chosen to use the male gender pronouns—*he, his, him,* etc. This gender rendering should not be viewed as a political or chauvinistic choice but rather as a means of greater clarification, making it easier to distinguish between the patient, who is always a *she,* and the doctor. On the same note, the baby is often referred to as *he* to distinguish it from its mother. From a scientific point of view, this designation is not completely correct, since in the United States, almost half of all newborns are girls. Statistics show that 1.9 million boys are born each year, as compared to 1.8 million girls.

Preface

Today women decide to have babies at different stages of their lives. My pregnant patients are young women who want to start families right away, businesswomen in their thirties who long to be mothers, and women over thirty-five—often in their forties—who achieved personal goals before choosing parenthood. These expectant mothers, and their partners, intuit their ideal times to conceive.

Having a baby is an emotional, not an intellectual, decision, and whenever the moment of conception occurs is "right." I have even examined newly pregnant women who had thought they would forgo motherhood for careers and, suddenly, they just changed their minds. A woman who decides on motherhood and finds herself pregnant, however, should take her pregnancy as a sign of nature's perfect timing.

What's important is that you're going to have a baby, and for nine months, no one can safeguard your pregnancy and care for your soon-to-be-born daughter or son as well as you can. I advise every expectant mother to feel good and to *take charge.* Throughout pregnancy and during childbirth, you are heading a team that includes you, your partner, and your obstetrician. Your choice of a knowledgeable, skillful physician whose advice you can trust is your first big decision. This is an important selection, because your doctor will be your counsel during these nine months, and many questions will arise.

Although today's expectant mothers are incredibly well informed about their options during pregnancy, they are often confused about which choices are "right" for the health of their unborn babies. My own patients, for example, find themselves in sudden quandaries. Should they eat a certain food? Take a medication? Pass through the detection system at an airport? They are also faced with decisions about genetic testing, amniocentesis, childbirth methods, episiotomies, and much more. Even with awareness, a woman often feels in conflict during pregnancy. She may seek the advice of her doctor, friends, and relatives before she selects a course of action.

After participating in seminars and being interviewed on television and radio subsequent to the publication of my recent books, I received telephone calls and letters from pregnant women all over the country who shared the questions and conflicts of my own patients. I have noticed that expectant mothers often rely quite strongly on the opinions of friends or relatives, and I have found myself saying, "But it's your pregnancy, not hers." Sometimes even the doctor's word is heeded much too automatically. For example, if you are well informed about the pros and cons of amniocentesis, the decision to have the procedure, no matter what your age, is yours!

It's Your Pregnancy grew from the questions I heard most often, from my own patients and from women who called and wrote from long distances. This book is designed as a guide to help all expectant mothers sort through the choices they must make as they move from conception to childbirth. At many points along the way, an expectant mother asks herself, "What is best for my baby?" I want her to know. Every woman deserves an honest answer.

I cannot emphasize enough that you are in control. With insight into the latest research and technological advancements, which are described in this book, you will be prepared for the tough job of decision-making during pregnancy. You, your partner, and your doctor are the team, but you are the captain. You are creating the perfect internal environment for the growth of a healthy human being. It's your pregnancy, and, finally, it's your beautiful baby.

Niels H. Lauersen, M.D., Ph.D.
Professor of Obstetrics and Gynecology,
New York Medical College,
New York City

7777777333

333

CHAPTER 1

You Are in Charge

IT'S YOUR BODY

In the seventies, health activists encouraged women to educate themselves about their bodies. The call to awareness was so widely heeded that today you probably take for granted the fact that you have a right to question your care. You can request a method of birth control that suits your life-style. You can seek a second opinion for surgery and inquire about the side effects of prescribed drugs, and you should never be less than inquisitive about the way your body works. The desire to conceive a child especially brings a need for great understanding. When you decide to become pregnant, knowledge of your body and alertness to your health options are particularly important. You are in charge of timing your conception, of creating a healthy internal environment for the developing fetus, of choosing a method of childbirth, and much more.

There are many decisions to be made during the nine months of expectancy. Do you want an obstetrician or a midwife to aid you? Where would you be happy giving birth? The foods you eat, the exercise you get, the tests you undergo are all under your control. You surely want your baby to have the best start on life, yet you can only achieve your goal by learning how to treat your pregnant body properly.

Even before you conceive, you must gain control of your body. You are preparing for your and your child's future by taking charge now. Eat a well-balanced diet supplemented with vitamins; eliminate alcohol and drugs that might be harmful to the unborn; and get plenty of rest.

Sometimes conception does not happen as quickly as you would like, and you may have to make an effort to become more attuned to your menstrual cycle. Within these pages, you will discover how to solve fertility problems. Traveling from chapter to chapter, you will be guided through conception, pregnancy, and childbirth. During pregnancy, you will be introduced to new monitoring and testing techniques, and you will hear about different approaches to childbirth. Both doctors and their patients must grasp the changing face of motherhood. You should aim to add your knowledge to your doctor's, and to strive for a perfect pregnancy.

An expectant mother must have special attention. Certain European countries require a pregnant woman to have ten to twelve prenatal checkups because so many conditions need monitoring. Through frequent screenings, complications such as high blood pressure that can lead to toxemia, the sudden onset of diabetes, premature labor, and the over- or underdevelopment of the fetus can be detected. Years ago women were not informed about the risks of pregnancy, and they suffered what today are better understood and often avoidable complications. *It's Your Pregnancy* aims to enlighten all women to their options. A woman has among her responsibilities the final word on her physician, power over her uterine environment, choices during labor and delivery. Each decision she makes affects not only her but her child, so naturally she wants her choices to be right.

The anxieties and difficulties of the months that may precede the birth of your offspring can be eased with information. Using your finely tuned instincts and the knowledge you derive from this book, you can carefully nurture the child in your womb. You may choose to experience pregnancy only once, so while it is happening, you should know that your life is being richly filled. This is a thrilling time. Soon you will be embracing the child you have conceived, and these nine months will be transformed into a gratifying memory.

THE MIRACLE OF PREGNANCY

Conception embodies all the mystery, drama, and action of life itself. For pregnancy to occur, the right egg has to link up with the right sperm, but before this encounter, a number of unbelievable events have to take place. By using only its dynamic thrust as impetus, moving as fast as a person swimming thirty miles per hour through a narrow tunnel, one sperm has to complete an awesome ten-minute mission. It has to force its way through the cervical barrier, beyond the uterus, and rush toward its target—the ovulated egg in the fallopian tube.

Millions of sperm begin that journey after ejaculation, but only a few thousand ever connect with the egg. Large numbers of sperm die in the vagina in the first few seconds of their existence. Others drop off at different points along the way as they swim toward their destination. The sperm that successfully make contact with the ovum (egg) are caught up in an intricate dance around it as they try to penetrate its outer membrane. Finally, when one sperm breaks through and enters the nucleus of the egg, a woman conceives. A chemical change in the egg then stops all other sperm from entering.

The next epic journey is the fertilized egg's seven-day trip from the fimbriated (fingerlike) end of the fallopian tube to the uterus. The egg is helped in its passage by the cilia, microscopic hairs that line the inside of the fallopian channel and nudge the egg along with their constantly swaying movements. If the egg encounters no obstructions in the tube, in five to seven days, it will firmly implant itself in the endometrium, the vascular lining that has been building in the womb since the beginning of the menstrual month. Once it is secured, the fertilized egg gains nourishment from this complex web of blood vessels, which in a week or so will become the placenta, as the egg will become an embryo.

All the elements must be right for a new life to begin. A hardy sperm must meet a receptive egg, which can only be fertilized within twenty-four hours after ovulation, in an internal environment that will promote and continue conception. Emotional attitudes, physical health, and timing are so variable, conception can seem incredibly chancy when you think about it. Yet the miracle of pregnancy will repeat itself time after time as each new generation of women becomes mothers.

When you were a teenager, you probably learned that all you needed was intercourse once without contraception and you could become pregnant. The teenage years are exceptionally fertile ones, and while the warning, "All it takes is once," may apply to those under twenty, as the years progress, the ability to conceive changes and once is sometimes not enough. Every menstruating woman must keep herself fit to enhance her fertility.

Today's women frequently postpone motherhood, preferring to establish a career first. Sometimes a couple chooses to have only one child rather than plan for a brood, and that child is carefully scheduled. Modern women are more than ever before deciding when and how they want to experience pregnancy. Whenever a woman does begin to attempt conception, however, she should be in good health. You are in charge of your body, and now that you are going to make it a nine-month home for your future daughter or son, some preparations are in order.

THERE IS NO "RIGHT TIME" TO HAVE A BABY

There really is no way to pinpoint a time in a woman's life when having a baby would be ideal. If you were considering only physical factors, you would be able to generalize and say that usually in her early twenties, a woman's reproductive organs and pelvic bones are at a stage that she could easily conceive, carry, and deliver a child. Fertility patterns change when a woman passes thirty, and conception can take longer then. But what about all the other variables in a woman's life? Her physical condition is only one part of the overall picture. The psychological, financial, and professional aspects of her life also influence her timing.

The most fertile period for a woman is in her teens, but few people would advocate pregnancy until later in life, when a woman has had a chance to develop emotionally. Yet a woman in her thirties, a person who is psychologically prepared to raise a child, is statistically less able to conceive. That is not to say that some teens might not be mature enough to become parents or that a percentage of women over thirty might not easily get pregnant, but generally, there is no time when a woman can be advised, "This is it. This is when mind and body are in concert, and you are ready to become a mother."

When you think about conception, you must look at the facts about reproduction, assess your life-style, and let your feelings about motherhood come to the fore. Yet do not plan too precisely. I have patients who have waited for the right moment to get pregnant because they were busy for a few years with this or tied up for a few months with that, and when they were finally ready, their bodies did not cooperate. Think about the timing of your children, but be flexible. I have watched couples find the greatest happiness in their lives after unplanned children have been born.

Perhaps you will be able to or already have been able to conceive exactly on schedule. Nevertheless, you should know that researchers have discovered interesting facts about fertility. The results of a study conducted by Dr. Christopher Tietze of the World Population Council show that one in ten previously fertile women will be infertile by the age of thirty-five, one in three by age forty, and seven out of eight women will be infertile by the time they are forty-five. A recent French study seems to confirm that the optimal reproductive years for a woman are those between twenty and thirty, but the extent to which fertility changes after thirty is another question. In a study of 792 unplanned first pregnancies, Dr. Alan Guttmacher discovered that on the average, women fifteen to twenty-four years old took 2 months to conceive, while those ages thirty-five to forty-four conceived in 3.8 months. Conception took longer for the older women, but only 1.8 months longer.

So women really have to know their own bodies and sense when they are drawn toward motherhood. In a study under the auspices of the Wellesley College Center for Research on Women, eighty-six couples who became parents in various decades of their lives were questioned about the timing of their children. The study showed that couples who had given birth to their first child in their early twenties later wished that they had postponed parenthood so that they could have developed more as couples. Early parenthood puts psychological and financial strains on a marriage. As a result of their findings, the researchers recommended that partners consider postponing parenthood until they reach the end of their twenties and are entering their thirties. During this delay, they can attain a coherent sense of self and develop resilient relationships.

17

I feel that the timing of parenthood is an intimate, individual, and at the same time shared decision. In my practice, I have seen young couples give birth with the strong support of their families. I never hear a word of regret about their decisions. On the other hand, I have watched couples in their forties, people who have finally achieved comfort and security in life, deliver offspring without any worries about having waited.

A difficulty in waiting, however, is that a woman over forty may have irregular ovulation, and conception may take a little time. Then, when she does conceive, she has to consciously pamper herself because the incidence of miscarriage is higher in this age group. These facts should not be discouraging to women who wait, because great care is being taken to see that high-risk pregnancies—which include over-forty pregnancies—are carried to term trouble free. Perinatology, or high-risk obstetrics, has become a more popular and more available medical specialty with the rise of expectant motherhood among older women. In fact, the U.S. Bureau of the Census has estimated that births to women age thirty-five and over will increase 37 percent in the 1980s. A woman who seeks the care of a competent perinatologist is giving herself the best possible chance for a good healthy pregnancy.

Now it must not be forgotten in all this talk about waiting that men who postpone parenthood are also going to be affected. An older woman's difficulty conceiving can be due to the fact that her partner is older too. The sperm of a forty-year-old is not the same as the hardy, fast-swimming sperm of a twenty-year-old. Sperm slows with age. Also, conditions such as varicocele, a bulging of the veins near the testicles, can develop. When a man has this condition, his veins do not carry the blood from the testes, and sperm motility (movement) drops. The man who thinks that the right time to start a family will be when he has a fat bank account should weigh his fertility factor too. Most lives are constantly in flux, and if two people wait for all the facets of their partnership to fit perfectly together, they may be waiting forever. Ultimately the right time to have a baby arrives when your heart says *now*.

AFTER CONTRACEPTION

Often women come to me asking whether the Pill or the intrauterine device (IUD) can affect their fertility. Some concerns over these contraceptives are sound, but misinformation also exists.

Scientists have never been able to name the Pill as a cause of infertility. In fact, women who have difficulty conceiving are sometimes put on the Pill to regulate their cycle and promote conception. If a woman develops health problems, such as high blood pressure, amenorrhea, or fibroid tumors while on the Pill, she should stop taking it and allow her hormones to balance themselves naturally. Her medical problems should then be alleviated. A number of statistical studies from the Centers for Disease Control in Atlanta have shown the Pill to have protective health benefits. It appears to reduce the incidence of ovarian cancer, pelvic inflammatory disease (PID), fibrocystic breast disease, and endometrial cancer.

Another plus for the Pill is that it may slow the spread of endometriosis, vascular tissue that, if unchecked, can grow and inhibit conception. While the Pill does not cure this condition, it is often used to prevent a recurrence following treatment with medication such as Danocrine (danazol).

On the minus side, however, two recent studies have suggested that oral contraceptives may increase a woman's chance of developing chlamydia, the most common sexually-transmitted disease and a known cause of infertility. So far, these studies are noteworthy but not conclusive. Also, the Pill may stimulate the growth of fibroid tumors, and large fibroids can make implantation of a fertilized egg very difficult and sometimes impossible. A woman with fibroids should be monitored carefully by her doctor. If a woman on the Pill has no health problems, she should have no worries. Three months after she ends her contraception, her hormones are usually back in balance and baby-making can begin.

Doctors trying to help couples overcome infertility are not finding Pill-related problems, but they are concerned about the aftermath of the IUD. IUDs have been scientifically connected to fertility troubles. The plastic devices such as the Lippes Loop and the discontinued Saf-T-Coil and Dalkon Shield, which are much less frequently used than the copper-covered devices, seem to be the most harmful. Nevertheless, IUDs as a group have been linked to the growing incidence of PID (pelvic inflammatory disease), an infection of the reproductive organs that can scar the fallopian tubes. The theory is that the tail of an IUD acts like a wick that bacteria travel along to the womb. The more sexual partners an IUD user has, the greater her chance of infection. Risk is highest during the first few months after the IUD is inserted; later on, there is much less likelihood of harm.

Once a tube is scarred as a result of PID, the delicate cilia—the fine hairs lining the tube—become damaged and cannot successfully aid the passage of the fertilized egg as it journeys to the womb. If conception occurs at all, an ectopic (tubal) pregnancy may result and surgery will be needed to remove the conceptus. When an ectopic pregnancy is not discovered early, it grows and eventually bursts the tube. The internal bleeding that ensues can then threaten the life of the mother. Doctors, now alert to the prevalence of ectopic pregnancy, are especially concerned when a pregnant woman complains of abdominal pain or vaginal bleeding. Taking these symptoms quite seriously, a physician will perform a quantitative blood pregnancy test and order an ultrasonography to find out whether an expectant mother's pregnancy is inside or outside her womb. One recent study estimated that 88,000 women in the United States might not be able to have children because they were IUD users. Many of the women with IUD-caused tubal damage might, however, be helped if the problem is diagnosed early. Tubal damage can often be corrected through microsurgical techniques that are able to shift the odds and make a normal pregnancy more likely than an ectopic one. (See Chapter 2 for more information about infertility.)

Other contraceptives such as the condom, diaphragm, cervical cap, sponge, and spermicidal jellies and creams leave no scientifically proven aftereffects, but these are all less effective methods of birth control than the Pill and the IUD. A woman who wanted the greatest protection before she decided to have a baby might understandably have chosen the Pill or the IUD. No matter what method of birth control you have used, however, now that you are ready to get pregnant, you should visit your doctor for an internal examination, prenatal vitamins, and general guidance on how to prepare your body for pregnancy.

PREPARING YOUR BODY FOR PREGNANCY

Many women do not know they are pregnant until five, six, or even eight weeks after they have conceived (when the fertilized egg attaches to the wall of the uterus and begins to grow). (See

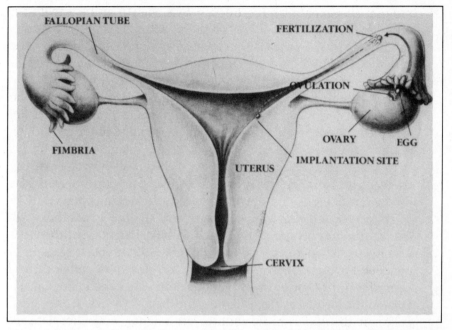

Figure 1-1. *Female reproductive organs. The relationship between the uterus, the ovaries, and the fallopian tubes is illustrated. Pictured is ovulation with the release of an ovum, the subsequent fertilization of the egg in the fallopian tube, and the implantation of the embryo.*

Figure 1-1.) Yet those early weeks are crucial for the baby, because it is during this time that the brain and nervous system are being formed, and alcoholic beverages, cigarettes, and drugs can interfere. If you really want your body to be a safe home for your baby, you should eliminate habits that can hurt.

Alcoholic beverages. Any alcohol you consume enters your bloodstream—and the unborn's—in the same concentration. Therefore, every time you drink, so does the baby. Eventually nature reacts, and a fetus in the womb of an expectant mother who drinks heavily arrives in the world as a newborn with fetal alcohol syndrome (FAS). An infant with FAS can have low birth weight, small head size (microcephaly), distorted facial features, damage to the central nervous system, and mental retardation. This is a serious situation. In New York City, restaurants have been ordered to post health warnings to prevent pregnant women from drinking.

Cigarettes. The nicotine and carbon monoxide that enter your system when you smoke can cause serious complications during pregnancy. Smoking can stunt a baby's growth and lower its IQ. Miscarriage is greater among smokers, and problems such as placental separation, which can threaten the child's existence, may occur. You should make a real effort to quit smoking before you conceive so that you are not tempted after pregnancy.

Drugs. Your body should be drug-free, since most prescription and nonprescription medications cross the placenta and affect the fetus. It's possible, for example, that Valium and other tranquilizers have subtle, long-term effects on the development of a baby's nervous system. Different drugs may cause lesser problems, but all drugs are suspect. So before you conceive, try natural remedies for minor illnesses and purify your body as much as possible.

Too much caffeine may be harmful. Caffeine is another substance that has been linked to possible birth defects, but the studies on rats are inconclusive for humans. Still, if you are trying to conceive, it might be best to reduce or eliminate caffeine from your diet until further investigations define its effects. For a start, you might switch to decaf coffee and herbal brews. Coffee, tea, cola soft drinks, over-the-counter stimulants, and chocolate all contain caffeine.

What to add:

Good nutrition and the power of vitamins. A woman who eats a well-balanced diet before she conceives is giving her future child the best start on life. I encourage every woman to eat plenty of fresh fruits and vegetables, whole grain products, lean meat, fish, poultry, and dairy foods, and to avoid refined and processed products. Once you have a good, healthy diet, you can only improve with vitamins.

The B vitamins, B_6 in particular, seem to have an effect on the brain hormones that direct the menstrual cycle. I suggest that women trying to get pregnant take a daily multivitamin, a B-complex vitamin that contains 100 milligrams of vitamin B_1, and an additional 100 to 200 milligrams of vitamin B_6. British studies have shown that babies borne by women who took multivitamins and iron had fewer birth defects than the newborns of women who were not taking vitamins. You cannot go wrong taking vitamins throughout your lifetime. Also, since the water-soluble B vitamins are excreted from the body, you do not have to worry about the effects of an overdose.

Exercise. Exercises such as aerobic dancing, bicycling, and swimming are good for toning the reproductive organs. These activities help you prepare for the extra stress that your body will experience during pregnancy, but be careful not to overexercise. It is hard to say how much exercise is too much, but if you are a competitive athlete or just a serious jogger who does not enter races or marathons, you may notice that your monthly cycle and/or your menstrual flow are different. These changes are signs that the exercise in your life interferes with your chance of conception. So if you are having difficulty getting pregnant, scale down your physical activity a bit.

HOW YOUR DOCTOR CAN HELP

You should stop taking the Pill or remove your IUD at least three months before you plan to become pregnant, because your hormones need time to flow naturally again. During this period of readjustment, make an appointment with your doctor for internal and breast examinations and a Pap test. Ask him if there's anything in your medical history that might give you trouble during pregnancy, and then discuss the tests that you may need. It might be helpful when you're talking to him to refer to the following list of conditions and tests that influence pregnancy:

• *Pelvic pain.* Abdominal pain just before your period is a symptom of endometriosis—also called the career woman's disease—a condition in which part of the endometrium, the lining of the uterus, flushes backward into the abdomen rather than leaving the body as menstrual blood. Endometriosis can prevent pregnancy if it is not cared for in its early stage. Right now, danazol is the only FDA-approved medication for treating endometriosis, but other drugs are being researched. (NOTE: Birth control pills, sometimes used in high doses in the past, are no longer recommended for endometriosis, but surgery is still occasionally performed to remove large endometriotic tumors.) So bring up the possibility of this condition with your doctor if you have pain before your period. And don't ignore pain during sex and difficult menstrual cramps, because they can also mean endometriosis.
Pain in the middle of the cycle may not be significant at all; it may just be what is called mittleschmerz, or pain during ovulation, which occurs for no particular reason. However, just in case your mid-cycle pain may be signaling endometriosis, again, discuss your discomfort with your doctor.

If you have pain right after your period, particularly if you use an IUD, bacteria may have entered your reproductive organs. If an infection creeps into your fallopian tubes, it could give you acute PID. Since PID is a serious condition that can make you infertile, it must be treated right away. In fact, if you have had any past problems with your IUD or have a history of ectopic pregnancy, your doctor may suggest a hysterosalpingogram, an X ray of your uterus and fallopian tubes, before you plan to get pregnant. From this X ray, your doctor can tell whether your tubes are open or blocked by scar tissue.

• *Vaginal infection.* A recurring vaginal infection can kill healthy sperm, so your doctor should do a Pap test and order vaginal cultures for venereal disease and the identification of any infection you feel. Douching with Betadine iodine solution can bring relief while you're waiting for the lab report.

• *Fibroid tumors.* Fibroids, benign growths on the uterus, can cause miscarriage or premature birth if they grow. If you have fibroids, you and your physician should decide whether you should have them taken out before you become pregnant. The choice operation is a *myomectomy*—removal of fibroid tumors without a hysterectomy. (If your doctor wants to do a hysterectomy, always request a second opinion.)

• *Thyroid problems.* The thyroid influences the hypothalamus and pituitary gland in the brain, which, in turn, control the menstrual cycle. So a sluggish thyroid may mean that you don't ovulate. To make sure that your thyroid is not going to cause a terrible fertility problem, ask your doctor to perform a blood test for thyroid values before you try to get pregnant.

• *High blood pressure.* Since hypertension can create a hostile environment for the baby in your body, a blood pressure test is an essential part of your prepregnancy checkup. Diet restrictions and exercise can often lower high blood pressure, but if your doctor feels that they aren't enough, he may prescribe blood pressure medication.

• *Rubella vaccination.* Although a mild case of rubella, commonly called German measles, may hardly affect you, it can cause brain damage, deafness, and blindness to an unborn baby. This is the time to find out if you've ever been exposed to the disease. If your blood test shows *no rubella antibodies*, then you should be vaccinated at least three months before you plan to conceive. Remember, the vaccine is live and needs those three months to integrate itself into your system. *The wait is important!* If you become pregnant during this interval, you'll be exposing your baby to the disease.

• *Test for toxoplasmosis.* Toxoplasmosis is a disease caused by a parasite that lives in the intestines of cats, cattle, sheep, and pigs. Lately women have been worried about getting toxoplasmosis when they change kitty litter, since the parasite can be found in cat fecal waste. Although the disease only causes mild flulike symptoms, if a pregnant woman catches it, there is a chance that it may cause brain damage and blindness in her child. Fortunately, since a house cat doesn't hunt its dinner in the wild, it is not likely to carry toxoplasmosis. The virus usually breeds in cats that eat wild prey or uncooked meat. However, before pregnancy, a blood test can determine whether you have toxoplasmosis antibodies, and if you do, you've already been exposed to the disease and are immune. There is no vaccine against toxoplasmosis, so if you *do not* have its antibodies, you may want to take extra precautions around your pet. When you become pregnant, ask someone else to change the litter and wash his or her hands before touching you. I've never met a pregnant woman who minded giving up cleaning the litter!

• *Genetic testing.* Tay-Sachs disease is a rare and fatal biochemical condition that usually ends a child's life before he or she is four. Although anyone can get Tay-Sachs, the disease appears with greatest frequency among a relatively small ethnic group: Jewish couples of Ashkenazi, or eastern European, descent. One in twenty-five Jewish-Americans carry the gene; however, both parents must be carriers for an offspring to be affected. Testing for the trait should be done before pregnancy, because it's hard to identify the Tay-Sachs gene after conception. You should ask your doctor whether a test for Tay-Sachs or any other genetic disease—sickle-cell or Cooley's anemia, for example—would be a good idea for you.

FOR THE FATHER-TO-BE

Can a man prepare his body for the conception of his child? A man does not become pregnant, of course, but he can initiate health habits that will strengthen his sperm for the task of fertilization. Sperm cells are fatty cells, and fat has the capacity to bind substances such as the chemical components of drugs and alcohol. Although the studies are not conclusive for humans, researchers have found that marijuana affects the sperm of animal subjects and inhibits fertility. If marijuana can make a monkey sterile, imagine what it can do to a man! Considering the possibility of sperm damage, a man who wants to become a father would be wise to avoid alcohol, cigarettes, and all drugs. A healthy life-style can definitely improve his contribution to this joint venture called pregnancy.

When couples have difficulty conceiving, 30 percent of the time the man is the source of the problem. Varicocele, a swelling of the veins near the testicles, can slow sperm practically to a halt. Sometimes a former bout with gonorrhea or infections such as T-mycoplasma, nonspecific urethritis, and chlamydia can affect fertility. Varicocele can be surgically corrected, and bacterial infections can be identified and treated if conception is elusive, but even before a man encounters a problem—which he may not—he should be trying to enhance his potency.

Daily supplements of B vitamins can help. Stress depletes the body's store of B vitamins, which are already in short supply due to contemporary diets. A man who is under a great deal of pressure needs the Bs to improve his well-being and boost the quality of his sperm. By taking one or two vitamin-B-complex supplements a day—I recommend a supplement that includes 100 milligrams of B_1—a man will be caring for himself and his reproductive capacity.

Vitamin C has also been shown to have positive effects on sperm. In a study headed by Dr. Earl B. Dawson at the University of Texas Medical Branch in Galveston, vitamin C reduced infertility. Men with sperm agglutination—sperm that stick together and thus lose their potency—were given pure ascorbic acid (vitamin C) in 500-milligram capsules, and they were told to take one dose every twelve hours. After what researchers estimated was only three or four days later, the sperm separated and swam without difficulty. With this clear correlation between vitamin C and sperm motility, I suggest that men take 500 milligrams of vitamin C three times a day.

I also warn men who are trying to conceive children not to allow their genitals to become overheated. The testicles hang in the scrotal sac outside the body, where they remain one degree lower than body temperature, the level needed to produce fertile sperm. Sometimes when a couple is having a hard time getting pregnant, the man has unwittingly elevated the temperature of his testicles by wearing nonporous synthetic clothing during vigorous exercise. Nylon jogging shorts, for instance, contain the heat generated during physical exertion. When the testicles grow hotter than normal, sperm cannot survive. Tight athletic supporters, skimpy briefs, even body-hugging jeans can kill sperm, as can long soaks in a hot tub. "Wear loose cotton clothing during workouts and limit your time in steam baths, saunas, and hot tubs," I tell prospective fathers. Then I remind them that they are creating another life and this child-to-be needs their concern before birth as much as after.

DO YOU WANT A SON OR A DAUGHTER?

No one can guarantee a way that you will have a boy or a girl, but researchers never stop seeking a surefire method. Lately scientists are trying to separate sperm in a centrifuge so that the smaller male sperm will be parted from the larger female types. This technique is not successful yet, but it is being perfected.

There are also the Sephadex technique and filtration. In the Sephadex technique, sperm are put in a special Sephadex tube. The fast-moving male sperm immediately begin to swim through, but the Sephadex filter traps the larger, slower female sperm. The smaller, faster male sperm collect at the bottom of the tube. The male sperm are then gathered and used for artificial insemination. The filtration method is based upon the same principle—the separation of male and female sperm—but in this case, the filter is not a Sephadex material but human serum albumin, extracted from blood, which slows sperm speed. Sperm are placed in a glass column that is filled with the serum albumin. The rapid male sperm race through the substance and reach the lower end of the column much faster than the female sperm. The male sperm, then concentrated in the lower end of the glass, can be separated. Both these separation techniques rely on artificial insemination with the chosen male sperm. Sex selection with these methods is mostly designed to help couples conceive sons.

The most popular methods of sex selection remain the ones developed by Dr. Landrum B. Shettles more than a decade ago.* He based his instructions for having a boy or a girl on the timing of intercourse and before-sex douching.

* *Your Baby's Sex: Now You Can Choose,* David Rorvik with Landrum B. Shettles, M.D. (New York: Dodd, Mead Inc., 1970).

The following conditions are thought to favor a boy:

1. intercourse about the time of ovulation, preceded by abstinence from the beginning of the menstrual cycle
2. an alkaline (baking soda) douche (2 tablespoons baking soda to 1 quart warm water) before intercourse
3. intercourse with female orgasm preceding male orgasm
4. deep penetration during male orgasm, to be sure the sperm are placed close to the cervix
5. vaginal penetration from the rear

The following conditions are thought to favor a girl:

1. intercourse 2 to 3 days before ovulation
2. an acidic douche (2 tablespoons vinegar to 1 quart warm water) before intercourse
3. intercourse without female orgasm
4. shallow penetration by the male during orgasm
5. the "missionary" position

It is a fact that approximately 49 percent of all births are females and 51 percent are males. It is not understood why, but this ratio is reversed in cases of earlier infertility and among test tube babies. One possible explanation is that the Y-chromosome (male) sperm are more susceptible to injuries that render them less able to fertilize the egg. It has also been found that men with low sperm counts have a high incidence of female offspring. It has been suggested that the factors that reduce sperm count might adversely affect the Y-chromosome sperm to a greater degree. For example, it has been found that a higher percentage of female births has been associated with failure of the rhythm method of birth control, when women have had intercourse before and after ovulation. During those times, the cervical mucus is relatively scant, acidic, and generally hostile to male sperm.

Even with all the knowledge we have about ovulation, consistency of cervical mucus, and sperm speed, however, no method of sex selection is guaranteed. New ovulation predictor kits, which can indicate the time of ovulation up to thirty-six hours in advance, are helping to enhance the moment of conception and may actually favor male offspring, since the closer to ovulation that conception occurs, the greater the chance of conceiving a male! A commercialized sex selection kit called Gender Care, marketed by ProCare Industries Ltd., Englewood, Colorado, is available (in drugstores) for about $50, but this kit is basically a packaging of the Shettles technique. A woman may learn from the kit's booklets and materials, which help her to chart her menstrual cycle for three months, but she would probably have the same chance of conceiving a son or daughter by reading the information in this section or purchasing Dr. Shettles's book. (For additional information on how to gauge the best time of the month to conceive, see Chapter 2.)

In the end, I feel that your baby's health is far more important than his or her sex. It may be fun to try sex selection techniques, but please do not forget to prepare a wholesome internal environment for the child you will be nurturing.

WHOM WILL YOU TRUST TO DELIVER YOUR BABY?

Your mother may not have carefully chosen her obstetrician. She may simply have remained under the care of the gynecologist who confirmed her pregnancy. Today's pregnant woman and her mate are different. The voice of each expectant parent is heard in the choice of that one experienced person who will ease and aid the birth of the long-awaited baby. Both women and men have learned that there are many decisions to be made about labor and childbirth, and the first important one is: who will deliver our child?

When the high number of unnecessary cesarean sections became known, the popularity of birthing centers rose. Couples began to see that hospitals might not be the only places in which newborns might arrive. Some expectant parents even gave birth at home. Many hospitals responded to the need for diverse and expanded facilities as women and men demanded the right to natural childbirth, in environments that would allow active participation by husbands. Some medical centers created midwife services, rooming in, birthing rooms, and nursery centers for newborns, and asked patients to suggest improvements. Maternity floors became sites for innovation.

Now a couple has the happy task of investigating hospitals and, if they so choose, birthing centers to find out where their needs can best be met. When you select a doctor or a midwife, you are also consenting to his or her affiliated facility. You are agreeing to a package deal that should include a competent professional and a facility equipped with the latest technology.

Chapter 4 is designed to help you reach decisions that will enrich the childbirth experience for you and your mate. Whomever you trust to be with you when you deliver should be an easily accessible person. It would be wonderful to have a private obstetrician at your side for the entire nine months, but since you probably won't, you are the one who is going to monitor your daily ups and downs. You have to be able to tell your doctor everything you think is important.

As you go through Chapter 4 and weigh the qualities of the doctor you would like to have, you might consider that his personal availability should be equal to his competency. An obstetrician should always be ready, not only to answer questions but to comfort and console.

To help my own patients understand how I am going to care for them, to alert them to signs of trouble and assure them of my concern, I give my expectant mothers the following letter:

Dear Expectant Mother:

I am very pleased to congratulate you on this pregnancy. Please be advised that we will constantly be available in this office to answer any questions and problems that should arise during the pregnancy.

I would generally prefer to see a pregnant patient every three weeks until the thirty-second week of gestation, and then every two weeks for the following months, and every week for the last four weeks of the pregnancy. If there are any high-risk problems or complications, you might be asked to come even more frequently.

If there are any questions, dilemmas, or misunderstandings that have not been addressed during each follow-up visit, please feel free to call the nurse or myself at any time.

Each patient will be managed individually but it is extremely important that you avoid drugs, tobacco, alcohol, or any other damaging environmental agent during your pregnancy to offer your baby the best conditions for intrauterine growth.

The labor and delivery will be handled as naturally as possible and intravenous infusion, shaving and enemas during the admission to the hospital will only be used if absolutely necessary.

It is advisable for each person to have prepared childbirth education, but it is not a must.

If there are any doubts or feelings of unhappiness, please mention them at any of the follow-up visits or call me personally. When the office is closed, the answering service responds, and immediately contacts me. Please advise the answering service when you call that you are a pregnant patient. Please indicate your month of pregnancy and your complaint. The service will then recognize the urgency of the call and page me right away. This information is extremely important if you have symptoms of miscarriage or premature labor.

If you call during office hours, please advise my staff or myself that you are a pregnant patient, since if you are newly pregnant, the staff might not have familiarized themselves with your condition.

If any drugs or medicines are advised for other health problems, please ask the nurse or myself if these are safe during pregnancy. This is one time that you cannot be too careful, and misunderstandings must be avoided.

I hope that we will be able to help you through a wonderful pregnancy and that you will be sure to take extra care of yourself during this time. Remember, the best way to ensure a happy outcome to this pregnancy is to take extra care from the moment of conception until the birth. You are never alone; pregnancy is a time for union and teamwork—teamwork among yourself, your husband, your family and your doctor.

Best wishes for a wonderful pregnancy.

—NIELS H. LAUERSEN, M.D., PH.D.

ALWAYS STAY IN CHARGE

During your pregnancy, you are the one who will physically and psychologically experience the growth of new life. Frequently this experience will be ecstatic, but at times you will have twinges, aches, worrisome symptoms. Never ignore something that troubles you. Sometimes a woman will feel inhibited about "bothering" her obstetrician, but she is the one in charge. You should inform the doctor, his partner, his nurse, whomever answers the phone in the physician's office of your condition. Symptoms can be interpreted and questions can always be answered. If you are planning a trip, taking medication, undergoing dental work, planning to dye your hair, or expect to do anything out of the ordinary, check with your doctor. He, and sources such as this book, will give you the knowledge you need to direct your own safe and healthy course through pregnancy to its fulfilling culmination— the birth of your child.

CHAPTER 2

When . . . and How. . . to Get Pregnant

YOU CAN'T WRITE THE SCENARIO, BUT . . .

A few years ago, a book with a catchy title precipitated its author onto "Donahue" and other talk shows. The book was called *The Baby Trap,** and in it, author Ellen Peck provocatively advocated resisting societal pressures to have children in favor of a guilt-free child-free life. In the impassioned media debate that followed the publication of the book, thousands of those who joined the argument, pro and con, wrote in support of Ms. Peck's contention that the joys of parenthood were largely hype. Yet, little by little, as the childless mid-seventies became the eighties, something hap-

* New York: Pinnacle Books, 1971.

pened. Patients who had regularly come in for gynecological examinations saying, in effect, "Children? Not for me; I'm not the baby-making type," were suddenly phoning in for the results of their pregnancy tests, excited and optimistic about the new chapter in their lives. A *Time* feature writer, surveying the mini baby boom, asked whether it could be something in the water, or a side effect of jogging, that had made those adamantly childless women so abruptly change their minds.

Hard as it is to tear up the scenarios we've carefully crafted for ourselves, it is best to admit that over the years, wishes, hopes, and dreams are bound to change. A woman's childbearing future may be clouded by ifs, buts, maybes, or apparently decisive nos, but whether she's eighteen, twenty-five, or thirty-nine, a woman can't listen to her body too closely or know too much about the way she functions best. The body is made to be tough and resilient, but fertility nonetheless is delicate—it can be damaged, and it can be lost, even in an age of test-tube babies and other scientific marvels.

To see how choices can affect childbearing options, take an apparently ordinary scene: a doctor's office where a woman in her early twenties is hesitating over the selection of a good, reliable form of contraception. At that moment, is she or the doctor sitting opposite her thinking of what she might want when she is twenty-nine instead of twenty-one? Probably not. Yet a decision pro or con for a birth control device or the Pill could affect her fertility in the future. A form of contraception that makes sense in the short run is not necessarily a good long-term investment.

In the sixties, millions of women loved the Pill for its simplicity and reliability, yet later, thousands of them would temporarily be infertile following the years that the original high-estrogen/high-progesterone Pill had suppressed their ovulatory cycles. With the modern low-estrogen/low-progesterone Pill used nowadays, most women go back to a normal ovulation and menstruation pattern immediately after discontinuing its use. In fact, the Pill can sometimes make a woman who had had irregular cycles more regular and fertile. Later, the favored form of contraception of the early seventies, the IUD, was known to have increased the incidence of fertility-destroying pelvic infections among young childless women. Before choosing any particular type of contraceptive—and that means any contraceptive, even one bought over the counter—always ask your doctor what effect it might have on your fertility. Enough options exist even in this imperfect world so that a shortsighted choice could impose an unnecessarily heavy burden later on.

Cultural attitudes, too, can be unexpectedly harmful. Women pride themselves on being the tougher sex, but a woman who grimly battles severe menstrual cramps each month because she isn't going to give in or complain could, little by little, be surrendering her future to a terrible disease like endometriosis, the silent factor in many cases of infertility. Early warning signals should never be ignored or explained away, and if one doctor doesn't have an adequate explanation for your symptoms, keep changing doctors until you find one whom you respect. Don't give up, even though a doctor may make you feel like a fool because he can't find anything wrong. If you know your body, and you know something is amiss, recognize that you are probably a better fertility expert than the experts themselves.

KEEPING THE OPTIONS OPEN: HOW TO BE YOUR OWN FERTILITY SPECIALIST

How can I live my life and still keep my options open? It's a question every woman should ask herself periodically if she wants to keep an eye on her fertility.

Becoming your own fertility specialist is not as awesome a task as it might seem. Often all it requires is simply *knowing your body* and *listening to your body*. No one can be 100 percent sure that she is fertile unless she has conceived, but the normal everyday working of the body is a very good clue to its fertility. Just the simple events that happen between two menstruations are a reliable guide to the balance of the all-important hormones in a woman's body. A grossly irregular menstruation usually means the meticulously timed ebb and flow of estrogen and progesterone has been disturbed, so that a woman is ovulating infrequently or not at all. A woman with a reasonably regular menstrual pattern, by comparison, ovulates in about nine out of ten menstrual cycles (it is normal for a healthy woman to skip ovulation once or twice a year). First, look for confirming signs in the change in the amount and appearance of the cervical mucus, which at mid-cycle is copious and almost ribbonlike if caught and stretched between the fingers. An easy, inexpensive, and more accurate way to corroborate the timing and frequency of ovulation is for a woman to take her basal body temperature every morning before she gets out of bed (movement will cause a rise in body temperature) and jot down the results on a basal body temperature chart. Body temperature normally fluctuates throughout the monthly cycle, dipping slightly about fourteen days after the start of the last menstrual period and then rising about one degree at the time of ovulation. Three months or more of basal body temperature readings should give a reasonably accurate guide to the day-to-day hormone fluctuations from menstruation to ovulation and back to menstruation once again.

The second item on the fertility checklist is the absence or presence of known enemies of fertility in a woman's medical history. A severe pelvic infection contracted a few years previously might, for instance, have been the culprit if a woman finds she is unable to conceive. And since gynecological disorders only worsen with neglect, warning signs should always be heeded and acted on immediately, even if the first symptoms don't seem very threatening. Any uneasiness about a known or suspected complication is best dealt with by a skillful infertility specialist and possibly diagnostic testing. Some important items in a woman's medical history include:

Venereal diseases. These are potent enemies of conception. It takes only one episode of gonorrhea or chlamydia to cause serious scarring of the fallopian tubes and ovaries, which can lead to infertility. The more sexual partners a woman has had, the more likely it is that she will contract one or both of these diseases. Although a condom offers some protection, every woman who has had more than one sexual partner should ask for gonorrhea and chlamydia screening tests when she has her routine gynecological examination. Gonorrhea and chlamydia caught early on will respond to antibiotics, thereby sparing a woman's reproductive organs from irreversible damage.

Pelvic inflammatory disease. This is another serious inflammation of the uterus and tubes. The risk of pelvic inflammatory disease, or PID, is again higher if a woman has had more than one sexual partner. She is more susceptible, too, if she is using an intrauterine device. Warning signs of PID are pain and tenderness in the lower abdomen, characteristically beginning during menstruation, when cervical cramping acts as a conduit for bacteria that are sucked up into the uterus. Pain and inflammation will persist after menstruation is over. Under the stress of the infection, the frondlike ends of the fallopian tubes close to seal off the abdominal cavity, but this natural defense system prevents the normal functioning of the tubes by creating a sticky mass out of the free-flowing fimbriated ends.

Several abortions or an abortion followed by complications. A single uncomplicated abortion done by a reputable doctor or clinic usually does not interfere with fertility. Several abortions or an abortion followed by infection, however, can lacerate the cervix or leave behind intrauterine adhesions, sticky masses that interfere with implantation by gumming up the tissues of the uterine lining. Symptoms of a damaged uterus include amenorrhea or a decrease in the amount of menstrual flow, but a diagnosis should be confirmed by an X ray of the uterus and tubes. A D&C (dilatation-and-curettage) will often clean out the uterine adhesions and free the uterus for conception.

Endometriosis. If the rule of thumb in detecting PID is pain *after* menstruation, with endometriosis, the warning sign is pain, usually felt as severe menstrual cramps, *before* a period begins. Endometriosis, a disease in which the uterine lining is pushed into the abdominal cavity (the pain occurs when tissue built up before the period is sprayed onto the ovaries and tubes), is still confused with the more familiar pelvic inflammatory disease by many doctors. Stress related and a major cause of infertility, endometriosis has blighted the lives of millions of women. Nourished by the menstrual cycle, endometriosis strikes at a woman's ability to conceive right at the most fertile time of her life. More information about endometriosis is provided later in this chapter, since it is so prevalent. In fact, the condition has been labeled the career woman's disease because it is frequently diagnosed among women in the labor force. Such women often postpone childbearing to have careers, but work creates emotional pressure. Research suggests that endometriosis may be a physical effect of emotional pressure, but, of course, all women, not just those involved with careers, may be subject to this stress.

Hormonal imbalance. Once the female hormones are out of sync, the normal menstruation/ovulation pattern is disrupted. Grossly irregular ovulation will leave a woman gambling blindly with her chances of conception and will sharply cut down her likelihood of conceiving within a given number of months. Uncertainty and discomfort go together, since many women with irregular ovulation experience acute premenstrual syndrome

(PMS), which only adds to an existing infertility problem because the inadequate level of progesterone in the last two weeks of the cycle increases uterine cramping and decreases the chances of an egg adhering to the lining of the uterus. A doctor may recommend a mild fertility drug, usually Clomid, to regulate the timing of ovulation and allow a woman to conceive. Vitamin B_6 given in tablet form will help balance estrogen and progesterone just before a period, and natural progesterone, given in suppository form, often reduces excessive cramping when a woman has proved hormonally related infertility.

And third: A woman delaying childbearing should, paradoxically, *give herself time.* An entry on a birth certificate is only one clue out of many where fertility is concerned; nonetheless, women and men are usually more fertile in their twenties than in their forties. It's not only that fertility declines naturally with the passage of time (witness the increased number of anovulatory cycles by the mid-thirties); the additional bad news is that health conditions that inhibit conception tend to worsen with age. One obvious culprit is endometriosis, which often worsens as the years go on. Also, by their thirties, over 20 percent of women have fibroid tumors of the uterus. A fibroid nesting within the endometrial lining may expel the fertile egg. Additionally, with the natural aging of the immature eggs, which have been present in the ovaries since birth, come chromosome breakages and other genetic injuries that contribute to numerous early miscarriages among older women. One such miscarriage does not, of course, mean that a woman could not or should not try again. By the middle thirties, though, each disappointment pushes the timing of conception on a few more precious months.

Although the bad news should not make a healthy woman race to get pregnant to meet some hard and fast deadline (there is usually no clear cutoff point beyond which a woman cannot conceive), the pregnancy timetable would certainly need some hasty readjustment if a new circumstance were to cast doubt on her ability to have children. Anyway, to be slightly uneasy at thirty and downright uneasy by thirty-five is understandable and realistic, given that the odds only lengthen as the years go by. Pregnancy over thirty-five, however, can still be a safe, healthy experience for an expectant mother and her baby. Many facets of late pregnancy are covered in Chapter 11, Over 35: Is Your Pregnancy Safe?

The infertility workup. A detailed description of the complete infertility workup is to be found in a number of books, including my own book on gynecology, *Listen to Your Body: A Gynecologist Answers a Woman's Most Intimate Questions.** Although the extensive coverage of infertility is really outside the scope of this book, I would stress one important point: both partners should work together to solve the mystery of an inexplicably delayed conception. It is hard to believe, but some gynecologists still treat infertility as a woman's problem. In reality, as men and women age, both partners are often less than fertile: he could have a low sperm count, she could have an erratic ovulation pattern. Together, they need help.

QUESTIONS ABOUT DIFFICULTIES IN GETTING PREGNANT

How Do I Know if I'm Ovulating?

Recently someone told me that you could have your period and not be ovulating. I never knew that. I thought that if you got your period every month, you were fertile. My cycle can be shorter or longer from month to month, but I didn't think that mattered. Now I'm beginning to wonder whether I'm normal and whether I'm ovulating. I'm twenty-eight years old, and my husband and I have been trying to have a baby for two years now. Nothing has happened. I thought this would be easy and wonderful, but instead, I feel like a failure. What can I do? How do I know if I'm ovulating?

L.G.
Decatur, Illinois

Ms. G. can assess her ovulation without ever having to visit her doctor. Today women are gauging their fertility by themselves, in the following ways: charting their daily basal body temperature readings, checking their cervical mucus, and using the new ovulation predictor kits sold at most pharmacies. These are all good indicators of ovulation, but before describing each technique individually, I would like to respond to the fact that Ms. G. has irregular periods.

Sometimes irregular periods can signal Stein-Leventhal syndrome, a condition that, besides menstrual irregularity, includes excessive hair growth and *polycystic ovarian disease,* a hereditary condition in which the ovaries enlarge and develop hard shells.

* New York: Berkley Press, 1984.

This is a common condition, and Ms. G. should not become alarmed. What happens is that the hardened outer shell of an ovary entraps the egg that would normally be released during ovulation. The imprisoned egg then becomes a fluid-filled sac, a cyst within the ovary. As more and more eggs are trapped in the ovary, more and more cysts develop, and the ovary grows bigger and bigger.

Oversize ovaries produce excessive hormones—estrogen, progesterone, and testosterone. It is not as easy to spot excessive estrogen and progesterone as it is to see an overabundance of testosterone. Too much testosterone can cause *hirsutism,* excessive hair growth. If, along with her irregular periods, Ms. G. has pubic hair that grows upward toward her navel, if she notices hair around her nipples or facial hair, she may have Stein-Leventhal syndrome. During an examination, a doctor should be able to detect the enlarged ovaries of polycystic ovarian syndrome and see noticeable hairiness.

With Stein-Leventhal syndrome, ovulation is erratic and it is difficult to select the best time of the month for conception. Eggs do escape from the ovaries from time to time, however, and opportunities to become pregnant do arise. Before consulting with her physician, Ms. G. should chart her ovulation pattern for at least three months. A three-month record will help her physician evaluate her fertility.

I am saddened to learn that Ms. G. waited two years before questioning her fertility. When a woman trying to become pregnant is involved in a healthy sexual relationship, she should not allow more than six months to pass before she consults with her physician. A couple's fertility problem should be targeted and treated right away, before frustration and anxiety occur.

Ms. G., or any woman trying to conceive, can find out exactly when she ovulates by using one or a combination of the following techniques:

Basal body temperature readings. By taking her temperature—an oral reading is fine—when she wakes up every morning, Ms. G. will get a sense of her ovulation pattern. She should start taking her temperature on the first day of her menstrual cycle, which is the first day she begins to bleed. She should keep a thermometer at her bedside, and in the morning, before she has any activity, eats, drinks, or even stands up, she should take her temperature and write it down. To keep track of her readings, she can request basal body temperature charts from her doctor, or she can note her findings on a calendar. Usually a woman's morning temperature is 97.5 before ovulation. At ovulation, her temperature either dips slightly or remains steady. A day or two after ovulation, however, the temperature rises one degree to 98.5, where it stays until immediately prior to menstruation, when it drops. (If Ms. G. becomes pregnant, her first sign of conception will be a temperature that remains high.) She should record her basal body temperature for three complete menstrual cycles in order to assess the timing of her ovulation. Her records will considerably help a doctor's evaluation of her in the future.

Cervical mucus checks. Right after the end of menstruation, the mucus is usually undetectable, but toward the middle of the menstrual cycle, the mucus starts becoming more obvious. By inserting her index finger and thumb into the opening of her vagina,

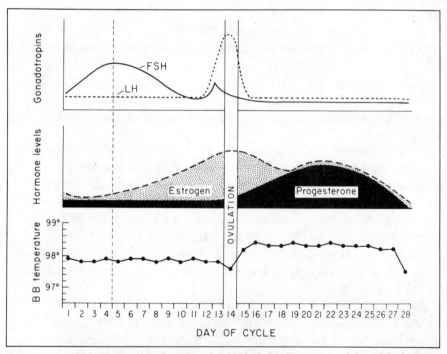

Figure 2-1. *The relationship between hormonal fluctuation and basal body temperature. The top graph shows the level of the brain hormones FSH (follicle-stimulating hormone) and LH (luteinizing hormone) during the menstrual cycle. The center graph shows the level of the ovarian hormones estrogen and progesterone throughout the menstrual cycle. The bottom graph indicates basal body temperature. Note how the temperature rises immediately after ovulation.*

Ms. G. should be able to withdraw her mucus. Near mid-cycle, it will have the clear, thin consistency of raw egg white. This is a sign that her estrogen is increasing. Soon the mucus will become abundant and very stretchy. During ovulation, there will be so much mucus that she will be able to create about a two-inch stretch of it between her fingers. When the mucus is plentiful and wet, she is ovulating. This is the best time for conception. After ovulation, the mucus seems to diminish, but in actuality, it just becomes thick. Ms. G. will not be able to withdraw or stretch it. If she checks her mucus every day from a few days after the end of menstruation for three menstrual cycles, she will be able to judge her ovulation by changes in its wetness and stretchability. Usually I suggest that my patients take basal body temperature readings at the same time that they check their cervical mucus. Then they have two ways to determine whether, and when, they ovulate.

Ovulation predictor kits. These are newly marketed products that take advantage of hormonal changes in a woman's urine. One such kit comes with specially treated sticks, and each day one stick is dipped into a cup containing the first morning urine. As the menstrual month proceeds, hormonal changes cause the sticks to display a color progression. The sticks change from white to pale blue to dark blue as a woman nears ovulation. The ovulation predictor kit indicates the amount of LH, the luteinizing hormone that determines ovulation. When the LH surges, ovulation

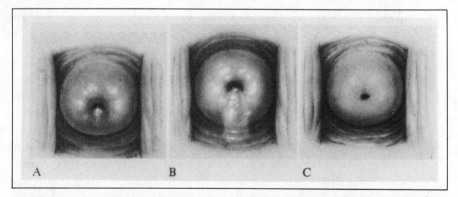

Figure 2-2. *The cervix (the mouth of the womb) as it appears during a gynecological examination. A) Immediately after menstruation the cervix is closed and only a minimal amount of mucus is present. B) During ovulation the cervix is open, facilitating sperm penetration. The mucus is copious and stretchable, permitting easy passage of the sperm. C) The cervix in the luteal phase, shortly before menstruation. The cervix is closed, and the mucus is thick, forming a natural shield.*

41

occurs twenty-four to thirty-six hours later. Intercourse should therefore be timed to occur after the darkest, bluest color appears.

While Ms. G. uses one or all of these methods to assess her ovulation, she should also be eating nutritionally balanced meals and increasing her intake of B vitamins. If each day she supplements her diet with 100 milligrams of B-complex along with 500 milligrams of B_6, she will be helping to maintain a good hormonal balance in her body. If after three months she still is not pregnant, she should consult her physician. To aid the doctor's evaluation, she should bring the records of her ovulation, whether they be basal body temperature notations or ovulation predictor kits.

Her physician will check her for endometriosis, pelvic inflammatory disease (PID), and the previously described Stein-Leventhal syndrome—three of the major causes of infertility among women. He will probably order blood tests to evaluate her hormonal levels and thyroid function, and he may suggest that she have a hysterosalpingogram, an X ray of her uterus and fallopian tubes that reveals whether her tubes are obstructed or clear. All these are standard procedures involved in an infertility workup. It is my hope that Ms. G. will become pregnant once she is able to determine her ovulation, but if she needs an infertility workup, she should also remember that her husband may need one too. A sperm count should be performed before a woman undergoes any extensive testing.

INFERTILITY: DON'T FORGET YOUR PARTNER

About 40 percent of all infertility problems are caused by the male. A man may have a low sperm count, sperm with poor motility (movement), or sperm with strange morphology (structure, shape). Infertility can also be due to an undescended testicle that lowers sperm production, or the absence of the vas, the sperm-carrying duct from the testicle to the penis. *Varicocele,* a bulging of the veins near the testicles, can also be the reason for a low sperm count. The veins actually become like varicose veins, which do not efficiently carry the blood from the testes. Another physiological reason for infertility in men is the presence of a silent infection (one that shows no symptoms). A man may have had a bout of gonorrhea in his past, or he might be harboring chlamydia or a microorganism called mycoplasma, which give no signs of their existence.

On the other hand, a man may be reacting to environmental or psychological factors. Exposure to pollutants or toxins, such as the Agent Orange cited by Vietnam veterans, may adversely affect sperm. Smoking, jogging, wearing tight-fitting pants, excessive drinking, and stress are a few of many far-ranging causes of infertility among men. A physician will try to pinpoint the problem.

First, a doctor must determine a man's sperm count. A man must abstain from orgasm for two to four days before he ejaculates for the count. Some men worry that a sperm count is an assessment of their masculinity, and they have great trepidation about allowing the test to be done. I assure men that a sperm count is only a routine part of a couple's infertility workup. Women undergo far greater analyses than men do.

A man usually releases from 3 to 5 cubic centimeters (cc) of semen with a pH ranging from 7.05 to 7.80. Today a normal sperm count is somewhere above 40 million per cc. During the sperm analysis, a portion of the semen will be cultured to rule out the possibility of infection.

Infertility is a sensitive issue that two people share. Until the problem is overcome, loving partners need comfort and support from each other.

Can I Try Fertility Drugs?

I was a young widow with a toddler when I met my present husband. He had been divorced after five years of marriage, and he has a son. Even though we each have a child, we want one of our own. I'll be thirty next year and I don't want to wait any longer. I say this because we haven't been able to conceive after eighteen months of trying. I've had all the tests and the doctors tell me I'm fine. My tubes are open, and I'm ovulating. My husband has a slightly low sperm count, but the doctors don't seem concerned. They all tell me to relax and nature will take its course. Well, I'd like to help nature along, but they refuse to give me fertility drugs. Why not? Aren't they safe? I'd like your opinion.

E.V.

Shreveport, Louisiana

Ms. V. writes that she has had "all the tests," but I wonder if she has undergone a blood test for thyroid function. Sometimes a lab reports that the level of thyroid hormone in a patient's blood is normal but on the low side. I have found that when a woman having difficulty getting pregnant has a low/normal reading, she can sometimes conceive after taking a small amount of Synthyroid, a thyroid medication. A low dosage of Synthyroid, 100 micrograms a day, can stimulate the metabolism enough to aid conception.

When she asks her doctor whether she has been tested for thyroid function, Ms. V. should also inquire about the possibility of endometriosis. As explained later in this chapter, endometriosis is a disease in which the tissue that forms the endometrium, the lining of the uterus, spreads to other organs. The condition, which is a major cause of infertility, can be difficult to diagnose. Ms. V. might want to find a doctor who has experience in diagnosing and treating endometriosis before she embarks upon a schedule of fertility drugs.

A heartening fact is that Ms. V. and her husband have both conceived children before. The likelihood is that they will both be able to conceive again; however, their bodies may have changed in the interim. Ms. V. mentions that her husband has a slightly low sperm count. I suggest that she use an ovulation predictor kit, as described in How Do I Know if I'm Ovulating? and that she and her husband refrain from sexual intercourse for three or four days before her indicated ovulation. Her husband's sperm will then have time to build and acquire potency. Within twenty-four to thirty-six hours after the indicator in the ovulation kit turns darkest blue, Ms. V. is fertile and she and her husband should have sexual intercourse. After relations, Ms. V. should slide a pillow beneath her buttocks so that her pelvis is propped at an angle. If she can remain in this position for at least thirty minutes, she will be giving the sperm an opportunity to pass more easily through her cervix, and her chance for conception will be improved.

As for fertility drugs, if Ms. V. is unable to become pregnant after all the tests for causes of infertility have been exhausted, and she has had at least three months of intercourse timed with her ovulation, then I believe she might be aided by medication. First, she might try Clomid (clomiphene citrate), a fertility drug in 50-milligram tablets. She should take two tablets daily from day 5 to day 9 of her menstrual cycle. Three to seven days after she stops taking the Clomid, she should be fertile. She might check her ovulation with an ovulation predictor kit. If she does not conceive after taking Clomid this way for three menstrual cycles, then she might try three tablets for one or two cycles. If she still does not become pregnant, she might request a combination of fertility drugs.

Much of our current knowledge about fertility drugs has grown from the research and efforts of physicians at in vitro (test tube baby) centers. Clomid is now being given in combination with injected Pergonal (human menopausal gonadotropin), and the results are quite successful. The drugs, carefully monitored by a fertility specialist, are safe for mother and baby. When a drug regimen is meticulously supervised, the chance of a multiple birth is relatively small. Two 50-milligram tablets of Clomid are given daily from day 5 to day 9 of a woman's menstrual cycle. Then, on days 10, 11, and 12, two ampules of Pergonal are injected. The Pergonal helps to stimulate the ovulating egg and a woman's estrogen level improves. On day 13, she should receive an injection of 10,000 units of HCG (human chorionic gonadotropin), which triggers ovulation. Intercourse should occur on day 14, but a woman might also be fertile on days 13 and 15. This drug regimen has helped many women to become expectant mothers while they are being cared for by fertility specialists. Such physicians conduct regular blood tests of estradiol (estrogen) levels and monitor ovulation patterns with sonograms.

Meanwhile, British in vitro centers have produced an even newer drug combination. In England, women are now being given Clomid, in doses of two tablets daily, from day 2 to day 6 of the menstrual cycle. On days 5, 7, 9, and 11, three ampules of pure FSH, the follicle stimulating hormone, are injected. On day 12, a woman receives an injection of HCG, and on day 13, she is fertile. This technique, involving pure FSH, (Metrodin) is now available in the United States for women who do not respond well to the Clomid/Pergonal combination. The drugs must be administered and monitored by a fertility expert who understands their effects.

Ms. V.'s fertility may be improved by Clomid, Pergonal, or a combination of these two drugs. With the drugs, her fertility may be increased, which, in view of her husband's lowered sperm count, may be just what they need to have their own family. Many of my patients have conceived when they began eating nutritionally balanced meals, taking vitamin supplements, and following a fertility drug program. I also advocate the use of natural progesterone suppositories if a woman's basal body temperature is low in the last two weeks of her menstrual cycle. Anywhere between 25 and 100 milligrams of natural progesterone can be given in suppositories each day during the last ten to twelve days of the menstrual cycle. The added progesterone can help to maintain conception.

Ms. V. should ask for recommendations for a fertility specialist in her area. She impresses me as an aware woman who wants to be an active participant in her own health care. I appreciate her question and encourage her to seek a doctor who is capable of helping her.

Why Wasn't I Told How Much Fertility Changes with Age: Have I Lost My Chance of Having a Baby?

I'm a married professional woman in my early thirties. I've worked hard for the last three years to get my MBA, and now I'm planning on a new career as a financial analyst. In a few years, my husband and I should be able to start a family without it being too much of a strain on our careers. When I went for my last checkup, my doctor looked me over and said that as far as he could see, I was perfectly okay and could probably have a baby anytime I wanted. I have one thirty-five-year-old friend who stopped using her diaphragm and got pregnant within a couple of months. Now I find there's some study that has proved many women my age to be infertile. In other words, I could be over the hill as far as having children is concerned. How could my doctor not have given me the right information? Talk about fading options—except we're not even allowed to make a choice because the information we've been given is inaccurate. Or is the study wrong? I do want children, but I don't want to rush into becoming pregnant. What would you advise a woman in my position to do?

B.G.
New York, New York

Ms. G. was only one of many women who were surprised and shocked by media reports of a recent French infertility study. Results of the study, first published in the United States in a 1983 edition of the *New England Journal of Medicine,* caused outrage and anxiety because they contradicted the widely held belief that a woman's chances of becoming pregnant remain favorable up to her thirty-fifth birthday. Instead, the group of women investigated by the study, who were twenty to forty years old, experienced a dramatic 13 percent drop in conceptions just before and after their thirtieth birthdays, followed by a more gradual decline between the ages of thirty-one and thirty-five. An editorial accompanying the article even suggested, in light of the study's finding, that women might want to reverse current trends by going back to having children in their twenties and waiting to work on their careers until their thirties. A common reaction among women interviewed by the press was that this conclusion was unrealistic. Many women, like Ms. G., felt bitter and betrayed.

Does this one study mean that Ms. G., a healthy woman in her early thirties, is over the hill? Of course not. There is nothing from her letter to suggest that she couldn't have a child even if she waits a few more years. Ironically, the shock of finding out that she could be less fertile than she thought might help her keep her options open; it is all too easy to avoid looking at the calendar and to allow the most fertile years simply to slip away.

She naturally wants to know what she should do and whether the study is even accurate. I would not advise any woman to rush precipitously into pregnancy due to the results of one study, whether it is accurate or not. The simple, inescapable fact, however, is that fertility does decline with age. Over their reproductive life spans, women are most fertile in their teens and middle twenties, certainly less fertile in their thirties, and considerably less fertile in the years just before menopause. (The twenties are also the most fertile time for men, although there is no male equivalent to menopause.) The French study shows a drop of percentage points starting at the age of thirty, another decline at thirty-five. A woman beyond her twenties should not always assume it will be harder for her to conceive. The findings do not mean it *necessarily* will be harder; only that it might.

Ms. G. has already begun to keep an eye on her fertility. To make doubly sure, she could write down her medical history, jot down the dates her periods begin and end, and ask herself the following questions: First, has she ever been pregnant? She doesn't mention any previous conception that would establish her fertility at some time in her life. Second, how regular is her menstrual cycle? Is she ovulating every month? A simple fertility check will establish that an egg is being produced in most, if not all, menstruations. A woman's ablity to conceive is probably more closely related to the regularity of her ovulation/menstruation pattern than to her exact age. Third, does she now or has she ever had a gynecological disorder that might affect her fertility? Should Ms. G. have or develop one of those conditions that inhibits fertility and becomes progressively worse with age, she may want to speed up her pregnancy timetable. Anovulatory cycles, for instance, usually become more common in a woman's thirties; so do fertility-crippling diseases like endometriosis. At the very least, a woman with a fertility problem should get used to the possibility that she may not give birth exactly when and how she originally planned. Even if no minuses appear on the fertility checklist, it would not be wise to let too many more years pass.

Waiting is terribly frustrating if a woman sees the passing months eating away at her chances of conception. Starting at virtually the eleventh hour also means there is less time to put things right, should a couple in their thirties need to get help. At her age, a consultation with an infertility specialist is highly recommended after six unsuccessful months of trying to conceive. Also, Ms. G. doesn't give her husband's age or a record of any previous conceptions. Since men in their thirties are quite often infertile or subfertile, it might be wise for him to have a semen analysis done a few months before Ms. G. plans to conceive, just to make sure.

Could That One Pelvic Infection Have Made Me Sterile? Who Is Right, My Girlfriend or My Gynecologist?

I've always been very healthy. I swim, jog, and play tennis regularly. At twenty-five, I went off the Pill because it made me put on weight. Instead, my doctor prescribed an IUD. I used it for about two years without any trouble, until last year, when I noticed an occasional sharp cramping just before I got my period each month. I put it down to premenstrual tension, and since I'm physically fit and hate complainers, I just ignored it. Then one day as I was crossing the street, I felt such a searing pain in my lower abdomen that I had to stop short to catch my breath. After my next period, I found I was spotting constantly, so I did go to the gynecologist. He said I had a pelvic infection and took out my IUD. I've used a diaphragm ever since. Recently I met a man I like very much. Really, at this point I'd love to get married and start a family, so you can imagine how upset I was when a girlfriend mentioned casually in conversation that having that infection probably means I'm sterile! My gynecologist has never said anything about my not being able to have children. Who is right, my girlfriend or my gynecologist?

R.B.

Wichita, Kansas

It's a pity that Ms. B. didn't see her doctor as soon as she noticed those first symptoms of infection instead of simply explaining them away. Any untoward symptom, however minor, should be looked at as a warning signal, even by a young and healthy woman. Ms. B.'s doctor didn't, I suspect, sufficiently describe the potential side effects of the intrauterine device, or I think Ms. B. would have detected the pelvic infection earlier on, before it became aggravated and caused her real pain. A woman with an IUD should be particularly alert because it comes with a higher risk of pelvic infection and tubal damage.

A minor intrauterine infection can usually be cured relatively easily with broad-spectrum antibiotics. Prompt treatment is important: an infection that is allowed to run wild can scar the delicate lining of the fallopian tubes or immobilize their fimbriated ends, the frondlike fingers that catch the egg and guide it into the tube. A seriously damaged fallopian tube could prevent conception altogether, or an obstruction in the tube might trap a fertilized egg, which would ultimately burst the tube (an ectopic pregnancy). I would doubt Ms. B. has experienced long-term damage from the infection, but if she is thinking of having children, it would be a good idea to go back to her gynecologist and review the situation. Right now she doesn't complain of any pain or tenderness in the pelvic area, so I would guess the pelvic organs are infection free. If she wants to make sure the tubes are open, she can ask her doctor to schedule a special X ray of the uterus and tubes, which is known as a *hysterosalpingogram*. The procedure is a little painful, but it is worthwhile if a woman is worried about her fertility.

I don't think a young, healthy woman like Ms. B. will have any trouble conceiving a baby. It's a pity, though, that she and her doctor made a shortsighted contraceptive choice when she stopped using the Pill. The IUD is a very good form of contraception for a woman who has children already or who has one steady sexual partner. It's not as good for a woman whose sexual partners change, because her immune system can't always handle the "foreign" bacteria introduced into the reproductive organs during intercourse. Ms. B. might have better accepted the slight weight gain and stayed on the Pill. Or she could have switched to the diaphragm, even though it is not quite as reliable as the IUD. Either would have been a better choice, unless Ms. B. had been fully alert to the side effects of the IUD.

NOTE: Women often ask their gynecologists whether a hysterosalpingogram is worth the discomfort, trouble, and expense. It is a diagnostic procedure that, like any other, should not be undertaken lightly, but in the aftermath of a serious pelvic infection or a complicated miscarriage or abortion, the test, which involves a dye being injected into the uterus and watching its passage through the uterus and tubes, will establish the configuration of the reproductive organs and show damaged areas, if any. Sometimes the test will flush out obstructions in the tubes and aid conception. If this does not happen, improvements in surgical techniques have made it possible for a skilled microsurgeon to enter the abdomen with fine surgical instruments and clean out or repair scarred areas in the uterus and tubes.

ENDOMETRIOSIS—IS IT DESTROYING YOUR OPTION TO HAVE A CHILD?

More than eight million American women suffer from the crippling, painful disease known as endometriosis. Yet many of them do not know it exists, let alone that they are victims of it. Struggling through recurrent episodes of pelvic pain and severe menstrual cramps, they may attribute the characteristic symptoms of endometriosis to the discomforts of a "normal" menstrual cycle. Months and years can go by before they seek help from their doctor, and even then, doctors unfamiliar with the disease may not know what it is. Meanwhile the endometriosis hidden inside a woman's body slowly, painfully incapacitates one after the other of her reproductive organs.

Endometriosis is a disease in which the endometrium, or uterine lining, spreads beyond the uterus to implant itself outside the womb. At the end of the normal menstrual cycle, rhythmic contractions of the uterus detach the endometrium and push the discarded tissue fragments out the cervix, to leave the body in the form of menstrual blood. With the onset of endometriosis, the normal pattern is disrupted. The hard spasmodic contractions evident to a woman as severe menstrual cramps flush the tissue fragments backward and up through the fallopian tubes instead of downward and through the cervix and the vagina. Tissue fragments flushed through the tubes are sprayed into the abdominal cavity, where they implant themselves onto the outside of the ovaries and the fallopian tubes and the outside of the uterus. Fed by the monthly production of estrogen and progesterone, the misplaced endometrial tissue thickens, bleeds, breaks away, and spreads throughout the abdominal cavity, to be joined by yet more tissue from within the uterus. With each monthly cycle, endometriosis takes a firmer hold, until it seems as though a woman's body has declared war on itself.

Symptoms of endometriosis include painful ovulation, severe cramps during ovulation, and a deep abdominal pain on one side or the other or an unspecific abdominal pain before or after menstruation. Women besieged by unremitting pain often say they have been taken over by the disease. But if pain is the first sign of endometriosis, infertility is the end result. Misplaced endometrial tissue, clinging like a parasite to its host, will eventually suffocate the ovaries, impeding the passage of the monthly egg. Tissue fragments creeping inside the fallopian tubes will block or scar the tubes. Even with a mild case of endometriosis, it is more difficult for a woman to become pregnant. With an advanced case, her chances are slim indeed.

Often the disorder is known as the career woman's disease, as though endometriosis were to be found exclusively among women with high-powered jobs. Understandably, endometriosis is seen more frequently among women who have put off childbearing, because pregnancy and breast-feeding disrupt ovulation and menstruation and put the hormonal cycle temporarily to rest. But any woman in her childbearing years could get endometriosis, especially in times of stress. Healthy, untroubled women have immune systems that protect them against the onset of the disorder. Their functioning immune systems are usually able to reject any endometrial tissue that might mistakenly be pushed into the abdominal cavity during menstruation. The immune system, however, is less efficient under stress; thus a tense woman might not be able to fight off the endometrial tissue growth inside her abdomen, just as a woman under stress is less likely to fight off the common cold.

Perfectionists, achievers, women who are hard on themselves because they want the best for themselves are the typical endometriosis victims, whether they are caring for their children or their law practice. Career woman or housewife, any woman who fits this profile *could* have endometriosis.

GETTING HELP

Inexplicable pelvic pain should never be ignored or explained away by a reassuring diagnosis. A woman trying to conceive who has suspicious pelvic pain that her doctor cannot seem to identify should not wait around for the symptoms to become easier to define. Her most fertile years are already slipping by.

A woman can usually find out if she has endometriosis by allowing a surgeon to perform the exploratory procedure called a *laparoscopy*. During a laparoscopy, the surgeon viewing the internal organs might spot the endometrial tissue right away. Unfortunately, the laparoscopy is only as good as the surgeon who is performing it, and arriving at a diagnosis of endometriosis is trickier than most people think. A surgeon will be able to see large masses of endometrial tissue if the disease is extensive, but if the endometriosis is minimal or located behind the uterus, it may elude his view and you may be told that you don't have it. This possibility of *hidden endometriosis* should not confuse a doctor familiar with the disease who believes in his ability to diagnose endometriosis from a woman's history and a straightforward clinical examination. A knowledgeable doctor who conducts an internal examination and who has the skill to feel small tender growths on or behind the uterus, ovaries, or tubes should, in my opinion, be able to *diagnose endometriosis without surgery*. This is important, since surgery should always, if possible, be bypassed because it exposes a woman to the unnecessary risks of both anesthesia and the operation itself.

If during a pelvic examination or a laparoscopy, a woman is diagnosed as having endometriosis, treatment should be started right away. An old form of treatment for endometriosis was the birth control pill. The Pill contains the hormones estrogen and progesterone, which create a pseudopregnancy and prevent the endometrium from developing to a greater extent each month. However, the Pill has enough hormones to continue to stimulate the endometrium so that the endometriosis tissue remains alive. Instead of incorrectly treating the condition with the Pill, knowledgeable doctors use a new breakthrough drug called Danocrine (danazol), a synthetic derivative of testosterone, which stops ovulation and thus provides a "pelvic rest." Danazol, the only FDA-approved drug for endometriosis, blocks the release of the brain hormones that set the menstrual cycle in motion. A woman's organs are not stimulated to release an egg, so there is no ovulation and estrogen and progesterone hormones do not increase. When a woman does not ovulate and her female hormones do not fluctuate, there is no buildup of the endometrium and no chance for endometriosis to grow. By taking Danocrine tablets every day for six to nine months, she is curtailing her hormone production and thereby cutting off the endometriosis from the hitherto continuous supply of blood vessels that it needs for its survival. The endometrial tissue dies, and like all dead tissue, it is slowly reabsorbed by the body and disappears.

In the past, doctors often recommended surgery for endometriosis; today Danocrine has made surgery unnecessary, except when a woman has large masses that must be removed. Doctors used to advise patients that they needed major surgery for endometriosis to "burn it all out," but inevitably the tissue will grow back over time. A surgeon cannot remove every bit of endometriosis by cutting or scraping at it, and the natural fluctuation of the hormones are not under his control after surgery. Should a woman with endometriosis need surgery, she ought to be placed on Danocrine for three months before the operation to reduce the endometrial growth and for three months after it to prevent a reappearance of the disease. New studies may add new agents that will aid in the fight against endometriosis, but at present, only danazol is approved and working.

I'd Like to Get Pregnant, but I Honestly Don't Know Where to Turn Next.

I've been in and out of hospitals and doctors' offices for over eight years now. I've had test after test, operation after operation, and still I don't seem to be able to get pregnant. The first doctor, whom I saw because I had such pain with my periods, told me I had fibroids. (I was only twenty-four at the time.) By the time I visited the second, the pain had gotten worse and I had also found it impossible to conceive. She told me it was some psychological problem that had stopped me from conceiving and recommended psychotherapy. Well, it wasn't all in my head. I really wanted a child and I wasn't afraid of being pregnant. Moreover, the pain was getting worse and worse and there didn't seem to be a time in between my periods when I wasn't spotting. What was crazy was that nobody except me seemed to think this abnormal! I did quit my job, which was stressful, I must admit, but that didn't help me conceive or even mitigate that terrible monthly pain. The next doctor I consulted did a D&C to clean out the uterus, as he put it. He also diagnosed gonorrhea! (I'm an orthodox Jewish woman and I have never slept with anyone but my husband.) Of course, the antibiotics didn't do

53

a thing for me, and the pain was getting worse and worse. Finally a friend in the medical profession, knowing I was looking for a new doctor, got me an appointment with a famous infertility expert who diagnosed my problem as endometriosis. He operated to remove what he said were massive adhesions behind the uterus and tubes, put me on Danocrine for three months, and told me I was fine—I could go ahead and conceive. Well, it was no go. The pain came back. I was on and off drugs for another few months; the same story over and over again. I wouldn't consent to further surgery because I was afraid of losing yet more pieces of my organs. Now my in-laws want us to adopt a child, the baby of a young woman who is known to our rabbi. Although I know they mean well, I feel terribly saddened and betrayed. I am just not ready to accept that I can't have children, even though I seem to have tried everything and I'm still infertile. I'm willing to keep going, but quite honestly, I don't know where to turn next.

L.E.

Los Angeles, California

Answer to Endometriosis Sufferers

When Ms. E. wrote this letter, she had experienced the frustration and heartbreak of consulting doctor after doctor, only to be told that the pain of endometriosis was all in her head, was correctable by antibiotics, or could be cured by surgery. Typically, the early symptoms of the disease hadn't been detected by her doctors, which often happens because a doctor palpating the abdomen to find pelvic masses doesn't find the smaller tissue fragments clinging to the ovaries and tubes. Consequently women with endometriosis often wage a lonely war with the disease, while their doctors try ineffective treatments, usually antibiotics; give up on them altogether; or, worse, convince them that a hysterectomy, the surgical removal of the reproductive organs, is the only way to cure their suffering.

Fortunately, Ms. E. knew her pain was real and she persisted until she found a doctor who at least diagnosed the disease correctly. You might think her search would have ended here, but unfortunately it did not. The infertility specialist may have been a good surgeon, but he made an all too common mistake: he relied on surgery to get rid of the disease and then suggested more surgery when the tissue inevitably grew back. Admittedly, he did also correctly prescribe danazol, the only drug the FDA approves for her condition, but the endometriosis had gone so far in Ms. E.'s case that a medication prescribed in low doses over three months or so was only going to relieve the situation temporarily. At the time she wrote to me, Ms. E. was facing a predicament that is only too familiar to the endometriosis victim—where to go after surgery, the "answer" to endometriosis, has failed.

Ms. E. wrote to me when the physical and mental stress had driven her almost to the edge. Fortunately, a month or two later, a sympathetic friend referred her to a doctor known to be a specialist in endometriosis. A thorough look at her history, a physical examination, and an ultrasound examination confirmed the previous doctor's diagnosis. Instead of operating, he put her back on Danazol medication but this time with a dosage of a 200-mg tablet three times daily, without interruption, for twelve months. Little by little over the year, the antihormonal properties of the drug effectively blocked the hormones that had fed the endometrial tissue until the organs were free and clear and the foreign tissue had been reabsorbed into the now healthy body.

Don't bear the burden alone. This should be the catchphrase for any woman undergoing infertility analysis. Incredibly, in all those eight years, no one until the last doctor she saw had thought to test Ms. E.'s husband. As it turned out, the semen analysis the doctor had performed just as a precaution showed how he had contributed to his wife's problem with a problem of his own. By putting a sample of Mr. E.'s semen under the microscope, the laboratory doing the fertility analysis determined that the number of sperm in the sample was more than adequate but that the unnaturally warm environment inside the testicles (from varicocele, a cluster of varicose veins in the groin) had slowed the sperm and made them sluggish. Sperm motility was enhanced when Mr. E. used an innovative new technique, a kind of jock strap that contains a cooling device placed next to the testicles. It was an experimental alternate to removing the veins surgically, and it worked. After a year of treatment and repeated tests (Ms. E. even had to have thyroid medication to correct an additional, smaller problem of an irregularity in the menstrual cycle), the couple went off together for their first holiday in five years. Ms. E. conceived and had a wonderful pregnancy, the happy ending to an eight-year saga of pain, doubt, and disappointment. She is now the proud mother of a healthy boy.

Don't Give Up

Prolonged infertility is saddening. It is also debilitating and frustrating. Involuntarily set apart from other couples with children, all too often, hitherto-supportive loving partners become estranged under the stress of expectations dashed and hope continually denied. "What you don't realize until it happens to you is that infertility is often so lonely," said a patient of mine whose marriage had almost broken up in the three years of intensive treatment that preceded her first successful conception. One woman writing to an organization for infertile couples echoed that observation when she described the neat, orderly plans for conception that were suddenly, unexpectedly, not so neat and orderly. And yet patience and persistence *are* rewarded. With the right fertility treatments, at least 70 percent of infertile couples can be helped, even if those treatments sometimes take years. Infertility is often reversible; it is often curable, although it may require the courage and persistence of a Ms. E. to achieve a long-overdue conception. It is important, however, that a couple become actively involved in their fertility problems, reading and asking questions as well as looking for the best and most sensitive infertility specialist.

ABORTION: WILL IT AFFECT CONCEPTION?

With one and a half million abortions performed each year, this is bound to be an urgent question for the many women with an abortion in their pasts who are looking to the future and a much-wanted pregnancy and birth. Abortion is still an emotionally laden issue, and though most women don't regret terminating pregnancies they realistically could not have carried to term, an unforeseen uneasiness about the possibly long-term effects of an abortion does sometimes surface just as a woman is planning to conceive. Fortunately, the perilous back-street abortion is more or less a bad memory now, and women get early, safe pregnancy terminations that do not end in septic abortion or other potentially fatal complications. Still, an abortion isn't always simple, and there continue to be medical risks and emotional difficulties anytime a woman must terminate a pregnancy for whatever reason.

I've Had Two Abortions. Will I Have Trouble Conceiving?

I've had two abortions, one performed by menstrual extraction a few weeks after I got pregnant at the age of eighteen and the other three years ago, when my boyfriend (now my husband) and I conceived shortly after we met. The second time I waited until the thirteenth week of pregnancy before we finally decided that having a child just then would place an impossible strain on our relationship. The doctor performed what he called a D&E, which wasn't pleasant but at least was done in the hospital. I hadn't thought much about either abortion until a few weeks ago, when in the middle of trying to get pregnant, I've started having recurring dreams in which I'm looking for a lost child. Of course I wake up very upset and have to take sleeping pills to get back to sleep. As far as I know, there's nothing wrong with me, but now I can't shake this fear that I'm never going to get pregnant again, that the abortions have destroyed my chance to have a healthy child. Are these fears unfounded? Or could something have occurred after the abortions that might affect my plans to conceive?

A.K.
Buffalo, New York

An abortion could be anything from a simple one performed at a doctor's office very early on in pregnancy or a hospital abortion at twenty weeks with a more complex procedure and under general anesthesia. As a rule, the safest and best abortion method is the one that can be performed very early on, the miniabortion, or menstrual extraction. Up to six or seven weeks, the menstrual extraction procedure can be done without really interfering with the cervix or the uterus, so the risk of uterine infection after the procedure is minimized and the cervix, which is minimally dilated during the procedure, should remain intact and ready for future childbearing. (A healthy unlacerated cervix is able to hold on to the contents of the womb without opening prematurely under the pressure of the pregnancy.) In the hands of an experienced doctor, the vacuum extraction method of performing abortions is so gentle nowadays that the cervix should not be damaged, and the uterus, because it isn't scraped out or otherwise tampered with, usually heals right away. A woman who has had one abortion performed early in pregnancy—one that wasn't followed by excessive bleeding from a cervical laceration or a low-grade fever or other signs of uterine infection—can presume that she is not only fertile but just as able to carry a pregnancy to term as if she had never had the abortion. It is probably even true that a woman can have more than one early uncomplicated abortion without endangering her future childbearing, although the fewer times a woman runs even a slight risk of postabortion complications, the better.

A woman's future childbearing abilities are most at question with several abortions or an abortion or abortions done at a point in pregnancy, usually after the sixth or seventh week, when the cervix must be dilated mechanically to allow the procedure to be performed. The suction method used at seven to twelve weeks is still a gentle method of emptying the womb, but the cervix must be stretched wide enough to accommodate the procedure. Later on in pregnancy, at twelve to sixteen weeks, the cervix must be even more widely dilated to remove the contents of the uterus. With a D&E, a dilatation and evacuation, there is a greater chance that the cervix or uterus will be lacerated during the procedure and that there will be rupture and bleeding. And the more times a doctor forcefully opens a woman's cervix to perform an abortion, the more chances she has of having her cervix torn or rendered incompetent, unable to withstand the pressure of a growing fetus. Pregnant women who have had traumatic or multiple abortions sometimes need what is known as the Shirodkar procedure, a literal sewing together of the cervical tissues, with the stitches securely left in place until the pregnancy is at or close to term.

A doctor examining a patient's cervix should be able to tell whether it is long and firm enough to hold on to a pregnancy. A doctor might suggest an X ray of the uterus and tubes if his patient is among the 5 to 10 percent of women who have postabortion infections (even after legalization of abortion), because they don't always protect themselves after an abortion and a man's penis can push bacteria into the uterus. Nothing should be inserted into the vagina until the healing process is over, not even tampons. Ms. K. can go all the more confidently to her doctor because she doesn't remember complications from either abortion. Having a hysterosalpingogram will reveal unsuspected adhesions in the womb or blockages in the tubes. Adhesions would require her to have a D&C, as I have already described. Damaged tubes may be repaired by microsurgical techniques. Those are the sensible, practical steps I would urge any woman to take who, like Ms. K., is trying to control powerful emotions with sleeping pills or mood-altering drugs. She is less likely to conceive in any case right now, just because she is so confused. A delicate interaction exists between the brain and the reproductive system, and Ms. K.'s grief is probably upsetting her hormonal balance along with her normally tranquil life. That stress will show itself in irregular periods or maybe even a temporary loss of menstruation. Exercise, diet control, proper nutrition as well as vitamin B-complex (100 mg of vitamin B_1 and 100–300 mg of vitamin B_6) taken daily might aid in regulating her cycle and eliminating her stress. If this does not fully relieve her symptoms, therapy would be the long-term answer if feelings of grief persist. However, a straightforward, sympathetic evaluation might be enough to set Ms. K.'s fears at rest.

THE FINAL GOAL: PREGNANCY

Nothing is more satisfying than to conceive successfully after you and your partner have made the decision to start a family. Many women may find getting pregnant easy, but others may have to work hard for it, and things seem to get more difficult when you want them badly.

If conception seems elusive, many specialists in gynecology and infertility are available to help. Physicians trained in the fertility field have so much more knowledge and understanding than ever before that someone will most likely be able to lead you to pregnancy.

Never let time pass when you suspect that you or your husband might have a fertility problem, since conception only gets harder as you grow older. Think about your future as soon as you can, because today you are younger than you will be tomorrow.

CHAPTER 3

Just Pregnant

The first noticeable symptom of pregnancy might be anything from a slight change in skin color to a violent atypical reaction to a familiar scent or a favorite food. Surprisingly, the first faint hint often precedes the missed period by several days. At times, a woman will know something is different or odd or wrong without being able to say exactly how she feels until the missed period tips her off to what is happening to her body. Other women simply seem to know that they are pregnant. The experience depends so much on the individual that each woman more or less writes her own story when she becomes pregnant, with the important plot points being how she knew that she was pregnant and when she knew that she was pregnant. Four women have contributed their experiences to this book. Not all of them expected to be pregnant, but each one recognized pregnancy in a way characterized by her personality and her pregnancy.

Jean B., a pediatric nurse: "I knew I was pregnant right away. To start with, my breasts felt different. Just how different is difficult for me to say. It wasn't that they were painful or tense, as though I were about to get my period; it was just that I was more aware of them. In fact, I was simply more aware of every minute part of my body. That odd sensation was what tipped me off to what had happened. I know it couldn't have been more than a week and a half after I conceived that I turned to my husband and said, 'Look, Bill, I'm pregnant, I know I'm pregnant.'"

Laura E., a travel agent: "After those three long years of hoping I was pregnant every time my period was a day late, I was so tired of my husband asking, 'Well, are you or aren't you?' that I'd go to my doctor's appointment and then go home pretending I'd just had an ordinary day. One afternoon I was standing up on the back of the sofa rehanging the living room curtains when I slipped and fell smack onto the floor. The next moment, without thinking, I had picked myself up, put my hand on my stomach, and said out loud and to the empty room, 'My baby, oh, my baby.' It was six or seven days before what would have been the first missed day of my period."

Elizabeth A., a kindergarten teacher: "That night I got home from work exhausted and was irritable all evening. In fact, I blew up over a minor disagreement over our checking account, had a tremendous crying spell, and went to bed an hour earlier than usual. None of this is at all like me except I do get a bit moody just before my period. The next morning I slept through the alarm, got out of bed rather quickly, and found myself clinging to the dresser to keep myself upright. It wasn't that I fainted but I had this dizzy claustrophobic sensation, as though the room were closing in on me and I couldn't breathe. I never even connected the bad mood and the dizzy spell until I missed my period a few days later."

Judith C., a free-lance copywriter: "By Monday, my period was five days late. I was trying not to be too hopeful because I've been irregular at other times. That morning I walked the dog back into the kitchen, where one of the men decorating the house had brought in hash browns and eggs from the local coffee shop. As he poured ketchup over the food, the smell hit me with such force that I almost stepped backward to get away from the sweet, suffocating odor. Almost simultaneously, I felt that I was going to vomit—not the queasy sensation I'd been feeling intermittently for a few days, but an honest-to-goodness feeling that I was going to vomit up everything in my stomach if I didn't get out of that room immediately."

THE FIRST SIGNS OF PREGNANCY

The missed period is the first symptom that most women mention to their doctors because it is the least ambiguous. (See Figure 3-1.) Other symptoms, however, can be clear signs of pregnancy, especially when several are experienced at once. Sometimes early-pregnancy breast tenderness or a feeling of fullness masquerades in the guise of PMS symptoms, but the heaviness of the breasts is unusual, the bluish veins on the breasts tend to stand out more, and the nipple area darkens. A woman may experience a bloated, stuffy, headachy feeling, as though she were just about to come down with a minor intestinal ailment, or indeed her period, if that's how she normally feels just before she menstruates. Sometimes the slightly queasy feeling is accompanied by a heightened sensitivity to smells—generally, but not exclusively, unpleasant smells. There might be an increased urge to urinate, which occurs even this early in pregnancy because the hormone progesterone relaxes smooth muscle in the bladder along with the muscles of the uterine wall. Another subtle sign of pregnancy is a rise in temperature, which may or may not be noticed from the general warmth and texture of the skin. Women who take their basal body temperature regularly will notice that the one-degree postovulation jump in temperature persists beyond the ten-day or two-week period. A temperature that remains steadily at the higher level past the expected date of menstruation is a most reliable early clue to a successful conception.

If the list excludes that classic early pregnancy symptom morning sickness, there is a reason for the omission. Morning sickness (although that in fact is a misnomer, since nausea and vomiting can occur all day) is expected by almost ten out of ten women from day 1 of their pregnancies. Consequently women who have every other early pregnancy symptom except acute nausea and vomiting sometimes hesitatingly ask themselves, "Am I really pregnant?" The reassuring answer is that many women do have

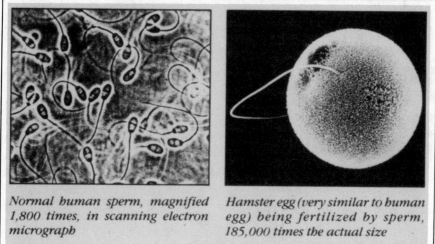

Normal human sperm, magnified 1,800 times, in scanning electron micrograph

Hamster egg (very similar to human egg) being fertilized by sperm, 185,000 times the actual size

DAVID M. PHILLIPS, PHD, POPULATION COUNCIL

Figure 3-1. *Semen and fertilization. Normal human sperm magnified 1,800 times, at left. Fertilization of hamster egg, at right.* Reproduced by permission of The Population Council.

milder related symptoms, often a queasy or bloated feeling, early in pregnancy, but severe nausea plagues far fewer pregnancies than most women suppose. (See Chapter 6 for more questions and answers on the subject of early pregnancy, nausea, and vomiting.) If a woman asks, "Will I have slight nausea?" the answer is probably yes, because nausea is experienced by many women. But actual vomiting? No, in all probability, although there is usually nothing to worry about if you do find yourself with a textbook case of morning sickness.

If there is one ubiquitous early pregnancy symptom in addition to the first missed period, it is fatigue; that tired, drained feeling begins very early after conception and often persists throughout the first twelve weeks of pregnancy. At times, women plagued by extraordinary fatigue describe themselves as having practically slept through the first trimester. Even if a woman maintains her prepregnancy level of seven or eight hours of sleep a night, her waking hours may be clouded by a persistent slight headache or a generally woozy sensation, which is a milder version of that "I am thoroughly exhausted" feeling. Women whose metabolism has a harder time adjusting to the new hormonal levels of early pregnancy are usually those who have the most fatigue. This fatigue may or may not be accompanied by breast tenderness, nausea, a bloated feeling, or other discomforts of early pregnancy. Hormonal changes may play havoc with the newly pregnant body, at least until the body has had time to marshal its defenses and fight back.

TESTS THAT DETERMINE PREGNANCY

The legendary rabbit test that used to confirm a woman's pregnancy is no more, but decades ago, it was really the only way to know whether a woman had conceived. A woman's urine was injected into a female rabbit, which would be killed so that its ovaries could be examined. If the urine had caused the ovaries to mature and develop blood spots, a doctor would then have positive proof of pregnancy. That does not happen today.

Urine tests. No rabbits are offering their lives for pregnancy testing anymore; however, a woman's urine is still used. Approximately two weeks after a woman misses her period, a doctor can perform a urine slide test in his office. HCG (human chorionic gonadotropin) is a hormone that rises during pregnancy. A physician can put a drop of a woman's urine on a slide and add a test solution and HCG antibodies. The results appear within two minutes. When a woman is pregnant, the mixture on the slide turns a milky white but remains smooth. When she is not pregnant, the mixture stays clear and gets a lumpy sour-milk consistency.

Another urine test is a lab analysis of a woman's morning urine. The urine is mixed with a testing solution and HCG antibodies in a test tube, where a reaction occurs. If a woman is pregnant, a whitish ring appears in the bottom of the test tube in approximately one hour. This test must also take place two weeks after a missed period.

A new urine test, however, can confirm pregnancy two to two and a half weeks after conception, which is usually just before a menstrual period is due to arrive. This highly sensitive test, called TestPack, marketed by Abbott Laboratories, is only available to doctors right now. A few drops of a woman's urine are added to an HCG reaction disc, a button-size disc treated with HCG antibodies. Within three minutes, either a plus or a minus sign appears, depending upon the reaction that occurs. A plus indicates pregnancy, and I can tell a woman that she is expecting before she leaves my office. TestPack has been very helpful in my practice.

Another fast way to find the answer to "Am I pregnant?" is with a blood test.

The radioimmunoassay (RIA) blood test. Theoretically, an RIA blood test can detect the beta-subunit of HCG, the placenta-produced hormone that rises during pregnancy, within a week or two after conception, even before a period is missed. Laboratories should be able to report the results of an RIA the same day if blood is taken in the morning. Another less frequently used but just as accurate blood test is the radioreceptor assay (RRA), which is also sensitive enough to confirm pregnancy within a week or two of conception.

Home pregnancy tests. The amount of HCG in a woman's urine can be detected with a home kit that costs about eight dollars. Just like the other urine tests, this one only gives accurate results two weeks after a missed period. Although the brand names of the tests are different, the testing method is basically the same for all of them. The package instructions for the test must be read carefully and followed explicitly to get an accurate reading. The home pregnancy tests are based on the same methods as those that are used in the laboratory: a few drops of urine are placed in a test tube containing the testing chemicals, water is added, and the tube is shaken and then allowed to rest in a special holder for at least two hours. The test tube must remain undisturbed or the results will be inaccurate. If the test is positive, a brown ring will appear, reflected in a small mirror underneath the test tube; if it is negative, the ring will not appear. A positive test taken at the correct time will usually be accurate—about 98 percent accurate, according to one manufacturer. But if the test shows a negative result, a woman should definitely take it again a few days later if meanwhile she has not started to menstruate. There is about a 20 percent chance that a negative test may be wrong, and a belief that you are not pregnant could have serious consequences.

THE NEW HORMONAL LEVEL: WHAT IT MEANS TO YOU

When a woman experiencing early pregnancy discomfort is glibly told that her body is simply adjusting to the new hormonal levels of pregnancy, a natural response is "Why?" and "How long will I go on feeling this way?" Without wishing to contribute to the pseudotheory that women (unlike men, of course) are dominated by their hormones, the first few weeks after conception really are a time when the familiar female hormones estrogen and progesterone behave in a unique way.

Initially, both hormones reach new peaks at the beginning of a pregnancy. Just before her period, a woman normally experiences high levels of estrogen or progesterone, but in most women, the hormones are in balance premenstrually. When they are not in balance, a woman may experience premenstrual syndrome (PMS). The reason classic premenstrual symptoms, including the bloated, tired, slightly nauseated feeling, appear in pregnancy just as they do before a period may be that estrogen and progesterone are not in perfect balance during the first couple of months of pregnancy. Later in pregnancy, when the hormones are in perfect balance, those symptoms disappear and a woman will begin to experience the "glow" of pregnancy.

Early in pregnancy, women may experience a tired, grumpy, overweight feeling similar to that frequently experienced by women in their first two or three months of going on the Pill. The Pill functions to suppress ovulation and even out the hormonal levels, so that the body goes into a permanent state of pseudopregnancy. When pregnancy is thought of as a sort of PMS-like state, the analogy is partly right and partly wrong. You may have PMS-like symptoms, but they are caused by the new balancing act between the high estrogen level and the equally high progesterone level, not the imbalance you are used to experiencing at the end of the monthly cycle.

Second, the disconcerting thing about this new hormonal situation is that it persists. You may be very used to a short period of discomfort at the end of every cycle, followed by a welcome feeling of relief as your period begins. In early pregnancy, the hormones remain at their new peak level and the body is consequently thrown into a temporary state of disequilibrium. It may take as long as two to three months for the renal system and the other body systems to adjust fully to the fact that you are pregnant. As the balance is achieved, the early pregnancy symptoms, from morning sickness and fatigue to a return of adolescent acne (a minor annoyance, but women often break out unexpectedly in those early months), often abruptly disappear. Then the new, steady hormonal levels may work to a woman's advantage. Not only does her normal energy come back, but being without her periods eliminates the monthly loss of iron, the premenstrual stress, and the other unwelcome side effects of menstruation. Vigorous, clear-skinned, visibly glowing with renewed energy, a pregnant woman can move confidently into the third or fourth month of pregnancy knowing that the worst of the early pregnancy symptoms have been left behind. Once the dreamlike state, good or bad, of the first trimester is over (many women talk about being in a fog in those first few months), most women wholeheartedly begin to enjoy their pregnancies.

QUESTIONS ABOUT EARLY PREGNANCY SYMPTOMS

Why Didn't I Know I Was Pregnant?

I have just spent two miserable months trying to explain away the symptoms of a mysterious illness, only to find that all I am is pregnant. I didn't miss my period because I'm a dancer and menstruate only every other month. But I did find I was hungry all the time, and I mean all the time. No matter how much I ate, a pit in my stomach never seemed to fill up. That bothered me a lot because I was eating my way out of my clothes at the same time that my energy level hit rock bottom. I've never been so tired in my life; I couldn't even drag myself to class, and getting to my part-time job and back exhausted me so much I would get home and sleep straight through until the next morning. My husband thought I had the flu, I thought I was hypoglycemic; finally I got so cold and shaky that my husband took me to the doctor. It was she who told me that I was two months pregnant! I can't believe I thought I was ill and I was really pregnant. Shouldn't I have known the difference? I would like to know if many women feel this drained and exhausted when they're first pregnant.

M.S.
Chicago, Illinois

Yes, for some women, this degree of fatigue is quite normal. Surprisingly, the women who notice acute early pregnancy symptoms often exercise strenuously and watch their weight with the hawklike attention of a dancer or an athlete. The reason is probably as much psychological as it is physiological. Almost every pregnant woman retains some water in the early months, and it is this water retention that gives her the headaches, the odd dizzy sensation, and the exhausted, slightly nauseated feeling. Athletic women, however, seem to notice the edema more quickly than women who spend more time at their desks than at the ballet class or the running track. It is not that athletic women actually have more early pregnancy symptoms than other women; on the contrary, they are better equipped than most women to carry a pregnancy gracefully. Living in a normally energetic, responsive, lively body, however, a woman who is used to exercising often realizes immediately that something is radically different. She might be eating the same foods and following the same exercise routines when suddenly she is tired—frustratingly tired, considering the brisk pace of her normal everyday schedule. If she continues to push herself, the tiredness only increases the frustration and the frustration only exacerbates the exhaustion, until she is caught up in a vicious circle in which her emotions are at war with her unexpectedly limited physical capabilities. After living with this degree of misery for a week or so, most women, tipped off by the first missed period, go to the doctor and get a pregnancy test. Ms. S. dragged herself around for two and a half miserable months. Had she thrown up or fainted, she might have suspected pregnancy sooner. As it was, she attributed the fatigue to hypoglycemia, thought her period was late because she did not have a completely regular menstruation, and went on working and dancing until she almost collapsed from exhaustion.

Fatigue due to pregnancy has a more insistent edge to it than do other forms of fatigue. Strategies for coping with normal fatigue help. If you eat better, sleep longer, and relax more, you will feel temporarily less tired. But the tired, dizzy, headachy feeling tends to persist even if you rest. The physiological reason is this: the brain as well as the rest of the body are thrown off balance by the extra water retention. Also, the burdensome sense of fatigue is only one of many messages the body transmits during pregnancy to guard the new life within the womb.

Certain antifatigue measures do help. Extra rest, of course, is important. If you are used to running four miles a day after work or sleeping only six hours a night, heed your body's signs; slow down, sleep more, spend a quiet evening at home instead of planning an evening full of activity. Dietary changes help, too. Avoid oversalting foods. The increased hormonal levels bind salt, which traps fluid and adds to the headaches and the bloated feeling. Vitamin supplements are never more useful than just before and during pregnancy. A lot of the extra fatigue can be eliminated by the simple precaution of taking extra vitamins: at least 100 mg of vitamin B_1 and 300 mg of B_6, 500 mg of vitamin C, and 500 to 1000 mg of calcium, starting a few months *before* conception.

Hormonally linked with fatigue are odd changes in appetite.

The hunger pangs and mood swings associated with fluctuations in blood sugar levels are particularly bewildering for women who have never experienced any form of hypoglycemia before becoming pregnant. Hypoglycemic reactions occur at the beginning of pregnancy probably as a response to the abnormal hormonal levels in the body.

Strategies for coping with errant blood sugar levels include eliminating refined sugars and eating small amounts of food regularly. Also foods high in the complex carbohydrates—vegetables, grains, and fruits—will supply a constant source of energy and help get rid of the ravenous feeling. Slower-burning high-fiber foods like vegetables and grains break down at a steadier rate than do red meats and simple sugars, which provide an instant high followed by an equally dramatic low. The common urban diet of starch and sugary foods eaten on the run may satisfy the appetite temporarily, but Ms. S. probably exercises off her coffee-and-danish breakfast within the first few minutes of her dance class.

Ms. S. thought she was hypoglycemic. Her husband thought she had a virus. Had she fainted, she might have thought she had low blood pressure. Had she been sick, she might have thought she had a stomach upset. The list could go on and on. Unless you think you could be pregnant, the "Why am I feeling this way" "What's wrong with me?" game can be played for weeks, with everyone concerned becoming more and more bewildered and confused. Because early pregnancy symptoms are often vague or apparently contradictory (How can I be sick *and* hungry at the same time?), a woman may put off calling or visiting a doctor's office until the symptoms become worse or more defined. At that time, the reason for the mysterious "illness" is usually obvious to her physician.

The temptation, meanwhile, is to try becoming your own physician. The medicine cabinet is close at hand and so is the local pharmacy. What was to prevent Ms. S. from dosing herself with over-the-counter drugs or using a prescription medication left over from a previous illness? People have become so used to connecting the words *aspirin* and *headache* that over-the-counter drugs are used more or less indiscriminately, and the scenario with certain prescription drugs is similar. Antibiotics are probably more widely overprescribed by American doctors than any other drug; many doctors simply prescribe them on the phone when a patient calls with virallike symptoms. Women have wrongly taken drugs at the beginning of a pregnancy when they have been misled by an apparently viral-induced stomach upset or the symptoms of the flu. They get an over-the-phone prescription for one of the antibiotics, like tetracycline, which is not recommended for use during pregnancy. (See Chapter 9 for specific information on the different antibiotics and other drugs and how they affect fetal development.) If the rule during pregnancy is, Never take a drug, even an over-the-counter drug, without your obstetrician's approval, the rule just before pregnancy should be, Don't play doctor. If you feel ill, get a pregnancy test before trying any kind of drug therapy.

Why Do I Have This Feeling That I'm About to Have My Period Any Minute?

I think I'm pregnant and so did my doctor when I called him, but it's too soon after missing my period to be sure. If I really am pregnant, why do I have this feeling that I'm going to have my period any moment? Although we haven't used birth control and I'm a week overdue, it's just the same vague crampy, stuffy, headachy feeling I always have in the last week of my cycle, except that maybe my breasts are a little heavier than usual. Shouldn't I have thrown up by now? Or felt faint? My sister was a mess at the beginning of her pregnancy, but at least she knew she had conceived. Could I possibly be having a delayed period? I almost never skip a period or run more than a day late.

D.B.

Bridgeport, Connecticut

The vague sensations Ms. B. writes about are very typical of early pregnancy. If Ms. B.'s menstrual cycle is as regular as she describes, chances are the delayed period plus the other symptoms mean she is pregnant. Headaches, breast enlargement, a slightly queasy feeling—these are all common early pregnancy symptoms. So are the menstruallike cramps Ms. B. is having. There is nothing mysterious about this cramping, although many early pregnant women think they are about to menstruate at any moment because of it. Mild early pregnancy cramping is caused by a spontaneous release of prostaglandins, the hormone that produces menstrual cramping, from a mind/body connection confused by the body's newly pregnant state. Although the uterus usually remains tranquil once the egg is fertilized (spasmic cramping has been known to dislodge the tiny conceptus from the uterine lining), signs of a pseudoperiod, including cramping and occasional spotting two weeks after conception, do sometimes occur during and after the days on which a woman would normally have menstruated. This may be due to a slight drop in progesterone before and during the former menstruation days, and even this slight decrease in progesterone will release the cramp-inducing prostaglandins, just as it does before a period. Cramping and/or spotting will usually decrease or disappear once the placenta begins producing its own progesterone, about the sixth week of pregnancy (although an episode of cramping from another slight dip in progesterone might be repeated four weeks later). Sometimes rather than occurring in episodes, the experience is more one of spasmodic cramping occurring on and off through the first few weeks of pregnancy. This is usually a side effect of the uterus gradually expanding to accommodate the placenta and the fetus.

Normally the cramping goes away once the progesterone level is fairly stable, and so does any slight spotting or staining. (See Chapter 13 for more on occasional bleeding during pregnancy.) Cramping can become quite severe at times, however, especially when it is accompanied by spotting, staining, or outright bleeding. Women who have experienced severe cramping during pregnancy often say it resembles heavy menstrual cramps. Noticeably heavy cramping is one of the first signs of miscarriage, as is bleeding a degree greater than a mere occasional spotting or staining. Miscarriage early in pregnancy may or may not be preventable, depending on whether the conception is a blighted ovum (a genetically flawed conception), which will not survive despite any efforts to prevent the miscarriage, or a good conception that the uterus is mistakenly trying to dislodge because the progesterone levels are not high enough to sustain pregnancy. The former is more common, but some women do experience several early pregnancy losses before their doctors determine that they are deficient in progesterone. Natural progesterone administered early in pregnancy by injection or vaginal suppositories may solve the problem. (Again, see Chapter 13.) Better for Ms. B. to call her doctor and ask him about the cramping than to ignore it and possibly risk an unnecessary miscarriage. Cramping in any case is a signal to slow down, rest more, and generally take it easy while the uterus is unusually sensitive to irritation.

71

Getting a pregnancy test is the next step. (See page 64.) If Ms. B.'s period is already overdue, a reliable pregnancy test can be performed. Through a local laboratory or doctor, she can have a blood sample tested and she will know the results within a few hours. This type of reliable, fast blood test will detect pregnancy immediately or even just before a woman misses her period. Early pregnancy symptoms are often confused with the symptoms that accompany delayed menstruation, and the only way to differentiate between the two is to take a pregnancy test. Most women do not have the dramatic early pregnancy symptoms of Ms. B.'s sister, but a woman experiencing late menstruation, breast tenderness, and a slightly queasy feeling probably is pregnant.

My Friend Doesn't Get PMS: Is This Why Her Pregnancy Is Different from Mine?

Can you tell me if there is any connection between PMS and early pregnancy symptoms? I've been sick almost from day 1 and my breasts are really giving me trouble they hurt so much. It is the same bloated, nauseated feeling I get before my period except much, much worse. My friend, on the other hand, who is in her second month, had experienced so few symptoms that she didn't believe the result of the first pregnancy test and had the doctor take it again. The only explanation we can think of is that I normally get PMS and she doesn't. Is this the reason? And if so, why?

P.M.
Union, New Jersey

Early pregnancy management could be simplified if a woman could differentiate her early pregnancy symptoms from her normal monthly cycle. But PMS-free women may feel just as exhausted, grumpy, and generally out of sorts at the beginning of a pregnancy as the chronic PMS sufferer. PMS symptoms may mimic those of pregnancy (or the other way around, if you prefer), but a PMS sufferer does not necessarily have the same symptoms when she is just pregnant that she gets before her period. Certainly the bloatedness, irritability, and nervousness, even that "odd" physical sensation that PMS sufferers know all too well, are very common at the beginning of pregnancy. So is breast tenderness, which is familiar to Ms. M. because she experiences a less severe form of it in the last few days of every monthly cycle.

On the other hand, Ms. M. could be one of those lucky women who never had PMS, and she might still have PMS-like symptoms in early pregnancy.

How pregnancy and PMS differ is essentially the difference in hormonal behavior before a period and during early pregnancy. A low progesterone level is characteristic of PMS; with it comes irritability and all the other PMS side effects. By contrast, in early pregnancy, progesterone is usually high even for former PMS sufferers, and this balancing with estrogen means that a woman with PMS may not get the same symptoms she gets before her period. In fact, some women who have severe PMS feel better than usual once they are pregnant. Natural progesterone has a diuretic effect, so a woman who is normally plagued with excessive water retention may actually feel less swollen during pregnancy than she does before her period.

Unfortunately for Ms. M., she is one of those women who have exactly the same breast tenderness, irritability, and other uncomfortable symptoms that she normally experiences before her period. In her case, progesterone may still not be completely balanced at the new level.

Cutting down on her salt intake and decreasing her caffeine consumption will at least help the breast tenderness. Some of the other symptoms, especially fatigue, can be partially counteracted by taking extra vitamins, especially vitamin B-complex and vitamin B_6, and the vitamins and minerals provided by a good nutritious diet.

Women combat everyday stresses much better when they eat well and have a reasonably good night's sleep. Without minimizing the difficulty of coping with early pregnancy discomforts, these discomforts have many causes, and I think a hidden factor in how women react physically is partially determined by how they deal with any kind of stress. A woman is not guaranteed a trouble-free pregnancy because she is relaxed and confident. However, she is much more likely to accept pregnancy discomforts like temporary exhaustion and occasional nausea with humor and a sense of perspective. A woman who is miserable at work and miserable at home is already starting pregnancy in a state of emotional bankruptcy. Add to that the petty annoyances, backaches, fatigue, joint pains, and other minor side effects, and you have an overburdened woman to whom every trivial irritant is a major aggravation. A woman has a much better chance of catching up physically if she is happy about herself and pleased with her pregnancy.

A NOTE ON PMS AND INFERTILITY: Recent studies of PMS victims have revealed some startling new solutions to some old problems. Not only is PMS definitely a factor in the large number of women who are treated every year for depression, it has robbed untold numbers of women of their chance to have a baby. The mischief is done in the last few days of the cycle, when the inadequate or wildly fluctuating progesterone level characteristic of PMS will release prostaglandin hormones. The severe uterine cramping produced by the release of prostaglandins will then displace and flush any conceptus that might have found its way into the womb. When surgeons experimenting with in vitro fertilization anticipated this problem, they protected the tiny laboratory-conceived conceptus by giving patients extra progesterone by injection in the first week after implantation. Women whose PMS is severe enough to make them infertile can often achieve the same end by simple changes in nutrition and vitamin intake. Or a fertility specialist might recommend natural progesterone injections or, better still, natural progesterone suppositories in the last ten days of the cycle. All these problems have been extensively dealt with in my book *PMS: Premenstrual Syndrome and You.**

A GOOD BEGINNING IS ESSENTIAL

Even before a pregnancy test confirms a woman's conception, her body can signal her expectancy. Sore breasts, frequent urination, and extreme fatigue are classic signs. Nature is letting her know that she must begin to take special care of herself because a new life is within. (See Figure 3-2.)

A pregnancy test, of course, is the only way to be certain of conception, and every woman who suspects that she is pregnant should be tested. A hormonal imbalance, trauma, stress—any number of situations—can cause a missed period; pregnancy is not the only reason.

Once a woman knows that she is an expectant mother, however, she has no time to waste in attending to her personal care. She will need a well-balanced diet, rest, and the right doctor to guide her through the nine months ahead. A caring obstetrician will screen her for problems, prescribe prenatal vitamins, and give her pregnancy a good start.

* New York: Fireside Books/Simon & Schuster, 1983.

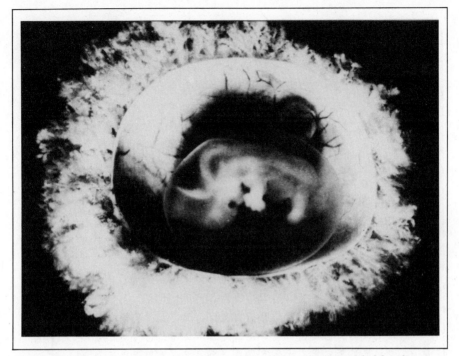

Figure 3-2. *Human embryo at forty days. The embryo is surrounded by the amniotic sac, which is surrounded by the placenta.*

HOW TO CALCULATE THE DUE DATE

Every obstetrician has a specially numbered pregnancy gauge that helps him estimate your due date during your first visit, but you can actually reach the same conclusion through simple arithmetic. If you have a regular twenty-eight-day menstrual cycle, take the date of your last period, add seven days, and count three months back. For example, if your last menstrual period began on July 5, count seven days ahead, with July 5 as day 1, and you will reach July 11. Count back three months from July 11 and the date you land upon is April 11, which is the due date. (See Table 1, When to Expect the Birth of the Baby, for calculated due dates.)

The due date is always an approximation, since menstrual cycles vary. Some women have cycles of over thirty days, while others may get their period every twenty-five days. A pregnant woman can usually expect her baby to be born at or around the due date; delivery within ten days before or after is part of the normal time frame.

Table 1.
When to Expect the Birth of the Baby

Month	1	2	3	4	5	6	7	8	9	10	11	12	13	14	15	16	17	18	19	20	21	22	23	24	25	26	27	28	29	30	31	
Jan.	1	2	3	4	5	6	7	8	9	10	11	12	13	14	15	16	17	18	19	20	21	22	23	24	25	26	27	28	29	30	31	
Oct.	8	9	10	11	12	13	14	15	16	17	18	19	20	21	22	23	24	25	26	27	28	29	30	31	1	2	3	4	5	6	7	Nov.
Feb.	1	2	3	4	5	6	7	8	9	10	11	12	13	14	15	16	17	18	19	20	21	22	23	24	25	26	27	28				
Nov.	8	9	10	11	12	13	14	15	16	17	18	19	20	21	22	23	24	25	26	27	28	29	30	1	2	3	4	5				Dec.
Mar.	1	2	3	4	5	6	7	8	9	10	11	12	13	14	15	16	17	18	19	20	21	22	23	24	25	26	27	28	29	30	31	
Dec.	6	7	8	9	10	11	12	13	14	15	16	17	18	19	20	21	22	23	24	25	26	27	28	29	30	31	1	2	3	4	5	Jan.
April	1	2	3	4	5	6	7	8	9	10	11	12	13	14	15	16	17	18	19	20	21	22	23	24	25	26	27	28	29	30		
Jan.	6	7	8	9	10	11	12	13	14	15	16	17	18	19	20	21	22	23	24	25	26	27	28	29	30	31	1	2	3	4		Feb.
May	1	2	3	4	5	6	7	8	9	10	11	12	13	14	15	16	17	18	19	20	21	22	23	24	25	26	27	28	29	30	31	
Feb.	5	6	7	8	9	10	11	12	13	14	15	16	17	18	19	20	21	22	23	24	25	26	27	28	1	2	3	4	5	6	7	Mar.
June	1	2	3	4	5	6	7	8	9	10	11	12	13	14	15	16	17	18	19	20	21	22	23	24	25	26	27	28	29	30		
Mar.	8	9	10	11	12	13	14	15	16	17	18	19	20	21	22	23	24	25	26	27	28	29	30	31	1	2	3	4	5	6		April
July	1	2	3	4	5	6	7	8	9	10	11	12	13	14	15	16	17	18	19	20	21	22	23	24	25	26	27	28	29	30	31	
April	7	8	9	10	11	12	13	14	15	16	17	18	19	20	21	22	23	24	25	26	27	28	29	30	1	2	3	4	5	6	7	May
Aug.	1	2	3	4	5	6	7	8	9	10	11	12	13	14	15	16	17	18	19	20	21	22	23	24	25	26	27	28	29	30	31	
May	8	9	10	11	12	13	14	15	16	17	18	19	20	21	22	23	24	25	26	27	28	29	30	31	1	2	3	4	5	6	7	June
Sept.	1	2	3	4	5	6	7	8	9	10	11	12	13	14	15	16	17	18	19	20	21	22	23	24	25	26	27	28	29	30		
June	8	9	10	11	12	13	14	15	16	17	18	19	20	21	22	23	24	25	26	27	28	29	30	1	2	3	4	5	6	7		July
Oct.	1	2	3	4	5	6	7	8	9	10	11	12	13	14	15	16	17	18	19	20	21	22	23	24	25	26	27	28	29	30	31	
July	8	9	10	11	12	13	14	15	16	17	18	19	20	21	22	23	24	25	26	27	28	29	30	31	1	2	3	4	5	6	7	Aug.
Nov.	1	2	3	4	5	6	7	8	9	10	11	12	13	14	15	16	17	18	19	20	21	22	23	24	25	26	27	28	29	30		
Aug.	8	9	10	11	12	13	14	15	16	17	18	19	20	21	22	23	24	25	26	27	28	29	30	31	1	2	3	4	5	6		Sept.
Dec.	1	2	3	4	5	6	7	8	9	10	11	12	13	14	15	16	17	18	19	20	21	22	23	24	25	26	27	28	29	30	31	
Sept.	7	8	9	10	11	12	13	14	15	16	17	18	19	20	21	22	23	24	25	26	27	28	29	30	1	2	3	4	5	6	7	Oct.

The bold type in each column denotes the first day of the last menstrual period. The light-face type immediately beneath it indicates the estimated date of delivery.

76

Calculating the due date becomes a little trickier when a woman has irregular periods or does not know when she last menstruated. This is when technology helps. A doctor can turn to ultrasonography and judge the due date by measuring the baby's head size on a sonogram, an image similar to an X ray created by sound waves that are safe to mother and baby. A blood test in which the level of HCG (human chorionic gonadotropin), the hormone that rises during pregnancy, is measured can also provide an estimated due date.

It is important to have a due date, not only for the convenience of planning your pregnancy but for the health of you and your baby. The due date tells you when a baby is premature and when it is overdue. The complications that arise from unformed organs when a child leaves the womb too soon (prematurely) are well known, but a woman may not realize that when an unborn child remains *too long* in the womb, the placenta begins to shrink, oxygen starts to diminish, and life is threatened. On the other hand, a child who is born close to the due date has a strong constitution and a good chance of surviving well in the world.

HOW OFTEN SHOULD I SEE MY DOCTOR?

As soon as you realize you are pregnant, you should make an appointment to visit an obstetrician. (See Chapter 4.) The first visit is usually the longest one because in it a doctor takes a complete medical history, conducts an internal examination, and performs a battery of tests. The usual tests are: a complete blood count, blood type and antibodies, a VD blood test, and a rubella test. Other blood tests may include tests for toxoplasmosis, sickle cell anemia, Tay-Sachs disease, or other conditions. A Pap smear is also taken during this first visit.

The consultation after the physical examination and testing is a good opportunity for you and your partner to question the doctor about any confusion or trepidations you may have. Do not hesitate to ask about sexual activity, travel, miscarriage, or other subjects that are on your mind. The doctor will outline a general health plan for you, with diet and exercise regimens, information on weight gain, and vitamin recommendations. (See Chapter 5.) Sometimes a doctor requests that you see him two weeks after the first visit to discuss the results of blood tests and laboratory analyses and to check the progress of your pregnancy. Then he will set a schedule of revisits. Follow-up appointments are usually booked this way:

from the first visit to 28 weeks	every 3 or 4 weeks
from 28 to 32 weeks	every 3 weeks
from 32 to 36 weeks	every 2 weeks
from 36 weeks to delivery	once a week

An obstetrician checks your urine, blood pressure, and weight gain at each visit. He is on the alert for signs of gestational diabetes, kidney problems, and any early symptoms of toxemia. A steady weight gain is good for the growth of the fetus, but both a meager rise and a great jump in poundage can be unsafe. The regular visits are important because an easy pregnancy may suddenly become complicated, and if trouble is spotted right away, it can be alleviated. Should toxemia, preeclampsia (see p. 109), high blood pressure, or diabetes arise, a doctor will discover the condition during a visit. The beginning of premature labor will be detected perhaps in time to avert premature childbirth. The low-risk pregnancy that becomes a high risk can be cared for with greater intensity. Pregnancy requires concerned watchfulness, and although babies are born every day, nothing in these nine months is really routine.

CHAPTER 4

Who Should Deliver Your Baby?

Your selection of the person who will guide you through pregnancy and help you deliver your baby should involve thorough and conscientious planning. Gone are the times, fortunately, when autocratic physicians controlled pregnancy and childbirth. Today the birth of a baby is a team effort, and it is up to *you* to choose your teammates. Making these decisions, however, can seem an overwhelming responsibility, particularly to a first-time mother. As with every aspect of childbearing, there are no set rules for finding an obstetrician, but there are several guidelines that can help you choose a physician with whom you and your partner can develop a trusting relationship.

WHAT DO YOU NEED?

In your book Childbirth with Love, *you suggested using friends and family recommendations as a way to choose an obstetrician. My sister-in-law and I are good friends, even though our personalities are very different. She is very outgoing and has a great sense of humor. When I discovered I was pregnant for the first time, she made an appointment for me with her obstetrician. Since she had been very pleased, and he has delivered her three children, I thought this was a good idea. Marie always seemed to enjoy her visits to the doctor, but I hate going. I never know when he's being serious, and he doesn't seem to pay attention to my questions. Is something wrong with me?*

A.P.

Akron, Ohio

My husband and I have an eight-year-old and we are expecting our second child in a few months. Our first child was born "naturally," and since our hospital now has several birthing rooms, we had been preparing our daughter for—and looked forward to—her participation in her new brother or sister's birth. Last week, however, my doctor became very upset when we said Sandra would be there. He said he wouldn't allow it and we were wrong to consider it.

B.V.

Baltimore, Maryland

I am expecting my first baby any day now and I am terrified. I have never been in a hospital, and since last month, when my obstetrician mentioned some of the equipment she might need to use while I'm in the hospital, I have been dreading labor. I've tried to talk about my fears with her, but she just keeps saying, "Don't worry. Everything will be fine." I can't seem to make her understand that this is all new to me and I'm very frightened.

C.S.

Lancaster, Pennsylvania

My husband and I are expecting our second baby this spring. Although we went the "natural route" with our first baby, we decided not to this time. In the first place, my husband found the experience very upsetting—which didn't help me any—and in the second place, he has a new job that involves a lot of travel and we don't want him under any additional pressure. We're fine, but my doctor keeps implying—and saying—that we're going about this all wrong. Why can't he respect our decision?

D.N.

Atlanta, Georgia

Obviously your primary concern—and that of your obstetrician—must be the safe delivery of a healthy baby. (See Figure 4-1.) To achieve this goal, you must first decide what *you* feel is necessary and important in order for you to have an emotionally fulfilling as well as a physically safe childbirth experience. If you do not take the time to sort out your own feelings and ideas before you begin to look for an obstetrician, your search will be more difficult. Are you looking forward to the birth of your baby with apprehension? With confident anticipation? Will you be most comfortable knowing that highly technical equipment will be available to you? Are you afraid of hospitals? How much information do you want a doctor to share with you? Do you need family

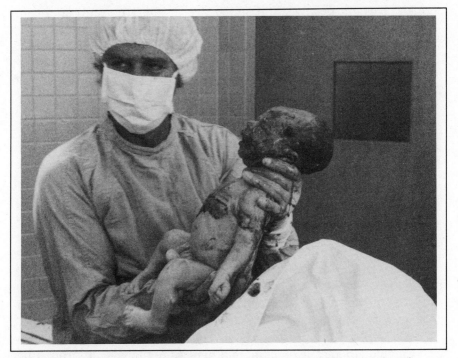

Figure 4-1. *Your doctor is your partner in childbirth. This baby is only a few seconds old, still attached to the mother's umbilical cord, and proudly posing for the photographer.* Courtesy of Madeline and Russell Kirk.

and friends around in stressful situations? These are but a few of the questions you should be asking yourself.

You should also consider the needs of your family. Although *you* are carrying your child and *you* will give birth, you are also creating or extending a family and, thus, your decisions will affect others. To what extent does the father of your child want to be involved with your pregnancy? Does he plan to come to your doctor's appointments with you? To be part of the delivery team? Do you have other children? What role do you foresee for them during the birth of their sibling? Are there future grandparents who are close to you? Do they need to be included in the birth experience? How? Consideration of your current family prior to delivery will avoid many problems that might otherwise arise in your future family.

Clarifying your own personal values will give you much peace of mind throughout your pregnancy. Since each woman's pregnancy is a totally unique experience, you will be hearing and reading many different versions of childbirth. Hopefully, most of them will be pleasant, positive, and supportive. If you are secure and comfortable with your own values, however, you will be much less apt to be swayed—or frightened—by any negative stories. Furthermore, until you are certain of your own beliefs, it will be difficult for you to transmit them to your prospective obstetrician, and without communication, there can be no trust.

A SOLO DOCTOR OR A GROUP PRACTICE?

A physician in a group practice usually has time for conferences, research, and his family. He also has medical consultants close at hand. Considering the advantages, doctors in group practices may proliferate in your community. You are then investigating not one but all the physicians in the office. For although you may be primarily under one doctor's care during your pregnancy, if that obstetrician is in a group, he may *not* be the one who ultimately delivers you.

Some women find it a plus that another member of a group practice, someone they have previously seen and spoken to, would be the physician present at delivery if their obstetrician was unavailable. In fact, expectant mothers sometimes seek groups because they worry that if they rely on an obstetrician in solo practice and he is not around on the day of birth, a stranger will take over the delivery room. (The truth is that doctors in solo practices usually know when their pregnant patients are due and they plan their vacations or trips out of town accordingly.)

The most important factor in choosing a doctor, whether solo or in a group, should be the care you will receive. If you are evaluating a doctor who is in a group, you will have a little more work because you will be meeting and questioning two, three, or four physicians, but the approach is the same. You will want to select an obstetrician who is well versed in the latest techniques and technological innovations, a doctor who has experience with fetal monitoring, believes in natural childbirth, and will respond quickly in an emergency. He should be ready to work with you as a partner, not against you as an adversary. You will want to ask him the percentage of cesarean sections he performs and how he feels about drug-free labor, birthing rooms, and even birthing chairs if you are interested in one.

Probably one doctor in a group will become your obstetrician more than the others. In a solo practice, the one-to-one relationship is a given. Since I find the doctor/patient relationship to be a special partnership, I am inclined to recommend solo physicians. Pregnancy and childbirth are emotionally and physically trying even though they are exceptional and wonderful experiences. You and your husband will be sharing these experiences with the obstetrician you choose. It is important that you both join in the selection and pick a person who is sympathetic to your needs. Even a group practice usually has a "personality," because the doctors in the group choose each other. Try for the personality that is a complement to yours. A solo doctor, of course, will either seem right or not.

Whether you are consulting a solo doctor or a group, notice whether the office is organized and efficient and do not hesitate to ask the other pregnant patients in the waiting room for their opinions. Your instincts, combined with information from family, friends, other patients, and the hospital with whom a physician is affiliated, will lead to good judgment.

A FEMALE OR A MALE DOCTOR?

A group practice may include female and male doctors, so you will be seen and cared for by both sexes. Still, some women have a strong preference for one sex or the other. Certain women feel more secure with a woman who may have given birth herself and is empathetic, while others are happier in a man's care. Your choice of obstetrician should really be based on the skill of the doctor, woman or man.

Years ago, there were few female obstetricians, but lately more women are becoming physicians and more female physicians are becoming obstetricians. In medical schools, women now constitute 50 percent or more of the physicians in training, and studies are showing that the female/male gap in number of patients treated and hours worked is closing. Female doctors were once thought to spend less time at work than males in the course of their careers, but in fact, women devote themselves more to the practice of medicine after childbearing, the time of life when men taper off.

The choice of a female or a male obstetrician should be based on the training and talent of an individual doctor. A woman who performs unnecessary cesarean sections is certainly less preferable than a man who does not. Follow the guidelines in this chapter, and make a careful evaluation of the female and male physicians you consult. Then, armed with the facts and your feelings, the choice will be yours.

WHERE DO YOU LOOK?

One of the most obvious starting places in your search for an obstetrician is your gynecologist. Most gynecologists are also obstetricians or they are in partnership with an obstetrician. If you have been pleased with the care your gynecologist has given you, you should by all means consider using him. But remember, the skills—and attitudes—required of an obstetrician are different from those needed by a gynecologist.

When my gynecologist informed me that I was pregnant, I was delighted, and naturally, since he had been my gynecologist for eight years and I was pleased with the care he had given me, I began using him as my obstetrician. Within months, I felt like I was seeing a different person. Before I was pregnant, I had never had the occasion to call my doctor, because I was always very healthy and always had all my questions answered during my visit. Now when I on several occasions have called with questions about my pregnancy, he's never available and takes days to return my calls. Also, in the past, I always scheduled an appointment for my yearly checkup months in advance, so I never had trouble scheduling my visit at my convenience. Now I find that I'm expected to come at times that are difficult for me, because it's very hard to get an appointment. And I had always assumed that my visits "happened" to coincide with "emergencies" and that was why I had to wait. I've discovered that my doctor is always running late and I'm forced to spend hours in his waiting room. Why didn't someone warn me?

E.C.
Red Bank, New Jersey

There is a very simple way Ms. C. could have discovered her gynecologist's "other" personality. If you are considering using your current gynecologist as your obstetrician, ask the pregnant women in the waiting room how they feel about him as an obstetrician. Use their observations *plus* your own personal requirements to reach your decision.

If you find yourself in the position of needing to look for a "new" physician, you may wish to consult your family or friends. Remember the position Ms. P. found herself in, however! Your most reliable referral will probably come from a woman whose personality and values most closely resemble your own. And even then, be sure you don't let yourself be pressured into accepting someone else's doctor until *you* decide that he's the right physician for you.

My husband began a new job recently and we've had to move across the country. I think I'm pregnant and would like to see an obstetrician but I have no idea where or how to find a new doctor. I have no family here and I haven't had time to make any friends, so I have no one to ask. I looked in the phone book, but I just can't choose a doctor from the Yellow Pages. Help!

M.F.
Sacramento, California

Ms. F.'s problem has become increasingly common in today's mobile society, and thus there are many more readily available solutions. The personnel departments of most large companies, for example, are well prepared to help the families of their new-to-the-area employees relocate, and among the many services they may be able to provide would be a list of doctors from whom you could choose.

If you're truly on your own, the best place to start is your local library. Ask to see *The Directory of Medical Specialists,* and look under your state and city for the listing of obstetricians. For each listed doctor, you will find age, address, medical school attended, hospital(s) in which training was completed, board certifications, specializations, and current hospital affiliation. Let's look at a fictitious entry from the 1987 edition:

> Smith, Robert Q. Cert OG b. 40 NYC MD Cornell 67. Surg Intern 67–68 Res in O & Gynec 68–72 Now Att Phys in O & Gynec (all at NY Hospital— Cornell Med Center) Staff (Lenox Hill Hosp NYC) Prof Dept O & Gynec. (Cornell) ACOG-AFS. 603 First Ave. 10001 Tel (212) 123-4567

"Cert OG" means that Dr. Smith is board certified by the American College of Obstetricians and Gynecologists (ACOG). To become board certified, after completing a rigorous resident's training program, Dr. Smith had to pass several very difficult examinations in order to be rated as a top professional in his specialty. You can be assured, furthermore, that Dr. Smith is governed by the rules of ACOG and, as such, will be apt to provide you with the finest care.

"b. 40 NYC" tells you that Dr. Smith was born in New York City and, in 1987, is 47 years old. His place of birth can be of use to you when you see where he received his MD license. As a general rule, you may want to question the qualifications of someone who was born in one country and received his MD in another. It would be more usual for a doctor to receive his MD in his native country and then seek further training elsewhere. You should also note whether the medical school is one of national repute. Although that will not guarantee that doctor will be "perfect," you can assume that he had the opportunity to receive excellent training. A word of caution here: do not pass over an obstetrician simply because he did not attend a "top" school.

Next the entry states where Dr. Smith received his training as an intern and as a resident, and it will indicate any specializations he had. This information is followed by the hospital with which Dr. Smith is currently affiliated and a listing of any other hospital affiliations as well as teaching positions.

Finally, you can clearly see where Dr. Smith's office is located and how to reach him.

You should be able to come up with a list of three or four doctors to consider, and the listing of the hospital(s) where they are now practicing will lead you to yet another source of referral: the hospital.

Often it is easier for someone outside the medical profession to rate a medical facility than to evaluate a medical professional. Call the hospitals in your town and ask to speak with the secretary in the Department of Obstetrics. Explain that you are new to the area and ask the following questions: Who is the chairman of the department? Is the hospital affiliated with a medical college? Does the hospital have birthing rooms? Are nurse-midwives routinely used? Does the hospital have a department of neonatology? Perinatology? Finally, ask to be sent a list of recommended obstetricians and ask when you can make an appointment to see the hospital facilities.

By coordinating the information you have obtained from neighbors, the library, and the hospital, you should be able to come up with two or three doctors who look like promising candidates. Now it is time for you to put your research to the practical test.

DID YOU CHOOSE THE RIGHT DOCTOR?

Call the office of the obstetrician at the top of your list, explain that you are pregnant, and ask for the first available appointment. If you are told that there are no appointments available for a month or more, go on to the next doctor on your list.

Consider Ms. R.'s problem:

Shortly after my husband and I moved to our new home five hundred miles from where we had been living, I discovered I was pregnant. I was very concerned that my new doctor be as excellent as my former one, so I chose the head of the obstetrics department at a nearby teaching hospital that has an excellent reputation. When I phoned for an appointment as a new obstetrical patient, I was told that I would have to wait six weeks. Since I was busy unpacking and settling us into our new home, I didn't question this. Two weeks later I began to bleed. I called the office and asked if I could be seen. By the time the doctor returned my call, my husband had taken me to the emergency room, where, after being admitted, it was confirmed that I had miscarried.

L.R.
Chicago, Illinois

All the most excellent professional credentials in the world will not be of any help to you if you can't get an appointment within a reasonable period of time. So when you call an obstetrician for a first appointment, be sure to tell the receptionist that you are pregnant and would like to be seen as soon as possible. If the appointment she offers is still several weeks away, ask to speak to the doctor personally. If you cannot get through to the doctor or if he is not willing to see you within a short time, try a different physician.

When you arrive at the doctor's office for your first visit, don't forget that this appointment should still be considered part of your search. You should be prepared to give your medical history, and this will be easier if you have already taken the time to write down important dates and information.

While you are waiting to be examined by the doctor, observe the office staff. Do they seem pleasant? Organized? Willing to help and explain? Although they will not be delivering your baby, it is often the receptionist (for appointments), the secretary (for billing and insurance), and the nurse (for simple medical questions and routine laboratory results) with whom you'll be dealing during the course of your pregnancy. You should also listen to what the other patients in the waiting room have to say. But remember to take any negative comments with a grain of salt—they may just be having a bad day!

As the nurse puts you into an examining room, she will ask you some preliminary questions and obtain some basic information (weight, blood pressure, urine sample) that will enable the doctor to be prepared to examine you. You should be made to feel comfortable by the nurse, and you may want to ask if there are other nurses whom you may meet during future visits. Also, you should be aware of how long (actual time, not how long it seems) you are in the waiting room prior to the arrival of the doctor.

Evaluating the examination given to you by the doctor is primarily a very personal matter. There should be no doubt in your mind, however, that he looked at your chart (containing your medical history and the nurse's notes) prior to examining you, that the examination was thorough, explained, and professional, and that the doctor seemed to listen and respond to any questions you asked.

Your meeting with the doctor after you have been examined is perhaps the most important part of your first visit. You should come with a *written* list of questions you would like answered. Writing down your concerns will prevent you from forgetting to ask anything important and will enable you to leave the doctor's office with your "research" completed. Here is a sample checklist that may help you:

1. Is the doctor board certified?
2. With which hospital is he affiliated?
3. Does the doctor practice with a partner?
4. What are the doctor's fees for a normal delivery? For a surgical delivery?
5. What insurance plans does the doctor accept?
6. How will you be billed?
7. What nutrition plan does the doctor recommend?
8. What weight gain should you anticipate?
9. How often does the doctor want to see you?
10. What facilities are available in the office?
11. For what tests might you have to go to a laboratory? The hospital? What fees are involved?
12. What labor and delivery facilities does the doctor's affiliated hospital have?
13. How does the doctor see the role of your partner? In office visits? At the hospital?

NOTE: The secretary may have been able to answer questions 1 through 6 for you.

Be sure to add any particular questions you and your partner have—and be sure to write down the answers.

I have great confidence in my obstetrician but I always seem to leave his office with more unanswered questions than when I went in. Since this is my first baby, I know he probably thinks my questions are silly and maybe that's why I always feel like I'm being rushed out of his office before I have a chance to say what's on my mind. Don't get me wrong—he always tells me what's happening and what I'm supposed to do, but I need to know more. Do I have to wait until I'm having my second baby to have my questions answered?

A.S.
Little Rock, Arkansas

Any competent, caring physician will be more than willing to answer your questions. If you sense a hesitancy on the part of the doctor to answer any of your questions in a clear and forthright manner, you may need to look elsewhere for your obstetrician.

It is by no means necessary for you to conclude your first visit by making an on-the-spot decision. You should return home and discuss your findings with your partner or evaluate them with a friend. If you feel that there are significant areas of conflict between you and the doctor, you may want to continue your search for an obstetrician. If you feel that all or the majority of your needs can be met by this physician you visited, you're ready to begin to create a mutually satisfying professional relationship.

PLAN AHEAD

Once you have selected your obstetrician, you cannot just sit back and let him or her take over. Particularly in the early phases of your pregnancy, you still have a lot of homework to do. It is essential that you trust your doctor, and this trust is best established through reciprocal communication. This means not only that you should have selected an obstetrician who is willing to listen to you but also that you have the responsibility of making sure your physician understands how you feel about your pregnancy and your imminent childbirth experience. Far too many women confine the questions they ask their doctors to purely medical ones and then are amazed and upset when their doctors fail to respond positively to their emotional needs. Once you have established this trusting relationship, however, it is time for you, your partner, and your obstetrician to discuss what will be the best delivery method for you and your baby.

With the approval and participation of my obstetrician, my husband and I decided to have our baby delivered at a birthing center located a few blocks from the hospital. We were very pleased with the relaxed but professional atmosphere and we had no qualms about the care we would receive when our baby was born. We were particularly reassured by the fact that the hospital was so close. When I went into labor, however, I sensed immediately that something was wrong: all my pushing was getting nowhere. After about two hours, the midwife decided to call my doctor because our baby wasn't descending properly through the birth canal. When he arrived, he confirmed her suspicion that there was an unsuspected disproportion between my pelvis and the baby's head. The ambulance arrived within minutes to take us to the hospital, but the baby's heart rate was already low and it was decided that I needed a cesarean section. Unfortunately, just as they began to operate, the placenta separated from the wall of the uterus and my baby's heart stopped. Although my son was revived after my surgery and is still alive today, he suffered extensive brain damage.

P.L.
Washington, D.C.

I went to a lot of trouble choosing my obstetrician, and so I was quite surprised to learn that the majority of my care was supervised by his nurse-midwife. At first, I was angry and considered changing doctors, but I gradually began to appreciate the extra time she was able to give me, and when my baby was born, I was very reassured by having her there as part of our team: I'm sorry now that I ever questioned the help "only" a nurse-midwife could offer.

F.M.
Richmond, Virginia

My first baby had to be delivered by cesarean section. I am now expecting our second child, and the hospital where my obstetrician practices has recently opened two new birthing rooms in their labor and delivery suite. I had hoped to be able to deliver my baby in one of the birthing rooms, but my doctor says this will not be possible because I've already had a C-section. Is he right?

C.N.
New York, New York

Recently I have been reading a lot about birthing rooms and I would like to deliver my baby in such a place. Where we live, however, the only hospital within a hundred miles of our home doesn't have any birthing rooms. Several of the women I've met in my obstetrician's office are also interested. How can we go about convincing our hospital to provide alternate delivery rooms?

T.O.
(name of town withheld)

What should be one of your most important concerns when selecting your obstetrician is a question too many women overlook until it is difficult to exercise any options: Where and under what circumstances will your baby be delivered? In the past, there was no decision to be made. Throughout the United States until well into the twentieth century, children were born at home, attended by people ranging in skill from a doctor to a midwife to a friend, neighbor, or family member. The trend in American obstetrics then led growing numbers of women to give birth in hospitals, directed by doctors and supported by specialized professionals. Today the various delivery options available can be overwhelming, particularly to a first-time mother.

SHOULD YOU CHOOSE A MIDWIFE?

The revival of the American nurse-midwife was inspired by the midwifery schools that still flourish in Denmark, England, and Holland. Those Western European countries never allowed their midwifery traditions to die out as we did here, and in Denmark, midwives attend every single birth, including forceps and cesarean deliveries—at which the hospital obstetrician, however, formally takes over. Both in Holland and Denmark, midwives work independently of doctors and function in effect as obstetricians supervising their patients' prenatal care and delivery in normal cases. Fifty percent of births in Holland still take place at home, with a midwife in attendance. In England, there are very few home births now, and a midwife usually works as part of a hospital team, with the doctor or doctors as the senior members.

The growth in this country of hospital midwifery services and independent birth centers now gives expectant parents the option to deliver under the care of a nurse-midwife. A *certified nurse-midwife* is a registered nurse who has graduated from an accredited, university-based program and is certified for practice by national examination. She (the majority of midwives are women) is different from a *licensed midwife*, who may be self-taught or may have apprenticed in a training program and received a permit in a state that grants one. A certified nurse-midwife is subject to national standards, but the qualifications of a licensed midwife may vary widely.

Few certified nurse-midwives run their own private practice; in fact, only 1.8 percent of the births nationwide are attended by midwives. Almost all nurse-midwives are associated with hospitals or birth centers, although they may attend home births. During her pregnancy, a woman might prefer the watchful counsel of a nurse-midwife who makes expectancy seem less clinical, perhaps, than an obstetrician. Either alone or in the presence of a doctor, a nurse-midwife will examine her during each of her visits to a hospital or birth center. A nurse-midwife is not trained to deal with high-risk pregnancies or medical complications. Only a woman who is in good health and appears to have a trouble-free pregnancy is eligible for her services.

During childbirth in a birth center, a nurse-midwife is able to prescribe painkillers and perform episiotomies, but she cannot handle complications that may require surgery, special drugs, or sophisticated methods of treatment. Usually a midwife tries to keep childbirth as natural as possible. She massages a woman's perineum rather than give her an episiotomy and stimulates her nipples to release internal oxytocin, which will speed up labor, rather than administer a drug such as Pitocin, which she is not legally qualified to do anyway.

A nurse-midwife in a hospital program may have complete autonomy or she may function primarily as a nurse who assists an obstetrician. In an autonomous hospital midwifery program, nurse-midwives offer prenatal care on a rotating basis to private and clinic patients. A midwife cares for pregnant women much as an obstetrician would and supervises childbirth in a delivery or birthing room equipped with fetal monitors and other technological aids. A senior resident or attending obstetrician is always present on the delivery floor to offer assistance.

The advantage of selecting a nurse-midwife in a hospital program is that if complications arise during labor and delivery, you are already within the building and can be treated immediately. If you are facing difficulty at a birth center, you would have to be rushed to the hospital, and during childbirth, every second counts.

If you are interested in choosing childbirth with a midwife in a hospital setting, find out exactly what the service entails. Is the program merely an auxiliary part of the obstetrical department, with midwives who have no say in the delivery room? Or are the hospital midwives autonomous, capable caretakers?

The best way to evaluate a hospital or birth center midwifery service is to visit the facility yourself. The centers usually welcome prospective patients and their families at special orientation sessions. Do not go into a midwifery program without carefully assessing it. Midwives vary as much as doctors do, and you should ask questions about the quality of care you can expect to receive.

A midwife is for you, though, only if you are having a low-risk pregnancy without any signs of trouble.

CHILDBIRTH AT HOME

In the seventies, before birth centers and hospital birthing rooms began to proliferate and offer alternatives to the delivery room, we experienced a return to childbirth at home. Couples wanted drug-free births, without monitoring equipment in the room and with family members present. The medical establishment worried because childbirth can be risky and complicated, and there are difficulties in delivery that cannot be overcome without the proper medication or surgical procedures. Most obstetricians declined to participate in home births, and couples who felt strongly had to learn how to do everything themselves. Husbands wound up "catching" the baby and cutting the cord. Were the babies all right? Studies that compare the mortality rates (numbers of babies who died during or within the first few weeks of birth) of hospital and home deliveries have found a higher mortality rate for home births. The chance of a baby dying during home birth is two to five times higher than during a hospital delivery.

Childbirth at home is an option for a woman only if she is in good health and has no pregnancy complications. She should be aware of the higher mortality rates associated with home birth and be willing to take a very positive, active role in the delivery. A woman who has a medical condition such as diabetes, heart disease, or anemia; whose baby is in the breech position; or who is expecting twins should give birth in the hospital.

If a woman is planning a home birth, she must still seek prenatal care and educate herself to spot pregnancy complications, and she should also enroll in a childbirth education program. It is not recommended that home birth be attended only by an inexperienced husband. Even if she accepts the risks of home birth, a woman should find a doctor or a certified nurse-midwife to assist her.

A successful home delivery can be a moving, rewarding experience for every member of the family, but before you decide that it is right for you, weigh the risks. Of course you desire a fulfilling childbirth experience, but you also want to hold a healthy newborn in your arms. Even though no birth center or birthing room in a hospital can replace the comfort of your own home, no attending midwife or physician can replace the security of having the best equipment available if a medical emergency arises during delivery.

THE BIRTH CENTER

A free-standing birth center usually has very strict rules governing acceptance into its program. A woman's age, her general health, and her past pregnancies are carefully evaluated at the first visit before she is accepted as a client. Then, if complications develop during her pregnancy, she will be asked to transfer out. The staff of a birth center is not prepared to handle high-risk pregnancies or serious complications during childbirth, but they do offer childbirth in a warm, tranquil environment.

In the majority of birth centers, a woman receives one-to-one prenatal care from a certified nurse-midwife who is present during childbirth. A "family" feeling prevails at birth centers, where the husband and any number of relatives may witness the newborn's arrival. Today over a hundred birth centers can be found in twenty-seven states. A recent survey showed that 45 percent of the centers are run by certified nurse-midwives, practicing with consulting physicians who receive referral and transfer of women with complications. In 29 percent of the centers that were surveyed, both physicians and nurse-midwives provide care, and 22 percent of the centers are headed by physicians with staffs of registered nurses and/or licensed practical nurses.

The homey atmosphere of a birth center is its strength, but the lack of emergency equipment and the inability to perform cesarean sections on the spot are its weaknesses. If labor does not progress well, if placental separation occurs, if an infection or some other unforeseen problem arises, a woman must be moved to a nearby hospital, and she loses time in transit. Minutes and seconds are crucial when new life is emerging. If placental separation or umbilical cord prolapse take place, oxygen to the baby may be cut off before a mother reaches the hospital emergency team.

This is not to say that birth practices in birth centers are careless or unsafe. Far from it. Midwives in birth centers are usually well trained, experienced, and competent, and they offer satisfying birth experiences to their low-risk clients. The centers are small and personal. And now many hospitals allow grandparents and children to live through the birth with the parents.

A birth center that provides proper care, is staffed by certified nurse-midwives, and has a backup hospital not too far away is much safer than and offers a birth experience that can be just as satisfying emotionally as a home birth. There are risks in giving birth in a birth center, but they are not as great as the dangers of a home birth improperly attended. The delivery in the birth center, furthermore, will most likely be reimbursed by your insurance company, which will not cover a home delivery. In my opinion, however, the best of all possible situations—a peaceful setting for childbirth, with modern medical treatments nearby—is the hospital birthing room. Here a woman delivers in a pleasant, homelike atmosphere, but she has the security of on-site hospital facilities.

THE HOSPITAL BIRTHING ROOM

Home births and free-standing birth centers became popular because women reacted unfavorably to the restricted, clinical environments of hospital delivery rooms. Many women felt that delivery-room atmospheres were conducive to the end of life rather than its beginning.

It took time for the medical establishment to respond to the needs of expectant mothers, but at last, hospitals are now "humanizing" the childbirth experience with the birthing room. A woman may deliver in a pastel-painted, warmly decorated bedroom with a sofa, chairs, a television, telephone, and lamps that may be dimmed. During labor, she may walk around in the company of her partner. Some hospitals might also allow children, other relatives, and possibly friends in the room. A fetal monitor and intravenous equipment may or may not be in the room, depending on the circumstances of the birth. The homelike ambience of the birthing room replaces the sterility of a delivery room, yet a woman is still within a hospital. Doctors, surgical facilities, equipment, and medications are immediately available if a complication strikes.

Birth at home or in an independent center can be dangerous if everything does not go absolutely smoothly. The lifesaving personnel and equipment that mother and child may need may be a few miles away, and the trip may hinder survival. The birthing room, however, has the advantage of offering an alternate birth experience while keeping mother and baby close to emergency operations.

Each hospital usually has its own rules about how many people may attend a birth in a birthing room, aside from the obstetrician, nurse-midwife, or nurses who may be present. It is my hope that restrictions will be listed as birthing rooms proliferate. Expectant mothers benefit from the support of loved ones, and since 30 percent of babies are now being delivered by single mothers, the "husbands only" regulation seems inappropriate.

I believe that every woman should negotiate for a birthing room delivery if she has the option. Sometimes, if the birthing rooms are occupied, an available labor room may be an appropriate substitute for a delivering mother. Then, after birth, bonding may occur without physically and emotionally disturbing a mother and child by moving them to a different location. As a mother touches her precious newborn, the childbirth experience continues.

THE FUTURE

Besides offering birthing rooms, your hospital may have birthing chairs for the upright childbirth position, and rooming in, a practice that allows a husband to visit and sleep overnight in a room with his wife and baby. These are some of the accommodations made by hospitals that have responded to women who speak out for changes in childbirth.

If your local hospital or medical center does not provide options in childbirth, you may want to organize a women's group to press for innovations in the hospital setting. In England, hospitals often offer separate "low-risk" and "high-risk" locations for childbirth. In this way, a woman who will probably have an easy delivery will be in a tranquil environment, while an expectant mother with impending complications will be in a clinical area where she will be carefully watched. American hospitals may eventually want to follow the lead of the English, who are making childbirth a happier, safer event.

CHAPTER 5

Eat Nutritiously– You Are Not Alone

Now that you are pregnant, it is especially important to learn about good nutrition. You are not only feeding yourself but you are also nourishing your baby when you eat, and a hearty, healthy diet is a must. Do not try to streamline your menu. I remember examining a pregnant woman who was entering her fourth month and just beginning to show. Before her visit to my office, she had had lunch—cottage cheese, a sliced tomato, and carrot sticks. Her breakfast had been a glass of juice and a cup of herbal tea. These are all nutritious foods, but not enough to sustain an expectant mother's good health along with her baby's. Since this woman had always been slim, though, she had reacted to her sudden expansion by dieting. "Please don't starve the baby," I said, and explained that pregnancy is the time to *increase* your intake of the nutritionally balanced foods that make up your menu. Today we know that a pregnant woman must eat more, and properly, to produce *extra* life-giving nourishment for herself and her developing infant. (An expectant mother should be ready to put on between 25 and 30 pounds.)

Until the 1960s, most doctors believed that women could nourish their unborn children without watching their diets. It was thought that nature would direct a fetus to take what it required from its mother, and that the female body would automatically fill fetal needs. In actuality, however, an expectant mother must support the active prenatal environment through the nutrients she consumes daily. These nutrients reach the fetus through a network of veins and arteries that carry them in and out of the placenta. A constantly circulating blood flow delivers nutrients and oxygen to the unborn baby in the womb and removes fetal wastes. An adequate amount of blood must reach the fetus at all times, and the only way a woman can be sure that she is maintaining the fetus's required blood level is to eat the right energy-giving foods. Her blood volume will naturally, healthily expand. If she mistakenly eats for one, there will be meager sustenance for the fetus. Newborns who have not received the appropriate nourishment are often smaller, lighter, and frailer than those who were nurtured in a kinder prenatal environment. (These smaller babies, in medical terms, are called *growth retarded*.)

HOW MUCH WEIGHT SHOULD YOU GAIN?

The answer is 25 to 30 pounds—a range with a history behind it. At the beginning of this century, obstetricians advised their patients to keep their weight down during pregnancy so that childbirth would be easier. Women were risking their lives as well as the lives of their unborn children to give birth in those years before modern medical advancements. It was thought that smaller babies would lower the risk and bring safer deliveries. The notion that a small newborn was healthier for a mother lasted until the early sixties. A weight gain of not more than 15 pounds was consistently ordered by doctors who policed the developments of mothers-to-be in their care. Not only was ease of delivery considered, but physicians held that toxemia (a condition that develops from high blood pressure and water retention and can lead to seizures) would be prevented if added poundage was kept to a minimum. Yet no matter how hard they tried, many women could not help but gain over 20 pounds; in fact, surveys at the time showed that women put on an average of 24 to 27 pounds during pregnancy.

Finally, in the late sixties, the myth that smaller babies are healthier babies was exploded in a study conducted by Dr. Nicholson J. Eastman at Johns Hopkins University in Baltimore. The results of a study of twelve thousand pregnancies revealed that mothers who gained 20 or more pounds during expectancy delivered higher-birth-weight (an average of 7½ pounds) babies. These heftier infants subsequently had better survival rates and superior health, growth, and intelligence than did babies who weighed less. The upshot of these findings was that the recommended 25-to-30-pound weight gain was established. An average weight gain of 25 pounds might break down in the following way in the course of gestation:

At 10 weeks, you would expect to gain 1–2 pounds

At 20 weeks, you would expect to gain approximately 8 pounds

At 30 weeks, you would expect to gain approximately 15 pounds

At 40 weeks (term), you would expect to have gained a total of approximately 25 pounds

You might not, however, follow this pattern exactly. Your weight gain will vary with your height, your prepregnancy weight, the food you eat during pregnancy, and your obstetrical history.

Most of the weight gained early in pregnancy goes toward creating an internal support system for the fetus. (See Figure 5-1.) An expectant mother's womb expands, her placenta grows, and her fat and blood volume increase. The fat, which is concentrated on the hips, breasts, and thighs, acts as a nutritional reserve during the last weeks of pregnancy. (Afterward, the fat becomes

Figure 5-1. (OPPOSITE) *Distribution of a mother's weight gain during pregnancy. This distribution shows where the weight is found in an expectant mother who gains approximately 25 pounds.* Reproduced by permission of The American College of Obstetricians and Gynecologists: You and Your Baby: A Guide to Prenatal Care (ACOG Patient Education Booklet b-001). Washington, D.C., ACOG, October 1984.

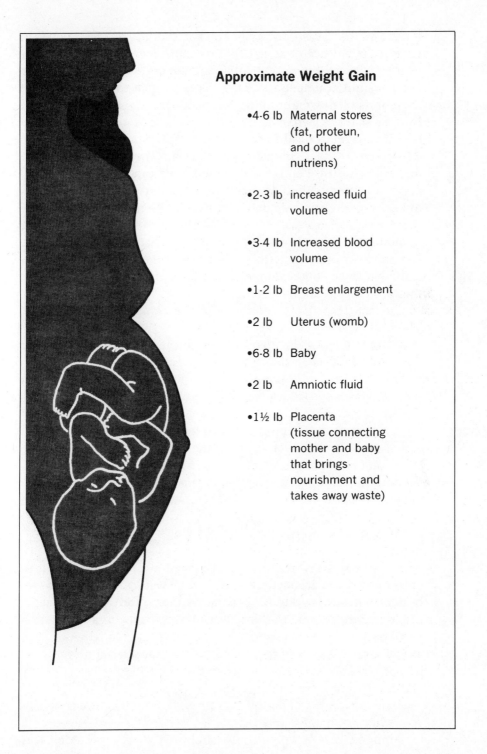

Approximate Weight Gain

• 4-6 lb   Maternal stores (fat, proteun, and other nutriens)

• 2-3 lb   increased fluid volume

• 3-4 lb   Increased blood volume

• 1-2 lb   Breast enlargement

• 2 lb   Uterus (womb)

• 6-8 lb   Baby

• 2 lb   Amniotic fluid

• 1½ lb   Placenta (tissue connecting mother and baby that brings nourishment and takes away waste) important to breast-feeding.) Toward the end of gestation, the weight gained goes to the baby, the amniotic fluid, and the placenta. In fact, there is a three-to-one ratio for fetal weight gain and other weight components of pregnancy. Since the baby acquires most of its birth weight in the last trimester, these are usually the hunger months, when you will notice a direct relationship between your sharpened appetite and weight gain.

How much food should you eat to gain the weight you need? According to the Food and Drug Administration, a healthy non-pregnant woman should be consuming about 2300 calories a day to keep up a reasonable activity level. Pregnancy changes calorie requirements, so a woman needs at least *300 extra calories a day* to maintain her prepregnancy activity level and put on a satisfactory amount of weight. By adding 300 calories, you bring your daily intake to *2600 calories,* an amount that has been linked to the births of higher-birth-weight (at least 7 pounds) babies.

The fact that bigger babies do better continues to be supported. The Collaborative Perinatal Project collected data on pregnancies that were followed in medical centers across the country from 1959 to 1967. Analysis of the data confirmed that babies who weighed more than 7 pounds at birth survive significantly better than do babies who are born a pound, or even a half-pound, lighter.

So eat more, but properly. It is important that the calories you add, for the weight you gain, come from a well-balanced diet. Chocolate chip cookies could give you the extra 300 calories, but they would not offer the nutrients that the baby needs to grow.

HOW AND WHAT SHOULD YOU EAT?

Your unborn baby requires a balanced combination of nutrients—protein, carbohydrates, fat, minerals, and vitamins—to become a healthy girl or boy. Usually an expectant mother's appetite, relatively normal in the first trimester, leaps to ravenous proportions in the second and third trimesters. This appetite shift seems to be nature's way of making sure that you eat more in the latter part of your pregnancy, when the fetus, in its greatest period of growth, increases its demands.

Snacking heavily or doubling your portions at mealtimes are not good ways to manage this heightened desire for food, however. I recommend that a woman have frequent meals, sometimes as many as five or six a day, from the beginning to the end of her pregnancy. Small meals at regular intervals maintain a steady blood sugar level and control the cravings that are more intense during the last few months.

The food at these meals should be planned according to the nutrient needs that arise during pregnancy. The developing fetus creates a demand for more protein and calcium than usual, and minerals and vitamins must be carefully balanced. Supplements for iron and folic acid are usually advised, but otherwise, most expectant mothers can fuel themselves and their babies through this recommended daily diet:

Four 8-ounce cups of milk or milk products, such as yogurt and cheese.

Four protein servings. A serving would be 2–3 ounces of cooked lean meat, fish, or poultry; ¾ cup of cooked dry beans, peas, or lentils; ¼ cup of peanut butter or 1 ounce of nuts.

Two servings of fresh, green, leafy vegetables. A serving is 1 cup raw or ¾ cup cooked.

One serving of fresh fruits and vegetables rich in vitamin C. Fruits such as oranges, mangos, grapefruits, pineapples, tomatoes; or vegetables such as broccoli, pepper, or cauliflower would be among the vitamin C group. You may choose a whole fruit or vegetable or juice.

One serving each day of a deep yellow or orange fruit or vegetable is recommended.

Four servings of grain products. One thick slice of bread; ½ cup rice, hot cereal, or cooked pasta; a muffin; or ¾ cup of unsweetened ready-to-eat cereal equals one serving. Whole-grain products are more nutritious than refined macaroni, breads, and flours, which provide calories but not energy-giving vitamins and minerals.

Plenty of fluids, at least 8–10 cups a day. You may count your milk intake in your quota.

Years ago, in line with the belief that a woman's weight gain should be minimal, doctors advised a high-protein/low-calorie diet with few carbohydrates. Your mother may remember eating a lot of meat and practically no bread when she was pregnant with you, and she may try to convince you to follow a similar plan yourself. As the suggested daily menu shows, however, we have now learned that a balanced diet, with protein from meat, fish, poultry, eggs, beans, and nuts, and carbohydrates from vegetables, fruits, and whole grains leads to a healthier pregnancy for mother and baby. In the first trimester, when nausea may be a problem, a little bread, pasta, or potatoes—all carbohydrate-containing foods— seems to bring relief more readily than other nutrients.

It's worth repeating, though, that more important than anything else, the foods you eat are supplying nutrients for your baby's growth.

HOW DO THE NUTRIENTS ESSENTIAL DURING PREGNANCY FUNCTION?

Protein

Protein contains amino acids, which are the building blocks of life—the creators and maintainers of body tissue. During pregnancy, to support the developing baby and her own newly formed gestational tissue, an expectant mother must increase the amount of protein in her diet by two-thirds, to about 75 grams a day. (See

Table 2.
Protein Content in Foods

Food	Amount	Protein (gm)
Meat, fish, poultry	3–3½ ounces	20–25
Soybeans	1 cup	20–25
Other dry beans, peas	1½ cups	20–25
Milk	1 glass (8 oz)	5–8
Brick-type cheeses	1 ounce	5–8
Cottage cheese	¼ cup	5–8
Egg	1	5–8
Nuts	1–1½ ounces	5–8
Peanut butter	2 tablespoons	5–8
Bean or pea soup	¾ cup	5–8
Bread	1 slice	2–4
Dark green vegetables	½–⅔ cup	2–4
Ready-to-eat cereals	¾–1 cup	2–4
Potato	1 medium	2–4

Table 2, Protein Content in Foods.) This protein is critical to the proper growth of fetal tissue, and it may also prevent the onset of toxemia.

Meat, fish, poultry, soybeans, and other dry beans and peas contain the highest amounts of protein, but there are other sources. Vegetarians can consume a proper balance of amino

Table 3.
Complementary Protein Sources

Protein Pair	Example
Legumes plus grains	Black beans and rice Kidney bean tacos Soybean curd, rice, and greens
Legumes plus seeds	Split pea soup with sesame crackers Garbanzo and sesame seed spread Peanut and sunflower seed tacos
Legumes plus nuts	Dry roasted soybeans and almonds Chili garbanzos and mixed nuts
Grains plus milk	Oatmeal and milk Macaroni and cheese Bulgur wheat and yogurt
Legumes plus seeds plus milk	Garbanzo beans and sesame seeds in cheese sauce
Legumes plus nuts plus milk	Mixed beans and slivered almonds with yogurt dressing
Legumes plus milk*	Lentil soup made with milk Peanuts and cheese cubes
Seeds or nuts plus milk*	Sesame seeds mixed with cottage cheese Chopped walnuts rolled in semihard cheese
Legumes plus egg	Cooked black-eyed peas with egg salad
Grains plus egg	Buckwheat (kasha) made with egg
Grains plus egg plus milk	Potato kugel Rice and raisin custard Cheese muffin
Seeds plus egg plus milk	Cheese omelet with sesame seeds

  * *Protein quality for this pair may not be as good as that of the other milk pairs.*

acids from a combination of legumes (beans and nuts) with grains, dairy products, or eggs. If she chooses, a mother-to-be who is a vegetarian can also pair grains with dairy products or eggs. (See Table 3, Complementary Protein Sources.)

Fat

Body fat, an internal source of energy, is absolutely necessary for getting vitamins A, D, E, and K—the fat-soluble vitamins—to the tissues. Since an expectant mother needs a real store of energy for all the work her body is doing in these nine reproductive months, some fat intake is a must. Now, as in any other time, however, her fat should come from nutritional foods such as cheese and eggs rather than from fatty meats, gooey desserts, or greasy, deep-fried things to eat. When cooking with oil or making salad dressing, the most beneficial oils would be unsaturated ones such as soybean and safflower. Olive oil, which is high in monounsaturated fatty acid, is currently being lauded for its positive contribution in the fight against artery-clogging cholesterol. A wise woman would include a moderate amount of carefully chosen fat in her diet.

Carbohydrates

Two kinds of carbohydrates—starches (complex carbohydrates) and sugars (simple carbohydrates)—are naturally found in fruits, vegetables, and whole grains. Without these carbohydrates, which supply protein, vitamins, and minerals, a person would suffer serious vitamin deficiencies, especially of C and the B vitamins, and be severely malnourished. Sometimes women think that they can compensate for the nutrients in natural carbohydrates by eating the "refined" starches and sugars in pies, cakes, cookies, candy, white bread, and most macaroni products, but they cannot. Refined carbohydrates are very low in nutritional value.

Although no carbohydrate requirement has been established for pregnant women, the need for carbohydrates cannot be minimized. (See the suggested daily diet on p. 103.) The glucose in simple carbohydrates fuels the human body and combats fatigue during pregnancy. Glucose also helps fat to burn energy efficiently. A diet that is too low in energizing carbohydrate-containing foods can lead to the production of toxic ketone bodies in the blood. A building of ketones creates fatty acids that may ultimately prove fatal to the fetus.

Natural carbohydrates are also important for the fiber, or roughage, they bring to your diet. The fiber in whole grains, fruits, and vegetables helps digestion and promotes bowel regularity.

Minerals for a Mother-to-Be

CALCIUM

A pregnant woman needs 1200 milligrams of calcium a day—50 percent more than before conception—to build the bones of her developing fetus and to keep her body functioning properly. If an expectant mother does not increase her calcium consumption, her unborn child, taking what it needs to grow, will be depleting the calcium content in her own bones. A quart of milk a day will meet the need for calcium during pregnancy, but as shown in Table 4, Calcium Content in Foods, other foods may be substituted for skim, low-fat, or whole milk. A cup of yogurt or 1½ ounces of Cheddar cheese contain the calcium found in an 8-ounce glass of milk. In fact, women who have trouble digesting the milk sugar lactose may get their calcium from yogurt, cottage cheese, natural cheeses, and buttermilk that does not have milk solids added. These foods are low in lactose and high in calcium. Sardines, salmon, oysters, and shrimp as well as bean curd, kale, mustard greens, and broccoli contain calcium, but the mineral is usually more easily absorbed from milk and milk products.

Also, you must have a proper calcium/phosphorus balance for calcium absorption. Phosphorus occurs in milk, cheese, seafood, eggs, meat, and onions, so there should be no problem maintaining an adequate phosphorus level. Carbonated soft drinks, however, contain phosphorus to prevent clouding. So if you consume a lot of soft drinks, you may elevate the phosphorus level in your body and cause a calcium/phosphorus imbalance. It may be wise, therefore, to moderate or avoid these beverages.

IRON

During pregnancy, the amount of blood in a woman's body doubles and dramatically increases her need for iron. This mineral is vital to the production of red blood cells, which carry oxygen to her own body tissue and that of her unborn child. The fetus, which is forming body tissue along with red blood cells of its own, is demanding in its need for iron and will take it from the mother whether or not she has it to spare—and she may not. Many women do not get enough iron in their daily diet, and their expanded blood volume, which is being drained by fetal requirements, puts great pressure on them to take in more iron. The recommended daily allowance (RDA) for a nonpregnant woman is 20 milligrams, and it is estimated that a pregnant woman needs 5 to 6 milligrams more.

A diet that includes iron-rich foods such as lean meat, liver,

Table 4.
Calcium Content in Foods

Food	Amount	Calcium (mg)
Skim milk	8 ounces	302
2% milk	8 ounces	297
Whole milk	8 ounces	219
Buttermilk	8 ounces	285
Low-fat yogurt	1 cup	415
Low-fat yogurt with fruit	1 cup	314
Frozen yogurt	1 cup	200
Cottage cheese, creamed	½ cup	116
Swiss cheese	1 ounce	272
Parmesan cheese (grated)	1 ounce	390
Cheddar cheese	1 ounce	204
Mozzarella cheese	1 ounce	183
American cheese	1 ounce	174
Sardines with bones	3 ounces	372
Salmon with bones	3 ounces	285
Oysters	1 cup	226
Shrimp	1 cup	147
Bean curd	4 ounces	154
Collard greens	1 cup	357
Turnip greens	1 cup	267
Kale	1 cup	206
Mustard greens	1 cup	193
Dandelion greens	1 cup	147
Broccoli	1 cup	136
Bok choy	1 cup	116

SOURCE: *United States Department of Agriculture*

NOTE: *Certain dark green leafy vegetables, such as spinach, Swiss chard, sorrel, parsley, and beet greens, contain a lot of calcium, but they also contain oxalic acid, which inhibits absorption of the calcium in these vegetables.*

leafy green vegetables, apricots, prunes, raisins, soybeans, peanut butter, and potatoes with the skins will boost a woman's iron supply; however, she will still probably not be able to absorb as much iron as she and her baby need. (Even the iron content in iron-rich food is not great—two slices of beef liver contain 6.6 mg.) To prevent the fatigue and anemia that may result from iron deficiency, a doctor will usually recommend iron supplements—ferrous gluconate, ferrous sulphate, or ferrous fumarate tablets—of at least 30 to 60 milligrams a day, since iron is more difficult to absorb from a supplement. A special note: iron absorption from food is considerably enhanced if you eat foods high in vitamin C, folic acid, and vitamin B_{12} along with your iron-rich serving. A fresh fruit cup after a lean steak or a salad of fresh greens and tomatoes with a chicken dinner will definitely aid iron absorption.

SODIUM: THE SALT STORY

Doctors used to prescribe diuretics and a restricted salt diet to reduce water retention, which they feared might lead to toxemia, a grave condition that, if it is not controlled, can endanger the lives of an expectant mother and her child. The cause of toxemia is still unknown, but the condition often occurs when the uterus of a pregnant woman does not receive an adequate blood supply. When a woman is carrying twins, for example, her uterus grows very quickly and the uterine blood supply, which provides the babies' nourishment through the placenta, may not be able to keep pace with her expansion. Toxemia, however, is not confined to multiple births; it occurs most often when a woman is only carrying one child.

What happens then is that the undernourished uterus sends an internal message to the kidneys to increase blood pressure in an attempt to bring more blood and oxygen to the womb. As the pressure increases, more blood is pumped through the vessels, and eventually the blood building within causes excess fluid to move outside the thin walls of the capillaries. Then water retention results. High blood pressure as well as the hormones that are being released from the kidneys may lead to kidney damage and may also change nerve impulses. A woman's nerve endings may become so overly sensitized that it takes very little stimulation for reflex actions to occur. A condition called preeclampsia, which is the forerunner of a seizure, could develop. If preeclampsia is not arrested, eclampsia, or seizure, may ensue. Ultimately, if seizure becomes a reality, the lives of both a mother and her baby are in jeopardy.

We now know that diuretics do not cure toxemia—they may even harm an expectant mother's kidneys and injure the fetus—and that salt intake really has nothing to do with the situation. The best way to overcome toxemia is to prevent it with good nutrition and bed rest. By eating a well-balanced diet of small, frequent meals, a woman will automatically be stimulating her blood supply, and by lying on her side in bed, she will be directing more blood to her uterus and less to her extremities. A healthy expectant mother does not have to increase or decrease her salt intake during pregnancy; however, a woman who has a tendency toward water retention should avoid ingesting extra salt.

The high estrogen level that occurs during pregnancy causes more salt than usual to be found in a woman's body. So sodium naturally rises, and fluid, which is a necessary reserve for the blood that will be lost during childbirth, builds. Since the body actually takes care of itself in many ways, I advise women to maintain their normal salting habits and to avoid oversalting. Do not add extra salt to your diet, because pregnancy will cause your internal sodium level to rise by itself. In fact, adding salt may cause problems. When women complain of pains in their joints due to water retention, I can usually trace their discomfort back to salty foods they have recently eaten. Chinese dishes, Cheddar cheese, canned soups, sausages, soft drinks, and seafood, for instance, are especially high in sodium.

If bloatedness or joint pain becomes noticeable, you may have to eliminate salt from your diet altogether. This, in combination with bed rest, will help you get rid of the extra fluid in your body without the need of dangerous diuretics.

OTHER MINERALS: IODINE, CHROMIUM, ZINC

Although the need for *iodine* and *chromium* has not been established, these trace minerals are necessary for a healthy pregnancy. Iodized salt and shellfish can provide an expectant mother with the iodine that her body requires to strengthen her bones and the baby's developing skeletal system. Chromium, which also strengthens bones, can be found in whole-grain breads and cereals.

An increase in *zinc,* an important component of the enzymes that maintain your body's metabolism, is also recommended. The

RDA for zinc is 15 milligrams, with 5 milligrams added for pregnancy and 10 milligrams more for breast-feeding. Almonds, eggs, peanuts, beef, walnuts, liver, herring, and oysters have high zinc content and should be included in a pregnant woman's diet.

Essential Vitamins

THE B VITAMINS

A number of the necessary B vitamins—thiamine (B_1), niacin (B_2), riboflavin (B_3), and B_{12}—are easily acquired through the recommended daily diet. (See p. 103.) Lean meats, whole grains, liver, seeds, nuts, wheat germ, and dairy products all contain these important Bs. There is an *increased* need during pregnancy, however, for *pyridoxine* (B_6) and *folic acid*.

The RDA for vitamin B_6 is 2.5 milligrams, and some researchers have suggested that during pregnancy that allowance should be raised to 10 milligrams. Vitamin B_6 is destroyed in the refining of white flour, but whole-grain products—whole wheat bread, bran muffins, natural grain cereals—still contain this vitamin, which is also in liver, meats, poultry, fish, leafy green vegetables, bananas, and nuts. Stress seems to deplete B_6, so the greater the stress, the more a woman needs this vitamin.

It is difficult to specify a daily amount between 2.5 and 10 milligrams that would be adequate for everyone, since stress varies so much in the life of each person. A woman may want to take up to ten times more than 10 milligrams—100 milligrams a day—when she is under a great deal of pressure. For B_6 to be properly absorbed, however, she will have to take a B-complex that includes 100 milligrams of B_1 in its contents along with the B_6, to balance the absorption of all the B vitamins. The B vitamins are water soluble, which means that excess amounts are excreted from the body. There have never been any reports of an overdose of B vitamins during pregnancy.

Finally, there is an essential need for a high amount of folic acid during pregnancy. Folic acid is necessary for the production of blood cells and fetal tissue, and a woman should have at least 800 micrograms a day. While most of the B vitamins can be consumed in the foods you eat, the need for folic acid is so great that your daily diet cannot provide enough. A doctor will usually prescribe a supplement, because if an expectant mother falls prey to a deficiency, she may suffer serious complications such as spontaneous abortion or toxemia. (A nutritional tip: one tablespoon of brewer's yeast sprinkled on your cereal in the morning gives you about 300 micrograms of folic acid, not to mention zinc, protein, iron, and B vitamins.)

VITAMIN A

Besides maintaining the good health of an expectant mother's skin and mucous membranes, vitamin A contributes to the growth and functioning of the baby's thyroid gland and to the future condition of her or his tooth enamel and hair. The recommended dose of vitamin A is 5000 to 6000 international units (IU) a day, which can usually be gained through a balanced daily diet. Dark green leafy vegetables are high in this vitamin. ⅔ cup cooked carrots contains 10,500 IU of vitamin A; one medium-size sweet potato, 8910 IU; ½ cup cooked green leafy vegetables, 7870 IU; half of a cantaloupe, 6800 IU. Unlike the water-soluble Bs and C, vitamin A is fat soluble and not easily excreted by the body. Vitamin A might accumulate internally and lead to toxicity. You can have too much and harmfully overdose. A pregnant woman should beware of supplements that might cause her to have an excessive amount of vitamin A. More than 50,000 IU a day is potentially harmful, since it could cause congenital malformation of the fetus, including abnormalities in the urinary tract.

VITAMIN C

Vitamin C helps a woman's body absorb iron, folic acid, and vitamin A. Without C, these other nutrients would be far less effective. C, however, has a role other than that of aid to a well-balanced diet. This vitamin is an important contributor to collagen, a protein found in skin, tendons, and bones. Collagen is vital to the strength of a newborn's bones, teeth, and gums.

The vitamin C requirement during pregnancy is 80 milligrams a day, which can be met through eating a variety of fresh fruits and vegetables. Strawberries, oranges, grapefruit, cantaloupe, broccoli, watermelon, tomatoes, and peppers are all rich in vitamin C. Stress can increase a pregnant woman's need for this vitamin, but she should be careful not to take more than 3000 milligrams a day. In megadoses, vitamin C may be harmful to the fetus. This vitamin is active metabolically and could cause excessive absorption of other nutrients.

VITAMIN D

Vitamin D helps the body use calcium properly, so with the rise in your calcium intake, your need for vitamin D grows too. The required amount during pregnancy is 400 international units (IU) a day, which is in a quart of fortified milk. Vitamin D is also found in other dairy products, tuna, sardines, canned salmon, and herring. It is one of the more unusual vitamins, in that you can receive it not just from food but from the sun. When you are exposed to sunlight, your skin manufactures vitamin D. A pregnant woman need not become a sun worshipper, though, because she will be getting her daily vitamin D from the milk that she drinks. A woman who has a lactose intolerance may get her vitamin D from a supplement, but her doctor will prescribe an exact dosage and she should strictly follow his recommendation. Vitamin D in doses over 2000 IU daily could become toxic. A pregnant woman's intake should always be less than that amount.

VITAMIN E

Vitamin E gained fame in recent years from the elaborate claims made for its effect on virility and fertility. Unfortunately, these claims have not been substantiated. Researchers experimenting with pregnant rats, however, have found that a serious lack of vitamin E appears responsible for reproductive disorders: the rats' red blood cells were destroyed, their muscles degenerated, and they suffered fetal loss. A link between a human vitamin E deficiency and pregnancy problems has not been discovered thus far, but vitamin E does have influence. It has been used to treat certain types of anemia that occur in newborns of low birth weight. And finally, vitamin E may help prevent respiratory distress syndrome in premature infants. Vitamin E is a very important substance in promoting lung maturation in the unborn child. In premature infants, it has been used to treat the lung damage that appears in early birth.

Also called tocopherol, vitamin E is present in vegetable oils, wheat germ, soybeans, broccoli, brussels sprouts, whole grains, and eggs. The recommended amount of vitamin E is approximately 400 IU a day.

VITAMIN K

When her baby receives a shot of vitamin K shortly after birth, a new mother may wonder why her diet failed to provide this vitamin. She should not be concerned. Vitamin K, which helps create and maintain the body's blood-clotting capacity, is not available through foods; it is internally produced by the bacteria in the human intestinal tract. A newborn does not have this internal bacteria until she or he begins feeding outside the womb. Once a baby's nourishment starts to come from breast milk or formula, these helpful intestinal bacteria, which are important to digestion, will grow. The vitamin K injection is a necessary safety precaution taken in case a baby should hemorrhage or have another kind of bleeding disorder before her or his small body has had a chance to develop vitamin K on its own.

The Debate over Supplements

No test can tell a woman which vitamins may be in short supply in her body, but we do know that when certain vitamins are lacking, pregnancy complications and problems in fetal development can occur. Nevertheless, a number of nutritional experts believe that with a well-balanced diet, a pregnant woman will receive sufficient vitamins and minerals, and that only folic acid and iron may require supplementation. I, on the other hand, feel that every expectant mother, even a woman who has a perfectly healthy diet, can benefit from overall supplementation with at least one prenatal vitamin taken daily. Why risk any chance of deficiency?

The different brands of prenatal vitamins vary in their concentrations of vitamins and minerals (see Table 5), and some contain stool softeners. I recommend that a prenatal vitamin contain at least 1 milligram of folic acid, 100 milligrams of vitamin C, and 60 milligrams of iron. A woman should try a brand of prenatal vitamins, see how her body reacts to it, and decide whether she wants to remain with that brand or try another that might be more compatible with her system.

One argument against supplementing a diet with vitamins is that they may prove toxic to your system, but a harmful effect would require massive amounts of vitamins that are internally retained beyond the body's need. Most vitamins do not fall in this category. The greatest danger in vitamin overdose could come from too much of the fat-soluble vitamins A and D if they were taken in extremely high amounts. The dosages in prenatal vitamins are not excessive or dangerous. In fact, I am so in favor of vitamin supplementation that I even recommend that in the second

Table 5.

Vitamin and Mineral Content of Prenatal Vitamins

	Filibon Forte	Materna 1.60	Natabec RX	Natalins RX	Stuart Natal 1 + 1
Vitamin A	8000 IU	8000 IU	4000 IU	8000 IU	8000 IU
Vitamin D_2	400 IU	400 IU	400 IU	400 IU	400 IU
Vitamin E	45 IU	30 IU	—	30 IU	30 IU
Vitamin C	90 mg	100 mg	50 mg	90 mg	90 mg
Folic Acid	1 mg	1 mg	1 mg	1 mg	1 mg
Vitamin B_1	2.3 mg	3 mg	3 mg	2.55 mg	2.5 mg
Vitamin B_2	2.5 mg	3.4 mg	2 mg	3 mg	3 mg
Niacinamide	30 mg	20 mg	10 mg	20 mg	20 mg
Vitamin B_6	3 mg	4 mg	3 mg	10 mg	10 mg
Vitamin B_{12}	12 mcg	12 mcg	5 mcg	8 mcg	12 mcg
Calcium	300 mg	350 mg	600 mg	200 mg	200 mg
Iodine	200 mcg	0.3 mg	—	150 mcg	150 mcg
Iron	45 mg	60 mg	30 mg	60 mg	65 mg
Magnesium	100 mg	25 mg	—	100 mg	100 mg
Copper	—	2 mg	—	2 mg	—
Zinc	—	25 mg	—	15 mg	—
Biotin	—	—	—	0.05 mg	—
Pantothenic Acid	—	—	—	15 mg	—

and third trimesters, when a fetus is experiencing an increase in bone and muscle formation, a pregnant woman take two prenatal vitamins a day. Any excess vitamins and minerals that a mother and her baby do not absorb are usually excreted with urine and stools. Vitamins are beneficial. A healthy, well-balanced diet along with vitamin supplementation provides the new life within you with a strong basis for survival.

Fluids

An expectant mother must drink a lot of liquid to compensate for her increased body fluid and to prevent bowel problems. As noted in the recommended daily diet (see p. 103), 8 to 10 cups of liquid a day—and four 8-ounce cups of milk may be included in that total—are suggested. Water, fruit, and vegetable juices are good choices. Soft drinks, which are high in phosphorus and low in nutrition, are best ignored, and coffee and tea should be kept to a minimum. Caffeine, which appears in coffee, tea, and cola beverages, easily crosses the placenta and enters fetal tissue. Since studies with rats showed that large amounts of caffeine—the quantity found in twelve to twenty-four cups of coffee a day— seemed to cause birth defects among the rodents, and that even rats taking only two to four cups a day had low-birth-weight off-spring, the FDA has advised women to be prudent about caffeine consumption. (See Chapter 9.) Decaffeinated coffees and teas are acceptable substitutes.

As for alcoholic beverages, there is evidence that even two drinks a day may contribute to birth defects among newborns. The alcohol that an expectant mother drinks reaches her baby in the same high concentration that is in her bloodstream. (See Chapter 7.) Alcohol must be considered a drug that is very dangerous to the well-being of your baby during your pregnancy. The safest practice, of course, is to avoid alcohol completely.

Constantly emerging facts about nutrition during pregnancy are causing doctors to question what is the "right" advice for their patients. Many expectant mothers, concerned about how they should eat for two, have written letters seeking help in planning their menus. So many questions have repeated themselves time and again that I have taken the opportunity to answer them here.

Should I Gain More Weight?

I'm four months pregnant, but I've only gained three pounds, and I'm very worried. When I came back from the doctor's office today, my mother was very upset with me because I had not put on an ounce since my last visit. She says I'm starving my baby, and I don't know what to do. I'm not really hungry and I don't like to force-feed myself. I tried it once and I got sick. Am I really harming my baby by not putting on more weight than I have?

E.S.
Tucson, Arizona

In early pregnancy, by eating small, frequent meals and drinking as much fluid as you can, you are creating a healthy climate for your baby. You should not worry about failing to consume 2600 calories a day at the beginning of pregnancy. Remember, some women have morning sickness and cannot even look at food in the first trimester.

The usual weight gain in the first ten weeks is only one or two pounds, and from ten to twenty weeks, it is about eight pounds, so you are really gaining on schedule. Your appetite will grow in the second and third trimesters—somehow nature works it that way—and you will eat more when the muscles and bones of the baby are developing. The second and third trimesters are the times when you really need 2600 calories a day and increased calcium intake. For now, be sure that you eat a well-balanced diet of protein, fats, and carbohydrates and that you avoid alcoholic beverages, cigarettes, and drugs. An expectant mother should aim for a clean environment for her baby before she counts her calories.

Is Milk the Villain?

I ended my pregnancy forty pounds heavier than when I conceived. Some of the weight came off immediately, but I'm six months postpartum and still twenty pounds heavier than I ought to be. Most of the weight went on in the last trimester, when my doctor told me to drink a lot of milk to help cure the painful leg cramps I was having. It made a difference, but I seem to be paying for it now. Couldn't my doctor have substituted calcium pills for milk when he saw how huge I was getting? Or is there another, more effective way to cure the leg cramp problem?
M.K.
Santa Fe, New Mexico

A high-calcium food like milk, in all its forms—milk, cheese, yogurt—supplies a balance of protein, vitamins, minerals including calcium, and calories that cannot be duplicated by a tablet or a powder. Your doctor encouraged you to eat well, and he is a more caring physician than one who simply hands out a bottle of pills or a packet of tablets. Also, the vitamins and minerals in foods are more easily absorbed by the body than the vitamins and minerals in supplements.

A pregnancy diet should always include an increase of calcium, especially in the second half of pregnancy when quantities of this mineral are forming fetal bones and teeth. Still more calcium is needed to maintain your bodily functions, teeth, bones, and the healthy working of your heart and nervous system. With this added need for calcium, a woman may fail to get enough in the second half of pregnancy, when leg cramps can become a problem.

117

Many women start pregnancy without a high calcium reserve. Dairy products, unfortunately, have a bad reputation for being fattening, and the calcium a woman does eat is subject to being lost through sweat and urine. Also, one popular consumption habit tends to decrease the body's ability to handle calcium. Carbonated soft drinks are high in another mineral, phosphorus, and ingesting large quantities of phosphorus affects the body's capacity to absorb calcium. (Drink fruit juices or sparkling water instead of soda—the phosphorus you need is readily available in nutritious foods like meat or eggs.) The popularity of carbonated sodas has caused reduced calcium among many pregnant women and the prevalence of bone disorders later in life due to poor calcium stores at menopause.

A diet of calcium-rich foods, however, will help reduce the incidence of circulatory disorders during pregnancy. A calcium supplement may be added to the diet, but I prefer to see women boost their calcium intake with natural foods and not depend solely on supplements. Low-fat milk and low-fat milk products drastically cut the fat out of milk without sacrificing its calcium content. Cheese and yogurt are acceptable substitutes if you cannot tolerate milk. (Many women have not drunk milk since it was forced on them at the family dinner table.) However, if you are unable to eat any calcium-containing foods at all, you must take calcium supplements. Calcium pills are perfectly safe. You can buy them in combination with carbonate, lactate, or magnesium (whatever you tolerate best), in quantities of 500 milligrams. Take one supplement two or three times each day.

Calcium helps monitor the nerve stimulation that causes muscle contraction. When calcium levels are low, control of the nerve endings is reduced, and muscles then contract more often. Frequent, rhythmic contractions, in turn, lead to muscle cramping. Those periodic attacks of muscle cramps are extremely painful. Cramping is especially difficult to cope with at night, when it often seems as though an invisible hand has caught the overtired muscles in a viselike grip. Besides eating more calcium-rich foods, take more rest periods than usual to decrease the chances of localized swelling irritating the tissues and causing bouts of cramping. Keep your legs warm and supported with a pair of support hose from a surgical supply store. Sitting at a desk with the feet elevated for as little as five minutes at a time will help bring the blood back from the extremities and reduce the chances of cramping.

High-heel shoes, which offer little or no support, should go to the back of the closet while you are heavily pregnant. In general, brisk walking is a good way to improve circulation and reduce muscular tension.

A stubborn weight problem after pregnancy is a subject discussed in Chapter 16. One of the simplest reasons the prebirth fat stays on after delivery is for breast-feeding. Part of the weight gain is deliberately retained so that you will have enough fat stores to breast-feed successfully. A woman who does not breast-feed is frankly going to have a harder time taking off the weight than a woman who does. A woman who is not breast-feeding, however, does not have to worry about getting enough nutrients for her milk supply, and she can more easily undertake a weight-loss diet. I suggest that Ms. M.K. review her diet, reduce the amounts of salt, refined carbohydrates, and fat, and try to get her calories from fresh fruits and vegetables, lean meats, fish, and poultry. By watching her diet and increasing her exercise, she should be able to lose those lingering twenty pounds.

A NOTE ON THE STATISTICS OF BREAST-FEEDING
According to the Surgeon General of the United States, 30 to 40 percent of new mothers start off breast-feeding their babies. The official goal of the Surgeon General's office is to double the number so that 75 percent of new mothers are breast-feeding by 1990. The women least likely to breast-feed are low-income women. Unfortunately, these are the very women who are most likely to become obese after pregnancy and whose babies could most benefit from the long-term health benefits of breast-feeding.

Aren't Doctors Supposed to Care About How Much You Weigh?

Must one listen to the authorities who tell you to eat this and eat that during pregnancy? I have a friend who was pregnant last year and who followed pamphlets she had been given to the letter. By the end of six servings of this and four servings of that, she had gained fifty pounds and couldn't even walk around the block to mail a letter. What's the point of following doctor's orders if it means eating excessively and becoming much too heavy? Aren't doctors supposed to care about how much you weigh as well as how much you eat?

J.B.
Providence, Rhode Island

119

Diet pamphlets are not meant to be followed slavishly. The four servings of this and three servings of that type of diet outlines a guide, at most. Its value, as is the worth of the recommended daily diet in this chapter, is that it usually covers all the nutritional bases. In pregnancy, you are aiming to eat a well-balanced variety of foods. A scanty supply of any food group, from protein foods to foods that supply essential vitamins, spells trouble. Although foods within the same group are often interchangeable—good sources of protein are fish, meat, fowl, and soybeans—you must have protein, complex carbohydrates, and fats to provide a balanced diet. You do not have to eat neatly calculated portions according to a precise timetable, but do eat when you are hungry. Do not ignore hunger pangs in the name of regular eating and suffer the low-blood-sugar reactions that are common in pregnancy. Six small meals a day are often more satisfying than three large ones, especially toward the end of pregnancy when you really cannot eat very much in one sitting.

Eating well is the first rule of pregnancy. Watching your weight comes second, though a very important second if you are experiencing a very heavy weight gain that occurs inexplicably. A fifty-pound weight gain is understandable if a woman started pregnancy twenty pounds underweight. Or she might be carrying a substantial amount of the weight in water. Women whose blood pressure remains normal (high blood pressure might be an early symptom of toxemia) sometimes gain ten to fifteen pounds in extra water. An overall feeling of fullness is the sign of healthy water retention.

If you begin carrying an inexplicable amount of weight, try keeping a nutritional diary for a few days to see whether the weight is caused by overeating, especially of refined sugar. A nutritional diary is a straightforward record of everything you eat and drink, from a banana to a full meal, jotted down under headings that indicate the day and date. The concept was popularized by childbirth educators practicing the Bradley method of husband-coached childbirth, but Lamaze-trained women find it equally useful. Although Bradley educators sometimes recommend keeping a diary for an extended period of time, it is perfectly acceptable to restrict your diary keeping to a few days so that you can quickly analyze the results.

Keep a diary for a week if you can. Try not to alter your consumption patterns; the point is lost if you artificially curb your food intake. After days of conscientious record keeping, you should begin to see a pattern emerging—too few pieces of fruit, perhaps, too many chocolate chip cookies, or more portions of ice cream than you had supposed. This is the one time a detailed calorie chart could be useful, because you will then have an accurate idea of how many calories you are consuming on a daily basis. A record of other nutritional imbalances will also emerge from your journal. Many women, for instance, find they are having plenty of vitamin C in the form of orange juice but too few vegetables high in the B vitamins, like broccoli and watercress. You may also find that your fluid intake is mostly in the form of coffee and tea. (The negative effects of excessive caffeine consumption are discussed in Chapter 9.) By the end of a week of honest record keeping, you may be able to see why you are running into nutritional difficulties, whether the problem is an imbalance of fat, protein, or refined sugars. Then it would be wise to take the diary to your doctor and discuss your findings with him.

Are Prenatal Vitamins Necessary Before Pregnancy?

I have a friend whose doctor prescribed prenatal vitamins before she became pregnant. I'm curious to know why he did so and why any doctor would prescribe medication designed for a pregnant woman for anyone who wasn't pregnant. I take an iron tablet daily and 100 mg of B₆ as antistress insurance. My doctor has never asked about my vitamin-taking habits and he certainly hasn't recommended prenatals even though he knows I want to get pregnant. Is there something special about my friend's pregnancy? Or am I missing out on something that is vitally important to my future pregnancy?

L.K.
Fresno, California

Doctors who are concerned about their patients' nutrition are beginning to pay more attention to remedying deficiencies before a woman becomes pregnant. This is a welcome change in obstetrics. Doctors have known for years that many women start their pregnancies with low iron and other mineral and vitamin deficiencies, and today's research is showing that what were once considered marginal lacks can have serious cumulative effects on the body.

In certain respects, you are already laying the groundwork for a successful pregnancy every day of your menstrual life. Supplementary iron is one vitamin/mineral supplement that every woman should take throughout her reproductive cycle. Iron is poorly provided for in the average diet, and what dietary iron does reach the intestinal tract is frequently not well absorbed. The best policy is to take a daily supplement that is high or relatively high in elemental iron. Many women do not realize that they are mildly anemic until their doctors take a hematocrit/hemoglobin test at the beginning of a pregnancy. Modern women have experienced tiredness for so long that they tend to ignore it rather than try to overcome it through dietary changes. As I have said before, changes in food intake always come first, but there are times when vitamin and mineral supplements become necessary.

Are you taking B_6 to counteract past oral contraceptive use? If you have been a long-time oral contraceptive user, your body will have been depleted of several of the B vitamins. Using B_6 alone, therefore, will not take care of your depleted reserve of B vitamins even though you are boosting your B_6 intake. If you need supplementary vitamins, the best way to take Bs is in a balanced form through a B-complex supplement. A complete B-complex preparation will ensure a balanced intake of the B vitamins, some of which are inadequately provided for in our overly refined modern diets.

The B vitamins play an important role in a woman's reproductive life. One physician at least believes they also can be the key to preventing certain birth defects. In experimental work done in Great Britain, where the central nervous system defects known as the neural tube defects are unusually prevalent, Dr. Richard Smitherells gave extra B vitamins and other minerals and vitamins to a group of low-income women who had had one child with a neural tube defect. After taking supplements for several months before conception, 90 percent of the women who conceived gave birth to children free of the defect. This represented a startling sevenfold drop in the expected incidence of neural tube defects among this high-risk population. And another study isolated folic acid (one of the B vitamins) as the vitamin whose absence was most closely linked to the defect. In this study, women were given folic acid supplementation, and neural tube defects were significantly reduced. (Low-income women tend to have folic acid deficiencies because they eat too few fresh vegetables, the main source of folic acid in most people's diets.)

Although no one knows exactly how neural tube defects occur, these studies should warn doctors to be on nutritional alert before a woman begins her pregnancy. Women who have eaten reasonably well since childhood are usually ensured against gross nutritional deficiencies, but since no one is immune to illnesses and the stresses of modern life, careful eating before pregnancy is important. As a good general precaution, ask your doctor to take a hematocrit/hemoglobin test to establish whether you are anemic. Using the general guidelines in this chapter, you can then work out a diet that covers most of your nutritional needs. Try to stay with it despite the everyday stresses and strains. Also, ask your doctor to recommend a supplement with a balanced quota of minerals and vitamins. This does not have to be a prenatal vitamin supplement, but prenatals generally offer more balanced combinations than over-the-counter multiple vitamins.

Unlike brand-name vitamins, prescribed prenatals provide a balanced quota of Bs, including folic acid. In fact, one of the great advantages of prenatal supplements is the greater margin of safety they provide as far as most minerals and vitamins are concerned. Because they are specially designed for pregnant women, they meet the special need for zinc, folic acid, and other minerals and vitamins that are diminished in modern diets of processed and refined foods.

What About a High-Protein/Low-Calorie Diet During Pregnancy?

I am confused. On my first visit to the doctor, the receptionist handed me a pamphlet that recommended far more calories than I usually allow myself on a daily basis. Since then, I have seen much the same information in a number of the books I've been reading. Yet when we've talked about controlling the little bit of nausea I've been having, my doctor has suggested I go on a high-protein/low-calorie diet for a few weeks until the morning sickness period is over. What's the value of a high-protein diet during pregnancy? And if I go on one, where will I get all these calories?

J.H.
Orange County, California

Your obstetrician is harking back to the calorie-conscious sixties, when high-protein/low-calorie diets were in vogue. The trouble is that doctors often pay lip service to the newer thinking on calories and then fall back on the old high-protein/low-calorie "solution" whenever patients run into nutritional difficulties during pregnancy.

The high-protein/low-calorie approach to pregnancy is inappropriate and unwise. You wouldn't consider breakfast as a balanced meal unless you were having protein and carbohydrates (eggs, orange juice, *and* toast), and neither should your doctor. An all-meat diet (high protein equals all meat in the diet books) means deliberately excluding the complex carbohydrates, so out go your vegetables, fruits, and whole grains. Imagine how you'd feel after a few weeks of pure protein eating: constipated, probably energy-less, and depressed. Sick, too, if you're in your first trimester. Nausea responds best to starches—bread, pasta, potatoes. Besides being easy to digest, these foods are high in vitamin B_6, the anti-nausea vitamin. A high-protein snack is useful before you go to bed—the slower burning protein will help counteract the nauseated early morning feeling when blood sugar is at a low ebb. Otherwise, a surfeit of animal proteins is likely to make you sicker, especially if you eat meat without legumes and dairy products to fill your protein requirement.

When a doctor suggests a high-protein diet (he may leave calories out of the conversation), he is imposing a hidden form of weight control on unsuspecting patients. The subject invariably comes up after the weekly weigh-in, when you have gained several pounds and your doctor asks you if you are having enough protein—by which he usually means more meat and less "starch." If you are already getting enough protein—and you should be if you follow the recommended daily diet—agree to cut down on sugars, *if* you think he is correct about your weight gain. Let him know that you intend to go on eating breads and potatoes because you need them (you do), but you will try to keep your intake of refined sugars to a minimum. Increasing your level of exercise may also help burn up some excess sugar, natural or otherwise. Perhaps you can come to a negotiated settlement rather than precipitate a head-on conflict about your weight or nutrition. Doctors frequently still treat carbohydrates as suspect substances, even though the recent research on pregnancy has officially dispelled the bad-guy image associated with carbohydrates and calories. A certain number of calories must be consumed to keep up a good weight gain. Besides, nutritious eating always means eating a variety of foods; otherwise, you tip the nutritional balance, which is potentially harmful during pregnancy.

A final note on the high-protein/low-calorie diet: it eats up protein. Anyone, pregnant or not pregnant, who goes on a high-protein diet and cuts out calories must consume huge quantities of protein to keep her body functioning. It is the concentration of protein that provides the body with extra energy to burn along with the unwanted fat. Even for the nonpregnant woman, the high-protein/low-calorie diet is an expensive, wasteful, and probably only temporary solution to a weight problem.

THE BOTTOM LINE

A pregnancy diet does not have to be troublesome or complicated, but it should be thoughtfully prepared. In the beginning of pregnancy, you do not have to worry about the quantity of the foods you eat as much as the quality. (Alcohol, caffeine, and drugs could be especially harmful to the fetus in the first few months.) Later on, as your pregnancy progresses, the recommended daily diet in this chapter, with vitamin and mineral supplementation, will give you a good, well-balanced eating program. An expectant mother who follows the guidelines offered here is doing as much as she can to make sure that the developing fetus will grow into a strong, healthy child.

CHAPTER 6

Everyday Encounters During Pregnancy—What Might Happen, What Is Safe

Every woman's pregnancy has its own profile. Childbearing always brings physical changes, from the incredibly common to the especially rare. A woman feels new sensations, sees her body reshape, and wants to know why. At the same time, she wonders how her environment will affect her and her baby's health. Suddenly activities like flying, getting a tooth filled, or dyeing her hair come into question.

In the course of a day, an expectant mother may be concerned about varicose veins, getting a suntan, stretch marks, or having an orgasm—about a lot of different things that arise from or may contribute to her pregnancy. The queries from pregnant women who are encountering physical surprises or facing unexpected decisions about what is best for the unborn baby are similar. In fact, a collection of often-asked questions has become apparent to many doctors.

At the root of the questions from women who have written or spoken to me are the basic concerns: "What should I expect?" and "How can I proceed safely?" When you puzzle over a bodily change or become perplexed about what is safe, look through the questions that follow; you will probably find your questions and be able to ease your mind with the answers.

WHAT MIGHT HAPPEN

A woman may live through her entire pregnancy without a twinge, or she may continuously be trying to understand her latest ailment. Every pregnancy is unique. Some expectant mothers feel different discomforts at different times. For instance, fatigue may overtake a woman during her first trimester, but by the fourth month, she may have drive and energy that turn tiredness into memory. A skin rash may suddenly plague her, however. Sometimes a symptom such as leg cramps appears, disappears, and returns at what seems like timed intervals during the nine months.

No one can predict exactly what will happen to you, but other women have experienced a variety of occurrences, including morning sickness, frequent urination, nosebleeds, varicose veins, breast changes, hemorrhoids, and backaches. You may feel some or none of these. Most unpredictable discomforts are fairly manageable and naturally fleeting. They are not likely to linger after childbirth. If the explanation for your problem is not among the questions and answers that follow, consult your doctor for advice. A mysterious condition should never go unchecked, especially during pregnancy.

Will My Morning Sickness Ever Go Away?

My morning sickness started right after I found out I was pregnant, and it has never really left me. I was vomiting so much in the first trimester that my doctor put me in the hospital in my second month. After a few days on intravenous feeding, I slowly began to feel better, but I have never been completely well. I'm in the sixth month now and i still feel nauseated off and on. Where is the glow of expectant mother- hood that everyone talks about? Is there anything I can do to get it be- fore this pregnancy comes to an end?

J.P.

Louisville, Kentucky

The nausea and vomiting of what is called morning sickness may really occur at any time during the day. Just why the condi- tion affects only some women is not known. Myth has it that women who are carrying boys are spared because the male hor- mone testosterone, produced in the gonads of the male fetus, pro- tects the expectant mother to some degree. Perhaps there is some truth in this bit of folk wisdom, but one can certainly find mothers of sons who will say otherwise.

The cause of morning sickness may more likely be the level of HCG (human chorionic gonadotropin), the pregnancy hormone, in the blood. HCG rises a few days after a missed period, which is when morning sickness usually starts. Continuously secreted by the brain and the placenta, HCG peaks at about eight weeks and dramatically falls at about twelve weeks. Suddenly a woman who has been sick and vomiting for months will awaken with barely a discomfort. Ms. P. has not yet reached a symptom-free day. She may be overly sensitive to food due to her pregnancy, and this sen- sitivity may be generating constant gastrointestinal problems.

Sometimes a woman becomes so ill with morning sickness that she cannot eat at all, and she vomits violently on an empty stom- ach. The nonstop vomiting then causes weight loss, and essential fatty tissue burns up. Soon ketones, acid-producing substances resulting from the breakdown of fatty tissue, begin to make the body acidotic. Since a high level of acidity can be dangerous to the developing fetus, a doctor will try to control the vomiting with medications such as Compazine or Tigan suppositories, and to neutralize the acidity with plenty of fluids. If this treatment does not work, then, like Ms. P., a woman will be admitted to the hospi- tal for an intravenous feeding of dextrose and water for a few days. Little by little, the intravenous feeding will wash out the acidity, strengthen a woman's body, and end the threat of harm.

Perhaps the best way to combat morning sickness before it has a chance to take hold is through prevention. When you are plan- ning ahead for pregnancy, increase the B vitamins in your body. A vitamin B-complex with 100 milligrams of vitamin B_1 included, and 200 milligrams of a separate vitamin B_6 every day, will help regulate hormonal fluctuation and defend your system against morning sickness. Fortification also comes from foods rich in iron and B vitamins (see Chapter 5).

If a woman does start to suffer, two prenatal vitamins with supplementary vitamin B-complex and B_6 may help alleviate the symptoms. In the morning, a woman should plan to move slowly when she first awakens. Sometimes, if she is already a mother with small children, she may have to spring into action early. If there is a way to take a few moments for herself, however, she should try. A woman with morning sickness needs special understanding and care from her husband and family. She is miserably ill, and if she does not have support from her loved ones, she will feel worse. She should be allowed to rest in a tranquil environment free from loud noise, visitors, and a ringing phone. Too many disturbances can prompt a bout of sickness.

Here is the best way to fight that nauseous feeling: keep a couple of crackers or dry toast at your bedside and nibble on them before you arise. Then sit on the side of the bed for a few minutes, and make sure that your stomach feels settled. Sudden movement may trigger nausea and vomiting, so you will want to stand up slowly.

A few bites of dry carbohydrate-containing foods such as toast, cereal, crackers, even plain popcorn can usually allay daytime nausea. Sometimes small amounts of ginger ale or cola are soothing too. When you are planning a menu, avoid greasy fried foods that might be upsetting, and if the smell of a certain food cooking makes you queasy, don't eat it. In fact, rather than schedule three meals a day, a woman should consume five or six small meals with tiny portions that will fill, but not upset, her stomach.

If a woman's nausea and vomiting continue in spite of her precautions, her doctor may prescribe Compazine injections or suppositories, a medication that has been used for many years for relief of nausea. A physician will only hospitalize an expectant mother after he has exhausted all avenues of treatment and has been unable to arrest the vomiting of morning sickness. Morning sickness will usually disappear after a week or two in the hospital. Afterward, when she is home, a woman should continue to rest and pamper herself with the love and kindness of her family and friends.

Why Do I Have to Urinate So Much?

I'm seven months pregnant and I'm having a terrible time controlling my bladder. It seems that I can't last more than ten minutes without having to go to the bathroom again. Urinary cultures do not show signs of cystitis or any other type of infection. Is this condition going to continue right up through childbirth, or will I have a reprieve?

K.V.

Wyandotte, Michigan

The urge to urinate is one of the early signs of pregnancy, but women often find that very little urine comes out when they act upon that urge. The feeling is nonetheless real, because bladder muscles relax with increased progesterone, and the nerves that direct the need to urinate send messages to the brain. Also, an expanding uterus puts pressure on the bladder. An expectant mother may visit the bathroom regularly until the middle months, when the uterus rises into the abdominal cavity and offers some relief. In the last trimester, however, the fetus drops down into the birth canal, and a woman's bladder is pressed once more. This time, though, the kidneys, which are receiving a greater blood supply due to the pregnancy, produce more urine.

Ms. V. is in her seventh month, so her urination is probably from the weight of the unborn baby resting on her bladder. When urination seems to be excessive, a woman should have a urinary culture, which Ms. V. did, to eliminate the possibility of a urinary tract infection. Ms. V. will continue to feel the pressure and go to the bathroom as the baby steadily grows, but there are a few ways in which she might ease her discomfort.

When frequent urination is a problem, a woman should try to avoid drinking fluids in the last hour or two before retiring. In this way, she can eliminate late-night trips to the bathroom. She may even be able to reduce the number of times she feels the need to urinate by making a conscious effort to empty her bladder completely when she voids. The Kegel exercises, which strengthen the muscles around the bladder neck and vagina, are also helpful. By tightening and then releasing the pelvic muscles that regulate the flow of urine, a woman will strengthen her bladder control. This contraction-relaxation exercise should be repeated ten to twenty times a day to be most effective; however, in spite of the Kegel technique, a urinary problem may still continue until after childbirth.

Why Am I So Tired I Can Hardly Move?

I'm eight weeks pregnant and I feel like I have some sort of sleeping sickness. I'm tired all the time. Some days I think I am twenty-two going on eighty. I'm taking vitamins and eating the right foods, but I can't seem to get any energy. My husband thinks I'm pretending to be this tired. He can't believe that a person who once had so much vitality could be so exhausted. Is there anything I can do to beat this fatigue?

B.B.

Elkhart, Indiana

The utter exhaustion that a woman feels in the first trimester of pregnancy is absolutely normal. Some women become so tired that they can hardly lift their heads in the beginning. The fatigue seems to be brought on by hormonal changes, specifically the increase in progesterone. In the last half of a menstrual cycle, the rise in progesterone often makes a woman extremely tired. It is also known that when it is injected into animals, progesterone brings on fatigue. The jump in progesterone during pregnancy is quite high, so Ms. B.'s tiredness is certainly understandable.

I also believe that an expectant mother's lack of energy in the beginning of pregnancy is nature's way of preventing her from excessive activity at a time when the life within her womb is only starting to secure itself. A woman who rests is allowing nourishment to reach the developing fetus in a calm environment. The fetus will begin to grow stronger in this peaceful state. Rest and a well-balanced diet promote a wonderful pregnancy.

Ms. B. might explain her hormonal change to her husband and let him know how valuable her fatigue is to giving their child a good start. He should be encouraged to help her around the house and to support the nap-taking that will only strengthen their future offspring. The overwhelming tiredness that has overtaken Ms. B. will disappear after the first trimester, and she will feel more vital than ever.

Why Do I Have Such a Craving for Ice Cream?

My first sign of pregnancy was not morning sickness but a tremendous craving for sweets. I'm in my fifth month now and the craving has not subsided. I stock my cupboards with chocolate bars and my freezer

*with gallons of ice cream. I'm gaining too much weight, I think, but I
don't know how to stop.*

L.H.
Canton, Ohio

Rather than becoming nauseated and eating less during pregnancy, some women find that they eat more, and the foods they choose are often sour, salty, or sweet. Pickles, potato chips, and chocolate are common cravings. Why? Once again, the rise in progesterone seems to be the trigger. Just as a woman can have a craving before her period due to increased progesterone, she can experience unusual eating habits during pregnancy for the same reason. Sometimes, though, there is a rationale for the craving.

Chocolate contains magnesium, and a chocolate craving may be a sign that a woman lacks this mineral. She may also be enjoying the effects of phenylethylamine, or PEA, in chocolate. Phenylethylamine is a neurotransmitterlike substance, similar to an amphetamine, which may contribute to feelings of elation and exhilaration. An ice cream craving may be brought on by the need for calcium. Also, increased progesterone makes body temperature go up one degree, and the refreshing coolness of ice cream is quite pleasant.

I worry that with cravings for sweets, my patients will gain too much weight, and I suggest that they try to limit the amounts they eat. A few bites of a chocolate bar or a couple of spoonfuls of ice cream calm a craving, but before a craving starts, a woman can sometimes stave it off with small portions of fresh fruits and vegetables.

When a woman who is prone to cravings allows more than three or four hours to elapse without eating anything, she is actually giving her blood sugar time to fall and create the craving itself. If she consumes the refined sugar in sweets, she will get a rush of insulin that will make her blood sugar drop. Other kinds of foods—proteins, whole grains, and carbohydrates in fresh fruits and vegetables—take time to metabolize into glucose, so insulin production occurs at a slow, even pace, and the blood sugar level remains steady. Kept at an even level, blood sugar cuts off a craving. Most women find that cravings intensify at some point during pregnancy but then fall off. On the other hand, there are those women who continue to have steady cravings throughout pregnancy. Ms. H.'s craving has not slackened, but she must not try to diet right now, in spite of the pounds she has added with sweets. Pregnancy is not a time to slim down. If Ms. H. attempts to reduce, she may burn up fatty tissue and create a dangerously acidic internal environment for the baby. Small, frequent meals are really craving stoppers.

What Can I Do About the Hemorrhoids I've Developed?

I've become so constipated with this pregnancy that now I have hemorrhoids. I've used an over-the-counter aid but it doesn't seem to help. Please help me find relief.

M.N.
Clarksville, Tennessee

Almost half of all pregnant women experience constipation, and unfortunately, painful hemorrhoids—varicose (or swollen) veins of the rectum—often result. When a woman strains to have a bowel movement, the rectal veins block and trap blood. With unrelenting constipation, the veins become itchy, painful, and may even protrude from the anus. Toward the end of pregnancy, the pressure of the baby also blocks blood from returning easily to the lower part of the body and aggravates the condition.

The best way to combat hemorrhoids is to alleviate constipation with a high-fiber diet of raw fruits and vegetables and whole grains. A woman should drink plenty of liquids, especially fruit juices such as prune. A natural laxative like Metamucil can soften the stool, and daily exercise, even if it's just a twenty-minute walk, also helps.

Ms. N. should not try to force a bowel movement. If she does strain, a little petroleum jelly just inside her rectum may ease elimination. Since her hemorrhoids are protruding, her problem is advanced. She might soak in a warm bath and try to push the hemorrhoids back with a lubricated finger. Afterward, to shrink the hemorrhoids, she can apply an ice bag or a washcloth soaked in ice water or witch hazel to the rectal area. If her hemorrhoids do not diminish, prescribed Anusol suppositories in a kit with medicated wipes (Tucks) may be effective. In the last trimester, a woman who lies on her side with a pillow propped under her hip will redirect her blood flow away from the hemorrhoidal area and ease the condition.

Bleeding or painful hemorrhoids should be examined by a doctor, because a thrombosed vein may have developed. A physician will make an incision into the thrombosed hemorrhoid under local anesthesia and empty the small blood clot.

Is There Anything I Can Do to Stop These Varicose Veins from Popping Out All over My Legs?

My mother had varicose veins, and I know they are hereditary, but I was spared during my first pregnancy. When I was carrying my son, I never had a sign of varicose veins, so when I got pregnant a second time, I thought I was probably immune to the problem. Not so! I am in my fifth month and my veins are bulging and my legs are aching. The pressure of this pregnancy is so different from the first. I've had to slow down much more due to this vein condition, which I would really like to stop if I can. Tell me, is there anything special I can do?

S.W.

San Luis Obispo, California

Varicose veins are swollen veins in the legs and sometimes in the pelvic area. They develop when the expanding uterus presses against the vena cava, the main vein in the body, and blocks the blood flow back to the heart. Ten to 20 percent of all pregnant women get varicose veins, a condition that is often inherited but may not appear until a woman has had more than one pregnancy. The pressure of a first pregnancy stretches and weakens the blood vessels; therefore, subsequent pregnancies extend an existing damage. Veins that have been weakened succumb to the added pressure of another conception. Although the veins may appear in the second or third months, they usually surface after the fourth month, as the fetus begins to grow more rapidly.

Ms. W., and any woman who knows that she is susceptible to varicose veins, should buy to-the-waist pantyhose and put on a pair as soon as she wakes up in the morning. Support hose pulled on before the veins fill with blood can prevent blockage of the veins by maintaining circulation. Ms. W. seems to have a serious case, so she would probably need the strong support hose sold in surgical supply stores (Jobst or Sivaris are the better brands).

In addition to wearing support hose, a woman can fight varicose veins by sitting with her feet elevated for several rest periods a day. She should not stand for long stretches of time, and if she does find herself standing to prepare dinner or to make a deposit at the bank, she should lie or sit with her feet elevated for at least a half-hour afterward. She should also take ten- to fifteen-minute walks every so often to increase her circulation. Another good exercise is to lie on a bed, a couch, or a floor near a wall. Lift your legs parallel to the wall and rest your heels on the wall. Two to five minutes in this position several times a day can combat varicose veins. At night, a woman might sleep with her feet elevated by pillows to enhance the blood flow.

Ms. W.'s husband can occasionally massage his wife's legs upward from the feet to stimulate circulation. Ms. W. should continue to wear support hose for a few weeks after the baby is born to prevent the onset of phlebitis (blood clotting in the legs). Her varicose veins may disappear forever after childbirth, but if they do not, she may want to investigate the surgery that is designed to eliminate the problem.

Why Is My Nose Bleeding?

Nobody ever told me that nosebleeds came with pregnancy. Does this happen to everyone? Why is my nose bleeding?
P.S.
Portland, Oregon

Nosebleeds are actually common during pregnancy, especially among women who are prone to allergies and sinus trouble. There is an increased blood flow to all parts of the body, including the nasal mucosa, during pregnancy, and if a woman is pregnant in wintertime, the cold, dry weather contributes to this already sensitive problem.

A nosebleed is rarely a serious problem, but it can be annoying. Ms. S. may be helped by a humidifier in her bedroom. Her nasal passages should be kept moist and lubricated at night with a few drops of 0.25 percent solution of menthol in white oil. If her nose does start to bleed, she should tilt her head backward and squeeze her nose tightly between her thumb and forefinger, pressing from side to side to create a blockage of the blood (hemostasis). If the bleeding persists, she might apply ice to the bridge of her nose between the eyes. She may prevent further occurrences with vaso-constricting nose drops such as Neosynephrine. If her nosebleeds are continual and severe, she should consult her physician. An acute loss of blood can require hospitalization.

Why Do I Have Such Painful Leg Cramps?

Sometimes I'm awakened in the middle of the night with a leg cramp so painful that I have to jump out of bed and hop around the bedroom. I've never had anything like this happen to me before. What can I do to prevent these muscle spasms?

T.A.

Key West, Florida

Leg cramps can become frequent in the last half of pregnancy, when the growing fetus is causing great pressure on the lower part of a woman's body. A woman who does not take walking breaks to increase her circulation may find that she is overtaken by a "charley horse" in her calf muscle now and then. Such a spasm can occur without warning and be blindingly painful.

When Ms. A. experiences a leg cramp in the middle of the night, she should extend her leg with her foot at a right angle. Her mate should then push down against her knee with one hand, and with the other hand, press against the sole of her foot. This maneuver extends and relieves the cramped muscle. He might also knead and massage her leg and foot, which should continue to be kept at a right angle. If Ms. A. is alone when she gets a cramp, she can hold onto the back of a chair while standing six inches away from it. Then she should slide the cramped leg backward as far as she can without lifting her feet from the floor. If she can hold this extended-leg position for a few minutes, the muscle will stretch and relax.

Sometimes leg cramps have been attributed to a lack of calcium. Ms. A. might ask her doctor to check the calcium/phosphorus level at the time of her next blood count. She should include plenty of calcium-containing foods such as milk, cheese, and yogurt in her diet, or take 500 milligrams of calcium two to three times a day if she has a lactose intolerance.

Ms. A. should avoid high-heel shoes. She should walk in comfortably cushioned low-heeled shoes and exercise moderately in the footwear appropriate to her activity. If her pain does not subside, Ms. A. might need heat therapy or muscle-relaxing drugs or injections into the muscle. As a last resort, a painkiller might even be necessary.

Will My Breasts Ever Stop Growing?

My breasts are becoming bigger and bigger and I'm beginning to get concerned. How much can they grow? I'd like to have my old figure back after pregnancy. Will my breasts be gigantic or will they return to their normal size?

I.M.
Independence, Missouri

Breast enlargement is one of the first signs of pregnancy. The breasts not only grow but the areola, the pigmented area surrounding the nipple, darkens and the veins in the breast become more apparent. As pregnancy progresses, these breast changes intensify. Breast expansion continues as mammary glands alter themselves in preparation for milk production. Additional veins appear, and the areola darkens even more. In the second trimester, the nipples themselves become large, dark, and erect. Colostrum, a thick yellowish fluid, may occasionally leak from the nipples in the later months, and a woman may find that she needs nursing pads in her bra to prevent staining. As the breasts engorge toward the end of pregnancy, a woman may decide to wear a nursing bra for extra support.

Ms. M. should check her weight gain with her doctor to make sure that she has not put on too much weight for the month of her pregnancy (see Chapter 5). If she is gaining too fast, her breasts may be enlarging so rapidly that she may notice stretch marks. These marks will not disappear after pregnancy. Ms. M. can, however, take preventive measures. She can stay within the limits of a proper weight gain, and she can massage her breasts with skin lotions. Creams or lotions that contain vitamin E, aloe vera, or cocoa butter may help ward off stretch marks. These creams and lotions soften the skin tissue so that it is less likely to tear as it expands.

After childbirth, if a woman does not breast-feed, milk production will stop and her breasts will return to their normal size. Unfortunately, stretch marks that have occurred will not disappear. Among breast-feeding women, there are great variations. Some women notice relatively little change in their figure after breast-feeding; others describe a certain maturity about their breasts. Often a woman who breast-feeds for more than a few months breaks down the fatty tissue in her breasts and finds them diminished once she stops breast-feeding. She may be able to enhance her figure, however, with upper body exercises.

Is My Backache Caused by Pressure on a Nerve?

I'm in my eighth month and I have terrible back pain. My mother says that the baby is probably pressing against a nerve. I don't think the problem is that serious, but I'm worried that she may be right.

W.E.

Muskogee, Oklahoma

I have often heard women with backaches ask whether their babies could be resting on a nerve, but this is not the case. In the last trimester of pregnancy, the added weight of the baby causes a woman to change her posture. She bends backward to compensate for her increasing girth. With this backward stance, a woman puts pressure on her lower back, an area that is weakened by pregnancy. One of the physical changes that occurs during expectancy is a softening of the pelvic joints and the discs of the lower back. This softening accommodates the growing fetus, but it also leads to backache.

Ms. E. may ease her pain in a number of ways. She should squat—bend from the knees—whenever she wants to pick up a child or an object. While holding the child or object close to her body, she should use her leg muscles to stand up slowly. Distributing her weight evenly on both feet and wearing cushioned low-heeled shoes will also offer relief.

The following exercise, called the pelvic rock, appears in a booklet on prenatal care offered by the U.S. Department of Health, Education and Welfare.* This exercise increases the flexibility of your lower back and strengthens your abdominal muscles. It not only relieves backache but will help improve your posture and appearance. Practice it every day, and try walking and standing with your pelvis tilted forward. This provides your baby with a cradle of bone in which to lie instead of your abdominal wall.

When you practice the pelvic rock standing up, you can use a chair for support. Stand about two feet away from the back of the chair and bend slightly forward from your hips. (See Figure 6-1.) Place your hands on the chair back and keep your elbows straight. Rotate your hips backward and sag with your abdominal muscles. You have a real "swayback" this way. (See Figure 6-2.) Flex your

* *Prenatal Care*, U.S. Department of Health, Education and Welfare, Office of Child Development, Children's Bureau, DHEW Publication No. (OCD) 73-17, Children's Bureau Publication No. 4, Rockville, Maryland, 1983.

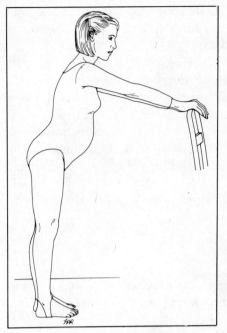 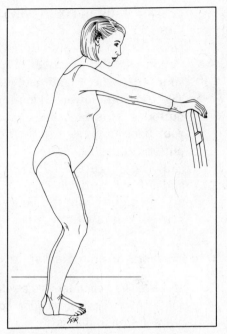

Figure 6-1. *Beginning position for standing pelvic rock exercise.*

Figure 6-2. *Completion of standing pelvic rock exercise.*

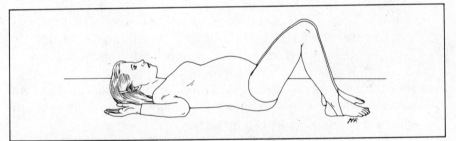

Figure 6-3. *Beginning position for supine pelvic rock exercise.*

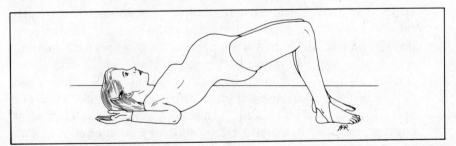

Figure 6-4. *Arched back pose for supine pelvic rock exercise.* Illustrations by Laurel Purington Rand.

knees slightly and then slowly rotate your hips forward. Tuck your buttocks under as if someone were pushing you from behind. Repeat this ten to twenty times a day.

You can also practice the pelvic rock lying on your back, with your knees bent and feet flat on the floor. (See Figure 6-3.) Tighten your lower abdominal muscles and the muscles of the buttocks. This causes the tailbone to be elevated and the small of your back to press into the floor. Then relax your abdominal and buttock muscles. As you do this, arch your back as high as you can. (See Figure 6-4.) Repeat the tightening of your abdominal and buttock muscles, and be sure that the small of your back presses tightly into the floor. The pelvic rock can be done in this manner ten to twenty times a day.

Can I Prevent Stretch Marks?

My sister had such terrible stretch marks after her pregnancy that she could no longer wear a bikini. I don't want that to happen to me. Can I prevent stretch marks?

W.T.
Asheville, North Carolina

Stretch marks are pink, slightly depressed streaks that may appear on the abdomen, breasts, thighs, and buttocks during the later months of pregnancy. Women under thirty seem to be more susceptible to stretch marks than older expectant mothers. Also, blondes, overweight women, and first-time expectant mothers are likely candidates. Just why some women are more prone than others to stretch marks is a mystery.

For generations, women have used various lotions and creams to fight stretch marks, and this moisturizing is effective. By massaging her body, particularly her breasts and abdomen, with a lotion or cream, a woman softens and elasticizes her skin. Cocoa butter and vitamin E cream are popular among pregnant women. A patient of mine, however, had great success with almond oil extract, which she purchased from her pharmacist. She massaged the oil into her skin every night for the last four months of her pregnancy, and after childbirth, her body was completely free of stretch marks. Other moisturizers may be just as effective as almond oil if they are also applied daily. Other effective ways to control stretch marks are to keep your weight gain within the range of twenty-five to thirty pounds and to firm your abdominal muscles with regular exercise. Do not gain too much weight too fast! After childbirth, stretch marks fade to an off-white color but they never completely disappear.

I'm Getting Blotches on My Face. Will They Go Away?

I'm in my fourth month and I've noticed that I'm getting dark blotches on my face. Someone told me that they come from pregnancy. Is this true? Will they go away after I have the baby?
S.S.
Amarillo, Texas

When a woman is expecting a baby, her hormonal shifts often give her a certain glow. Her skin seems clearer and more radiant than ever. However, a pregnant woman may also discover some skin changes that she does not welcome. Fortunately, her skin will return to normal after childbirth, but during these nine expectant months, she might notice:

- *Darkening of the skin.* The female hormones, estrogen and progesterone, may stimulate melanin, the chemical substance that affects pigmentation. A woman may see tan or brown patches on her cheeks, forehead, or around her eyes. Sometimes a dark area spreads out in a butterfly pattern across her cheeks, and if this happens, she is experiencing a condition called *chloasma,* or the "mask of pregnancy."

  In other parts of her body, she may also notice changes—a darkening of the areola, the area around her nipples, and the appearance of the *linea negra,* a line that travels from her navel to her pubic hair. The darkness of the areola sometimes remains after pregnancy, but the linea negra goes away.

  Whether or not she has deeper skin tones, though, a woman can sunburn very easily during pregnancy, so she should always use a sunscreen when she goes outdoors.

- *Dry or oily skin.* I hear some women say that their skin is drier than usual, while others complain of too much oiliness. A mild glycerine soap is probably the best skin treatment for dryness; an astringent after cleansing might help control oiliness. But whatever your condition, remember, it's only temporary.

WARNING: Moles, stimulated by melanin, may become darker and larger during pregnancy. A woman should ask her obstetri-

141

cian to monitor any changes in moles, because although they are usually benign, they can occasionally mutate into melanoma, a severe skin cancer.

Why Do I Feel Dizzy When I Stand?

Several times during the day, I get a dizzy feeling, a sense that I'm on the brink of fainting. Usually this sensation comes when I stand. I wouldn't worry if it just happened once in a while, but it's becoming a frequent pattern.

Y.R.
Eau Claire, Wisconsin

Sometimes in the first half of pregnancy, a woman may experience dizziness when she stands suddenly or rises from a sitting or lying position she has been in for a while. Blood pressure changes during pregnancy and a quick move may make her pressure suddenly drop. A plummeting pressure can bring on lightheadedness. If Ms. R. has hypotension (low blood pressure) already, she should try to avoid sudden moves. She should also drink extra fluids and take in enough salt in the summertime, when heat and humidity cause the blood vessels to dilate even more than usual. A higher sodium intake increases blood pressure.

Besides moving slowly, Ms. R. should inhale deeply to bring more oxygen to her brain. The added oxygen will raise her blood pressure and ward off that dizzy feeling. Several deep breaths if she ever feels faint can help to overcome that problem. To increase the blood pressure even more, she might press both index fingers on the sides of the upper part of her nose while she is deeply breathing.

A woman who has regular dizzy spells should consult her obstetrician. As mentioned, frequent dizziness can be a sign of hypotension, and if it is prolonged, low blood pressure can decrease the amount of oxygen reaching the fetus.

Is It Normal to Have a Lot of Saliva?

I have an embarrassing problem. Saliva fills my mouth to the point that I have to spit it out. Is this a normal complaint during pregnancy?

V.C.
Chester, Pennsylvania

The majority of pregnant women have an increased amount of saliva during the first few months of pregnancy. This is only a problem if it becomes excessive. The presence of excess saliva, called *ptyalism,* can add to a feeling of nausea in the first trimester. A woman who has this problem—which usually vanishes by the beginning of the second trimester—can control it by brushing her teeth frequently, using mouthwash, and sucking on peppermints or chewing gum. Eating refined carbohydrates and sugars may contribute to the problem, so Ms. C. might also reduce the amount of these foods in her diet.

Where Is This Discharge Coming From?

I never had a problem with vaginal discharge, but now that I'm pregnant, it's abundant. Where does it come from? Will it stop soon? I'm in my fifth month.

M.B.
Kansas City, Kansas

The normal white vaginal discharge that you sometimes see when you are not pregnant always increases during pregnancy. Hormonal changes alter the vaginal environment to promote this discharge, and, in fact, the vagina is also less resistant to bacteria at this time. So along with the discharge, pregnant women might experience one of the common "yeast" infections such as *Candida albicans* or *monilia.* This situation may last throughout the entire pregnancy.

To control discharge, an expectant mother should avoid eating refined sugars, which can contribute to a hormonal imbalance in the vagina. She should also wear loose-fitting cotton underwear. Pantyhose should be avoided, but if it is worn, the kind with a cotton crotch is recommended. Tight jeans or slacks can trap bacteria. All clothing should be loose enough to allow air to circulate and moisture to evaporate. Warm baths cleanse the area effectively and eliminate the need for douching. In low-risk pregnancies, douching with Betadine, an iodine solution, is considered safe, although it should be avoided during the last few weeks of pregnancy when the cervix begins to open.

If a yeast infection persists, a physician will probably recommend suppositories or a medication such as Mycostatin or Monistat. Since the uterus is fully protected by the neck of the cervix, suppositories are unlikely to have an adverse effect on the fetus, and Mycostatin suppositories have a good record for safe use during pregnancy.

If the Baby Is So Small, Why Is My Stomach So Big?

I'm only starting my third month and I've already gained almost ten pounds. My pregnancy books say that the baby is only about 1½ inches long at this time. If the baby is so small, then why is my stomach so big?

G.A.
Newark, New Jersey

It is true that in the ninth week of pregnancy, the fetus is approximately 1½ inches long and weighs about 1/15 of an ounce (close to 2 grams). The size of the fetus does not dictate a woman's weight gain, however. Some women have put on as much as 20 pounds in the first trimester, when the fetus only reaches about 3 inches in length and about 14 grams in weight. The growing unborn baby is not the only source of a pregnant woman's added weight. Water retention, increased blood volume, and stores of fatty tissues also contribute to poundage.

A woman's weight gain is related to her nutritional habits. In

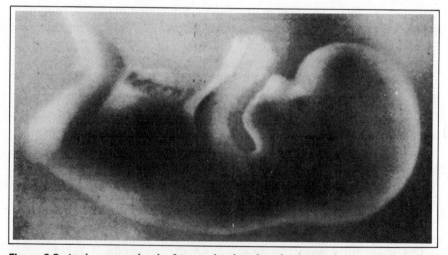

Figure 6-5. *At three months the fetus is developed to the extent that it now looks like a human being. Whatever activity you undertake during pregnancy, remember that you are not alone.*

Chapter 5, the recommended daily diet during pregnancy is described. Sweets and fattening foods should be avoided. Remember, metabolism often changes due to the high hormonal levels during pregnancy. Ms. A. should carefully watch what she eats, because a rapid weight gain may contribute to a prediabetic condition, which in turn may lead to an oversize baby and a complicated childbirth. Moderate exercise can also help burn calories.

A Few Words About Heartburn

Heartburn is not a pain in your heart but a burning sensation in your chest from acute indigestion, caused by the acid content in the stomach being pushed back into the lower esophagus from the pressure of the expanded uterus. This usually happens during the third trimester, when the womb is at its largest.

To prevent heartburn, avoid greasy, fried, and fatty foods, and just as if you had morning sickness, eat five or six small meals a day. Drinking plenty of fluids, particularly milk, which has antacid properties, brings relief. Even though you may watch your diet, however, you may occasionally still need an antacid such as Mylanta, Maalox, Riopan, Milk of Magnesia, or, if you prefer, antacid tablets such as Gelusil, Rolaids, Tums, and Milk of Magnesia. Do not use products containing baking soda or sodium bicarbonate (Alka-Seltzer is one), because their high sodium content can bind water and lead to high blood pressure. *A tip:* Some women say that chewing gum after meals lessens heartburn.

WHAT IS SAFE?

Today facts and rumors about what may be harmful to an unborn baby have become intermingled. A pregnant woman is often perplexed about the safety of her activities, and she hesitates to expose herself to different environments. She knows that certain pollutants cross the placenta, but which ones? Sometimes it seems that not a day can pass without a question: Can I have novocaine to have a tooth filled? Is it all right to make love? Can I dye my hair? Will airplane travel be dangerous?

Scientists are continually making new discoveries about how the daily life of an expectant mother affects the developing fetus. Yet these scientific findings can be exaggerated, and misconceptions can occur. Situations can seem more or less harmful than they actually are. A number of the current quandaries facing pregnant women are sorted out in this section. The facts that follow should help a woman overcome the confusions of everyday encounters.

Is Intercourse Safe During Pregnancy?

My husband has become more interested in sex since I have become pregnant. He is entranced by my growing breasts and body. He wants to make love almost every night, but I'm worried that intercourse might hurt the baby. I'm going into my fourth month and I'm not sure whether sex is supposed to be safer now or not.

N.S.

Norwalk, Connecticut

Sexual relations during pregnancy can be very fulfilling for a husband and wife. These months are a time of great closeness and, unless a pregnancy is a risky one, this time should be sexually shared.

In the first trimester, if a woman's pregnancy is problem free, she should not worry about harmful effects from intercourse. If she has complications, such as bleeding or staining, however, or is in a high-risk category due to certain health problems, intercourse may not be advised.

During intercourse, prostaglandins, contraction-causing hormonelike substances that are contained in sperm, are also released by the uterus. If a woman is having a problematic pregnancy, she may be risking a miscarriage by allowing the prostaglandins to build in her womb and possibly cause intense contractions. A woman who has been told she is a high-risk case, because she has experienced signs of a possible miscarriage or has other complications, may have to refrain from sexual activity throughout the entire course of pregnancy. Whenever a woman is in doubt about the state of her pregnancy, she should avoid sex and consult her physician.

If Ms. S. has had no pregnancy-related problems in her first trimester, she should not anticipate any complications during the second trimester. Intercourse should be safe. If she was an infertility patient who became pregnant and suffered staining and bleeding in the early months, she should be cautious about having intercourse. Even though she is now in her second trimester, she should still be considered at high risk and she should check with her doctor.

Controversy over the safety of intercourse arises during the third trimester for all pregnancies. A study of over 26,000 pregnant women, conducted between 1959 and 1966, found that frequent intercourse in the last half of pregnancy could be correlated with a rise of infection of the amniotic fluid surrounding the fetus. Mothers who had intercourse during the month before childbirth were also reported to be twice as likely to have newborns who suffered premature birth and related problems, such as low Apgar scores, jaundice, and respiratory distress. Other studies have reported contrary conclusions: that intercourse at the end of the last trimester *does not* contribute to the rate of infection of the amniotic fluid or prematurity.

Since a controversy does exist, I recommend that expectant mothers refrain from intercourse after the eighth month. In the last few weeks of pregnancy, the cervix (the mouth of the womb) may begin to open, and bacteria could enter the uterus. Since bacteria could be introduced through penile contact, no woman should have sex and take the risk. A woman is also avoiding the chance of bringing on premature birth, which can sometimes be the result of such an infection.

Important: The Safety of Orgasm

Pregnancy can heighten or diminish sexual desire. Until she is pregnant, a woman cannot predict how she will respond sexually—and she may be surprised. While a recent Swedish study reports that both intercourse and orgasm decline during pregnancy, many women feel more sensual at this time. And as a woman's body grows, a man often finds her voluptuous figure to be arousing. A wife and husband who have created a child together are often more emotionally and physically drawn to each other. Even without actual intercourse, the intimate touching that occurs can lead to orgasm.

Expectant mothers have heard numerous stories about the safety of orgasm, and many women are concerned. The folk wisdom passed down through generations is that orgasm in the first trimester may lead to miscarriage. Scientific data does not support this notion, yet the warning against orgasm continues to survive. There is more substantial research on orgasm during the last month of pregnancy. Here scientists diverge: some researchers believe that the uterine contractions of orgasm may bring on premature labor in the last month, but experts who oppose this view cite studies that find no connection between orgasm and prematurity.

The safety of orgasm ultimately depends upon whether a woman's pregnancy is low or high risk. A woman with a low-risk, problem-free pregnancy should have no fear of orgasm. If a woman has experienced premature labor in a previous pregnancy or if she now has complications such as spotting, threatened prematurity, or placenta previa, she certainly should refrain from orgasm. Every pregnancy is different, and a woman should consult her physician about how orgasm might affect her particular condition. No matter what her doctor might recommend, however, she should allow herself to enjoy the special intimacy that pregnancy creates between partners.

May I Dye My Hair?

I have felt so rundown and depressed in the first three months of this pregnancy. Finally, now that I've reached the fourth month, I'm starting to get more energy. I'd like to have my hair dyed or frosted, just for a lift. So many things are forbidden during pregnancy. Is there any problem with hair dye?

D.W.
Asbury Park, New Jersey

The safety of all hair dyes has been questioned, and Ms. W. should be concerned. Doctors do not have any definite word on how dangerous dyes might be, however, so for the present we are proceeding cautiously.

Research has shown that the coal-tar chemicals in permanent and semipermanent dyes and rinses can penetrate the scalp and enter the bloodstream. Since these chemicals have been linked to chromosomal damage and cell change, they cannot be taken lightly. The fact is, though, that there is no solid evidence specifying the harm that might be done.

The rinses do not seem to be as potentially harmful as the permanent and semipermanent dyes, since the coal-tar chemicals in rinses coat the hair shafts rather than penetrating the scalp. Hair frosting, tipping, streaking, and painting techniques, which only involve the hair shafts, are safer than permanent and semipermanent one-color processes that are rubbed into the scalp.

Probably the safest hair coloring product is henna, a reddish brown dye obtained from a tropical plant. Henna is a natural rather than a chemical product. If a woman does not like the reddish brown hue of the commonly available henna, she may be able to purchase a dark brown henna made from walnut leaves at her local health food store.

I usually suggest that my patients avoid all hair coloring during the first trimester, when the brain and nervous system of the fetus are developing. During this crucial time, no chances should be taken. Later on, in the second and third trimesters, risk is reduced. If a woman decides then to color her hair, a rinse would be safer than a permanent or semipermanent dye, but the safest product of all is henna. To eliminate all risk, no hair coloring should be used.

I Have a Terrible Toothache and I'm Going to Need a Filling. Can I Have Novocaine?

I have a toothache that gets worse every time I eat something sweet. My dentist says that if I don't have my tooth filled now, I may have to have root canal later. I'm in my seventh month and I don't want to do anything that will harm the baby, but I can't stand this pain. Would it be all right to have my tooth filled? I cannot stand to have my teeth drilled without a painkiller and I would like to have novocaine. Is novocaine safe?

M.G.
Council Bluffs, Iowa

As a general rule, I advise patients planning pregnancy to complete their dental care before they conceive. Only emergency dental work should be undertaken during pregnancy, since the anesthesias and X rays that are routinely administered in a dentist's office may affect the fetus.

Since Ms. G. is in pain, she undoubtedly needs dental attention. She should consult her obstetrician about any medication her

149

dentist may suggest. Today most dentists are well informed about which drugs are safe for their pregnant patients, but even so, it is always wise to check with the physician who is overseeing your pregnancy.

Studies have cast doubt over the safety of nitrous oxide, the "laughing gas" that can make tooth drilling seem "pleasant." Certain research has shown that women who work in dentists' offices or operating rooms, where they are exposed to anesthetic gases, have higher rates of spontaneous abortion and birth-defective babies than do technicians who have not been exposed. On the other hand, alternate investigations have concluded that there is no great difference in pregnancy complications among women who were exposed to gases and those who were not. As with other questionable areas of safety, since there is doubt, I advise my patients to avoid anesthetic gases altogether.

Dentists are now able to inject a short-acting, quickly metabolized novocaine (procaine), which should have less effect, if any, on a developing fetus. At present, we do not know if novocaine is detrimental to an unborn baby, but the medication will travel throughout the bloodstream after it has been absorbed by the gum tissue. It can lower a woman's heart rate as well as her baby's. This drop could then decrease the blood flow to the fetal brain. Since it is not certain to what degree novocaine influences the development of the fetal cardiovascular system, I suggest that pregnant women avoid it and all local anesthetics during the first trimester. If dental work must be done, it should be postponed until later in pregnancy. Since she is in her seventh month, Ms. G. should have less worry about serious problems resulting from a novocaine injection.

What Should I Do About an Abscessed Tooth? My Dentist Wants to Take an X ray and Possibly Perform Gum Surgery.

Recently I experienced incredible pain in my jaw and learned that I have an abscessed tooth. My dentist wants to take an X ray and possibly schedule gum surgery. I don't know what to do. I am in my fourth month and I don't want to expose my baby to radiation or drugs. I've been so careful until now, but the pain is pretty bad.

L.D.
Fresno, California

All X rays, even dental X rays, which only transmit a low level of radiation, should be avoided during pregnancy. If a dental X ray is required in an emergency situation, the dentist or dental assistant must safeguard you and the fetus by limiting the beam size, using an electric timer, and shielding your abdomen with a lead apron to prevent secondary radiation from hitting this sensitive area.

Ms. D. is in her fourth month, which makes the use of an anesthetic less risky, but I would still suggest that she try to put off her gum surgery. In the first trimester, when the intricate internal networks that will become the nervous and cardiovascular systems are forming in the fetus, no substances that might be potentially harmful should be permitted within a woman's body. The longer Ms. D. can wait to have her tooth treated, the more resilient the fetus will become.

If she postpones surgery, she may eventually be cured without it. Her dentist may be able to treat her with an antibiotic (see Chapter 9), which would centralize the infection and allow him to drain it. If Ms. D. does need the gum surgery, she should make sure that she consults her obstetrician about the anesthetic that would be used. As explained in the answer to the preceding question, anesthetic gases should not be administered.

How Long Can I Work?

I've been at my job as office manager for four years now and I've just learned that I am pregnant. My boss is a company man who has no patience with people who take personal and sick days off. Eventually he's going to see that I'm pregnant, but before he does, I want to be able to tell him how much time off I'll need. I don't want to do anything that would be detrimental to my pregnancy, so please tell me how long I can safely work. I'm afraid that if I don't work right to my limit, I may lose my job.

E.W.
Mount Kisco, New York

More than forty million women are in the work force, and 70 percent of them are between the ages of sixteen and forty-four, the major span of reproductive years. Over one million working women become pregnant every year.

Women used to be a much smaller segment of the working population, and in their minority numbers, they used to fear expectancy. Pregnancy often generated hostility from co-workers or forced a woman to resign. The 1978 amendment to Title VII of the 1964 Civil Rights Act changed behavior and attitudes when it legally ended job discrimination based on pregnancy and childbirth. Neither Ms. W. nor any pregnant woman can be fired for pregnancy. A pregnant woman who must take time off for childbirth has the same rights as an employee who is temporarily disabled. In fact, the U.S. Supreme Court recenty ruled that states may require employers to grant special job protection to employees who cannot work due to pregnancy.

If Ms. W. tells her boss that she is pregnant and requires time off, and he is threatening, she may complain to her personnel director. If she is in a union, the shop steward should be informed. Most businesses now have company policies for maternity leave, and Ms. W. might investigate her options before she approaches her employer. She should also remember to look into her coverage. She might have extenuating circumstances during pregnancy to consider.

If it happens that Ms. W. is expecting twins or she suffers complications such as an incompetent cervix, bleeding, high blood pressure, heart disease, anemia, or other conditions that would cause her obstetrician to regard hers as a high-risk pregnancy, she may have to severely curtail her employment. Since every pregnancy is different, it is really up to a woman and her doctor to decide how and when she should arrange her leave of absence. For a job that is rather sedentary, the average recommended time off is usually about a week and a half before childbirth; for a job that requires standing or walking, two and a half weeks; for physically exerting work, more than a month. These, of course, are *average* times; some women work right up until the moment of labor.

A physician will ask a woman about her working environment, and if she spends her days in an atmosphere that may be hazardous to the developing fetus, he may suggest an early departure from the job. Certain occupations put a woman at higher-than-average risk during pregnancy. A woman who must travel, physically exert herself, or be exposed to unusual pollutants or contaminants should be allowed by her employer to take a less strenuous job or an extended leave until childbirth. For example, AT&T recently banned all pregnant women from working on semiconductor production lines for computer chips because a high rate of miscarriage has been found there.

A woman who is in a low-risk pregnancy may find that she is bored if she leaves work early and waits at home until the baby is due. Many women discover that waiting for the baby is easier when they have work to distract them. If an expectant mother does not overexert herself with physical chores and she continues to eat small, well-balanced meals and get plenty of rest, she should be able to work as long as she wants. Anyway, it is sometimes better for a woman to schedule more time off after the baby is born rather than before. The most precious days are those following childbirth, when a new mother is breast-feeding and bonding with her infant. This is a time when she would not want work to interfere.

I'm a Pregnant Airline Attendant. Is My Job Risky?

I love my job as an airline attendant and I intended to keep flying until I showed, but now I'm worried. I've heard other attendants say that it's not safe to fly during pregnancy and that I should transfer to a ground job. What happens in the air?

A.R.
Los Angeles, California

Exposure to natural radiation increases with altitude, and in efforts to economize on fuel, jet planes are flying at much higher altitudes these days. The radiation exposure during a flight is said to be well within the safety limits of 170 millirems a year, a standard set by the National Council of Radiation Protection and Measurements; however, an airline employee is continually exposed. On a flight from New York to Los Angeles, exposure may be about 2.5 millirems, and from London to Los Angeles, about 10 millirems. Since we do not know what the cumulative effects of this exposure may have on the developing fetus, it would be wise for Ms. R. to request a transfer to ground work. If she stops flying, Ms. R. would also be avoiding contact with the ozone layer in the air.

Ozone, a colorless gas concentrated at 35,000 to 150,000 feet above sea level, has been known to cause changes in developing cells and to affect the bloodstream. Airline passengers have sometimes complained of ozone illness that created shortness of breath; drowsiness; headache; nose, throat, and chest pain; and eye irritation. Although it is not known whether the pregnancies of airline attendants can be harmed by ozone, it creates a health hazard that is best avoided.

About Airport Security: Are Body Scanners Safe?

Many pregnant women have asked me whether the body-scanning passenger entrance to airline flights is safe. When they walk through the metal-detecting gates, women wonder whether they are being exposed to radiation. Actually the body-scanning entry is a construction for a magnetic field that, when it is broken by metal objects, sets off an alarm. A magnetic field *does not use radiation;* it is simply a polarized area that, according to security experts, should not affect a pregnant woman or her fetus. The hand-held body scanners operate on the same principle and should also be safe.

Since long-range effects are unpredictable, however, I advise my first-trimester patients to request a body search rather than walk through the magnetic field. In the first three months, fetal cells are in a critical stage of development and should be well protected.

I have some concern about the X-ray equipment that inspects carry-on luggage. The equipment is lead shielded to prevent radiation leakage, and each airline is individually responsible for maintaining the equipment and its protective covering. For security reasons, airline personnel do not divulge the amount of radiation that is used in the inspection devices, but since X rays are the method of detection, pregnant women would be wise to distance themselves from the machinery. As a safety measure, a pregnant woman might ask someone else to handle her luggage.

Is It Safe to Fly from New York to Los Angeles in My Sixth Month?

I want to go to my high school reunion in Los Angeles but I'm in my sixth month and I live in New York. I've heard all sorts of horror stories about flying when you're pregnant, and I want to know the facts. Is it safe for me to fly?

L.G.
New York, New York

Airlines usually do not have restrictions against flying during pregnancy up until the sixth month. Regulations vary from airline to airline during the third trimester, when officials might require a doctor's note stipulating a passenger's due date. A few carriers do not permit a pregnant woman to fly under any circumstances in the ninth month, so before a woman makes any travel plans, she should investigate clearance requirements with the airline of her choice.

In one trip, a pregnant woman will not be exposed to the same hazards facing an airline attendant who is regularly in flight, but health problems can occur. In spite of the regulated air pressure in an airliner, the oxygen level at flying altitudes is lower than normal. As a result, the mother's and baby's heart rates increase, and less nourishing oxygen reaches the fetus. In the "thin" air of the mountains, there is less oxygen, and low-birth-weight babies are more common. The low oxygen level affects fetal growth. This being the case, the oxygen drop during extended air travel might potentially interfere with the development, especially the neurological development, of the fetus.

If Ms. G. remains in her seat for the long coast-to-coast trip, she is increasing her chances of developing thrombophlebitis (blood clots) and edema (swelling). She should take occasional ten-minute walks up and down the aisles of the cabin to prevent circulatory problems and water retention. Before she embarks for the airport, however, Ms. G. should check her travel plans with her doctor.

I prefer that my pregnant patients avoid airline travel simply because weather and flight conditions are so unpredictable. A particularly bumpy flight or an abrupt landing may create complications. I ask every pregnant patient who must fly to come for a checkup a day or two before takeoff to be sure that no problem has arisen and to confirm that the cervix, the mouth of the womb, is long and closed. If a woman has any sign of bleeding, threatened miscarriage, or premature labor, I advise against travel. If a woman is not at high risk and does take a trip, I suggest that she refrain from lifting heavy suitcases and ask for a body search rather than expose herself to the scanning devices at airports. Once on board, she should sit propped to one side by a pillow so that the uterus is slightly tilted and less apt to feel the pressure of landing.

Can I Continue Commuting to Work in My Car?

I drive to work in highway traffic. I travel about forty minutes each way, and I am beginning to wonder if this commute is safe for me. I am only

155

six weeks pregnant, so I still fit behind the wheel. My concern, though, is whether I will be more accident prone during pregnancy, and whether auto exhausts will affect the fetus.

S.L.

Boston, Massachusetts

A pregnant woman may drive as long as she is comfortable behind the wheel. In her third trimester, Ms. L. may find that her pregnancy interferes, however. She may have a little trouble coordinating her steering and braking, since her reflexes may slow a bit. If she notices such a slowdown, it would be wise for her to switch to a passenger seat and let someone else do the driving until childbirth. This is a precautionary measure, since statistics show that the always high risk of being in an auto accident is the same for pregnant and nonpregnant women, but cautiousness becomes more important as a due date nears.

A seat belt should be worn at all times, whether an expectant mother is in the front or back seat. A woman should fasten the belt below her pregnant abdomen, just above her thighs—not around her expanded stomach—and use the shoulder strap. The seat belt must be correctly attached to prevent a jolt to the uterus in the event of a sudden stop.

Carbon monoxide does reach high levels in heavily trafficked cities, and Ms. L. may be inhaling the fumes if her car is idling in traffic for a long time. The fetus may then be subjected to the deleterious effects of carbon monoxide, which are usually the concern of a pregnant smoker. (See Chapter 8.) On the other hand, if Ms. L.'s commute is fairly nonstop without much occasion for sitting in traffic, her exposure to carbon monoxide, while it is not good, may never reach a dangerous level.

Stay Away from X Rays

Every pregnant woman should say no to diagnostic X rays unless a life-threatening situation exists. The effects of radiation, even minimal radiation, on a fetus cannot be measured accurately, and there is no way to tell whether cell changes have occurred. Undetected chromosomal mutation may exist within a perfectly normal looking fetus that has had X-ray exposure. We are always told that there are "safe" levels of radiation, and this warning may sound unduly strong, since most X rays are given in doses of millirads

(1/1000 rad) and even a woman who has chest and gastrointestinal X rays still does not receive 2 rads, but the fetus is extremely vulnerable, especially in the first trimester.

Early in pregnancy, cell development is rapid as the embryo becomes a fetus and the fetal tissue forms. Since so many conceptions are inadvertently, and dangerously, exposed to X rays before a woman knows she is pregnant, it is essential that the "ten-day rule" of the American Association of Radiologists be followed: *If you are trying to conceive or suspect you have conceived, do not schedule any X ray of the pelvic, lumbar, or abdominal area any later than during the ten days immediately following the onset of your last menstrual period.*

The most dangerous X rays are the abdominal, pelvic, and lumbar ones, which expose the fetus to a direct beam. The amount of radiation is increased when the procedure involves continuing exposure through the use of a fluoroscope. (The fluoroscope shows the interior of the body in continuous motion rather than in one single exposure.) Unless a mother's life is at stake, these X rays should *never* be taken during pregnancy. Direct exposure of the fetus has been linked to growth retardation and possibly intelligence loss, a higher incidence of childhood leukemia, and menstrual and reproductive disorders among young women.

Other X-ray procedures, those that do not expose the fetus to a direct beam, are reasonably safe as long as the abdomen is fully shielded from any scattering of radiation, the technician is properly trained, and up-to-date equipment is used to minimize the exposure. The head, limbs, chest, and neck can all be X-rayed without exposing the fetus directly. But your doctor or dentist would be exposing you and the baby to unacceptable risks if he insisted on any X ray without proper indication. Don't hesitate to question his judgment if a situation arises in which an X ray of any kind is involved. If you need to visit an emergency room at any point during pregnancy, tell the nurse you are pregnant and refuse any X ray that seems unnecessary. Emergency rooms often take X rays "just in case."

NOTE: During labor, a woman may hear a doctor say that she needs an X ray. A procedure called *X-ray pelvimetry,* designed to measure the size of a woman's pelvis and the diameter of her birth canal, is an antiquated way to determine whether a cesarean section is needed. Today a physical examination of a woman and the circumstances of her labor can alert any physician to the appropriateness of a C-section. X-ray pelvimetry should not be called upon, except in extremely rare cases. When a breech birth presents itself, an obstetrician may perform an X-ray pelvimetry to be sure that a vaginal birth can succeed. In some instances of twins, X-ray pelvimetry may also be indicated.

Whenever this procedure is suggested, however, a couple should question its necessity, since it means that an expectant mother and her baby are going to be exposed to radiation, and the adverse effects of this exposure are cumulative.

Video Display Terminals (VDTs) and Pregnancy

Can the radiation emitted by computer VDTs be contributing to miscarriage and birth defects? As this book goes to press, the connection remains controversial. A couple of years ago, Nine to Five, the National Association of Working Women, received calls from women who worked with VDTs and delivered birth-defective babies. These women reported other pregnancy problems among co-workers. Based on these calls, Nine to Five was able to identify twelve clusters of employees, all working with VDTs, who seemed to have an unusual number of pregnancy complications. The National Institute of Occupational Safety and Health (NIOSH) investigated three of these clusters and reported that there was no evidence to support the claim that the low level of radiation emitted from VDT screens could cause fetal damage. Backing NIOSH, the Food and Drug Administration's Bureau of Radiological Health and the American College of Obstetricians and Gynecologists (ACOG) have agreed that the radiation level of VDTs is not high enough to be dangerous. Still, the reports from pregnant women continue, and Nine to Five is not satisfied that VDTs are safe.

In 1985, Nine to Five, with volunteers from Service Employees International Union, launched a four-year study on the effects of VDTs during pregnancy. Dr. Irving J. Selikoff, professor and occupational health investigator from Mt. Sinai School of Medicine in New York, heads the research effort. Between ten and twelve thousand female and male VDT workers will be studied for the effects of radiation, stress, and ergonomics (the way the body interacts with machines). This research is vital to the safety of the 65 percent of white-collar workers who use VDTs every day and to the health of unborn babies. Recent research from Spain (confirmed by two researchers in the United States) shows that when chick embryos are exposed to the same low-frequency radiation that is emitted by VDTs, biological changes occur. This finding adds to the consternation.

Until all the data are amassed and analyzed, Nine to Five— contrary to NIOSH, the Food and Drug Administration's Bureau of Radiological Health, and ACOG—recommends that pregnant women who work with VDTs transfer to other jobs until child-birth. NIOSH, the FDA's Bureau of Radiological Health, and ACOG—all reputable and prestigious organizations—continue to affirm the safety of VDTs. A recent study at the University of Michigan found that working at video display terminals for less than twenty hours a week has no effect on the risk of miscarriage. The researchers, who observed approximately seven hundred pregnancies, cannot comment on the risk when working time is increased, but they do feel that it is unlikely that VDTs have a large effect on the outcome of pregnancies. I tell my patients to do some investigating if they work with VDTs. I suggest that they check with their employer and the manufacturer of their machine to find out whether its safety has been researched. I also suggest that they try not to work over twenty hours a week in front of or next to a VDT that is in operation.

I Will Be Redecorating the House Before the Baby Is Born. Is It All Right to Be Around Indoor House Paint?

My husband and I are planning to redecorate the house now, before the baby is born. We are having new carpeting installed after the paint-ers arrive next week. I've suddenly grown concerned that the chemicals in the paint might be dangerous. Am I becoming overly alarmed? Is it all right to be around house paint?

C.V.
Madison, Wisconsin

It is not certain whether lead-free, brush-on indoor house paint, which releases noxious fumes, is dangerous to the fetus. Ms. V. would be taking the healthiest course for herself and for her baby if she stayed with a relative or a friend until her paint job was completed and the fumes had dissipated. Since we do not know all the chemicals that may affect a fetus, and since the fumes contain chemical components, Ms. V. is better off staying away from fresh paint.

The old lead-base paints, which are no longer in use, are very dangerous during pregnancy, and a woman who may be renovating an old house and scraping painted walls is at risk, since she may inhale lead from the scrapings and dust. Lead crosses the placenta and enters the fetal bloodstream, liver, and brain. At high internal levels, lead increases the chance that a woman may miscarry or give birth to a stillborn baby.

A woman should also beware of spray paint and paint remover. M-butyl ketone (MBK), a chemical found in spray paint, may impair neurological development of a fetus. Methylene chloride, an ingredient of turpentine and many paint strippers, turns into carbon monoxide when it is inhaled. If this chemical is breathed in for several hours, it lowers the oxygen in a mother's bloodstream and deprives the normally oxygen-nourished fetus. If Ms. V. cannot find other accommodations while her home is being redone, she should at least postpone the stripping and painting part of her redecoration until after the baby has arrived.

Is It Safe to Exercise During Pregnancy?

Today's physically active women jog, play tennis, pump iron, do aerobic dancing; and when they become pregnant, they do not want to slow down. As Jane Fonda writes in her *Workout Book for Pregnancy, Birth, and Recovery,* once she conceived and stopped exercising for fear of harming the fetus, she felt like "a sack of overripe tomatoes." Women want to keep moving, but many expectant mothers still have a nagging concern that exercise may be unsafe during pregnancy. Moderation is really the key.

Recently, the American College of Obstetricians and Gynecologists (ACOG) made known the "down" side of exercise. Certain physical changes do take place during pregnancy; a woman's heart rate increases, her ligaments and tendons soften, and her center of gravity shifts. When she exercises, she elevates her already high heart rate. She may also stress softened joints and find herself feeling off balance. What else happens? Exercise causes body temperature to rise, may bring on dehydration, and stimulates the release of two adrenal hormones, epinephrine and norepinephrine. While the former hormone has a calming effect on the womb, the latter may trigger contractions. These are all important facts to remember, but there is an "up" side.

Moderate exercise during a problem-free pregnancy can sometimes alleviate lower back pain and leg cramps. It improves circulation and strengthens pelvic muscles for childbirth. Many women have been told that exercise diverts oxygen intended for the fetus to the working muscles, but recent findings disprove this notion. At Loma Linda University in California, researchers have concluded that a pregnant woman's circulatory system naturally supplies nutrients and gases to the growing fetus and that moderate exercise does not interfere. Vigorous exercise could, on the other hand, be potentially harmful.

I recommend that a woman relax and exercise very little during the first trimester, when the risk of miscarriage is at its highest. Later on, in the second and third trimesters, when the fetus is securely implanted in her womb, mild to moderate exercise can ease the strain of expectancy. For a woman with high-risk complications, or signs of possible miscarriage or premature labor, no exercise should be allowed. If you are not certain about whether you are in the high-risk category, check with your doctor. In fact, whenever a woman has any questions during pregnancy, she should consult her obstetrician.

Snow or waterskiing, surfing, or horseback riding—sports in which jolts and falls are common—obviously should be avoided. Exercise that strengthens muscles with the least amount of resistance—walking, swimming, and stationary cycling—are the best. Swimming is especially beneficial during pregnancy, since it is a resistance-free way for a woman to tone her entire body. Saltwater swimming, as long as the sea is not rough, should be safe. In pools, I recommend short (15-minute) swims so that a woman will have limited exposure to the chlorine used to sterilize the water. She should always shower right after her swim. It is not known whether internally absorbed chlorine affects a fetus, but I prefer to err on the side of caution. One more reminder: a woman should always swim in calm, *warm* waters. A womb should always be a *warm* and secure home for a fetus.

The pregnancy exercise programs proliferating across the country are also helpful. Whether a woman enrolls in one of these programs or follows the workout suggestions in pregnancy exercise books, she will be improving her physical condition. A woman who regularly exercised before pregnancy, whether she jogged, golfed, played tennis, or attended aerobic dance classes, may continue her activities in moderation; however, it is always best, if she has any doubts, to check with her doctor.

The American College of Obstetricians and Gynecologists recommends that a woman's heart rate not exceed 140 beats per minute during a workout. According to ACOG, when you check your pulse, you should count no more than 23 beats in 10 seconds.

My pregnant patients continually say that the mild to moderate exercise they do helps them feel better psychologically as well as physically. Each expectant mother has her own individual limitations, but as long as her pregnancy permits, mild to moderate exercise should certainly ease the course of her days.

Women have always worried about how they could do the best for themselves and their unborn babies during pregnancy, and in the past, they have felt frustrated. They were unable to find answers to their questions, and often when they finally learned the safety of certain situations, they had already exposed themselves to hazards. Today both women and their doctors are more informed about the changes a woman's body undergoes during pregnancy and the vulnerability of the fetus. Many confusions are now resolved.

A woman should find most of her concerns dispelled in this chapter, but if she does not, her doctor is ready to alleviate her worries. A knowledgeable obstetrician knows the answers, or he refers his patients to the right source of information if he is in doubt. Scientists, physicians, and women themselves are working to make pregnancy the safest and most satisfying experience it can be, and no expectant mother should have trouble getting the facts.

CHAPTER 7

Alcohol: When You Drink, Your Baby Drinks Too!

Before the discovery of fetal alcohol syndrome (FAS) in the 1970s, expectant mothers never had second thoughts about drinking. Often alcoholic toasts were offered to celebrate their pregnancies, and they imbibed without realizing that their unborn babies were joining in the festivities. Today's pregnant women are much more aware that alcohol is a drug that can hamper fetal growth.

Two American researchers from Seattle, Drs. Ulleland and Jones, identified and described fetal alcohol syndrome in 1972. It is surprising that this discovery did not occur in Europe, where wine and beer are customary beverages at mealtime. Observations on the possible effects of alcohol on the newborns of women who drank heavily during pregnancy were made by German scientists in 1957 and French researchers in 1968, but the severity of alcohol's effects was not clear until the Americans delved deeper.

Drs. Ulleland and Jones reported that newborns whose mothers were alcoholics suffered smaller head circumferences, were smaller on the average in weight, and had delayed growth after their births. The Ulleland/Jones work was followed by a five-year study among women in the Boston City Hospital. This study supported the existence of FAS, and from then on, pregnant women were put on the alert. Yet confusions still abound. Many expectant mothers think that FAS is only a concern of alcoholic women.

Every pregnant woman must be mindful of her consumption of alcoholic beverages. The safest route, of course, is to avoid alcohol completely, but occasionally you may attend a special event at which cocktails are served. Doctors frequently hear the question: "Can just one drink hurt?" (A drink is considered to be 12 ounces of beer, 5 ounces of wine, or 1 ounce of hard liquor.) The answer is not a simple yes or no. No one can define *safe drinking*.

FAS is influenced by how much and how often you drink and other variables. Whether you binge drink; consume beer, wine, or hard liquor; even your race may affect your baby's susceptibility. Ingesting no alcohol means no fetal alcohol syndrome. The risks, if you do drink, are becoming more apparent through research. In the meantime, women are asking sound questions, and every expectant mother should understand exactly what fetal alcohol syndrome is.

UNDERSTANDING FETAL ALCOHOL SYNDROME (FAS)

When an expectant mother drinks, alcohol quickly enters her bloodstream. The baby's major body systems are much smaller than the mother's and are not fully developed, so the alcohol that is reaching them has a greater effect. Obviously the fetus cannot say no when it has had enough—which is much sooner than for an adult with a high tolerance—and the fetus suffers damage.

In the first trimester, when the brain, other vital organs, and the network of essential body systems are rapidly forming, the fetus is especially vulnerable to internal elements. At this point in pregnancy, alcohol from daily heavy drinking—the FDA has concluded that six drinks a day constitute a major risk—may bring on some or all of FAS's effects. A baby may be born with a small head size (microcephaly), low birth weight, and/or facial defects, which include a short, upturned nose with a flattened bridge, small eye openings, and a receding jaw. Other results of FAS are an impaired central nervous system, mental retardation, cleft palate, heart and kidney damage, and abnormalities in other organs. The small-size FAS-baby never "catches up" in growth and remains physically as well as mentally retarded.

In the second and third trimesters, drinking may not have as devastating an effect on the fetus as in the first trimester, but the unborn baby can still be harmed. Although visible birth defects may not appear, drinking in the latter trimesters may lead to intrauterine growth retardation (retarded growth), mental retardation, hyperactivity, and low IQ.

Babies born of seriously alcoholic women may exhibit the most FAS-related defects, but FAS may also appear at some level in children of women who drink moderately—two to three drinks daily—during pregnancy. For example, hyperactivity, extreme nervousness, poor attention span, and low IQ may be linked to FAS in children who have no major birth defects. The estimate is that FAS appears in one to two of every one thousand births—it is all too common.

Since 1980, the FDA has campaigned to educate women about the effects of drinking alcoholic beverages during pregnancy, and it issued a warning based on these findings:

- Significantly decreased birth weight among the children of some women who average only one ounce of absolute alcohol per day during pregnancy
- Sizable and significant increases in spontaneous abortions among women who consumed alcohol levels as low as one ounce of absolute alcohol twice a week
- The risks of physical and mental defects of FAS among children born of women who are alcoholics

The FDA also noted that if a woman who drinks heavily does not give birth to a baby with full-spectrum FAS, she is still more likely to have a baby with one or more of the birth defects of the syndrome.

In the years following the FDA warning, scientific studies have made more information available about drinking during pregnancy. The importance of the type of alcohol you drink, and how often, is in sharper focus.

WARNING: The scientific findings that directly relate birth defects to alcohol consumption have made government leaders as concerned as physicians. This concern is being widely communicated. While it is difficult to pass a law that forbids pregnant women from drinking, local governments have taken a creative stand. In New York City, the Department of Health has issued a warning to be posted in all bars and restaurants. This warning (see Figure 7.1) tells men, women, children—everyone—about the danger of drinking during pregnancy. FAS can be prevented!

Figure 7-1. *This warning sign must be posted in every establishment that serves alcoholic beverages in New York City.*

SMOKING AND DRINKING

Before I Knew I Was Pregnant, I Drank Wine and Champagne at a Party. Will the Alcohol Hurt the Baby?

I went to a graduation party for my brother and I did not hesitate to drink wine and champagne in his honor. Three weeks after the party, I found out that I was pregnant. Will the alcohol hurt the baby?

C.P.
Newport, Rhode Island

A few drinks on a single occasion before you knew you were pregnant are not going to harm your baby, but you should definitely stop drinking for the rest of the first trimester. In the first three months of pregnancy, when biological systems—especially the nervous system—are forming and the fetus is most vulnerable, alcohol can have a particularly damaging effect. As mentioned, when early research was conducted among pregnant women who were heavy drinkers, the fetal alcohol syndrome was discovered. Now, after years of investigation, we know that even babies of women who have had no more than two to four drinks a day may be born with abnormalities.

The FDA is unable to set a "safe" level for alcoholic consumption during pregnancy, but common sense should prevail. Do not drink any alcoholic beverages in the first trimester. Later on, in the second and third trimesters, the fetus is stronger, and although FAS can still occur, an occasional drink may be less harmful now than during the first trimester. Since alcohol absorbs the body's nutrients, if you do have a social drink, make sure that you increase your intake of essential nutrients and vitamins. And remember, habitual drinking will hurt the baby.

I'm very guilty about my smoking habit. I'm in the first trimester, and I've tried to cut down from the pack-a-day I smoked before I conceived. I know I should quit, but I do allow myself about three cigarettes a day. I just can't seem to stop completely. Now a friend has told me that since I haven't stopped altogether, if I ever have a drink while I'm smoking, I'll be doing terrible things to the baby. I know smoking is bad and drinking is bad, but is a combination of the two the worst thing that can happen to a fetus?

E.R.
Racine, Wisconsin

167

Cigarette smoking contributes to low-birth-weight babies. Nicotine and carbon monoxide enter the mother's bloodstream and reduce the oxygen supply to the fetus. (See Chapter 8.) Alcohol in the bloodstream, especially in the first trimester, attacks the cell membranes and the fetal organs. Often women who drink heavily are chain smokers, and they may sometimes be drug abusers too. These observations have led researchers to question whether nicotine, carbon monoxide, and other drugs or toxic substances might combine with the alcohol and intensify fetal alcohol syndrome.

Studies to sort out the controversy over whether the appearance of FAS traits can be brought on by substances other than alcohol, or mixed with alcohol, are ongoing. Smoking and drinking may cause your baby more harm together than separately, but researchers do not have conclusive evidence. Neither habit, however, will enhance the fetal environment. The first trimester is a dangerous time to drink. Avoid alcoholic beverages right now, and try to give your baby the best start in life by cutting out cigarettes today.

I Let Myself Go and Binged at a Party. Will My Baby Be All Right?

My boyfriend and I had been living together and finally decided to get married. At a prenuptial party, I really had a good time, threw caution to the winds, and drank a lot. I don't normally drink more than a glass or two of wine, but this was a special occasion. The next morning I had an awful hangover. A couple of weeks later, when the wedding was over, I learned that I was pregnant, and I remembered my binge. Will my baby be all right?

L.P.
Boulder, Colorado

Most of the studies on fetal alcohol syndrome were conducted among women who were habitual drinkers. Binge drinking, which is quite common, is now being scrutinized as well. Dr. Kenneth L. Jones, director of the birth defects clinic at the University of California–San Diego/School of Medicine, La Jolla, recently headed an investigation of eighty women who had one to three drinking binges early in pregnancy. He and his researchers examined the offspring of the women for six months, and no physical defects or growth retardation that would have signaled FAS appeared. Neurological function cannot definitely be determined until the babies are older, but so far, they seem perfectly healthy.

This latest discovery about binge drinking is good news, but it does not mean you can go to a bash and drink without worry. You binged before you knew you were pregnant. Now that you are aware of the new life you have created, you can protect it by not drinking for the rest of this pregnancy.

Scientists do not know exactly how fetal alcohol syndrome occurs, but alcohol appears to absorb certain nutrients and vitamins that should be nourishing the unborn baby. On a short-term binge, it may be that the absorption is less harmful than it is over time, with steady drinking. Your unusual binge is not likely to harm your baby, but future drinking might.

I advise my patients to eat several small, well-balanced meals a day (see Chapter 5), and if for some reason they do have a drink or two, to be strongly disciplined about their diet afterward. I suggest that they take extra prenatal vitamins with additional vitamin B-complex for a few days after they drink. If you eat nutritiously and drink nonalcoholically, you will be successfully nurturing your baby in the womb.

Is Beer More Harmful Than Wine?

I didn't think that the new light beers would be harmful during pregnancy, but my husband becomes anxious every time I take a sip. He says that beer is worse than wine. Is he right?
D.S.
Dedham, Massachusetts

Research is beginning to show that beer may actually be *more harmful* than wine during pregnancy. A recent study conducted by Dr. Robert Sokol, chairman of the department of obstetrics and gynecology at Wayne State Medical Center in Detroit, linked heavy beer drinking to low birth weights in newborns. Dr. Sokol did not find a connection as strong with wine and spirits. Interestingly, his conclusion about beer drinking supports a study that came out of France in 1968. A French research team followed the drinking patterns of ten thousand women and reported that heavy beer drinking could be associated with the births of unexpectedly small infants and an increased rate of stillbirths. According to the researchers, 13 ounces or less of wine a day *did not* contribute to a rise in the occurrence of low-birth-weight babies, congenital abnormalities, or stillbirths.

Here in the United States, Dr. Sokol and his colleagues, in an attempt to learn why beer would be more dangerous, speculated that a compound called thiocyanate (SCN), which is in beer but absent from wine, may make the difference. The American researchers noted that the greater the level of SCN in the blood of a newborn or its mother, the lower the birth weight of the baby. Other studies have suggested that high amounts of SCN in the blood of pregnant smokers may also be a reason for smaller newborns.

Ms. S. is obviously not safer drinking beer. Even if she is not a heavy drinker, she should eliminate beer, wine, and all alcoholic beverages from her diet. FAS is one risk that can be avoided.

I Was Drinking and Smoking Marijuana on the Night I Conceived. Is My Baby In Trouble?

My husband and I were drinking and smoking marijuana on the night I conceived. I wasn't trying to get pregnant and, in fact, used contraception. When I learned that my diaphragm had failed, I started to worry about the alcohol and the "grass." Is my baby in trouble?
W.M.
Atlanta, Georgia

You drank and smoked marijuana on the night you conceived, but you do not describe these activities as habitual. If you do not normally drink and smoke, your unborn baby should be developing healthily.

Fetal alcohol syndrome results from an expectant mother's intake of alcohol. Researchers have not yet proved that caffeine, nicotine, or other drugs work in combination with alcohol to heighten the syndrome. Whether you are pregnant or not, though, mixing alcohol and other drugs can be dangerous. Narcotics, barbiturates, sleeping pills, major tranquilizers, antihistamines, cold-relieving drugs, and motion-sickness drugs can severely depress the central nervous system and cause serious side effects when they are combined with alcohol. Now that you are pregnant, do not drink or smoke anything in the first trimester especially but throughout the entire pregnancy, if possible. In the second and third trimesters, when the fetus is more fully developed, an infrequent drink on a special occasion may be less harmful, but even so, for these nine months, you should be staying away from alcohol and all other drugs.

Can a Good Diet and Vitamins Counteract the Effects of Alcohol?

I've been reading so much about nutrition since I've been pregnant that I've begun to wonder about whether a balanced diet and vitamins could be powerful weapons against toxic substances in the body. If I had a drink or two, would proper nutrition counteract the effects of the alcohol?

R.M.
Rising Sun, Indiana

A nutrition/alcohol connection exists, but it is one to beware of. Alcohol absorbs nutrients and can lead to a malnourished fetus. If you drink, you must be particularly conscientious about the food you eat and maintain a well-balanced diet. Alcohol can diminish the potency of vitamins and minerals.

Dr. Sheldon Miller, director of the division of comprehensive alcohol and chemical dependency programs at the Sheppard and Enoch Pratt Hospital in Baltimore, recently found zinc deficiencies in alcoholic women. Astonishingly, these low zinc levels seemed more closely correlated with birth defects than did the amount of alcohol consumed. Dr. Miller theorized that the diuretic effect of alcohol caused the zinc to be washed out of the body, and the zinc deprivation contributed to FAS abnormalities.

A proper diet (see Chapter 5) is a must throughout pregnancy, and a woman who does have a drink should infuse her body with essential nutrients and extra minerals and vitamins. I suggest that my patients take two of their prescribed prenatal vitamins, which must contain zinc, as well as vitamin B-complex with vitamin B_6.

What Happens When an Expectant Father Drinks?

An expectant father's consumption of alcohol is critical *before* pregnancy. Men who are alcoholics or heavy drinkers often are impotent or have low sperm counts, and conception can be very difficult. A man who drinks may also smoke and have poor nutri-

171

tional habits that contribute to unhealthy sperm. Whether the sperm of an alcoholic man leads to FAS abnormalities is still unknown.

YOUR BABY'S CHANCE OF BEING AFFECTED BY ALCOHOL: WHAT THE STATISTICS TELL YOU

• *The risk factor.* Researchers at the National Institute of Child Health and Human Development recently collected data from 31,604 pregnant women to find out if there was a relationship between drinking during the first trimester and low birth weight. The percentage of newborns below the tenth percentile of weight for their due dates increased sharply with increasing alcohol intake. The results suggest that a woman who regularly consumes one to two drinks each day is putting her unborn baby at great risk, whereas a woman who consumes less than one drink a day will hardly be affecting her baby at all.

When compared to nondrinkers, the odds for producing a small-for-date newborn ranged from 1.1 percent for women drinking less than one drink a day to 1.96 percent for women having three to five drinks daily. The researchers strongly caution pregnant women who drink one to two alcoholic beverages a day that they are seriously hurting their chances of having healthy babies. Pregnant women should understand, however, that a regular intake of even one drink daily may still put a child in jeopardy. The safest advice I can give is to avoid alcohol altogether.

• *The race factor.* Although the nationwide incidence of FAS is 1 to 2 cases in 1,000 births, the numbers jump among minorities. On one American Indian reservation, researchers found that 40 percent of the children were affected by FAS. And a recent study by Dr. Robert Sokol, chairman of the department of obstetrics and gynecology at Wayne State Medical Center in Detroit, concluded that dose for dose of alcohol, black women appear to have a sevenfold greater risk than white women of giving birth to FAS babies.

The influence of race upon fetal alcohol syndrome must be studied further. These figures should, however, create an awareness that racial factors may exist in relation to FAS and that American Indian and black children may be particularly sensitive to the prenatal effects of alcohol.

HELP FOR THE ALCOHOLIC WOMAN

Alcoholism affects an estimated 2.3 million women in this country, and the numbers are growing. The deeply rooted problems that lead to alcoholism are not easily resolved, but it is known that support from family and friends helps in the fight against this addiction.

If you are the husband or close loved one of a pregnant alcoholic woman, encourage her to battle the bottle not just for herself but for her baby. Therapy, Alcoholics Anonymous, and your availability will all help. If you are an expectant mother as well as a heavy drinker, use these nine months to stop drinking, as the AA slogan goes, one day at a time. Your baby can be born with facial defects, physical and mental retardation, all or several of the FAS symptoms if you drink. With this pregnancy, you have a nine-month opportunity to purify your body and give your baby a good beginning. The life within you can be perfect.

I Was an Alcoholic. Will I Be Able to Have a Healthy Baby?

My divorce from my first husband was such a traumatic experience that I fell apart. I sank into a deep depression and began drinking. I never would have thought that an athletic person like me would have become an alcoholic, but I did. Finally, with the help of AA and my family, I was able to quit drinking and resume a sober life-style. I have been away from alcohol for two years now and I have met a wonderful man. We are planning to marry and start a family. I want to produce healthy children, but I'm worried that my former drinking may have destroyed my eggs. I'm eating well and exercising again to try to build up my body. Will I be able to have a healthy baby, or is it too late for me?

T.R.
Dallas, Texas

You are courageous to call yourself an alcoholic. Many women who go through difficult times define themselves as heavy drinkers and do not seek help. You were able to face your problem and conquer it.

Alcoholism, of course, is abusive to your body, but you are not alone in physically abusing yourself. Drugs, certain types of sexual behavior, and nutritional neglect are other health-destroying habits that women admit to having. Yet the body is amazing in its recuperative powers, and given rest and the proper attention, it can be returned to good health.

You have been on a healthy regimen for two years now, and your menstrual cycle should be back to normal. Continue to eat well-balanced meals of fresh fruits and vegetables, fish, poultry, and lean meats, and supplement your diet with vitamins. I suggest a multiple vitamin and a separate vitamin B-complex with at least 100 milligrams of B_1 included, 200 to 300 milligrams of vitamin B_6, and calcium, magnesium, zinc, and iron. Every formerly alcoholic woman can rebuild her body and have the same chance of a healthy and successful first-time conception as a woman who has not been a drinker. I congratulate you again for your strength, and I encourage every woman with a drinking problem to follow your example.

CHAPTER 8

Cigarettes and Pregnancy: Is Your Child Old Enough to Smoke?

Anyone would be horrified to see a three-year-old smoking. Yet if you are a pregnant smoker, you are permitting a much younger child—an unborn child—to have cigarettes. The nicotine, carbon monoxide, methyl alcohol, arsenic, and tars that you inhale with every puff reach the developing fetus. The onslaught of these substances endangers the baby's life, so why light up?

International studies from many countries, conducted over two decades, have documented the devastating effects of cigarettes on the unborn baby, but 30 percent of all pregnant women still smoke. In fact, statistics show that today's men are quitting while today's women are getting hooked on tobacco. Teenage girls are smoking more than teenage boys, 40 percent of all women over age twenty smoke, and lung cancer is beginning to outrank all other cancers in women. The National Institute of Child Health and Human Development has become so concerned about the damage done by cigarettes during pregnancy that the agency has sent information bulletins to obstetricians. Doctors are asked to remind their pregnant patients that:

- Up to 14 percent of all premature births are linked to a mother's smoking.
- Babies are born nearly a half-pound lighter to smokers than to nonsmokers, and this low birth weight leads to many problems throughout life.

Considering that the connection between smoking and fetal development is so strong, it is astonishing how many women continue to smoke during pregnancy. We now know that the risk of miscarriage rises with every cigarette smoked, so a pack-a-day smoker is creating a risk that is 50 percent higher than that of a nonsmoker. The good news from the researchers, however, is that if a woman *stops smoking before the fourth month* of her pregnancy, she can reverse the odds that forecast an adversely affected baby and improve her chances of having a healthy child. What better reason to say good-bye to cigarettes!

EARLY DISCOVERIES OF THE SMOKING CONNECTION

- *Low birth weight and smoking.* In 1957, a California obstetrician, Dr. W. J. Simpson, reported an average 200-gram (7-ounce) drop in the birth weight of newborns of women who smoked, when compared to newborns of nonsmokers. Her finding was challenged by other researchers, who felt that not just smoking but a woman's race, number of offspring, age, and socioeconomic status were contributing to her low-birth-weight baby. Over the years, forty-five studies involving more than a half-million births have consistently shown that regardless of other factors, women who smoke cigarettes during pregnancy have lighter babies than do nonsmokers. Today we even know that the effects of smoking are directly related to the number of cigarettes smoked. In one study, researchers calculated that light smokers (women who smoked less than one pack a day) were 30 to 170 percent more likely to give birth to smaller-than-average babies, while the children of heavy smokers (over a pack a day) had a 90 to 340 percent chance of being growth retarded.

• *Low birth weight, sex, and smoking.* In the early fifties, Dr. A. Lowe, a British physician, conducted a study in which he correlated the weight of newborn after newborn with whether mothers smoked, and if so, how much. His investigation convinced him that nonsmoking women gave birth to babies who were nearly a half-pound heavier than infants of smokers. He also found an interesting reversal in the usual relationship between the baby's sex and birth weight: boys born to smokers were appreciably lighter in weight than the girls of nonsmokers. Since newborn boys are usually heavier than newborn girls, Dr. Lowe could only presume that the boys were unusually affected by the smoking. His suspicion has been confirmed. Researchers have discovered that males are more vulnerable to several kinds of prenatal damage, including injury from the substances in tobacco.

• *Premature babies and smoking.* Dr. Simpson is also credited with discovering the relationship between cigarette smoking and premature deliveries. In the fifties, she created what came to be known as the Simpson Graph, which plotted the number of cigarettes smoked against the rate of premature delivery among smokers. The graph showed a steep curve that began with a 7 percent prematurity rate among women who smoked up to five cigarettes a day and ended in a staggering 33 percent prematurity rate among women who smoked close to two packs a day. Follow-up studies over the years have continued to support Dr. Simpson's findings. Since premature birth is responsible for 75 percent of

Figure 8-1. *Smoking is so dangerous during pregnancy that every woman should try to quit as soon as she knows she has conceived. Remember, when you smoke, your baby smokes too.* Reproduced from the Dept. of Health and Human Services, (PHS) 83-50198.

perinatal deaths—deaths before, during, or after delivery—the risks of smoking are unbelievably high.

How Do Cigarettes Do Their Damage?

When researchers isolated the components of the tobacco smoke/air mixture that a smoker inhales, thousands of toxic substances that cross the placenta were found. Among the harmful chemicals cigarettes bring to the baby are: nicotine, carbon monoxide, hydrogen cyanide, tars, resins, and known carcinogens such as nitrosamines. When these toxins enter the fetal bloodstream, they influence the development of the baby—if the baby survives.

Smoking increases the risk of spontaneous abortion (miscarriage), premature birth, and stillbirth. The perinatal death rate—the death of children just before, during, or just after they are born—is 25 percent higher for women who smoke heavily than for women who smoke less than one pack a day. *The extent of damage done to the fetus is directly related to the number of cigarettes smoked!*

One study estimates that due to the nicotine-diminished blood flow to the fetus, the risk of miscarriage may be as much as 70 percent higher among heavy smokers than among nonsmokers. Reduced blood flow from smoking also weakens the placenta and, in the latter months of pregnancy, two dangerous complications—abruptio placentae and placenta previa—may occur.

Abruptio placentae, or placental abruption, is a life-threatening condition for mother and baby. Recently researchers reported that just one cigarette could cut back the flow of blood across the placenta for up to fifteen minutes! When blood flow is decreased, fragile placental tissue begins to die. A placenta that decays around the edges may separate prematurely from the uterine wall. Suddenly either prematurely, close to, or at term, the placenta partially or completely detaches, and the baby may die or be born with brain damage. An emergency cesarean section is usually the only way that mother and baby may be saved. A smoker who quits before the fourth month of pregnancy, however, has a good chance of avoiding this potentially fatal condition.

The risk of *placenta previa* grows with the number of years a woman has smoked *before* her pregnancy. She can only improve her odds if she stops smoking a few months before she attempts conception. With placenta previa, the damage is done beforehand.

Within a week after an egg is fertilized, the placenta attaches itself abnormally low in the womb. Badly positioned, the placenta and its developing fetus are in danger, because the blood flow to the area is inadequate. With placenta previa, the chance of vaginal bleeding, miscarriage, placental separation, premature birth, and fetal death increases. Also increasing is the risk that the mother may suffer fatal hemorrhaging if one of these conditions becomes a reality.

Smoking has also been named as a contributor to *sudden infant death syndrome* (*SIDS*), better known as crib death. The exact cause of crib death is not known, but the theory is that a baby may succumb because its breathing, swallowing, and coughing mechanisms have not properly developed. When asleep, a baby who does not have optimum respiratory reflexes may experience blocked breathing. It is widely believed that one cause of underdeveloped respiratory capability is smoking.

Exactly *how* do cigarettes do their damage? Nicotine moves into the arterial blood supply and causes constriction of the arteries and veins. In a laboratory, when nicotine was injected into animals, the blood flow to the uterus and placenta and the oxygen supply to the fetus all dropped. Although researchers cannot measure the uterine blood flow within a pregnant woman, they have been able to observe that a fetus slows or stops its breathing movements when an expectant mother smokes. Scientists have concluded that nicotine reduces the blood flow and the amount of oxygen available to the fetus.

Carbon monoxide also deprives an expectant mother and her baby of oxygen. By crowding out the oxygen in the hemoglobin (red blood cells), carbon monoxide molecules reduce internal oxygen by 12 percent. A fetus that is oxygen starved grows more slowly.

Considering the effects of nicotine and carbon monoxide— without even examining the other toxins in cigarettes—a fetus never receives the proper nourishment. A survivor of this environment is often a low-birth-weight or premature baby whose growth and development have been affected.

WHAT PROBLEMS FACE A LOW-BIRTH-WEIGHT BABY?

The more an expectant mother smokes, the more she reduces her unborn baby's supply of oxygen. In what appears to be an effort to protect itself, an oxygen-deprived fetus grows at a slower rate. A smoker's baby will weigh almost a half-pound less at term than a nonsmoker's. Outwardly an oxygen-starved infant is lighter, shorter, and has a smaller head circumference than a properly nourished baby, but inner growth may also be stunted. The cells that form the brain, tissues, and major biological systems may not divide to capacity. A smoker's baby may be born frail and susceptible to illness in its early months. Later on in childhood, the effects of the brain's growth retardation may appear in lowered IQ scores and reading levels.

Investigating a group of seven-year-old schoolchildren, researchers found that the offspring of mothers who had smoked during pregnancy were three months behind their classmates in reading ability and were 3/10 inch shorter than the children of nonsmoking mothers. In Finland, a fourteen-year follow-up study of the offspring of 12,068 pregnant mothers confirmed the fact that the children of the smoking mothers were more prone to respiratory diseases than were the children of nonsmokers. The smokers' children were also shorter and had poorer aptitude levels in school.

A relatively new association has been made between hyperactivity in children and smoking. A hyperactive, or hyperkinetic, child sleeps infrequently, throws temper tantrums, quickly reacts to sensory stimuli, and has a lack of concentration. The brain abnormalities seen in hyperactive children have been discovered in the sons and daughters of women who smoked heavily during pregnancy.

The hyperactivity/smoking link was originally made when researchers discovered that of twenty hyperkinetic children, sixteen were the offspring of women who smoked heavily and four were born during traumatic deliveries. Speculation that a smoking mother is an anxious woman who is more likely to have a hyperactive child has been disproved. Siblings born to women who smoked in one pregnancy but not in the other are different: hyperactivity is more apparent in the child of the smoking pregnancy.

The low-birth-weight baby, outwardly and inwardly growth retarded, is always just a step behind. Knowing this, why smoke?

Other Birth Defects Linked to Smoking

In a sense, a smaller newborn is a defective newborn, but low birth weight is really a subtle defect. Other more obvious birth defects are also sadly connected to babies born to heavy smokers. Smoking can cause serious damage to the central nervous system of the fetus. A correlation has been made between certain *neuro-tubal defects,* such as *spina bifida* and *anencephaly,* and heavy smoking, and there may also be a greater chance of *cleft lip* (harelip) or *cleft palate* in babies of moderate to heavy smokers.

As for future problems, scientists suspect that prenatal exposure to the chemical components of inhaled tobacco smoke may contribute to heart and arterial disease in adulthood. Since the chemical ingredients in cigarettes include carcinogens such as diazobenzopyrene, anthracenes, nitrosamines, hydrazines, and urethane, researchers also theorize that a smoker's baby may be more vulnerable to cancer as an adult. The increased susceptibility of laboratory animals to cancer after exposure to carcinogens in the womb lends credence to the theory.

The guesses go on, and the future is undefined, but scientists do have one definite statement: Don't smoke during pregnancy.

I've Been Smoking for the First Two Months of My Pregnancy. Will I Lose the Baby?

I'm a pack-a-day smoker, but since I've become pregnant, I've cut back. I'm smoking abut half the amount of cigarettes I used to, but everyone tells me that cutting down is not enough. I've tried to quit before and I couldn't. I feel like I'm doing the best I can, but a couple of friends keep insisting that I'm going to lose the baby, that I have to stop completely. Can't I just keep the number of cigarettes down? Will I really lose the baby? Aren't my friends being a little extreme?

J.B.
Dill City, Oklahoma

Your friends are not being extreme. They are giving you prudent advice. Statistics show a direct correlation between smoking during pregnancy and the incidence of spontaneous abortion (miscarriage) and stillbirth. Pregnant women who smoke a pack a day or more have about a 50 percent greater risk of losing their babies than nonsmokers do. The infant mortality rate for you, a woman who is smoking less than a pack a day, is about 25 percent greater than a nonsmoker's—a figure that should activate concern. The numbers are worrisome. In one New York study, the risk of miscarriage alone was estimated to be as much as 70 percent higher among heavy smokers than among nonsmokers.

Your chance of miscarrying rises every time you light up. There is a direct relationship between the number of cigarettes smoked and the extent of damage that can be done to the fetus. The more you smoke, the greater the harm. Although it is better to smoke fewer cigarettes, unless you quit completely, you continue to seriously endanger the life of your child.

Animal studies show that the substances contained in tobacco smoke, besides interfering with fetal metabolism and endocrine function, actually alter the genetic makeup of the unborn. A normal fetus can become abnormal due to a mother's smoking habit. When normal development is disrupted, the baby often cannot survive. Early in pregnancy, the fetus may miscarry; later on, it may be stillborn. One in five unsuccessful pregnancies occur in women who smoke regularly. It bears repeating that pregnant smokers have a higher incidence of spontaneous abortion, stillbirth, and premature delivery than do nonsmokers. Also, since the nicotine in cigarettes reduces the blood flow to the baby, the umbilical cord becomes thin and weak. With little pressure in the cord, it easily bends and curves and may strangle the baby or be squashed by the baby's weight. The result, again, is a tragic stillbirth.

There is hope for your baby if you stop smoking now. Researchers have discovered that if you quit *before the fourth month,* your baby regains its chance to be born healthy. Quit now, and your risk of losing the baby or having a low-birth-weight baby drops to that of a nonsmoker. (Placenta previa is the exception to this rule, however.) So throw away your cigarettes, eat a well-balanced diet (see Chapter 5), and rest often. Lie on your side to allow more blood to flow to the placenta and strengthen it. Before your pregnancy gets one day older, you can create a safer environment for your future son or daughter.

What Happens if I Begin to Smoke in the Fourth Month?

In my first trimester, I completely lost my taste for cigarettes. The thought of a cigarette made my stomach turn. Then something happened. After the first trimester, my craving came back. I wanted to smoke so badly that I finally gave in. In my fourth month, I was smoking a few cigarettes a day, usually after meals. I stopped after an en-

counter with my doctor. He happened to be in the same restaurant where my husband had taken me for dinner. He walked right over to my table and ordered me to stop. I was so embarrassed and guilty that I did. Now I worry about whether my return to cigarettes will have an effect on the baby. I don't dare ask my own doctor. Can you help me?

W.P.

Lynchburg, Virginia

You do not mention how long you smoked prior to the pregnancy. A condition called *placenta previa,* which occurs when the placenta positions itself low in the womb, can be experienced by women who have been long-time smokers. The risk of placenta previa, which is potentially fatal to mother and baby, increases with the number of years a woman has smoked before pregnancy. Placenta previa takes place within a week after conception, and the condition remains even if you stop smoking. If you do not have placenta previa, you will probably have a normal pregnancy. Your baby should greet you with a healthy mind and body.

You did not smoke during the first trimester and you smoked only briefly in the fourth month. It is not likely that your short relapse, although it was undesirable, has caused any lingering harm. Smoking reduces blood flow and oxygen supply to the fetus. The fetus begins its greatest period of growth as you enter the third trimester. This is the time when the demand for blood flow and oxygen—fetal nourishment—rises. You have not allowed your smoking to continue throughout the second and third trimesters, so you have not diminished your baby's nourishment.

Your doctor was wise to take a strong stand against your habit. I am frankly surprised that your husband did not attempt to stop you himself. Whenever a pregnant woman lights up, a loved one should remind her about the devastating effects of smoking during pregnancy.

FETAL BREATHING AND SMOKING

Now in my sixth month, I feel like the baby is really living and breathing inside me. With the moving and kicking, I have a sense of life separate from my own. My big problem, though, is that I am a smoker who has never been able to kick the habit completely. I'm down to about six cigarettes a day, but I can't seem to go cold turkey and quit. Yet now that

183

I'm more aware of the baby, I can tell that when I smoke, it moves less. What is happening? Do my cigarettes slow down my child?

T.K.
Winona, Minnesota

The fetus does exercise its breathing capability in the womb. In fact, a forty-week (full-term) fetus takes about sixty breaths a minute. If an expectant mother smokes, though, she reduces fetal breathing rhythm. Fetuses have been observed through ultrasonography while their mothers smoked, and researchers found that breathing and movement decreased. Five minutes after a pregnant woman smokes a cigarette, a depressed fetal breathing pattern occurs. This slowed breathing may last up to an hour. You can imagine, then, that smoking a pack of cigarettes may lead up to 20 hours of diminished breathing.

Since smoking constricts the blood flow and oxygen supply to the fetus, the lack of movement may be a natural effort to conserve energy. At any rate, the reduced movement is not normal. You are in the sixth month and you are still smoking. Please stop and give your baby a chance to grow in good health. There is no fail-safe way to stop smoking. The best advice I can give is to tell you to think about how you are hurting your unborn child, and to quit cold turkey.

Why Didn't I Know That Smoking Could Lead to Bleeding Problems?

I am now in my seventh month but I smoked until my fifth month. I stopped because I became incredibly frightened. No one knew I was still smoking, and one night, in my fifth month, my husband and I had just made love. I went to the bathroom to sneak a smoke and I noticed that I was bleeding. The bleeding became so heavy that my husband had to rush me to the hospital. The doctor did a sonogram and told me that I had placenta previa and I would need a cesarean if I went to term. He told me that my condition was being seen in more and more women who smoke. I never thought I would bleed and risk losing the baby just from a few cigarettes. Why aren't pregnant women more informed?

E.V.
Wyckoff, New Jersey

The National Institute of Child Health and Human Development, the American Cancer Society, the American College of Obstetricians and Gynecologists, midwives, and obstetricians are all working to inform pregnant women of the hazards of smoking. Today we know that two very serious complications—abruptio placentae and placenta previa—are more likely to be suffered by smokers than by nonsmokers.

Abruptio placentae, or placental abruption, is the deterioration and separation of the placenta. The placenta, which is already small because it is receiving a nicotine-reduced blood supply, begins to wither at the edges and fall away from the uterine wall. This separation may occur at any point from about the sixth month on, and it is signaled by sudden bleeding and/or severe abdominal pain. Sometimes only one symptom may appear. The risk of abruptio placentae increases 24 percent in moderate smokers and 68 percent in heavy smokers. If a woman develops bleeding during pregnancy, she should expect her doctor to order a pelvic ultrasound to determine the cause and the location of her placenta.

Ms. V.'s condition, placenta previa, rises 25 percent in moderate smokers and 92 percent in heavy smokers. Placenta previa—an abnormally low in the womb placenta—occurs among women who have smoked for some time. The location of the placenta is defined within a week of conception, so the fact that a woman stops smoking after she conceives will not change the situation.

Once her condition was diagnosed, Ms. V.'s pregnancy became a high-risk one. Placenta previa can lead to premature birth and stillbirth. The best treatment is bed rest to lessen the pressure and stress on the placenta. She should have no intercourse from the onset of bleeding until the end of her pregnancy. She might need to be hospitalized if bleeding begins again or appears quite heavy. In the hospital, her doctor will be able to observe her closely. A cesarean section will be the only way to deliver the baby if the placenta covers the entire birth canal.

If I Don't Smoke but People Around Me Do, Will My Baby Be Affected?

I'm four months pregnant and I work in an office where a lot of people smoke. I don't smoke because I know cigarettes are unhealthy for me and my baby. Sometimes I would like to ask my co-workers not to smoke around me but I'm not sure if I have the right. Does their smoking affect my baby?

N.G.
Roseville, Michigan

If a pregnant woman's husband, friends, or co-workers smoke, they are exposing her to toxins from their cigarettes. Ms. G. is the victim of "passive smoking." She is inhaling carbon monoxide and creating an unhealthy environment for her unborn baby. She has every right to ask her co-workers to stop smoking around her, because it is possible that heavy passive exposure to cigarette smoke may slow fetal growth. It is certainly known that a child in a household of smokers becomes more prone to ear, nose, and throat infections, bronchitis, asthmatic attacks, and respiratory difficulties. So please ask those who are close to you to refrain from smoking while they are in your company. They will be helping you to have a healthy pregnancy.

Is Marijuana Safer Than Tobacco?

My husband and I occasionally smoke pot. Now that I'm pregnant I've told him that I don't think I should smoke anything. He says that marijuana is safer than tobacco, and I argue that he is wrong. Please tell me who is right.

B.B.
New York, New York

Marijuana is a drug that exposes your unborn baby to psychoactive chemicals. A Boston University School of Medicine study of 1,690 mother-child pairs showed that marijuana smoked during pregnancy seemed to contribute to infants born with the characteristics of newborns that have fetal alcohol syndrome (FAS). (See Chapter 7 for details about FAS.) Marijuana use was linked to diminished fetal development and low birth weight. In fact, one Boston physician noted that women who smoked marijuana three or more times a week gave birth to infants who were smaller than the low-birth-weight newborns of women who smoked a pack or more a day of cigarettes.

You should be alert to the fact that marijuana is *more dangerous* than tobacco. Marijuana is a drug that crosses the placenta and affects the fetus. Even before conception, a woman should stop the use of all recreational drugs and purify her body for pregnancy. Ms. B.'s husband is obviously the loser in this argument.

Don't Some Women Smoke During Pregnancy and Have Healthy Babies?

I consider myself a social smoker. I like my cigarettes after meals and now and then at parties. My doctor keeps telling me to quit because I'm pregnant, but I don't think I'm doing that much harm. I have a neighbor who smoked during her pregnancy and her son is three years old now and totally healthy. Is smoking really that bad?

W.F.

Monterey, California

As mentioned several times in this chapter, smoking during pregnancy is associated with miscarriage, stillbirth, premature birth, placenta previa, abruptio placentae, and crib death. Smoking is also responsible for growth retardation, which may create physical and mental difficulties in childhood. Now there is no doubt that the adverse effects of smoking are directly linked to the number of cigarettes an expectant mother smokes while she is pregnant. The more you smoke, the greater harm the fetus will suffer.

Every woman, and every pregnancy, is different. A woman's age, health history, diet, and smoking habits are her own. Ms. F. should not compare her situation to her neighbor's. Although her smoking friend's child appears to be healthy, Ms. F. does not know all the details of her friend's habit and how the child might have been affected by it. A child who appears normal might have been gifted if the mother had been a nonsmoker! Smoking is detrimental to the growth and life of a fetus. If Ms. F. wants to give her future son or daughter a sound foundation for good health, she should never smoke another cigarette.

SMOKING IS A FORM OF CHILD ABUSE

Although a public outcry for the unborn's right to life can be heard, there is no stand taken for the quality of that life. Over fifty million Americans still smoke. They are endangering their own

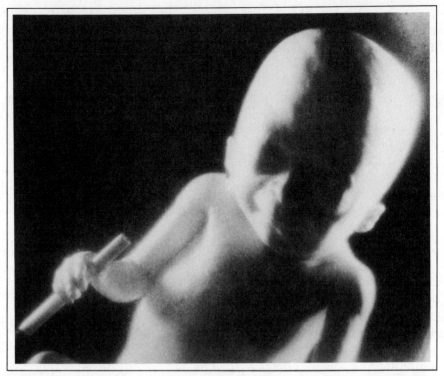

Figure 8-2. *This controversial antismoking message depicting a simulated fetus puffing on a cigarette was rejected by CBS and NBC as too graphic.* AP/Wide World Photos.

well-being, but they are also injuring and potentially destroying the lives of children who are yet to be born. This form of child abuse is rampant and tragic. Yet a public service announcement that featured an image of an unborn baby smoking a cigarette was rejected as "too graphic" by major television networks. This is unfortunate, because information about the life-threatening effects of smoking during pregnancy must be proffered.

A recent study of American women showed that nearly one-half did not know that pregnant women who smoke have a greater chance of losing their babies than do nonsmokers. Of the 306 million women who become pregnant in the United States every year, nearly one-third smoke. Doctors must keep reminding their patients of the danger of cigarette smoking. You, an expectant mother, should follow your doctor's advice and tell your female friends and relatives that no good can come from keeping the tobacco habit during pregnancy.

IT'S NEVER TOO LATE TO STOP

As mentioned before, recent studies have given hope that if an expectant mother who smokes quits *before her fourth month,* she has a good chance of preventing growth retardation in her baby. Then there is time for the smoking-reduced blood supply and oxygen content to return to normal gestational levels as the fetus enters its greatest period of growth. The best approach, of course, is for a woman who smokes to quit before she conceives. If she does continue her habit, the opportunity to make a safe inner world for her baby is still there. She should stop smoking in the first trimester, and for her future and her baby's, she should never start again.

CHAPTER 9

The Unseen Chemicals in Your Environment and the Drugs in Your Medicine Chest

Although it sometimes seems as if contaminants are overtaking the environment, we are probably just more informed about the chemical and radioactive substances that exist. In a sense, an expectant mother may be safer now than in the past. The news about a Love Canal or Three Mile Island is shocking and scary, but these events open new areas of scientific exploration into the effects of environmental pollutants on the unborn. More attention is currently focused on chemicals that a pregnant woman may be exposed to in her home and on her job.

During the first three months of a fetus's development, its fragile structure is especially vulnerable. In Chapter 6, the effects of everyday activities such as dyeing your hair, painting a room, commuting in traffic, and working in front of a computer video display terminal (VDT) were explained. An expectant mother learned whether during a normal day, she was exposing her unborn baby to chemical substances or the possibility of radiation.

This chapter describes other circumstances that may put you and the child you are carrying in contact with potentially hazardous materials. You may be getting ready to do a little gardening around the sprayed fruit trees, or to turn on the microwave oven, and you might need extra protection. You may work in a plant where toxic chemicals are used. Do you know what substances are harmful? By understanding your "invisible" surroundings, you will sense whether to continue or to change routine habits.

Highly visible substances—drugs—on the other hand, are easier to comprehend. If you become ill during pregnancy, you may automatically reach for an antihistamine or an antibiotic that was previously prescribed. You will see as you read through this chapter that certain drugs may interfere with the safe development of your baby. Even caffeine is a drug that you should reconsider. You can actively decide to create an inner world that is just a little bit better for your baby. The choices are not hard.

PURIFY YOUR BODY BEFORE CONCEPTION

Scientists do not know every drug and chemical that might be potentially harmful to reproduction, but a wise woman will not take a chance that any drug is safe. If you are in a situation in which recreational drugs are offered, decline and keep your body cleansed. Marijuana, cocaine, hallucinogens such as LSD (D-lysergic acid diethylamide) and PCP (phencyclidine hydrochloride), amphetamines, barbiturates, and narcotics will not enhance your internal environment. LSD and a number of narcotics have been linked to chromosomal breakdown, and other drugs are suspect. You can never be sure what chemical substance will have a lasting effect. Agent Orange, a highly toxic dioxin that contains the contaminants 2,4, 5-T, and TCDD, was not considered biologically hazardous during the defoliation of Vietnam. Vietnam veterans, however, brought a class suit against Dow Chemical Company, manufacturers of Agent Orange, for serious health problems of their own and birth defects among their offspring. The veterans claimed that they had been affected by exposure to the herbicide. The case was settled out of court when Dow Chemical agreed to establish a $180 million fund for the veterans, but studies of the veterans' health in relation to Agent Orange continue.

The most recent reports from the Centers for Disease Control (CDC), as published in the *Journal of the American Medical Association* (JAMA) in August, 1984, have shown a slightly increased incidence of spina bifida ("open spine") and anencephaly (no brain) among the offspring of Vietnam veterans who were exposed to Agent Orange. The study also indicated that a significantly higher proportion of veterans who believed they were exposed to Agent Orange had more than one child born with birth defects, when compared to fathers of babies who felt they were not exposed. Researchers emphasize that the slightly higher incidence of birth defects among children of soldiers who were exposed to Agent Orange might be due to "some other unidentified risk factor." The CDC is currently conducting studies to answer the many questions that continue to be asked about Agent Orange.

All this news about the effects of drugs and chemicals should convince women and men who are thinking about starting families to stay drug free. You may not be able to avoid a pollutant in the environment, but the thrill of taking recreational drugs is not worth the risk of harming your future son or daughter. Exercise, eat well-balanced meals, and supplement your daily diet with a vitamin regimen that includes at least 100 milligrams of vitamin B-complex, 100 to 200 milligrams of vitamin B_6, 500 milligrams of vitamin C two or three times a day, one or two iron supplements a day, and calcium tablets if your diet is low in this mineral.

MAKING SAFE CHOICES AT HOME

During the first trimester, the baby's vital body systems are rapidly forming. If a harmful substance, a teratogen, reaches the fetus in these early months, its development may be impaired. A newly expectant mother should not be afraid, but she should be cautious. This is not the time to try different detergents, cleaning fluids, artificial sweeteners, or food substitutes. Redecorating should be postponed, since, as mentioned in Chapter 6, the chemicals in solvents, paint, varnish, paint strippers, and thinners may affect the vulnerable fetus. In fact, if you have a choice about whether to expose yourself to a chemical product, choose to stay

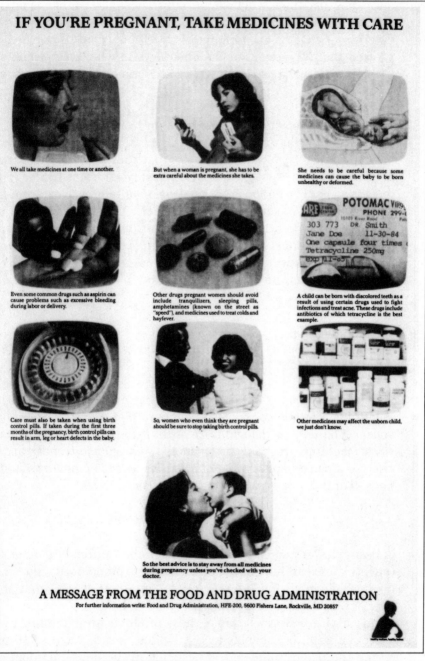

Figure 9-1. *This FDA drugs-and-pregnancy poster speaks for itself. It tells every expectant mother to watch out for all drugs.* Reproduced by permission of the Department of Health and Human Services.

away, because there will be many substances you cannot avoid. In 1981 and 1982, research from blood, urine, and breath samples to determine what types of chemicals were prevalent in our bodies showed that 90 percent of the chemicals to which the people in the study were exposed came from the home. Let your husband spray pesticide in the vegetable garden or apply spot remover to the soiled shirt.

If you are suspicious of your drinking water, you may want to install a water filter or purchase purified water during your pregnancy. You will also want to be sure that your home is well ventilated in case you have gas leaks from a stove or space heater. The question about radiation from a television or microwave oven is always asked by concerned women. Since science has not given us an absolute answer, it is probably best to stay a safe distance away from the appliances. Never dwell on unseen hazards, however, because anxiety will build, and then you may constrict the blood flow to the fetus. Be informed and cautious, but most of all, be yourself.

QUESTIONS ABOUT THE HOME

Are Insecticides Dangerous?

I live in a well-maintained apartment building in New York City. Once a month the exterminator comes to spray so that cockroaches will not appear. I have never thought twice about the insecticide he uses, but since I became pregnant last month, I've begun to wonder about whether it could have harmful effects. The smell is pretty bad, and I worry that I may be breathing in dangerous chemicals.

V.W.
New York, New York

Pesticides are considered to be a possible source of danger to the fetus. Researchers have not been able to pinpoint exactly what might happen to fetal development, but they do feel that the chemicals in pesticides and insecticides hold the potential of harm, and they worry because these products are plentiful. In a survey of 8200 households in the United States, 9 out of 10 reported the use of some sort of pesticide in the house, garden, or yard.

Pesticides contain toxic substances that are in the air you

breathe after fumigation. Fruits and vegetables are often sprayed and should be washed before you cook and eat them. I would suggest that Ms. W. open the windows and air her apartment during and after her monthly extermination. She should also remain away from her home for most of the day. Since Ms. W. is only in her first trimester, when the fetus is most vulnerable, she might be wise to postpone the monthly exterminating. This is not a time to take chances.

Does Radiation Ever Leak from a TV, a Microwave Oven, or Any Other Household Appliance?

When I hold my hand in front of my television set, I feel a glittery sensation. Is radiation being emitted? Is a TV set hazardous to my unborn baby? I'm very worried about household appliances like the TV and the microwave oven, and I'm scared about what I may not have considered. Is there anything I can do to make sure I'm not around anything that's dangerous?

Y.P.
Sioux City, Iowa

A television, especially a color TV, does emit a low level of *nonionizing radiation*, which lacks the energy and hazardous potential of the *ionizing radiation* produced by X rays and nuclear materials. However, no type of radiation can be dismissed, and high levels of nonionizing radiation have been associated with incidences of cancer, sterility, and nervous disorders. The research, though, is controversial and inconclusive.

Color TVs manufactured after 1975 emit much lower levels of nonionizing radiation than do models that were sold earlier, and it is not likely that you have to worry about prenatal problems from your set. Since you are being protective of yourself and your unborn child right now, you might always sit at least six feet away from the TV screen. You are trying to avoid all sources of radiation, and even though a television set is not considered a prime risk, you may as well be extra safe.

Microwave ovens also emit nonionizing radiation. Before 1976, the ovens were manufactured in ways that allowed leakages to pass through the closed doors during use. Today the oven doors are made to seal in the microwaves, but even so, I do not recommend that women use these ovens during pregnancy. Especially during the first three months, I advise my pregnant patients to put their microwave ovens in storage and to cook with a standard electric or gas stove. If you feel you must prepare food in a microwave oven later in pregnancy, stand away from the appliance while it is on, and use it infrequently.

Other possible sources of nonionizing radiation in the home are radios, computer video display terminals (VDTs), burglar alarm systems, and garage door openers. Alone, none of these appliances is likely to harm fetal development, but since you may be in contact with nonionizing radiation from more than one of these gadgets and mechanisms, try to avoid exposure wherever you can. (See Chapter 6 for a report on the safety of VDTs.)

MAKING SAFE CHOICES AT WORK

Some jobs may be too dangerous to continue while you are pregnant. If you work around radiation or with chemicals, your baby may be at risk. Dental and X-ray technicians would be wise to request leaves of absence while they are pregnant. As mentioned in Chapter 6, even airline attendants are exposed to radiation while in flight at high altitudes, and office workers who sit in front of video display terminals (VDTs) every day may be in contact with risky levels of nonionizing radiation. (See Chapter 6.)

As for chemicals, if you work at a dry-cleaning establishment, perchloroethylene, a dry-cleaning chemical, may be harmful. Lead fumes from paint and pottery materials should also be avoided. Hospital and dental personnel who administer anesthetic gases—especially nitrous oxide (laughing gas)—have been found to have an increased rate of birth-defective babies and spontaneous abortions. Pollutants such as carbon monoxide and mercury vapors may also affect an unborn baby. If you are in an office of smokers or, as discussed in Chapter 6, if you commute a long distance to work in heavy traffic or are a bus or taxi driver, you are likely to be inhaling carbon monoxide. Dentists and dental assistants may be breathing in mercury vapors as they prepare fillings for cavities.

So think about whether you are exposed to radiation or chemicals on the job. If you are, you should really weigh the possibility of alternate employment while you are pregnant. And make sure that you are not in a physically demanding job, no matter what the environment is. A pregnant woman should not be climbing ladders or carrying heavy loads. Think about how you feel as you progress through pregnancy. As your baby grows in your womb, perhaps part-time work would make you more comfortable.

Remember to consult your obstetrician if you have any apprehensions about the safety of your workplace or the suitability of your job. These nine months are a time to pamper and protect yourself and your baby.

I'm a Subway Conductor. Is My Job Jeopardizing My Pregnancy?

I'm a conductor on a New York City subway and I just found out that I'm pregnant. I'm worried because the train stops suddenly and often bumps and rattles along. Will all the jolts and shakes of the train make me miscarry? My friends tell me that I should get off the train and ask for an office job until I have the baby. What do you think?

L.C.

Richmond Hill, New York

It is important for every pregnant woman to take it easy in the beginning of pregnancy. An embryo implants itself into the womb's placenta, a warm and secure environment. Until the embryo has evolved into a developing fetus, a woman should try to stay physically relaxed. In a healthy pregnancy, strenuous activity or an environment such as a shaking train may have no effect on the fetus, but at the start, you never know if a pregnancy is problem free.

I would suggest that Ms. C. take no chances with her baby. Her friends recommend a desk job, and I think they have the right idea. Even after miscarriage is no longer a risk, if she continued to be a conductor, she would eventually find it difficult to move through the train with ease. Her size would throw her off balance as the train bumped along and shook her from side to side. A moving train is not a safe place for a pregnant woman, and noxious fumes, confined underground, may also be unhealthy.

Do I Have to Leave My Job if I Work for a Company That Uses Chemicals?

I am a shipping clerk for a company that manufactures commercial inks. Although I don't work in the plant itself, the loading dock is nearby and I know that I am breathing in the fumes of chemicals that are used. I've asked one of the lab technicians what I may be exposed to, and she said that there are solvents such as toluene, benzene, and xylene used every day, and also pigments. One of the pigments, benzidene yellow, is carcinogenic and the men wear overalls and masks when they work with it. Carbon black has tiny particles that fly through the air like dust. I'm worried about breathing in these chemicals or eating them in my food. Do I have to leave my job? I like it here; in fact, I met my husband at this company.

C.R.

Rahway, New Jersey

Ms. R. is fortunate that a lab technician informed her of some of the chemicals that are used in the company plant. Benzene and xylene have been linked to low-birth-weight babies in animal studies, and toluene has been connected to low-birth-weight babies in at least one human study. The pigments, one of which is a known carcinogen, may also be potentially hazardous, although I am not aware of studies on how these *specific* substances affect the fetus.

Any pregnant woman who is employed by a company that uses chemicals should check with her superiors about the exact substances she may be breathing and touching. A company should have safety standards for their employees, but once you know the names of the chemicals in your environment, you can also consult your physician.

If Ms. R. believes that her company's safety measures are inadequate, she should request a leave of absence. A business should be responsible for protecting its employees, but sometimes an environmental situation, such as an air-conditioning system that circulates chemical vapors throughout the premises, cannot be overcome. You must weigh the risks to the fetus when you decide whether to remain on the job.

DRUGS AND PREGNANCY

Medical experts used to believe that the placenta acted like a filter between the expectant mother's body and her unborn baby, but after 1961 and the sadness of seeing "thalidomide babies," we all began to realize how vulnerable the fetus really is. The placenta is not an impenetrable protective barrier. Research in the effect of drugs on the fetus was intensified after the thalidomide tragedy, but even with the extensive studies, it continues to be extremely difficult to know how each individual drug will affect an unborn baby. Thalidomide was tested on pregnant mice and rats, which did not show any effects. In fact, human fetuses only seemed to be sensitive to the drug between 27 and 40 days after conception.

Considering the thalidomide experience, an expectant mother should avoid all drugs early in pregnancy, when vital cells are dividing and the baby's brain and major biological systems are forming. (See Figure 9-2.) Yet according to a study conducted by the Drug Epidemiology Unit at the Boston University School of Medicine, the average pregnant woman still uses as many as four drugs during early pregnancy when the embryo is at highest risk. The

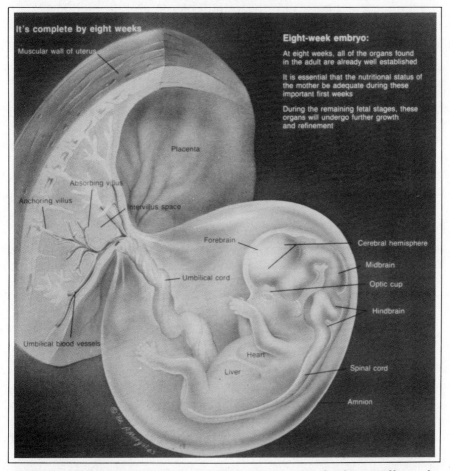

Figure 9-2. *An embryo at eight weeks. The major organs develop rapidly at this time, and can easily become damaged by drugs and environmental agents.*

study names nine consistently used drugs, among them aspirin and Seconal. Tylenol (acetaminophen), which is regarded as being safer than aspirin for use during pregnancy, tops the list.

When expectant mothers ask about drugs, they usually want to know about aspirin, antibiotics, cold remedies, sleeping aids, and tranquilizers. Some women have taken drugs for specific conditions before they became pregnant, and they wonder whether they may continue. Doctors can name drugs that have been clearly labeled unsafe, and some of these are the antiinflammatory drugs indomethacin and naproxen, the anticonvulsant Dilantin, the anticoagulant warfarin, high-blood-pressure drugs thiazide and reserpine, and iodine. Even the vitamins C, D, and K; calcium; and copper have been found to be toxic at high levels. Almost all the drugs labeled unsafe would probably have to be taken at regular intervals for several days to be harmful. Still, if you have a choice, do not take a chance.

On the other hand, even if you have no intention of using a drug during these nine months, you may fall prey to accident or illness. If you need medication, talk to your doctor before you reach for a bottle of pills. Never take a drug, even a seemingly safe over-the-counter drug, without consulting your physician. Your medicine cabinet is high-risk terrain right now, and your doctor is your guide. If you want to learn more about pharmaceuticals on your own, investigate the *Physicians' Desk Reference* at your local library. This volume, which is updated annually, lists side effects and warnings for all the latest medications.

While no drug can be guaranteed to be safe during pregnancy, some drugs are less risky than others, and now and then even a risky drug, at a minimal dose, is prescribed when a woman's health is at stake. There are so many circumstances that can occur during pregnancy that it is difficult to set iron-clad rules for all drugs, and there are always new drugs being made that may be exceptions to the rules. When you think about the millions of pregnant women who took medications before safety was a question, you realize that at one time, the possibility of fetal harm was never given a second thought. Today the risk cannot be denied, but it should not create a fearful pregnancy.

While it is impossible to analyze every drug in the confines of this chapter, I have highlighted the medications that seem to be the most worrisome to my patients. Expectant mothers are puzzled about how to find relief from various aches, pains, and illnesses if they do not take drugs. No matter what knowledge you gain from these pages, however, remember that above all else, you are in partnership with your doctor during pregnancy. Any drugs that touch your life should be evaluated by you and him together, and together you will share in a problem-free childbirth.

What Can I Take for a Headache?

I am suffering from headaches that have become unbearable as my pregnancy has progressed. Now I'm in my fifth month and I'm at my wits' end. My doctor says that the headaches are due to pregnancy tension and he does not want to prescribe any medication. I don't care! Isn't there anything I can take?

> P.D.
> Galveston, Texas

Headache in pregnancy is not uncommon. It is often caused by the higher hormonal levels in your body and possibly by increased water retention, which can lead to swelling of the brain tissue. Stress may also contribute to headache pain. During pregnancy, most doctors will try to treat a headache without medication, because the healthiest pregnancy is a drug-free one.

Ms. D. may be able to lessen the pain with a change of diet. Reducing salt and sugar intake may bring relief. Salt binds water, so by decreasing her salt intake, Ms. D. may lessen the water retention that swells brain tissue and brings on pain. She may have a tendency toward hypoglycemia, and lowering her sugar consumption will regulate her blood sugar level and eliminate a hypoglycemic headache.

Not every headache is due to water retention, hypoglycemia, or stress, however, and her condition should be evaluated carefully by her doctor. Is she normally subject to migraines? Does she suffer from sinus trouble? On occasion, I have seen women experience severe and unpredictable migraine attacks in the second and third trimesters. An antimigraine medication that contains ergotamine should be avoided during pregnancy, since it may bring on contractions that may lead to miscarriage or premature delivery. Now and then, a Tylenol (acetaminophen) tablet or capsule, however, is reasonably safe.

Most doctors prefer to recommend Tylenol to their pregnant patients, since a minimal dose of this over-the-counter analgesic has not been found to cause debilitating side effects or congenital malformations. If Ms. D. continues to suffer, she may be helped by Tylenol. Her doctor should be consulted for his approval, though, since he knows her health history. At any rate, Ms. D. should never just reach for an aspirin. Aspirin may be harmful, especially in large amounts (more than twenty-five aspirin tablets a week) during late pregnancy. Aspirin may alter the clotting capacity of maternal and fetal blood by preventing the coagulating capability of platelets, the cellular bodies that internally repair blood vessels. As a result, a new mother may suffer excessive bleeding before and after delivery, and a newborn may be at risk of fetal hemorrhage. Considering that prostaglandins, contraction-causing substances in the body, are also inhibited by aspirin, large doses of aspirin may delay and prolong labor. Researchers have also found that aspirin may be responsible for the premature closing or narrowing of the *ductus arteriosus*, the blood vessel that carries fetal blood from the right to left side of the heart. This vessel should remain open until after birth, and its early closure may lead to stillbirth. I recommend that my patients stay away from aspirin throughout their pregnancies.

During the first trimester, when an unborn's vital organs are rapidly forming, an expectant mother should avoid all drugs. Later on, an occasional Tylenol should be safe for headache relief. Newer medications—Nuprin and Advil (both ibuprofen), nonprescription analgesics—may also be safe, but they, like aspirin, are prostaglandin inhibitors and if taken in high doses may delay or prolong labor. They may also result in the premature closing of the ductus arteriosus.

You should always consult with your obstetrician before you even open a drug-containing bottle. The inserts included in nonprescription drug packages usually carry warnings for pregnant women, but it is certainly best to check with your doctor. He is living through your pregnancy with you, and he will know what is safe.

My Hay Fever Is Worse Now That I'm Pregnant. Is There a Safe Antihistamine?

I've had allergies all my life, and I suffer especially during hay fever season at the end of the summer. It's that time of year right now, and my pregnancy seems to make my itchy eyes and runny nose worse than ever. I don't think I can get through too many more days without medication, but I'm worried about the baby. Is there a safe antihistamine?

C.S.
Walla Walla, Washington

A runny nose, postnasal drip, and congestion—normal signs of a cold or an allergy—are common during pregnancy. Ms. S. may have a bad bout of hay fever, but she may also be experiencing the cold that seems to come and go as her baby grows. Considering that nasal stuffiness is so frequent during the trimesters, it is surprising that more extensive research has not been conducted on the effects of antihistamines.

So far, we do know that Dimetane and Dimetapp, which contain brompheniramine, and Triaminic (phenylpropanolamine hydrochloride, pheniramine maleate, pyrilamine maleate) should not be prescribed during pregnancy because they have been linked to fetal malformations. Benadryl (diphenhydramine), when taken in the first trimester has been connected to an increased risk of cleft palate but is considered safe in the second and third trimesters. Actifed (triprolidine hydrochloride and pseudophedrine hydrochloride) has not been tested sufficiently for safety and should probably not be used during pregnancy. Other antihistamines requiring further testing are: Optimine (azatadine maleate), Sudafed (pseudophedrine hydrochloride), and Co-Pyronil (pyrrobutamine and cyclopentamine).

No evidence has traced congenital defects to Chlor-Trimeton, Histaspan, and Teldrin, (chlorpheniramine maleate) or PBZ (tripelennamine), but these antihistamines should be used cautiously, since researchers say that there are many variables in studies and more extensive investigations are needed.

If Ms. S. can withstand the onslaught of the hay fever season without medication, she will be making the safest choice for her future newborn. The safety of antihistamines in tablets, capsules, liquids, and nose sprays is still rather dubious, and even after childbirth, during breast-feeding, some of these drugs may inhibit lactation, and if they enter the breast milk, an infant may react very sensitively to them.

Is There a Safe Antibiotic?

I have a tendency toward recurring bronchitis and I usually take penicillin. Now that I'm pregnant, I wonder if it is safe for me to continue

*taking this drug, and I'm also concerned about what happens if I get
sick in some other way. Is there a safe antibiotic for a pregnant woman
to use?*

Y.T.
Duluth, Minnesota

Antibiotics are medically grouped according to the bacteria they
combat. A number of antibiotics are safe to use during pregnancy,
but others should be avoided. Here is how a wide range of antibiotics are currently regarded:

Penicillins (ampicillin, amoxicillin, carbenicillin, dicloxacillin,
cloxacillin, methicillin, nafcillin, oxacillin, Penicillin G, Penicillin
V: *Natural and synthetic penicillins are the safest antibiotics to
take during pregnancy*. Penicillin, in fact, is the antibiotic used to
prevent infection during fertilization of a test tube baby. Although
penicillin compounds do cross the placenta, there appear to be no
harmful effects to the fetus. Ms. T. may continue to take penicillin
for her bronchitis. If a woman has allergic reactions to penicillin,
however, she will still be susceptible during pregnancy, and she
should tell her doctor about her sensitivity.

Erythromycin: If you are allergic to penicillin, erythromycin
may be prescribed instead. This antibiotic crosses the placenta at
low levels and, like penicillin, has not been shown to harm the
fetus. Erythromycin should be avoided by women who have a history of liver disease, but for otherwise healthy pregnant women,
the drug is safely prescribed.

Cephalosporins (Ancef, Kefzol, Anspor, Keflex, Keflin, Velosef,
Mefoxin, Ultracef, Duricef, Cefadyl, Ceclor): The cephalosporins
fight both staphylococcal and streptococcal infections. Illnesses as
diverse as strep throat and pelvic inflammatory disease (PID) may
be treated with cephalosporins. So far, animal studies have not revealed harmful fetal effects from this group of antibiotics, even
though they do cross the placenta. Before recommending cephalosporins, penicillin, a cheaper and safer drug, should be the first
line of treatment.

Aminoglycosides (Amikin, Garamycin, Kantrex, Nebcin, Streptomycin): If you are suffering from tuberculosis, peritonitis, or
any infectious abscesses, you may be injected or treated intravenously with one of the aminoglycosides. Streptomycin and Kantrex

especially should be avoided in the first trimester, and a course of medication should never exceed 20 grams during pregnancy, since these two aminoglycosides have been associated with auditory nerve damage and deafness in newborns. The other aminoglycosides, which also cross the placenta, have not been linked with any birth defects, but for safety's sake, doses should be kept to a minimum. When an expectant mother is seriously ill and can only be helped by aminoglycosides, then there is no question that she should be treated. In comparison, the risk to the fetus is small and the benefit to the mother, great.

Tetracyclines (Panmycin, Terramycin, Vibramycin, Declomycin, Minocin, Sumycin): These popularly prescribed drugs are *not recommended* during pregnancy, especially not in the second and third trimesters. Tetracyclines rapidly cross the placenta and find their way into developing bones and teeth. Reaching the fetus in the second and third trimesters, tetracyclines may slow bone growth and permanently discolor teeth. If you took a tetracycline before you knew you were pregnant, however, do not become alarmed. For serious damage to be done, you would have had to consume large amounts of the antibiotic over a long period of time.

Sulfonamides (Gantanol, Gantrisin, Thiosulfil Forte, Azo Gantrisin, Azo Gantanol, Bactrim, Septra): Bactrim and Septra are sulfonamides combined with the drug trimethoprim, which has been linked to an increased incidence of cleft palate and fetal death. *Bactrim and Septra should not be taken during pregnancy.*

Azo Gantrisin and Azo Gantanol are sulfonamides combined with Pyridium (phenazopyridine hydrochloride), which creates reddish orange urine. The sulfonamides are most frequently prescribed to relieve urinary tract infections, but they should only be recommended in the first and second trimesters. In the last three months, these antibiotics may lead to jaundice in a newborn baby. A nursing mother should also avoid sulfonamides, since her infant will continue to be susceptible to jaundice as it receives the drug in breast milk.

Since new antibiotics are routinely produced by pharmaceutical companies, it is impossible to offer a comprehensive listing of every drug that is used to fight infection. Consult with your doctor, and trust that he will have the latest information about any antibiotic he is prescribing for you.

I Take Dilantin to Prevent Convulsions. What Does a Woman Like Me, Who Is Not Completely Healthy, Do During Pregnancy?

A few years ago, I was in a car accident, suffered a concussion, and became a victim of seizure disorder. I'm in the care of a neurologist and I regularly take Dilantin to prevent seizure. What's going to happen now that I'm pregnant?

S.S.
Clarksville, Tennessee

If you suffer from epilepsy or seizure disorder similar to Ms. S.'s, you may be taking phenobarbital, Dilantin, Mysoline, or Tegretol. A woman who suffers from epilepsy has a 90 percent chance of giving birth to a normal baby, but anticonvulsant medications do cross the placenta and increase her risk of delivering a child with congenital malformation. Anticonvulsants, if possible, should be avoided during pregnancy, but the options must be weighed. The onset of a seizure is dangerous to a fetus. Phenobarbital, an older drug with a better safety history than the newer medications, is preferred by most obstetricians who care for women with seizure disorders. Ms. S. should tell her obstetrician immediately that she is on Dilantin. He will then consult with her neurologist to determine whether she may be placed on the safer phenobarbital for the course of her pregnancy. Phenobarbital should lessen any potential teratogenic effects that may be attributed to seizure medication.

May I Keep Taking Inderal?

I have high blood pressure and have been on Inderal for a long time. What effect will all these years of medication have on my pregnancy?
F.P.
Pineville, Pennsylvania

It is usually best to stop taking Inderal at least six to eight weeks before conception, so the drug can be eliminated from your body. Now that you are pregnant, your doctor may suggest that you switch to another medication. Inderal (propranolol) is a beta-blocker that has been associated with growth retardation in the fetus, hypoglycemia and breathing difficulty in the newborn.

Many doctors are reluctant to prescribe Inderal during pregnancy, although it may be safe in limited use.

Aldomet (methyldopa) is the preferred antihypertensive drug for expectant mothers, since it has been tested and found to be safe during pregnancy. If it is taken for more than six months, however, a woman may notice some adverse side effects, such as headache, dizziness, and mild depression, so its use should be carefully monitored.

I would advise Ms. P. to avoid all drugs containing *reserpine*, which has been linked to severe, and possibly fatal, breathing problems in the fetus. Sandril, Serpasil, Raurine, Regroton, Diupres, Unipres, and Harmonyl are a few reserpine-containing drugs. Another drug, Apresoline (hydralazine), which was once thought to be safe, has recently been found to be teratogenic in mice, and this medication should also be avoided.

I Took Diet Pills Before I Knew I Was Pregnant. Have I Harmed My Baby?

For about a month before I knew I was pregnant, I was taking diet pills to lose weight. I didn't get them from my doctor; they were the over-the-counter kind. Have I hurt my baby?

A.E.

Appleton, Wisconsin

You were not taking diet pills for a long time, and you appear to have stopped as soon as you learned you were pregnant, so no harm should come to your baby. Most malformations in the fetus occur between the fifth and tenth weeks of gestation, when cell division and fetal development are rapid.

Women who are searching for methods of weight control are often prescribed appetite suppressants that contain *amphetamines*, such as benzedrine, biphetamine, and dexedrine. These "uppers" should not be taken during pregnancy, since animal studies show that they may lead to cleft palate and heart defects in the fetus. In the rare case of chronic narcolepsy, an amphetamine may be prescribed during pregnancy, but otherwise, there should be no reason for an amphetamine to be recommended. This is a time not for cutting down on calories but for eating a hearty, well-balanced diet to nourish you and your unborn baby.

IS THERE ANYTHING TO RELIEVE MORNING SICKNESS?

Many women have written to ask about relief from morning sickness. There is really no surefire way to eliminate the nausea that arises in early pregnancy, but, as explained in Chapter 6, if you do begin to suffer, two prenatal vitamins, with supplementary vitamin-B complex and B_6, may help alleviate the symptoms. Bendectin, a drug that is now off the market, was once prescribed for morning sickness when women became violently ill. Although no studies were able to prove directly that Bendectin was harmful to the fetus, it was considered too controversial to continue manufacturing.

In a severe situation, when a woman cannot eat and is vomiting so much that the acidity is increasing in her body, a doctor may recommend medications such as Compazine (prochlorperazine) or Tigan (trimethobenzamine). Both these antinausea drugs, which have been used for many years, appear to be safe for the fetus. (See Chapter 6 for daily tips on how to combat morning sickness without medication.)

May I Take a Tranquilizer Now and Then Just to Help Me

I've been so nervous about having this baby that my insomnia has returned. The other day I found a few Valiums I had left over from an old prescription. Would it be all right if I took a Valium now and then, just to help me sleep?

C.N.
Flagstaff, Arizona

The effect of tranquilizers on the fetus has long been the subject of controversy. In a study done more than a decade ago, the tranquilizers Miltown (meprobamate) and Librium (chlordiazepoxide) were reported to cause birth defects, but a follow-up study then rescinded the findings. For years, tranquilizers were prescribed without concern, but then in the mid-seventies, when the safety of drugs during pregnancy became an issue, tranquilizers were more carefully scrutinized. Their safety has never been positively confirmed, and so many questions keep recurring that it is best to avoid them during pregnancy.

Valium (diazepam), which Ms. N. is contemplating taking, has probably been evaluated more than any other tranquilizer. Years ago, a doctor would not find any warning for Valium in the *PDR* (*Physicians' Desk Reference*), a volume that describes all prescription drugs. Eventually, however, Valium became associated with the occasional trouble a newborn had in regaining its body temperature after a birth in which the drug was administered. Animal studies also implicated Valium, other tranquilizers, and barbiturates in the development of cleft palate. The news about Valium was not good, but recent studies have shown that it may not be as harmful as the initial investigators made it seem.

One researcher has reported that 121 different insults, including poor nutrition, environmental toxins, age of expectant mother, and even stress may lead to cleft palate—Valium cannot be singled out of all these variables. In 1983, a study jointly conducted by researchers from Boston University School of Medicine, Harvard Medical School, and Tufts University School of Medicine, published in the prestigious *New England Journal of Medicine*, concluded that exposure to Valium did not materially affect the risk of cleft lip with or without cleft palate or of cleft palate alone. However, the controversy itself makes Valium too risky to be prescribed, and there is always a question of what happens when one tranquilizer is combined with another, or with a barbiturate. I would advise Ms. N. to throw away her pills.

Tryptophan, an essential amino acid available in capsules, 500 milligrams taken before she goes to bed, may help her to sleep at night. Sometimes phenobarbital, in doses of 30 milligrams taken three or four times a day, can relieve nervous symptoms and bring on sleep. If Ms. N. thinks phenobarbital may help her, she should consult her doctor about her health history and whether he would consider this drug appropriate. The safest choice, of course, is to choose to stay away from medication.

I Got Pregnant on the Pill. Can This Hurt the Baby?

I am one of those rare cases doctors cite when they say that the Pill is not 100 percent effective. I became pregnant while taking oral contraceptives. I guess I must have taken two weeks' worth between conception and my pregnancy test, and now I'm worried. I remember the DES scare of the past, and I'm concerned that exposure to the hormones in the Pill may cause birth defects in my baby.

R.D.

Torrance, California

You have probably been on the new low-dose birth control pill, and since you have only taken it for a short time at the onset of pregnancy, the chance that anything will happen to the fetus is slim. Problems are not likely to occur if you stop taking the Pill before the seventh week of gestation. The risky period is from the seventh week on, when the Pill's hormonal contents may affect the formation of the female genitals, should you be carrying a girl.

We now know that the female hormone estrogen, in synthetic or natural forms, and synthetic progestins lead to fetal abnormalities during pregnancy. DES (diethylstilbestrol) was a synthetic estrogen–based hormone given to pregnant women in the 1950s to prevent miscarriage. The practice of hormonally supporting a pregnancy, which was what the DES treatment was intended to do, ended with the DES scare. In 1966 and 1967, researchers discovered that a rare cancer, clear-cell adenocarcinoma, could be found in daughters of women who had taken DES. Over the years, the risk of developing this cancer has turned out to be low—perhaps only one in ten thousand DES daughters—but still, both female and male offspring of mothers who took DES may have reproductive problems when they try to have their own children. DES is no longer prescribed during pregnancy, and we are all much wiser about the detrimental effects of estrogens and synthetic progestins.

Natural progesterone, however, may be prescribed when a woman has an inadequate luteal phase (the second half of the menstrual cycle), spotting at the beginning of pregnancy, or a history of miscarriage. Natural progesterone has not been shown to harm the fetus; in fact, it has been linked to a positive effect—a higher than average IQ among the children whose mothers took the hormone. The side effects for the mother, though, may include weight gain, occasional lethargy, and vaginitis. Use of the hormone stirs debate among doctors who are skeptical about administering hormones during pregnancy, but so far, it is the synthetic progestins that seem to put the fetus at risk.

WARNING: Do Not Take the Acne Medication Accutane

Accutane (isotretinoin), the wonder drug for severe cystic acne, makes the risk of having a birth-defective baby twenty-five times higher than normal—about the same as that of thalidomide. In a study of 154 drug-exposed mothers, there were 26 normal births, 21 malformed newborns, and the rest of the pregnancies ended in spontaneous or induced abortions.

Accutane was not designed to be taken during pregnancy, but some pregnant women have used the medication without realizing its danger and others have conceived without stopping treatment. If you are using Accutane, you should always be using birth control. A pregnancy test should be taken before a woman is exposed to Accutane, and she should use an effective form of contraception one month before, during, and one month after treatment with it. If you want to become pregnant, you must end your Accutane treatment one to two months before conception, to cleanse your body of the drug.

THE CONTROVERSY OVER THE ARTIFICIAL SWEETENER ASPARTAME

Aspartame (L-aspartyl-L-phenylalanine methyl ester) is better known as NutraSweet, the food additive, and Equal, the tabletop sweetener. It is an ingredient in a range of foods that includes cereals, puddings, and diet soft drinks from the Coca-Cola, Pepsi, and Seven-Up companies. Recently a controversy has erupted over the safety of aspartame, especially one of its components— the amino acid phenylalanine. Since aspartame raises the phenylalanine level in the blood, foods containing this sweetener now bear a warning for people who suffer from phenylketonuria, or PKU, and are unable to metabolize the amino acid.

Dr. Louis Elsas, director of the division of medical genetics at Emory University in Atlanta, has advised that pregnant women and infants under six months old stay away from aspartame because the phenylalanine may lead to brain damage in the fetus or baby. He is especially concerned about the unborn children of women who have the PKU gene, which he estimates is carried by about 2 percent of the population.

Dr. Richard J. Wurtman, director of the clinical research center at the Massachusetts Institute of Technology, reports that the effect of phenylalanine in the brain is doubled when aspartame and carbohydrates are combined. Since no one knows what a safe amount of phenylalanine is, he suggests that pregnant women should be among those who might consider themselves especially sensitive to its effects.

The Centers for Disease Control in Atlanta received six hundred complaints from people who said that they suffered dizziness, headaches, blurred vision, or grand mal seizures after consuming aspartame, and in 1985, a $2 million lawsuit was filed

211

against G.D. Searle & Co., the makers of NutraSweet, on behalf of a five-year-old boy in Maryland. Although the suit did not specify the amount, it charged that consumption of NutraSweet had caused irreversible brain damage.

Studies from Searle's research department and a review from the American Medical Association do not find aspartame to be hazardous to anyone but those who suffer from PKU and must control their phenylalanine intake. The FDA continues to approve the safety of aspartame, and the Centers for Disease Control, after interviewing complainants, reported that although certain individuals may have an unusual sensitivity to the product, the data did not show that aspartame caused serious, widespread, adverse health consequences. I suggest that the expectant mothers in my care stay away from diet sodas or drugs that contain aspartame.

IS THERE A CAFFEINE CONNECTION?

Since caffeine is so prevalent in foods, a woman may forget that it, too, is a drug. Coffee, tea, cola soft drinks, chocolate, cocoa, and a number of nonprescription drugs contain caffeine, which easily passes through the placenta and into the fetal bloodstream. During pregnancy, caffeine lasts twice as long in a woman's circulatory system, so an expectant mother who boosts her energy level with coffee is definitely stimulating her baby.

In the last decade, researchers concerned that there may be a connection between caffeine consumption and birth defects have conducted investigations on mice. The U.S. Food and Drug Administration oversaw tests in which mice were given as much as twelve to twenty-four cups of coffee a day. Birth defects discovered in the animals' offspring indicated a link to caffeine consumption, which was further supported by the low birth weight found among newborns of mice who only had two to four cups a day. Based on these findings, in 1980, the FDA warned pregnant women to limit caffeine consumption.

So far, it has not been proved that birth defects in humans can be caused by caffeine, and most people do not drink the large amounts of coffee administered to the mice. An extensive study in 1982, at Brigham and Women's Hospital in Boston, however, reported that women who drank more than four cups of coffee a day were more prone to having premature rupture of the membrane or a baby in a breech position.

Table 6.
What Has Caffeine?

Beverage/Food	Average Mg of Caffeine
Coffee (5 oz)	
Brewed, drip method	115
Brewed, percolator	80
Instant	65
Decaffeinated, instant	2
Tea (5 oz)	
Brewed, imported brands	60
Brewed, major US brands	40
Instant	30
Iced (12 oz)	70
Soft drinks (12 oz)	
TAB	46.8
Coca-Cola	45.6
Diet Coke	45.6
Dr. Pepper	39.6
Pepsi-Cola	38.4
Diet Pepsi	36
Mountain Dew	54
Cocoa (5 oz)	4
Milk chocolate (1 oz)	5–10
Bittersweet chocolate (1 oz)	20–30
Chocolate cake (average slice)	20–30

All such averages are widely variable. For example, loose tea has more caffeine than do tea bags. Also, the dosage of caffeine per cup of tea increases an average 20 mg for every extra minute you brew it. Brewed coffee will have similar variations in caffeine content.

Nonprescription Drug	Mg Caffeine/1 Tablet
Weight control aids	100–200
Alertness tablets	100–200
Analgesic/pain relief products	30–65
Diuretics	100–200
Cold/allergy remedies	16–30

SOURCE: *FDA Consumer*, March 1984.

The caffeine connection is far from being called absolute, but the FDA continues to stand behind its warning, and physicians generally recommend that expectant mothers curtail their caffeine intake, especially during the first trimester, when the developing fetus is most vulnerable. Fortunately, in the beginning of pregnancy, many women lose their desire for coffee because it upsets the stomach. If you do crave the flavor of coffee while you're pregnant, you might choose a safer, water-processed decaffeinated brew. (See Table 6.)

Today the knowledge that is available about chemicals in both the environment and drugs can protect the unborn baby from harm. From the sixth to tenth weeks of pregnancy, fetal development is at a crucial stage. Vital organs and major biological systems are forming, and dangerous substances that pass through the placenta at this time may alter normal growth. These are the weeks to be most careful, and I know that informed expectant mothers are cautious. A recent survey showed that in early pregnancy, many women still take an average of four drugs, but such women often do not realize the potential harm that can come from these substances. Once alerted, every expectant mother should become a watchful woman.

The problems that can arise from exposure to chemicals usually come from *prolonged* exposure. If a woman mistakenly takes a pill early in pregnancy, the single error is not likely to lead to fetal damage. Do not fret about a solitary pill taken in haste, but try to correct your mistake by initiating a super-healthy regimen that will last until the end of pregnancy. A woman can assure herself that she is giving her baby the best start in life by avoiding all drugs and known environmental hazards, eating a well-balanced diet, and taking vitamins with iron. Her pure and healthy program will make her body a safe haven for her baby.

CHAPTER 10

Will My Baby Be Okay?

Every expectant mother wonders whether her baby will be all right. When a woman gives birth, the first question she asks about the baby is: "Is it okay?" The answer is usually: "She (or he) is beautiful!" Rarely is an unhealthy baby born, but concern is natural, and wise.

Although most infants are born perfectly healthy, a low 2 to 3 percent may have some type of birth defect, and another 4 to 5 percent may sustain a minor imperfection. If you and your husband have health histories free of genetic disorders and you are unaware of anyone in either of your families suffering from an inherited disease, your baby is not at high risk. But whether or not a risk exists, we can all feel comforted that modern technology and genetic counseling have broadened knowledge and created options.

The causes of birth defects are not always known, but many have been found. We know, for example, that expectant parents in certain ethnic groups are at high risk for specific genetic disorders. Jewish couples of Ashkenazi, or eastern European, descent may carry Tay-Sachs disease. Cooley's anemia, or thalassemia major, affects people of Mediterranean descent, and sickle cell disease is generally confined to the black and Hispanic populations. Blood tests can detect these and other diseases, just as amniocentesis can signal the presence of Down syndrome. Years ago, a pregnant woman over thirty-five lived with the worry that she might give birth to a Down-syndrome baby. Modern science has alleviated this concern. Even the birth defects that are brought on by environmental toxins or prenatal exposure to radiation have been more isolated by technology. With new screening and counseling methods becoming increasingly available, we are no longer in the dark about ways to protect our children.

UNDERSTANDING THE GENES

A female egg and a male sperm each contain twenty-three chromosomes, tiny chemical structures that are crucial to every cell in the human body. At conception, the egg and the sperm unite to form forty-six chromosomes, which arrange themselves in twenty-three pairs. You and your baby—and all human beings—have forty-six chromosomes in twenty-three pairs.

One pair of the chromosomes created by an egg and a sperm is responsible for the baby's sex. A normal egg always carries the X chromosome, but a sperm will carry either an X (female) or a Y (male) chromosome. A baby's sex is therefore determined by the father's sperm. If a sperm fertilizes an egg and the result is an XX pair of chromosomes, the baby will be a girl; if an XY union occurs, a boy will be born.

Everything in a newborn's physical makeup comes from the chromosomes, which hold within them many microscopic genes. Like the chromosomes, the genes also form pairs, with one gene in each pair coming from each parent. Working together, the genes are responsible for a person's sex, appearance, and growth. All inherited characteristics are housed within the genes, but the ones that predominate depend upon the individual pairings.

Genes can be dominant or recessive. The trait of a dominant gene will prevail whether the other gene in the pair is dominant or recessive. Only the linkage of two recessive genes will cause the appearance of a recessive trait. Blue eyes, for example, are in recessive genes, and both parents must carry the recessive gene for blue eyes to have a blue-eyed baby. A mother or a father may have brown eyes, or both parents may have brown eyes, but they may carry the recessive gene without knowing it.

Hundreds of thousands of genes are within every human cell, and time after time, they fall perfectly into place. There are occasions, though, when something goes wrong and a baby is born with a birth defect.

How Do Genetic Disorders Occur?

There are three reasons genetic disorders, which create birth defects, may occur:

1. Among the many genes that exist, a woman or a man may carry one or more defective genes that they don't know about. The chances of having a defective gene increases among people with genetic disorders already in their families. A "faulty" gene may be dominant, recessive, or linked to the X chromosome.
2. Chromosomes may have abnormal shapes or patterns.
3. A combination of genetic and environmental factors may cause what is called a multifactorial defect.

A *"faulty" gene*. When a parent has a single *dominant* abnormal gene, there is a fifty-fifty chance that the disorder it carries may be passed to a newborn. On occasion, an unborn baby has a dominant gene that abnormally changes on its own, but this is rare. Huntington's chorea, the disease that slowly degenerates the nervous system in adulthood, is a dominant genetic disorder.

A *recessive* genetic disorder can only appear in a child when both parents carry the same abnormal recessive gene. In this case, the odds are one in four for each child conceived that the disorder will appear. Chances are one in two that a child will be an unaffected carrier of the disorder, just as the parents are carriers. There are also one in four chances that a child will be normal and neither have the disease nor be a carrier. Cystic fibrosis, a disease that affects the lungs and sweat glands, is a recessive genetic disorder.

An *X-linked*, also called sex-linked, genetic disorder can be carried by a woman who appears perfectly healthy because her other dominant X chromosome cancels the effects of the defective one. If this woman has a son, however, he has a 50 percent chance of inheriting the X-linked disorder. A daughter has a 50 percent chance of becoming a carrier like her mother. (There is also a 50 percent chance that both a son and daughter will be free of the X-linked disorder.) Hemophilia and certain types of muscular dystrophy are well-known X-linked disorders.

A chromosomal abnormality. A chromosomal abnormality is usually caused by an imperfect egg or sperm. A baby may have broken chromosomes or, perhaps, too many chromosomes and be born with physical handicaps as well as mental retardation. The likelihood that a chromosomal abnormality will occur increases with age. Down syndrome, which results from chromosomal abnormality, appears in 1 out of every 385 children born to thirty-five-year-old women. When a woman becomes pregnant at age forty, the chance that her baby will have Down syndrome increases to about 1 in 100, and if she waits longer to conceive, her risk grows. Fortunately today's older expectant mother may take advantage of amniocentesis and through the analysis of her amniotic fluid be informed about whether Down syndrome is present.

A multifactorial defect. Scientific researchers are continually learning about birth defects that are associated with outside forces, such as a virus, a drug, or a pollutant. Cleft lip, cleft palate, heart defects, and clubfoot are often traced to chromosomal abnormality from an external influence, either a drug or an environmental agent. This may be the one cause of birth defects that can be avoided, if a woman becomes aware of her exposure to hazardous substances.

WHEN THE GENES AND CHROMOSOMES ARE FINE: WILL THE BABY LOOK LIKE YOU?

The sex of your child is determined by the sex chromosomes carried in the father's sperm. A baby is conceived with twenty-two matching pairs of autosomal chromosomes plus one set of sex chromosomes—XX for a girl and XY for a boy. The conceiving sperm brings with it that crucial X or Y chromosome that creates a girl or a boy. Who will this daughter or son look like? Facial features, height, and body build will depend upon the inherited genes within the chromosomes.

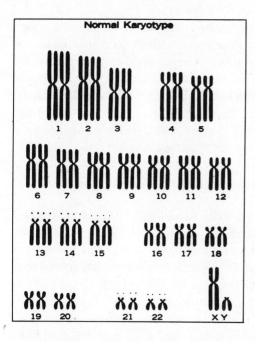

Figure 10-1. *Normal human chromosomes—forty-four autosomes and two sex chromosomes. When chromosomal analysis is performed, the chromosomes are always lined up in this manner. In this case, the sex chromosome (XY) indicates a normal male. If two X chromosomes had been seen, this would have been a normal female.*

One pair of genes is largely responsible for hair color, and another pair of genes creates the color of the eyes. Hair and eye coloring result from the way the dominant and recessive genes couple. For example, parents who have brown hair may each carry a hidden, recessive gene for blond hair, and their child may be a blond-haired baby. Only the hair and eye coloring come from single pairs of genes, whereas other features and traits arise from gene groupings.

Facial characteristics, such as the shape of the head and nose, and the jawline, are fashioned by a combination of genes contributed by both parents. One cluster of genes may make a child look more like one parent than the other, but that particular cluster only happens once. Another child from the same mother and father will be conceived with a different mixture of genes and look different.

Height will also spring from a combination of genes. Research has shown that the sons of tall men usually aren't quite as tall as their fathers, and the sons of short men usually aren't quite as short as their fathers.

That unseen trait, intelligence, is produced by an intermingling of genes and influenced by environment. Children of intelligent parents seem to have above-average IQs, and children of parents with below-average IQs are likely to be below average. Studies have revealed that the IQs of adopted children are closer to the IQs of their biological rather than their adoptive parents. Whatever the intelligence quotient of a child, she or he can be shown how to use brain power to the fullest. For example, musical talent, mathematical ability, and a fluency for language are inherited qualities that need nurturing. Genes may provide a basic intelligence, but a stimulating environment helps it flourish.

GENETIC COUNSELING: UNDERSTANDING YOUR OPTIONS

Elizabeth had grown up with a retarded sister, and she was afraid to have a baby. Her husband Bill wanted a child, but Elizabeth worried that she would pass on "bad" genes, that her sister's retardation might be in the family. Elizabeth's doctor suggested that she and Bill talk to a genetic counselor, who would be able to explain whether her fear was well founded.

Most large medical centers have established genetic counseling and testing centers for couples who feel they may be at risk of transmitting birth defects. (Your doctor should be aware of a trained genetic counselor in your area.) Elizabeth and Bill visited a counselor, who asked for the health histories of both of their families, including their own physical examinations and blood tests for chromosomal abnormality, and an analysis of Elizabeth's sister's chromosomes.

The genetic counselor evaluated the records and was able to assure Elizabeth and Bill that they had good chances of conceiving a perfectly healthy baby. The retardation in Elizabeth's sister was not due to defects in her chromosomes. The handicap may have been caused by exposure to environmental toxins, drugs, or an infection, such as rubella, during her mother's pregnancy.

Genetic counseling is now allowing couples who were afraid to have children to give birth to beautiful babies. Others who are counseled are able to prevent future babies from being born with tragic disabilities. Couples seek genetic counseling for various reasons. They might want to know whether they have or are carriers of a genetic disorder; whether having had one birth-defective child, they might conceive another; if the woman is over thirty-five, whether fetal chromosomes are normal.

With new staining techniques, chromosomes drawn from blood or amniotic fluid can be scrutinized carefully for differences. Each person has chromosomes that band together in a unique pattern. Under a microscope, modern staining makes alterations in the pattern visible. Down syndrome, for example, is seen as an extra chromosome in the twenty-first pair. Over three thousand genetic diseases have been identified, but not every disease can be detected prenatally. Fortunately, healthy genes usually overpower unhealthy ones.

Most couples are relieved after a visit to a genetic counselor, but sometimes both a wife and her husband are found to be carriers of a genetic disorder. Then the counselor is there to help them sort through their options, which may include adoption, sterilization, artificial insemination, or diagnosis during pregnancy.

TESTS FOR GENETIC DISORDERS

Before Pregnancy

Today tests that can accurately detect carriers of certain genetic disorders are available. If a woman or man suspects that either or both of them might be carrying a specific genetic condition, they may be tested before they try to conceive a child. Blood tests exist for finding the recessive-gene disorders Tay-Sachs, sickle-cell disease, and thalassemia in couples who are thinking about starting their families. (As yet, there is no screening for cystic fibrosis.) If a chromosomal abnormality is discovered, a couple may choose to go ahead with conception and to rely on testing during pregnancy to tell them whether the baby is affected.

During Pregnancy

Amniocentesis has been a remarkable breakthrough for genetic testing. Performed between the sixteenth and eighteenth weeks of gestation, the procedure involves inserting a slim, hollow needle through the abdomen into the womb, and withdrawing a small amount of amniotic fluid (the "water" in the sac surrounding the fetus) for testing. A local anesthesia is administered. To ensure that the placenta will not be punctured and the fetus harmed, ultrasonography (the picture of a fetus created by ultrahigh-frequency sound waves) is performed before the needle is inserted.

The cells within the amniotic fluid are analyzed for any possible chromosomal abnormality. A extra chromosome on the twenty-first pair of chromosomes (trisomy-21), for example, would signal Down syndrome. At present, amniocentesis can detect a total of three hundred chromosomal conditions and about sixty hereditary defects of biochemical origin, if specific analyses for biochemically inherited diseases are carried out. The test is recommended for expectant mothers who are thirty-five or older, because older mothers—and fathers—are statistically at higher risk of conceiving a child with chromosomal defects. Although amniocentesis slightly increases the chance of miscarriage, its benefits are far greater than the small 1 percent possibility of complication.

Women who are Rh negative should receive an injection of Rhogam after an amniocentesis, since a small amount of fetal blood may reach the maternal bloodstream due to the procedure. Then antibodies may form that could eventually destroy the baby's cells. (See Why Is the Rh Factor So Important? in this chapter.)

One of the significant tests of the amniotic fluid is for the level of alpha-fetoprotein (AFP), a protein produced by the fetus as it grows. A certain amount is a sign of healthy development, but if the AFP is higher than normal, a multiple birth, a miscarriage, or a neural-tube defect in the fetus may occur. Neural-tube defects result from the improper development of the brain and the spinal cord. Two neural tube defects are anencephaly, a missing brain, and spina bifida, an opening in the spinal column.

Under special circumstances, an expectant mother who is not planning to have an amniocentesis may request a *blood test for alpha fetoprotein*. If a neural-tube defect is in her or her husband's health history, or if she has previously given birth to an affected baby, a blood sample taken in the sixteenth week of gestation may be analyzed for its AFP content. A high amount of AFP would lead to a second test. If the second blood test confirms the first, then an ultrasound examination would follow. Using the ultrasound technique, a multiple pregnancy or a visible neural-tube defect such as anencephaly might be viewed, and would account for the high AFP. In the event that an ultrasound does not reveal a reason for AFP elevation, an amniocentesis would be performed. A very high amount of AFP in amniotic fluid is almost always due to spina bifida, because AFP-containing fluid leaks through the opening in the fetal spine, which gives the disorder its name. A couple should seek genetic counseling if the amniocentesis indicates high AFP. They may want to discuss pregnancy interruption or special care for their future newborn.

As time goes on, other tests may be used to detect genetic disorders during pregnancy. One procedure that is drawing enthusiasm from doctors is the *chorionic biopsy*. With the exception of neural-tube defects, chorionic biopsy can find the same chromosomal and biochemical abnormalities that amniocentesis does. During a chorionic biopsy, an ultrasound image is required to help the doctor guide a soft, thin tube through the cervix, the mouth of the womb, to the chorionic villi (tissue from the *fetal side* of the placenta). A sample of the tissue is aspirated, cultured, and analyzed. The laboratory results arrive much faster with a chorionic biopsy than with an amniocentesis—from twenty-four hours to one to three weeks, depending on the laboratory, as opposed to from three to four weeks for amniocentesis results. A chorionic biopsy can be performed from the sixth to tenth weeks of gestation, which is much earlier than the sixteenth to eighteenth weeks, when an amniocentesis can be done. The future looks hopeful for the still-experimental chorionic biopsy, but as with all new ventures, we will wait to see whether it ever replaces amniocentesis.

Chorionic biopsy is not without its drawbacks. The chance of miscarriage is 15 to 30 percent with this procedure, and if tissue is mistakenly removed from the *maternal side* of the placenta, the analysis will be of the mother's rather than the unborn's chromosomes. An error-free chorionic biopsy means that no miscarriage occurs. If a woman learns that she is carrying a healthy boy, there is no doubt that the tissue sample was taken from the correct side of the placenta. If she is told that she is carrying a girl, she can never be sure whether the tissue sample was from her or her future daughter's side of the placenta.

Fetoscopy, a delicate procedure that has been attempted in the last nine or ten years, requires great skill and precision. With the aid of ultrasound, a specialized physician directs a fetoscope, a slim, periscopelike instrument, through a small abdominal incision, beyond the abdominal wall and into the amniotic sac. An expectant mother is given painkillers and tranquilizers during a fetoscopy, but she does not need general anesthesia. More birth defects can be detected with this procedure than with other techniques.

A doctor can look through the fetoscope and see whether the face, head, fingers, toes, major joints, and different areas of the fetal spine are normal. The fetoscope is also a tool for taking blood and tissue samples from the fetus. A geneticist can analyze the blood sample for certain hemoglobin disorders, including sickle cell anemia, beta thalassemia, hemophilia, and disorders of the white blood cells and the serum proteins. Tissue culture can reveal the level of drugs and other teratogens in the fetal environment.

A concern about fetoscopy centers on the 5 to 10 percent increase in miscarriage that is associated with the technique. This risk is falling as the procedure is being perfected, and fetoscopy, in a safer stage, may eventually expand prenatal diagnosis of crippling blood disease and severe birth defects.

After Birth

Do not become alarmed if you learn that your newborn is being tested for certain genetic disorders. Blood samples of infants are routinely tested for disorders such as phenylketonuria (PKU) and hypothyroidism. When they are detected and treated early, these diseases can be prevented from causing serious disabilities, so newborns are usually screened.

QUESTIONS ABOUT GENETIC DISORDERS

The question "Will my baby be okay?" is always asked by expectant mothers, and, of course, most babies are perfectly healthy at birth. Yet with the availability of tests for genetic disorders, every woman has the opportunity to ease her mind before and during pregnancy. Sometimes questions about specific disorders nag at couples who think the problems may be in their families, and these queries require thoughtful responses. The diseases most frequently at issue are explored in letters I have received from concerned expectant parents. These questioning letters and my responses are presented here so that all wondering couples may understand their options.

Will My Children Have Thalassemia?

My wife is what most people consider frail. She is thin and anemic, and gives the impression that a strong breeze could blow her away. I have always found her fragility attractive, but now we have learned that "thalassemia trait" is responsible for her anemia, and I'm worried. The doctor says that as long as she takes care of herself, she will remain healthy. We're really concerned about whether any children we may have will get the trait, or even the disease. We're consulting several

*doctors in an effort to compile all the information we can before we try
to have a baby.*

S.H.
Foxboro, Massachusetts

There are a number of different thalassemia disorders that produce anemia, a deficiency of the red blood cells. The most prevalent types affect hemoglobin, the oxygen-carrying protein in the
cells. With about 2500 people hospitalized for treatment annually,
thalassemia is one of the most common hereditary blood diseases.

The various thalassemias range from the very severe thalassemia major, or Cooley's anemia, to the barely noticeable thalassemia minor or minima. Thalassemia minor may not show up in
symptoms, but blood changes do occur. Thalassemia minima,
which has literally no effect on a person, may only appear on blood
tests or in genetic studies.

Ms. H. seems to be living with the trait for thalassemia minor,
which is a mild, controllable form of iron-deficiency anemia. A
person with severe thalassemia major, on the other hand, must
have frequent blood transfusions, and then may still die young.
Iron buildup in the heart and the other organs as a result of the
transfusions leads to heart failure.

Ms. H. has thalassemia trait, which she inherited. Thalassemia
is strictly a genetic condition. It is not contagious, and it is not one
of those diseases that surface later in life. Most of the people who
have thalassemia are of Italian, Greek, Middle Eastern, southern
Asian, or African ancestry. Perhaps Ms. H.'s heritage is among
these?

For a child to inherit the disease, both Mr. and Ms. H. would
have to be carriers of the thalassemia trait, which a blood test can
detect. If both future parents are carriers, then there is a 50 percent chance that their child will be a carrier, a 25 percent chance
that the baby will be normal, and a 25 percent chance that the
newborn will have the disease. (See chart.) Basically the odds are
the same for every recessive-gene disorder. If a child is a carrier of
thalassemia, she or he can lead a healthy life as long as a little
extra attention is devoted to nutrition. Daily supplements of folic
acid and iron are needed.

When Ms. H. does become pregnant, if her husband *is not* a
carrier, their baby has no chance of getting the disease itself, and
no further testing is needed. If her husband *is* a carrier, the baby

225

will have a 25 percent chance of inheriting thalassemia, and a doctor might recommend an amniocentesis or fetoscopy to rule out the presence of thalassemia in her unborn baby.

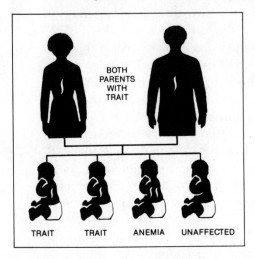

Figure 10-2. *If both parents have sickle cell trait, there is a 50-percent chance that their child will have sickle cell trait, a 25-percent chance that the child will have sickle cell anemia, and a 25-percent chance that the baby will be disease-free.* Reproduced by permission. March of Dimes, Genetic Series, "Sickle Cell Anemia."

I Have Sickle Cell Trait. Is My Baby Getting Bad Blood?

I was born with sickle cell trait, and doctors have always told me that I have nothing to worry about, that I am a healthy person. Now that I'm pregnant, though, I worry about whether the sickle cells in my blood will hurt my baby. Is my baby getting bad blood?

B.W.

Little Rock, Arkansas

Sickle cell anemia is an inherited blood disease that causes the normally round red blood cells to change into crescent or sickle shapes. These sickled cells are destroyed by the spleen, but then a shortage of red blood cells occurs. A person with sickle cell anemia, for which there is no cure, may suffer pain, shortness of breath, and fatigue. Vital organs may eventually become damaged; infections may arise, and life may end in childhood.

About 1 in every 400 to 600 blacks and 1 in every 1000 to 1500 Hispanics inherit sickle cell disease. One out of every 10 black Americans carries the gene. The disease also affects some people of Arabian, Greek, Maltese, Sicilian, Sardinian, Turkish, and southern Asian ancestry. Sickle cell anemia is not contagious; a person can only get it genetically.

The chance that Ms. W.'s baby will have sickle cell anemia depends upon whether her husband also carries the sickle cell gene. If he does, the odds of the baby having sickle cell anemia are one in four. (See Figure 10-2.) A blood test can indicate whether a person has the trait or the disease. During pregnancy, if both parents are carriers, a fetoscopy can determine whether the fetus bears the trait, has the disease, or is unaffected.

Ms. W.'s blood is not going to harm her baby, but she may have to take special care of herself due to her sickle cell trait. She may have an increased susceptibility to urinary tract infections and anemia. Her urine should be analyzed for signs of infection, and her blood count checked frequently. To safeguard her well-being, Ms. W. should drink cranberry juice, take extra folic acid and iron, eat a well-balanced diet, and get plenty of rest.

I'm Two Months Pregnant. Is It Too Late to Be Tested for Tay-Sachs?

My husband's father is Jewish. There is no Jewish heritage in my family and I completely forgot about being tested for Tay-Sachs. I'm two months pregnant. Is it too late?

E.H.
Westport, Connecticut

Tay-Sachs disease, a rare and tragic biochemical disorder, has fortunately been brought under control by prenatal testing. People of Jewish heritage have been especially aware of the disease since descendants of central and eastern European (Ashkenazi) Jews have been primarily affected. About 1 out of every 25 American Jews carries the Tay-Sachs gene, but members of any ethnic group are liable to have it too. The rate of occurrence is much lower in other groups, but it does exist.

Tay-Sachs strikes healthy-looking babies at approximately six months old. These children do not usually live beyond their fourth birthdays. A blood chemical, specifically hexosminidase, an enzyme that is essential for breaking down certain fatty deposits in brain and nerve cells, is missing in Tay-Sachs victims. Soon their cells become clogged (see Figure 10-3), and the entire nervous system collapses. A Tay-Sachs baby loses mobility, cannot reach out, and gradually becomes blind, paralyzed, and unaware of the world.

227

Figure 10-3. *An illustration of a normal brain cell and a Tay-Sachs brain cell with extra fat deposits that create the disease.* Reproduced by permission. March of Dimes, Genetic Series, "Tay-Sachs."

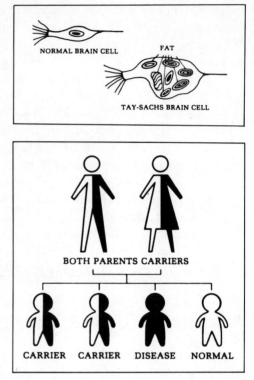

Figure 10-4. *A graphic illustration of the probability of transmitting Tay-Sachs disease to offspring. If both parents are carriers, there is a 50-percent chance that a child may become a carrier, a 25-percent chance that the child will have Tay-Sachs disease, and a 25-percent chance that the child will be completely normal.* Reproduced by permission. March of Dimes, Genetic Series, "Tay-Sachs."

This devastating disease can be detected through a blood test that measures hexosminidase. Tay-Sachs carriers have half as much of the chemical as do noncarriers, but they can still lead normal, healthy lives. All couples who fall into the high-risk ethnic groups should be tested for Tay-Sachs *before conception.* Later on, pregnancy hormones interfere with a screening. A test for Tay-Sachs is therefore considered inaccurate during gestation.

The chance of Ms. H. being a carrier is slim, and yes, it is too late for her to be tested. Her husband, however, should have a blood test, and if he is not a carrier, there is no problem. If he is a carrier, there probably will still not be a problem, because *both parents* must have the Tay-Sachs gene for the disease to appear. To find out whether Ms. H. is also a carrier, her doctor can order more extensive analysis of her blood. The chance is one out of four that the baby will be affected if both parents are carriers. A fetoscopy to aspirate fetal blood for analysis can eliminate worry. (See Figure 10-4.)

Should more questions about Tay-Sachs come to mind, a couple may write to the National Tay-Sachs and Allied Diseases Association, 922 Washington Avenue, Cedarhurst, New York 11516.

Do Potatoes Cause Spina Bifida?

You may think I am crazy, but a friend of mine told me not to eat potatoes during pregnancy because they cause spina bifida. Is there anything factual in what she is saying? Am I really to believe that potatoes are dangerous?

P.H.
High Point, North Carolina

Spina bifida is a neural-tube defect that affects the nervous system. Technically, an opening in the spinal column occurs and nerves protrude, causing a cyst or lump under the skin. A baby may be mildly or severely affected. The defect may not be discovered until later in life in a slight case, but in a severe instance, it may paralyze the lower body. Spina bifida may also be accompanied by hydrocephalus (water on the brain), due to spinal fluid collecting in and around the brain.

About one in two thousand babies are born with spina bifida every year, and it seems to be most prevalent among the Irish, Welsh, and English. Jewish families rarely experience spina bifida. What causes this defect? We don't know, but researchers theorize that genetics combine with some sort of unhealthy situation in the womb.

Ms. H.'s inquiry about potatoes is not as crazy as she may think. In 1972, a Dr. Renwich suggested that blighted potatoes might be a link to neural-tube defects. He could have been trying to find a common denominator among high risk people in the United Kingdom. Potatoes may have been prevalent in their diet. Current research has not found a connection between potato consumption in expectant mothers and spina bifida in their offspring, but facts about good nutrition have come to light.

Folic acid supplementation has recently been shown to be effective in curtailing the recurrence of babies born with spina bifida to mothers who had previously given birth to such children. I have always urged my patients to take vitamins and eat a well-balanced diet, and this news about folic acid's possible ability to inhibit spina bifida only confirms my belief in the value of good nutrition.

Prenatal tests—the blood test for measuring the level of alpha-fetoprotein, and amniocentesis—can detect spina bifida, but proper nutrition and a healthy environment may help lower the number of times the disorder ever shows up.

A BREAKTHROUGH IN UNDERSTANDING CYSTIC FIBROSIS

Researchers in the United States and Canada have recently discovered a genetic marker, a DNA segment, that will help them pinpoint the faulty gene responsible for cystic fibrosis. With this latest discovery, diagnosis of cystic fibrosis in early pregnancy will be possible in the future. Right now there is no routine prenatal test to detect cystic fibrosis. A complicated skin test can help people with cystic fibrosis in their families to learn whether they are carriers, but no general screening is available.

Cystic fibrosis alters the function of exocrine glands, and they then produce thick secretions that clog the lungs and block airways. Lung infections, coughs, colds, and pneumonia are frequent afflictions for a person with cystic fibrosis. The pancreas and digestive system are also affected. A baby with cystic fibrosis can survive childhood but will probably not live beyond the twenties. The current breakthrough, however, holds hope for detecting and eventually curing this disorder.

I Am 34 Years Old. Do I Need an Amniocentesis for Down Syndrome?

I am thirty-four years old and I have just learned that I am pregnant. I will be thirty-five by the time the baby is born and I wonder if I will need an amniocentesis. They say that if you are thirty-five or over, you should have the test, but I am right on the borderline. I don't want to have a baby with Down syndrome. What is your advice?

N.M.

Stillwater, Oklahoma

Down syndrome comes from a chromosomal abnormality. In a normal conception, the sperm and the egg each contribute twenty-three chromosomes, but when a baby with Down syndrome is conceived, either the sperm or the egg usually brings one

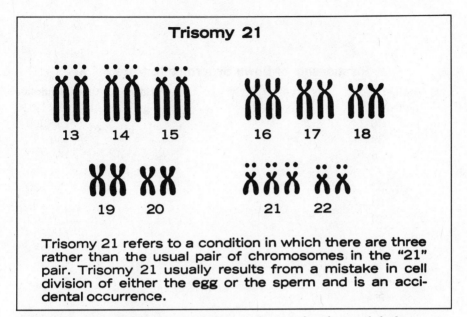

Trisomy 21 refers to a condition in which there are three rather than the usual pair of chromosomes in the "21" pair. Trisomy 21 usually results from a mistake in cell division of either the egg or the sperm and is an accidental occurrence.

Figure 10-5. *This chromosomal analysis indicates the abnormal findings associated with Down syndrome. (Trisomy 21)*

extra chromosome. That extra chromosome, which signals Down syndrome, appears on the twenty-first pair of chromosomes and is called Trisomy 21. This chromosomal abnormality can be seen in a laboratory analysis of the amniotic fluid drawn during amniocentesis. (See Tests for Genetic Disorders in this chapter.)

If Trisomy 21 appears, a woman may choose either to interrupt her pregnancy or to continue with the knowledge that her baby will be born with Down syndrome. A child with Down syndrome usually has distinct features—almond-shape eyes, a dropping tongue, a short neck, a head that may be flat in the back. She or he remains short in stature and appears to be physically flexible throughout life. Mental deficiency also accompanies Down syndrome, but great strides have been made in improving the life condition of an afflicted person. With education and a good home environment, Down syndrome children are developing more skills today than ever before.

The likelihood of having a baby with Down syndrome is less than 1 in 1000 for expectant mothers under thirty. (See Table 7.) After age thirty, the incidence begins to increase and grows to 1 in 400 at age thirty-five. The dramatic jump in risk has given physicians reason to set age thirty-five as a cutoff point. Also, years ago,

Table 7.

Relationship of Down Syndrome to Maternal Age

Mother's Age	Incidence of Down Syndrome
under 30	less than 1 in 1,000
30	1 in 900
35	1 in 400
36	1 in 300
37	1 in 230
38	1 in 180
39	1 in 135
40	1 in 105
42	1 in 60
44	1 in 35
46	1 in 20
48	1 in 12

SOURCE: *National Institute of Child Health and Human Development, 1984.*

one woman who was not told by her doctor about the change in risk at age thirty-five was not offered an amniocentesis, gave birth to a baby with Down syndrome, and sued her doctor. This suit only emphasized the fact that thirty-five is the age at which a woman should be given the opportunity to have an amniocentesis. It is, of course, up to you and your mate to decide whether you want an amniocentesis. If religious or personal beliefs would lead you to choose against pregnancy termination even with a diagnosed fetal abnormality, then there is no reason to expose your unborn baby to the risk of the test.

Ms. M. writes that she will be thirty-five by the time the baby is born. Usually doctors recommend that if you are going to give birth by age thirty-five, you should have an amniocentesis. Since Ms. M. has already stated that she is concerned about Down syndrome, the procedure can alleviate her worry. If Ms. M.'s husband is ten or more years older than she is, the test becomes even more desired. Little is mentioned about the expectant father's age in relation to Down syndrome, but it is certainly a factor. The extra chromosome that creates Down syndrome may originate in the sperm as well as the egg, and a doctor should consider the age of both future parents when he advises a woman to have an amniocentesis.

What Good Is It to Know About Genetic Disorders I Cannot Control?

I have been reading about all the things that may happen to the baby I am going to have, and I'm fed up. What good does it do to know about genetic problems that I cannot control?

T.G.
Summit, New Jersey

Birth defects are rare, and most expectant mothers will have beautiful, healthy, normal babies. While no woman should dwell on genetic problems, which occur in statistically few cases, it is smart to be informed about testing for these disorders. Genetic counseling offers choices that were not available a decade ago.

Today we also know that a number of birth defects seem to be created by a combination of factors. Inheritance is a strong influence, but the food an expectant mother eats, the drugs she may take, and her living environment also touch her unborn baby. Disorders such as spina bifida, cleft lip, cleft palate, and clubfoot may be affected by a pregnant woman's life-style and health habits, in addition to heredity.

Every woman has some control over the child she will produce. By taking exceptionally good care of herself, eating well-balanced meals, and staying away from drugs, an expectant mother can offer her child-to-be the healthiest and best start in life.

OTHER HEALTH ISSUES

When it comes to thinking about whether her baby is okay, an expectant mother turns over many questions in her mind. Does she really understand the Rh factor? Can she be vaccinated during pregnancy? Is ultrasound safe? Such lingering questions are answered here.

Why Is the Rh Factor So Important?

I have Rh-positive blood, and my husband is Rh negative. I know that there is a problem if an expectant mother is Rh negative, but what happens when the father is the one with the Rh negative blood?

K.C.
Mount Kisco, New York

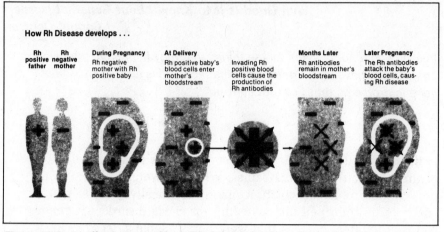

How Rh Disease develops . . .

Rh positive father	Rh negative mother	During Pregnancy	At Delivery		Months Later	Later Pregnancy
		Rh negative mother with Rh positive baby	Rh positive baby's blood cells enter mother's bloodstream	Invading Rh positive blood cells cause the production of Rh antibodies	Rh antibodies remain in mother's bloodstream	The Rh antibodies attack the baby's blood cells, causing Rh disease

Figure 10-6. *An illustration of how Rh disease develops.* Reproduced by permission of Ortho Diagnostic Systems Inc., Raritan, New Jersey.

The Rh factor is a substance found on the red blood cells of 85 percent of white people and 95 percent of the black population. A person who has the Rh factor is identified as Rh positive, and someone without the factor is Rh negative. (The "Rh" labeling is coined from the word *Rhesus.* Rhesus monkeys were used in laboratory studies of red blood cells.) The presence or absence of the Rh factor does not affect the health of a woman or a man at all. The Rh factor is only an issue during pregnancy, and then *only a woman who is Rh negative must be concerned.*

Ms. C. is Rh positive and her husband is Rh negative, so she will not have to deal with any problems involving the Rh factor. Complications may arise when the opposite combination exists— when an expectant mother is Rh negative and her husband bears a positive factor. An Rh-negative expectant mother whose partner is positive may have conceived an Rh-positive baby. The blood from the Rh-positive baby can occasionally enter the mother's bloodstream. Once the baby's blood combines with the mother's, her immune system treats the Rh factor as a foreign substance. Antibodies attack the Rh factor, which has never before appeared in her body. As a mother's antibodies increase, they may enter the baby's bloodstream, and there they can do great harm. The antibodies can kill the baby's red blood cells and cause Rh blood disease. The fetus may then suffer brain damage or prenatal death.

Usually in a first pregnancy, a woman's body does not build the amount of antibodies that would do serious damage to a fetus. But any antibodies that are ever created remain. If an Rh-negative woman had a previous pregnancy, whether full-term, ectopic, or shortened by an abortion or a miscarriage, fetal blood cells with the Rh factor might have found their way into her bloodstream, and antibodies may have formed. After amniocentesis, an Rh-negative woman should also receive an injection of Rhogam (Rh immune globulin), because the procedure may cause placental bleeding and subsequent development of antibodies. A transfusion with Rh-positive blood may also have caused some antibodies to form. To prevent Rh disease, an Rh-negative woman should receive a vaccination with Rhogam after any pregnancy, amniocentesis, or erroneous transfusion. (She should only be receiving her own blood type in a transfusion.) Rhogam prevents a woman's body from producing antibodies that could attack the positive Rh factor in a future unborn child.

An Rh-negative woman should receive an injection of Rhogam after each pregnancy if the baby is Rh positive. If she has not been immunized, she should have blood tests at regular intervals during pregnancy to see whether she is developing antibodies. A woman should be screened for antibodies at twenty-six, thirty-two, and thirty-six weeks of gestation. If no antibodies appear by the twenty-eighth week, it has now become standard practice to give an injection of Rhogam at that time. This injection prevents the spontaneous immunization that may occur in the last three months of pregnancy.

If antibodies do appear during a screening, she may need an amniocentesis to find out how severely the baby is affected. Sometimes an unborn baby can be given a blood transfusion in the womb. A newborn can also be transfused immediately with Rh-negative blood, and a mother may be given medication to induce an early delivery.

Rhogam has significantly reduced the incidence of Rh disease in newborns, but many women still do not know about the vaccine. Every woman should learn her blood type and Rh factor as she enters her first trimester. And remember, only a woman who has Rh-negative blood must be careful.

Can I Get a Rubella Vaccine Now That I'm Pregnant?

My mother said that she does not recall my ever having had German measles, and sure enough, my blood tests came back today, and I have no rubella antibodies. Can I be vaccinated now? I only found out that I was pregnant three weeks ago.

T.F.

Calumet City, Illinois

Rubella (German measles) used to be considered a mild condition, since it only lasts about three days and a person usually doesn't experience more than a skin rash and a slight fever. In 1964 and 1965, however, a rubella outbreak resulted in birth defects among more than twenty thousand babies whose mothers were exposed to the disease. To prevent such an epidemic again, a rubella vaccine was made available in 1969, and since then, all children, teenagers, and adults, especially women of childbearing age, have been urged to get the vaccine.

A simple blood test, which Ms. F. had, shows whether a person has rubella antibodies and is now immune to the disease. If a woman does not have rubella antibodies, she is susceptible. During pregnancy, if she catches the disease, her baby may be born deaf, blind, or with brain damage. A woman who wonders whether she has had rubella should have a blood test done, and if no rubella antibodies appear, she should be vaccinated at least three months before she conceives. The three-month wait is essential. A woman cannot be vaccinated against rubella while she is pregnant, because the injected live virus would produce an effect just as if she had caught the disease. Ms. F. must make an effort to stay away from anyone who might have rubella, especially during her first trimester, when the fetus is particularly vulnerable. Until childbirth, she should beware of large gatherings of people, especially family get-togethers filled with children.

A Word About Hepatitis During Pregnancy

The nausea, vomiting, and fatigue that accompany hepatitis may at first be considered normal signs of pregnancy. The jaundice that sets in may also be mistaken, so a woman who has these symptoms should undergo a battery of tests for diagnosis. If antibodies for hepatitis, which may be carried in the virus type A or B, appear in her blood test, her doctor will recommend that she continue her pregnancy in hospital isolation. Her body needs time to build more antibodies to combat the disease.

Hepatitis does not adversely affect pregnancy, but all newborns whose mothers have tested positive for the hepatitis B antibody should be given one dose of hepatitis B immune globulin at birth, with hepatitis B vaccine started soon afterward. Eighty to 90 percent of the time this treatment prevents a baby from becoming a carrier.

What Is a Low-Birth-Weight Baby?

I'm four months pregnant, and my doctor has told me that I'm not gaining enough weight. He says that I should eat more so that I don't have a low-birth-weight baby. As long as an infant is healthy, what's the difference how much it weighs?

E.V.
Stockton, California

A baby has a much better start on developing normally and living successfully if it is born at what doctors now consider an optimum weight—7½ pounds. A newborn who weights 5½ pounds or less is a "low-birth-weight baby."

There are two types of low-birth-weight babies: preterm and small-for-date. A *preterm* baby is born before the full 37 weeks of gestation have been completed. Such a baby usually weighs under 5½ pounds and is at risk for many complications. A *small-for-date* baby may be born at its due date but may still be low birth weight.

Ms. V. has misunderstood the issue of low birth weight. A baby who is very small is not a healthy baby. A low-birth-weight infant may not be able to breathe properly, and if the lungs do not function well, the blood supply and body tissues are not receiving enough oxygen. Other problems low-birth-weight babies face include hypoglycemia (low blood sugar); jaundice, which means the liver is not working properly; and anemia (low red-cell blood count). A low-birth-weight baby can be growth retarded and slow throughout life.

Perhaps Ms. V. is not eating a hearty, well-balanced diet, and she should heed her doctor's advice. A woman who eats nutritiously (see Chapter 5), takes vitamin supplements, and rests frequently is giving her baby a chance to grow to a healthy size. Also, if Ms. V. lies on her left side, she will be allowing a strong supply of blood to move to her heart and be pumped out again as clean, oxygenated blood with added nutrients. Resting on her right side, Ms. V. would be blocking the vena cava, the large vein that carries the blood from the legs to the heart. With a healthy regimen of good nutrition, rest, and a body free from drugs, she will have a robust baby.

Do I Have to Get Rid of My Cat?

My husband and I have had a beautiful Persian cat for the last seven years. We think of him as a member of the family. I am four weeks pregnant, however, and I have recently learned that cats can carry a virus called toxoplasmosis, which can cause birth defects. I don't want to give away my cat. What are my chances of catching this disease? Is it highly contagious?

R.C.
Arlington, Virginia

A cat that feeds on wild prey or raw meat may harbor toxoplasma, a parasite that settles in the intestines of cats, cattle, sheep, and pigs. Excreted in the feces of these animals, this parasite may travel to humans and cause toxoplasmosis, a disease similar to a mild flu. Most domestic cats only eat commercially packaged pet food and are not likely to spread toxoplasmosis. A woman who takes in a stray, however, risks exposing herself to the disease. (A woman who eats underdone red meat or pork is also risking infection.)

Toxoplasmosis is such a mild illness that a woman may have thought she was slightly under the weather, perhaps caught the flu for a day or two, when she actually had the disease. Although it hardly affects adults, toxoplasmosis can cause severe fetal damage. Blindness, deafness, and mental retardation may result.

A woman who has already had toxoplasmosis will carry antibodies for the disease in her blood. These antibodies can be measured in the titer level of a blood test. Ms. C. might ask her doctor to test her for toxoplasmosis, and if the lab report is positive, she has had the disease in the past. Her body has already fought off the virus. If the titer is very high, however, she might currently have the disease and she may need another blood test to determine whether her baby is being affected. If Ms. C. tests negative, she should be especially careful to eat properly cooked meat and to stay away from her cat's litter. Toxoplasmosis rarely afflicts pregnant women, but when it does, there is a 40 percent chance that it will reach the fetus. Ms. C. should be careful. She does not have to get rid of her pet, but her husband should take charge of the litter.

If she appears to get a viral flu during pregnancy, her doctor should take a second blood test. If the titer rises, she has caught the disease. A pregnant woman who becomes infected should speak to a genetic counselor, since her unborn baby may have been injured. Toxoplasmosis is so rare, though, that most blood tests show a low titer. A pet that has been in the family a long time is not likely to be infected. Strays are another matter. Pregnancy is not the time for adopting a lovable stray cat, even if you think it is irresistible.

I Have a History of Herpes. Will I Need a Cesarean?

I've heard that every woman who has had herpes has to have a cesarean section because if the baby passes through the birth canal, it will catch herpes and be born blind or die. Is this true? I'm not worried about the cesarean, but I am concerned about the danger my baby may be facing.

A.G.
Athens, Georgia

Estimates are that as many as 25 million Americans may suffer from sexually transmitted herpes, or, more specifically, the herpes simplex virus. There are two main kinds of this virus—type 1 (HSV-1) and type 2 (HSV-2)—and they each may appear in oral, genital, or anal areas. When a person becomes infected with the herpes virus for the first time, a fever, fatigue, and weakness may occur. It is usually HSV-2 that is transmitted to the genitals, and a woman who is experiencing an attack of genital herpes will feel an itch; then a blister or cluster of blisters will surface in or around her vagina. These tender, painful blisters will burst and become oozing sores. A vaginal discharge may also be produced by this onslaught of the virus, which will not subside for about three weeks. Once the sores have healed, the virus may remain dormant within the cells of the spinal column—dormant until emotional stress, illness, or menstruation weakens the immune system. Then the herpes virus may flare again, but subsequent attacks are usually not as severe.

Newborns do not have fully developed immune systems, and if they are exposed to an outbreak of herpes while passing through the birth canal, they may not survive. About 50 to 100 percent of the infants who are contaminated by the herpes virus die, and the ones who live may suffer severe handicaps, such as blindness and permanent damage to the nervous system. Safety precautions exist, however, to prevent such tragedy.

If Ms. G., or any other pregnant woman, has visible herpes sores when she is in labor, of course her baby should be delivered by cesarean section to avoid contact with the virus. Since Ms. G. has a history of herpes, her doctor should take periodic vaginal cultures to see whether the virus is alive in the birth canal. If Ms. G. has had negative cultures and no sores up until two to four weeks before she is due to deliver, she can have a vaginal childbirth. A cesarean is a must only if the vaginal culture is positive or if a fresh herpes sore is visible just prior to delivery.

After childbirth, Ms. G.'s baby will be observed in the newborn intensive care unit. If her baby shows any signs of infection, Zovirax (acyclovir) injections can be administered successfully. Zovirax, the new herpes medication, stops the spread of the virus.

ARE SONOGRAMS SAFE?

Every time a pregnant woman participates in a sonogram—a screen image created by ultrasound waves—she asks, "Is it safe?" "Yes," answer the researchers. Ultrasound technology was invented by a Scottish researcher in the 1960s and was initially used by the commercial fishing industry to spot schools of fish in the ocean's depth. The similarity between the fish in their watery environment and the fetus in its amniotic sac soon became obvious to medical researchers. They transformed ultrasound into a diagnostic tool. Originally used in obstetrics, ultrasound is now available for many diagnostic purposes.

During ultrasonography, an obstetrician moves a hand-held transducer over a woman's abdomen, and ultrasound waves travel to and from the womb through a cluster of quartz crystals. These ultrasound waves vibrate at an extremely high frequency, much too high pitched to be heard by the human ear. They form sonograms—reflections on a televisionlike screen—when they bounce off the surface of a nonmoving object.

Ultrasonography, which does not use radiation, has been continually researched for safety. No side effects have been found in human beings—adults or children—who were exposed prenatally. In one study, very high levels of diagnostic ultrasound, levels far more intense and powerful than those used during pregnancy, were found to produce mild cellular damage in laboratory animals. At the low levels and brief exposures used during pregnancy, ultrasound is considered quite safe. In the countless numbers of sonograms produced every day throughout the world, no abnormalities have ever been associated with the procedure. Long-term follow-up studies of patients exposed to ultrasound twenty years ago in Europe have consistently found the technique to be safe. An ongoing study in Canada, which has been in existence for nine years, has also failed to show any harmful effect. All this data have proved ultrasound to be one of the safest forms of diagnostic testing available to pregnant women.

Why Do Some People Say Ultrasound Is Dangerous?

Since I've become pregnant, my doctor has taken several sonograms of my baby. When I told a girlfriend of mine how thrilling it was to see the baby, she was horrified. She said that sonograms are dangerous, that they cause birth defects, and that I should stop having them. Is she right?

S.F.
El Paso, Texas

Ultrasonography is considered to be an important and *safe* diagnostic tool. Experts have found at least twenty-seven different ways in which ultrasound is helpful during pregnancy. The needs that are filled range from determining the precise age of the fetus to detecting survival problems in the womb. The technique has been used since the sixties, and it continues to be evaluated.

Ultrasound, which uses high-frequency sound waves to produce an image on a television-type screen, has consistently been proved safe. This technique does not hold the danger of the X-ray method, and they should not be compared. In a limited number of animal studies, however, long and intense exposure to ultrasound showed that cell damage may occur and fetal growth may be slowed. These studies, though, were conducted with extremely high levels of ultrasound, and exposure was often under test-tube conditions. Follow-up investigations have been unable to reproduce these early results. The validity of these early animal studies have, therefore, been questioned. Modern scientists do not believe that any adverse effects from ultrasound exist.

Among humans, ultrasound has, in spite of the numerous studies, never been found to be harmful or dangerous. In fact, long-term American studies on seven- and twelve-year-olds who were prenatally exposed to ultrasound have not uncovered any long-term ill effects.

Long-term European and Canadian studies on thousands of children up to age nine—groups exposed to ultrasound, when compared to control groups not exposed—have also failed to show any adverse effects from the technique. These positive results were somewhat expected, since ultrasound does not employ radiation.

Physicians in other countries routinely screen their pregnant patients with full (30- to 45-minute) sonograms twice during pregnancy, but in the United States, we are much more conservative about using the technique. Doctors here believe that an expensive diagnostic tool such as ultrasound should only be used when necessary. If Ms. F.'s doctor is suggesting ultrasound, he probably has a reason, and Ms. F. can be secure in the knowledge that the procedure is safe.

Some doctors use ultrasound more frequently than others; nevertheless, the procedure shold not be performed casually, just to "see" the baby. Ms. F. might ask her doctor why he is monitoring her womb so carefully. I, for example, will not perform a full sonogram very often, but I will screen the fetus two or three times a trimester, for thirty to sixty seconds, to ascertain proper fetal development, a good growth pattern, fetal movement, placental location, and amount of amniotic fluid, and to watch for visible congenital abnormalities. When complications such as bleeding occur, ultrasound is the only way to find out what is wrong. It is essential for determining treatment.

The Sonogram of My Baby Has Removed All My Fears

I was worried when I didn't feel my baby move the way it had been, but then my doctor did an ultrasound scan and changed my outlook. The picture showed a healthy baby boy—we were able to see the sex—and I'm ecstatic. I feel closer to my child, and this picture is going to be the first one in our baby book.

M.K.
Monterey, California

The psychological effect of a sonogram is new to the pregnant woman, and it is a remarkable emotional event. Concern about what might be happening inside your body is normal. Most women worry if a certain pattern changes, if movement is different. When a woman can actually see her baby, she is relieved and happy. Viewing a developing human being, its arms and legs, its head and spine, is awesome, and taking home a Polaroid snapshot of the image is real proof that your child exists. Bonding seems to begin even before the baby is born. This unexpected effect of ultrasound brings added joy to expectancy.

THE SAFETY OF AMNIOCENTESIS

Often, by the time a woman over thirty-five has reached the end of her fourth month and is ready for an amniocentesis, she is nervous. She has heard that the needle is painful, that the baby can be damaged, or that the procedure will cause miscarriage. A physician who is experienced at performing amniocentesis will find the position of the baby using ultrasonography, and a woman and her unborn baby will be at very little risk.

The doctor will mark the exact point where he can safely enter the abdomen with a needle. The area will have a free flow of amniotic fluid, with no placenta involved. A woman's abdomen will be cleansed with a sterile iodine solution. Some physicians choose to numb the area with an injection of novocaine before inserting the needle to withdraw the amniotic fluid; others feel that the novocaine injection is as uncomfortable as the needle for amniocentesis, and they perform the procedure without the numbing.

At most, an amniocentesis takes two to three minutes, and the skin puncture heals within three to five days. Although there is a small risk of internal bleeding, skilled physicians can overcome it. Injury to the fetus is a hazard that is not likely to occur when a woman is in the hands of a practiced obstetrician; in fact, fetal complications are so infrequent that the risk has been difficult to determine. There is a small, perhaps 1 percent, increase in the miscarriage rate for women who have amniocentesis, and due to this risk, I advise my patients to rest for twenty-four hours afterward. A woman should be accompanied, preferably by her husband, to the doctor's office or hospital on the day of her amniocentesis. Once the procedure is over, she should be escorted home, where she should plan to recuperate in bed for at least one day.

How Is an Amniocentesis Performed if I'm Carrying Twins?

My doctor says he hears two heartbeats and he thinks I'm carrying twins. He says he will know definitely when he does the ultrasound before my amniocentesis. I want to know how a doctor can do an amniocentesis on a woman who is carrying twins. Isn't there a chance that one of the babies will be hurt?

P.J.
Braintree, Massachusetts

In the case of fraternal twins, a skilled physician will view both amniotic sacs and fetuses. He will not insert a needle unless he has marked a safe spot. A problem with fraternal twins arises not because there is added risk to the fetus but because two sacs are involved. A doctor must know that he has taken a sample from each sac. So after a doctor aspirates fluid from a sac, he injects it with blue or red dye as an indicator. He will be sure he is tapping the second sac when the fluid is clear. Red or blue fluid would mean he has mistakenly entered the first sac. The dye will remain in the fluid for a few hours and then be absorbed by the body.

Do You Want to Know the Sex of Your Child?

One of the results of an amniocentesis or a chorionic biopsy is that the sex of the child is revealed. At first, most expectant mothers and fathers wanted to know the sex. The doctor knew, his staff knew, so why shouldn't they? Planning the nursery was easier once they knew whether it was a girl's or a boy's room.

Today, however, many couples say they don't want to be informed. They look forward to the thrill of childbirth, when the sex of the baby is discovered in the delivery room. Of course, the doctor and his staff have to be especially careful not to mention "son" or "daughter" to a woman who wants the secret kept. She enjoys the feeling of anticipation right up until the last moment. It's a choice more and more expectant couples who experience prenatal testing are making.

GENETIC COUNSELING: A POSITIVE EVENT

By staying on a healthy, well-balanced diet, taking vitamins, remaining free from drugs, being alert to toxins in her environment, and getting plenty of rest before and during pregnancy, a woman will be doing everything possible to have a healthy baby. Technology and genetic counseling will then give her the best science can offer. If genetic disorders are in her or her husband's family, modern screening methods can often alleviate concern.

This chapter is meant to eliminate fear through understanding. If a woman is over thirty-five, amniocentesis can remove the worry that comes with having a baby at that age. Older women feel much better about becoming pregnant today. Women over age thirty currently comprise almost 30 percent of all pregnant women in the United States. Many of these women fall into the high-risk classification because they are older, but they are more educated about pregnancy. They feel that they benefit from the demystification of fear thanks to advanced techniques. This positive attitude generated among expectant parents creates a healthier intrauterine environment—and future—for our babies.

CHAPTER 11

Over 35: Is Your Pregnancy Safe?

An expectant mother who is over thirty-five is no longer a rarity, and women who are over forty are becoming pregnant more often. Their mothers no doubt married young and devoted themselves to raising families, but these women chose different paths. They may have postponed pregnancy because they wanted time to fulfill academic achievements, to develop careers, to travel, or to explore personal endeavors. For many, marriage and the desire to have a baby did not come until their thirties, when they were ready to settle down. In fact, if you are reading this chapter, you may easily relate to some of these life choices.

If you are over thirty-five and pregnant, or ready to become pregnant, you are not alone. About one-quarter of my obstetrical practice is comprised of expectant mothers who are over thirty-five. Some may have become pregnant quite easily; others may have needed extensive fertility work (see Chapter 2); and occasionally women who thought their fertile days were behind them conceived unexpectedly.

Certainly, starting in the early thirties, fertility begins to decline somewhat, and I encourage women who think they might want to be mothers to consider conception before age thirty-five. With the current focus on fitness and good nutrition, however, women and men are able to maintain healthy, youthful bodies much longer than their parents did. Often, knowing that their options are fewer with age, older couples educate themselves about pregnancy and childbirth in much greater depth than younger couples do. Still, questions arise: How risky is pregnancy at an older age? What is the chance of miscarriage? Is a cesarean always necessary?

This chapter is designed to clarify confusions and misconceptions. For instance, although many cesareans are performed on older expectant mothers, a woman in her forties is frequently capable of giving birth vaginally, naturally. I enjoy caring for older pregnant women. They have boundless love and appreciation for the babies they have conceived. They become excellent mothers, and I know that one day they will be doting grandmothers.

THE BIG QUESTION: WHEN IS IT TOO LATE?

About a year ago, two patients came into the office on the same day to ask me the same question: "Is it too late for me to have a baby?" The first woman, Elizabeth B., would soon be thirty-seven. Not a woman to settle for second best, she had waited a long time to meet a man she loved enough to marry. Now, suddenly, she had a nagging sense that time had robbed her, that at thirty-seven, she would be too old to have a child. Jane S., on the other hand, had spent years meticulously planning the right time for her first pregnancy. Her life had been carefully plotted, from her graduate school degree to the partnership in her law firm, to marriage and motherhood. She had not expected any snags, but now she was a few weeks away from her thirty-fifth birthday. She and her husband had been trying to conceive for more than a year, and when Jane S. came into my office, she was bewildered, angry, and hurt. She felt that her body had betrayed her and she would never be a parent.

As it turned out, it wasn't too late for either of these women to have children. Elizabeth B. was pregnant within three months of being married; Jane S. conceived after I diagnosed a minor irregularity. But the Elizabeths and the Janes are known to every obstetrician / gynecologist with a specialty in infertility, as thousands of women who would once have been thought to be slightly beyond childbearing are planning their first pregnancies. Now that it is fashionable to become a mother in one's thirties or forties, that archetypical first-time mother is the heroine of countless magazine articles: the articulate, assured woman who plans her pregnancy with the same élan that she conducts a boardroom meeting. It is a seductive image; besides, it acknowledges the obvious financial and professional advantages of delaying childbearing. Nonetheless, a woman who believes it unquestioningly could be gambling against impossible odds if her overconfidence deceives her into waiting too long.

A gynecologist, when asked the anxious question, "When is it too late for me to have a baby?" often faces a dilemma. He doesn't want to frighten his patient. But he can't, if he's a good physician, gloss over the hard facts either. Once such inescapable fact is that after age forty, only half of all women are still able to conceive; another is that women appear to be at their most fertile between the ages of eighteen and twenty-four.

QUESTIONS ABOUT PREGNANCY AFTER 35

I'm 37. How Risky Is It for Me to Have a Baby?

I'm thirty-seven and my fiancé and I have just set our wedding date. I have never been pregnant and I am beginning to long for a child. When I discussed this with my girlfriend, however, she scared me. She said that my chances of conceiving a baby at my age were much lower, and that if I do become pregnant, it could be very dangerous for me, and my baby would be far more likely to be born with some abnormality. Do I dare risk trying to have a baby at my age?

D.V.
Denver, Colorado

In the past several years, obstetricians have seen a steady increase in the number of first pregnancies in women over the age of thirty-five, and although the morbidity rate for both mother and

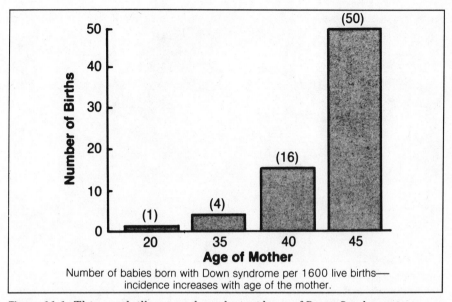

Number of babies born with Down syndrome per 1600 live births—
incidence increases with age of the mother.

Figure 11-1. *This graph illustrates how the incidence of Down Syndrome increases with age. This increase is the reason why a woman over thirty-five should undergo amniocentesis.*

baby might be higher in pregnancies that occur after the age of thirty-five, many new studies indicate that in reality, a woman of that age might be better off than a younger one. Statistics show that childbirth after the age of thirty has become very popular. This is the age group with the highest increase in birth rates in the past ten years. Among women between the ages of thirty and thirty-four, the birth rate increased from 56.4 per 1,000 in 1976 to 60 in 1980 to 72.2 per 1,000 in 1984.

Ms. V.'s friend was correct when she said that it is more difficult for older women to become pregnant, especially if they have never been pregnant before. Infertility in women over thirty can be caused by many conditions: hormonal imbalances, fallopian tubes damaged by previous infections, pelvic adhesions, and, particularly in career women, pelvic endometriosis. Furthermore, merely the general effects of age can damage a woman's eggs. Thus there is no doubt that an older woman may have a somewhat harder time conceiving, but with modern technology, it is certainly very possible to get pregnant. It is, however, important that a woman be aware of the potential difficulty of conceiving should she decide to postpone having her first baby, and that she make

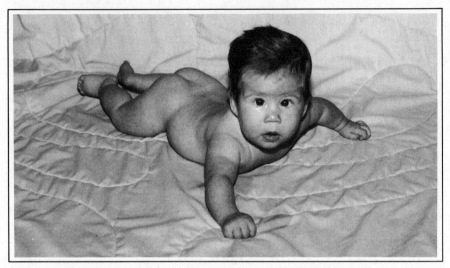

Figure 11-2. *A healthy baby is everyone's dream, and with good nutrition, rest, avoidance of drugs, and careful monitoring, a woman of any age should have this dream fulfilled.* Photo of Sarah Velazco reproduced by permission of her parents.

every effort to keep herself in the best possible health, by following a sound nutritional regimen and by taking the correct vitamin supplements throughout her lifetime.

Once an older woman does conceive, she will face far fewer problems today than she would have even ten years ago. Studies have shown that women who have the healthiest babies are women who obtain early and regular prenatal care. Indeed, women who are older often do have healthier babies, perhaps partially because they are more educated about the importance of proper prenatal health. This added maturity, coupled with new advances in obstetrics, can relieve many of the former legitimate fears of older first-time mothers.

Ms. V. should, by all means, be encouraged to realize her dream of having a baby, but she needs to be sure that her obstetrician is skilled and experienced in handling high-risk pregnancies. Early in her pregnancy, Ms. V. should avail herself of genetic counseling and amniocentesis. When a woman is over thirty-five, her pregnancy is more vulnerable. The possibility of miscarriage increases, and so does the chance that some type of chromosomal abnormality may occur. The most well known age-related chromosomal defect is Down syndrome, or mongolism. Since the incidence of this condition increases with age, and quite rapidly after age forty, women who are over thirty-five should have their pregnancy monitored by ultrasound and amniocentesis. (See Table 7, p. 232.)

Some of my infertility patients who have become pregnant have asked me about a new test, chorionic villi biopsy, which they have heard can replace amniocentesis. (See Tests for Genetic Disorders, p. 221, for a further discussion.) I do not advise a woman who has been infertile for a long time to choose chorionic villi biopsy over amniocentesis. The technique is not as yet perfected, and over 20 percent of the women who have this sampling end up miscarrying. There is also a rather high rate of infection, and there have even been some reports of septic shock with renal failure after a chorionic villi sampling.

In addition to being familiar with genetic counseling, Ms. V.'s doctor should be prepared to screen and monitor the development of her baby carefully throughout her pregnancy. Today thorough obstetrical care and skilled use of modern technology make it possible for Ms. V. and other women in her situation to safely enjoy their pregnancies.

As the time to deliver Ms. V.'s child approaches, she needs to be aware of potential delivery complications, not so that she becomes frightened but so that she and her doctor can work effectively as a team to make her delivery as easy and as safe as possible.

More than 25 percent of my own obstetrical patients are now over the age of thirty-five, and they have all had wonderful pregnancies and births that have been no more complicated than a

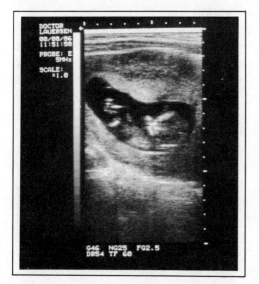

Figure 11-3. *An ultrasound image shows that a fetus only eleven weeks old is already fully developed. The head is at the right; the baby is sucking its thumb, and the legs are up "in the air" to the left. Through careful monitoring, a woman over age thirty-five can be more secure about the health of her baby.*

251

younger woman's. At all times in my own practice, I have had a great number of women who were above the age of forty when they conceived. Many were in their mid-forties, and I recently delivered a patient who was forty-nine. I, therefore, do not believe that age should be a limiting factor for a woman deciding whether to become pregnant, since a woman in her forties can have a pregnancy as healthy or even healthier than that of a younger woman.

Is It Better to Conceive with a Younger Man?

I'm forty-four and my husband is thirty-eight. I was not trying to get pregnant, and when I skipped my period, I thought that I might be facing the start of menopause. Imagine my surprise when I found out that I was going to have a baby! I really think I conceived because my husband is a younger man, with younger sperm. Am I right? I'd also like to know whether it's better for the baby's health when you conceive with a younger man. Is there less chance of birth defects?

T.D.

Santa Rosa, California

A woman who has regular, pain-free menstruation, and no history of infections, bleeding disorders, pelvic conditions such as endometriosis, or other reproductive problems can usually consider herself to be fertile until the first signs of menopause. If she continues to have a good ovulation pattern, even if she is over thirty-five, her chance of conception is good.

As mentioned in Chapter 2 and in this chapter, however, both sexes face a decline of fertility with age. A woman who is over thirty-five is less fertile than she was at twenty-five, and a man her own age is also less fertile than he used to be. This mutual drop in fertility certainly makes trying to conceive with a younger man's sperm seem more advantageous. It seems that Ms. D. may have benefited from the relative youth of her husband. It is misleading to say sweepingly that it is better to have a baby with a younger man, however,

About 40 percent of all infertility problems are male related, which means that many younger men have poor sperm counts, defective sperm, or other reproductive difficulties (see Chapter 2). Meanwhile, some men in their fifties, sixties, and seventies have become new fathers of healthy newborns. I know one recent case in which a thirty-nine-year-old woman conceived with her husband, a sixty-two-year-old man, on their first attempt. The woman had checked and timed her ovulation; her husband had received a sperm count, and they were sure of their fertility. I encourage every older couple who want to conceive to check their own fertility, as this couple did. A woman can use an ovulation predictor kit, which is sold at pharmacies, or, as described in Chapter 2, she can take basal body temperature readings and check her mucous. Her mate, if he is older, can request a sperm count from a physician.

The father's age plays some part in the need for amniocentesis, but it is less significant than the mother's. The chance of Down syndrome occurring increases with the *mother's* age, and Ms. D. is definitely a candidate for this procedure. It is the mother's age, which is an indication of the age of the fertilized egg, that is the criterion for testing for chromosomal abnormality. Ms. D. should feel pleased that she is pregnant, and with good nutrition, rest, and proper prenatal care, she is likely to have a fine and healthy newborn.

I'm Concerned About Miscarriage. Should I Spend the First Trimester in Bed?

This is my first pregnancy and I'm thirty-eight years old. My doctor told me that older women have a greater chance of miscarriage and he warned me to "take it easy." Actually, he scared me. Now I'm afraid to go to work because I get jostled on the commuter train. Should I spend the first trimester in bed?

L.W.
Mamaroneck, New York

It is true that as a woman gets older, her chance of having a miscarriage increases. A woman in her thirties is more susceptible to miscarriage than a woman in her twenties, and a woman in her forties may miscarry sooner than a woman in her thirties. The older an egg is when it is fertilized, the greater the chance that it is a bad egg ("blighted ovum") or that it contains a chromosomal abnormality. Sometimes a chromosomal abnormality can lead to a congenital defect that is so incompatible with life that a miscarriage occurs. As described in Chapter 13, miscarriage is often nature's way of ridding the body of a poor conception.

Although an older expectant mother may be more likely than a younger woman to conceive a blighted ovum or a chromosomally defective egg, many women over thirty-five have perfectly normal, healthy eggs and pregnancies, and beautiful babies. I suggest that Ms. W. keep herself strong with a well-balanced diet and daily vitamin supplements—100 milligrams of vitamin B-complex, 500 milligrams of B_6, 1000 milligrams of calcium, extra folic acid and iron, and 1000 to 1500 milligrams of vitamin C. If she has ever had a miscarriage before, she might request a blood test for her thyroid function. As explained in Chapter 13, sometimes a sluggish or low/normal thyroid can contribute to repeated miscarriage. A low dose of Synthyroid, a synthetic thyroid medication, can correct the thyroid deficiency and help protect the conceptus. If Ms. W.'s doctor is concerned about miscarriage, she should heed his advice—try to stay off her feet in the first few weeks of pregnancy, and perhaps refrain from sexual intercourse. I also suggest that she lie on her left side to increase the blood flow to the fetus. If she lies on her back, the weight of her pregnancy may cause pressure on the vena cava, the large vein to the heart, and restrict the nourishing supply of blood that is traveling to the womb. Occasionally during early pregnancy, I recommend natural progesterone suppositories for expectant mothers who might need extra hormonal support. In double-blind studies, natural progesterone has been found to be safe and helpful; it is a relaxant for the uterus as well as an aid in the development of the fetus.

As Ms. W.'s pregnancy progresses, she should know that when she reaches about her eighth week of gestation, she will be able to hear the fetal heart rate, and the chance of miscarriage will lessen. The probability of miscarriage drops even lower at the tenth week, with the beginning of fetal movement. By the twelfth week, or third month, the fetus is fully formed and the chance of losing the baby through miscarriage is very slim indeed. Sometimes when a woman is very concerned about the possibility of miscarriage, I suggest that she refrain from telling many people about her pregnancy. Then, as she approaches her third month, she can share the news without anxiety and with joy.

I often remind my patients that there are times when women have tried—and failed—to rid themselves of their pregnancies by falling, horseback or motorcycle riding, even jogging to the point of exhaustion. A healthy pregnancy just keeps growing! Ms. W. should "take it easy," but I would not want her to be fearful of a slightly bumpy ride on a commuter train. If she rests frequently, eats nutritionally balanced meals, and takes extra vitamins, she will be doing her best to protect a healthy pregnancy.

Can I Refuse an Amniocentesis?

I know that when you're over thirty-five, it's wise to have an amniocentesis to find out if the baby is all right, but I don't want to. I'm thirty-six and I don't think my risk is great. After thinking about it, I don't think I would have the abortion even if the test showed something wrong. I believe that I will have a healthy baby anyway. Can I refuse an amniocentesis?

A.E.

Savannah, Georgia

When a woman is older, the chance of her conceiving an egg with a chromosomal abnormality increases. Recognizing this increased risk, doctors recommend that women over thirty-five undergo amniocentesis, a diagnostic procedure that can detect a large number of chromosomal defects, most particularly Down syndrome. As pointed out earlier, the incidence of Down syndrome especially rises after age forty, but doctors use thirty-five as the age to begin recommending amniocentesis, although a pregnant woman of any age could benefit from a chromosomal analysis.

Several years ago, a physician in the New York area was sued by a thirty-five-year-old woman who gave birth to a baby with Down syndrome. The woman contended that her doctor had not advised her that she faced increased risk of Down syndrome as an older expectant mother, and he had not given her the option of having amniocentesis. The woman won the case, and since then, doctors have felt an obligation to advise women who are thirty-five or older about the statistics on chromosomal abnormalities and the availability of amniocentesis.

As explained in Chapter 10, amniocentesis is a safe procedure that is performed with the guidance of ultrasound. After creating a small abdominal incision, a physician gently inserts a needle and withdraws a sample of amniotic fluid from a woman's womb. The fluid is analyzed for its chromosomal makeup and many, *but not all*, defects can be determined. (NOTE: Amniocentesis remains safer than the new chorionic villi biopsy for determining chromosomal abnormalities.) The ultrasound image can also provide a view of overall fetal development, and if a woman is carrying more than one baby, she will see her additional offspring.

Every woman has a right to accept or refuse the option of amniocentesis, and a number of my patients have declined. They feel that they would not choose to terminate their pregnancies even if their babies were going to be born with some abnormalities. Every physician respects a woman's right of refusal. On the other hand, I have noticed that occasionally a woman who is sure that she would retain her pregnancy no matter what the findings of an amniocentesis still chooses to have the test. Couples are beginning to feel that they want to know the baby's chromosomal status in order to prepare for its arrival. If they are going to give birth to an impaired infant, they want to be ready beforehand. If the baby is perfectly normal, they can enjoy the peace of mind.

Ms. E. should know that having an amniocentesis does not mean that she must interrupt her pregnancy. The procedure is a way of giving her greater insight into the health of her baby.

Should I Stop Work Early?

My doctor is gently trying to convince me to stop work in my seventh month. I'm a receptionist, so my job is not physically strenuous, but at forty, I am an older expectant mother. He says that at my age, I need more rest. Isn't the first trimester the riskiest one? Is he being overly cautious? Should I stop work early?

S.F.
Silver Spring, Maryland

The first trimester is a time of concern for pregnant women of all ages. The possibility of miscarriage is real. An older expectant mother, as mentioned earlier, is at greater risk of having conceived a problematic egg, and she should be especially careful not to exert herself. An older woman should, in fact, be quite cautious throughout her pregnancy. Babies conceived by older parents need more protection. Whenever Ms. F. has the opportunity to lie down, she should rest on her left side. This position permits optimum blood flow to the fetus.

Ms. F. writes that she does not have a physically exerting job, and this is to her benefit. Her physician appears to be choosing a conservative, responsible approach that I can understand. In the case of an older pregnancy, it is often better to be safe than sorry. He obviously does not want her to try to push herself beyond her capabilities in her last trimester. As explained in Chapter 13, complications such as toxemia can arise in the last trimester, and a woman may also be faced with premature labor.

Ms. F. should let her employers know that she may have to go home from work early sometimes, and may have to elevate her feet now and then. Certainly an early leave of absence is preferable. During her last trimester, Ms. F. should be alert to any warning signs of trouble—bleeding, staining, painful cramps, premature contractions (see Chapter 13).

If ever Ms. F. has a warning sign, she should contact her doctor immediately. Physicians have a number of avenues of treatment for complicated pregnancies. For example, if Ms. F. is experiencing premature labor, she can be treated with a medication called Yutopar (ritodrine), which relaxes the uterus and allows the fetus more time to grow. Also, a technologically sophisticated at-home monitoring device called TERM GUARD, from the Tokos Medical Corporation headquartered in California, can be worn on an abdominal belt (see Chapter 13). This device transmits signals by telephone to nationwide monitoring centers staffed with nurses. The centers keep doctors informed, and if signals warn of premature labor, a woman can be admitted to the hospital for immediate treatment.

Pregnancy protection is the key. Ms. F. should follow her doctor's advice, be aware of her body, and treat herself delicately. An older expectant mother should know—and let others know—that for her baby's sake, she must be a little more careful.

Will I Need a Cesarean Because of My Age?

I will be forty by the time the baby is born. I'm going to natural childbirth classes, but I've been told so many times that someone my age automatically is given a cesarean that I'm mentally preparing myself for one. Yet I want to deliver naturally. Am I kidding myself? Will I need a cesarean because of my age?

E.N.
Middletown, Rhode Island

Statistics do show that after age forty, there is a higher rate of cesarean section performed on women who give birth for the first time. An older expectant mother is more likely to encounter a complication during labor and delivery, and her baby is also more likely to suffer fetal distress. For these reasons, and because physicians are aware of how important a child is to a woman who becomes pregnant near the end of her fertile years, a cesarean section is a more frequent consideration. (See Chapter 15 for fur-

257

ther information about cesarean sections.) These facts do not mean, however, that older women cannot give birth vaginally.

A mother's physical condition, the size of her baby, and the strength of her labor will vary. If a woman has no pregnancy or labor complications, is in good health, and her labor progresses smoothly, then there is every reason to believe, even if she is older, that she can deliver vaginally. If a complication occurs, however, and the survival of the fetus is threatened, then intervention may be necessary. A woman may have to have oxytocin, an epidural anesthesia, and a cesarean.

Ms. N. should remain optimistic about her chances to have natural childbirth. As long as she watches her weight, eats a nutritionally balanced diet, takes vitamin supplements, rests often, and stays fit throughout her pregnancy, she will not automatically be marked for a cesarean. Should her labor and childbirth take a turn that requires a cesarean, however, her husband may be permitted to be present during the surgery.

Ms. N. should discuss the possibility of a cesarean with her doctor early in pregnancy. She should know his approach to childbirth, and be sure that if a cesarean is needed, he will make a bikini incision, which will leave less scarring. (See Chapter 15.) Being an older expectant mother, Ms. N. doubtless is very aware of the best way to maintain her health and her baby's. Unless an unforeseen complication arises, a vaginal delivery can probably take place. Every expectant mother, no matter what her age, should feel confident about the chance for natural childbirth.

In the last decade or so, national attention has been paid to maintaining a strong, fit body and mind. With regular exercise, good nutrition, and increased awareness, today's forty-year-old woman is much healthier than her mother or her grandmother was at her age. This new health consciousness has made pregnancy much more feasible for a woman over thirty-five, a woman who can now decide to have a baby later in life. If you are an older expectant mother, you might consult with a perinatologist, an obstetrician who specializes in older and high-risk pregnancies. A doctor who is shocked by your conception may not provide proper care. My advice to pregnant women over thirty-five is always: choose a physician who believes in tomorrow rather than yesterday. Surround yourself with a supportive team—your doctor, your partner, and you.

CHAPTER 12

Dreams and Emotions During Pregnancy: Do They Affect Your Baby?

In her eighth month, Sharon walked out of her house at nine o'clock at night, got in her car, drove to her sister's house, and spent the night there. During her office visit the next day, she told me that she had been frustrated and angered by her husband John. He had promised to come home early from work so that they could shop for a crib. When he greeted her late, at eight thirty, she became enraged. Sharon felt that John was not showing any interest in her pregnancy or their baby. When were they supposed to furnish the nursery? After the baby was born? She had stormed out of the house.

"I blow up at John all the time lately because he acts as if nothing is happening," Sharon said. "I never thought I had a temper, but I fly off the handle regularly. The funny thing is, I feel justified. Having this baby is a big event, and I don't think John cares. But if you talk to him, he'll tell you that now that I'm pregnant,

I've grown self-centered and impossible. You know, before I got pregnant, we hardly ever fought. But I think he's trying to blame my pregnancy for his shortcomings."

Sharon and John were really only discovering that pregnancy is a physical and a psychological experience. Two people are facing the unknown with wonder and trepidation combined. A woman, especially in a first pregnancy, is contemplating the meaning of becoming a mother, a role she has never before filled. She is concerned about whether she will be able to care for her child. Will she be a *good* mother? How will she be the same or different from her own mother? Questions without answers collide in her mind.

Even the most physically trouble free pregnancy is a life passage that, emotionally, is not easily traveled. Female psychiatrists Dr. Helene Deutsch in the forties and Dr. Grete Bibring in the fifties wrote about the identity changes that women undergo during pregnancy. Today's researchers in the field of psychology continue to explore the ways in which these nine transitional months emotionally affect expectant parents, and the one fact they affirm is that this is not a period of calm.

Sharon was delighted to be pregnant, but her happiness was sprinkled with intervals of edginess. She was preoccupied with thoughts of whether her baby would be normal. She fretted about whether her body would ever return to what it had been, and she was worried about her relationship with her husband. How would this child change their marriage? Her pregnancy was taking her on the emotional roller-coaster ride that most expectant mothers take. A woman may be content, involved in her daily routine, when something goes wrong. In Sharon's case, her husband was late arriving home. Normally a woman might be irritated, but in a pregnant state, an emotional outburst may be quickly triggered.

The stress of added weight, physical fatigue, and overall discomfort is heaped upon psychological pressure during pregnancy. A life change is occurring along with a tremendous physical transformation. It's a wonderful, volatile time.

HORMONES PLAY A PART

Pregnant women have complained to me that frequently when they are upset, friends or co-workers will say, "We understand; you're pregnant." These women dislike having their pregnancy used as an excuse for their moods and feelings. "Everything is so easily dismissed by the sentence, 'Don't worry, dear, it's hormonal,' " one pregnant patient told me. "People think all my actions are due to raging hormones. What about my feelings?"

While it is true that women are in a psychological as well as a physical upheaval during pregnancy, the influence of the physical side should be recognized. Anxieties and fears are real and should never be sloughed off with the sentence, "It's just your hormones," but on the other hand, hormones do influence emotional equilibrium. Scientific investigations into the causes of premenstrual syndrome (PMS) have identified the fluctuation of the female hormones estrogen and progesterone as one of the strongest reasons for the mood swings related to PMS.

Hormonal secretions are regulated by, and in turn regulate, the release of the brain's neurotransmitters, messengers that direct the flow of body chemicals. Progesterone, the female hormone that rises in the second half of the menstrual cycle and stays particularly high if conception occurs, has a physically tranquilizing effect. It relaxes the uterus and produces the tiredness that comes with pregnancy. High, imbalanced levels of progesterone and estrogen also influence brain chemicals and may lead to an inability to cope. Impatience and irritability are often linked with hormonal imbalance.

In pregnancy, an increase in progesterone and the fluctuation of estrogen and progesterone may exacerbate mood swings similar to those experienced by PMS suffers. These hormones affect the brain's catecholamines, neurotransmitters that initiate emotional ups and downs. The adrenal hormones also respond to pregnancy and enhance or detract from shifting moods.

The influence of hormones is real. In premenstrual syndrome, pregnancy, and postpartum depression, biochemistry definitely plays a part, but equally important parts are being played in other areas too. All those who are close to a woman contribute to her moods. The attitudes of her co-workers, her husband's feelings about their developing baby, the response of her own parents and siblings, and the spirit exuded by her doctor combine to create her outlook. When enthusiasm and encouragement abound, an expectant mother can feel good in spite of her hormones and her heightened sensitivity.

EVEN A WOMAN'S DREAM WORLD CHANGES

The profound emotional changes that are part of the pregnancy experience are reflected in an expectant mother's dreams. Each

261

trimester brings new conflicts and concerns, which are illumin-ated while she sleeps. As described by Eileen Stukane in her book *The Dream Worlds of Pregnancy,** dreams fall into a pattern dur-ing these nine months. During the day, a woman may be busy at the office or at home, but at night, her mind has time to explore nagging issues. In sleep, she cannot bury questions such as Will the baby be normal? or How will my marriage change? In dreams, these questions unfold like the plot of a play.

Early in pregnancy, a woman may dream about small, cuddly creatures that symbolize the new life within her womb. A woman who is pregnant for the first time may not yet be able to visualize herself as the mother of an infant, but she recognizes the concep-tion that has taken place. This is a time when patients have told me that they dream of kittens, or bunnies, or sometimes baby chicks. As the first trimester progresses, worry about the possibil-ity of miscarriage may bring on more frightening dreams. In *The Dream Worlds of Pregnancy*, a dream in which a pregnant woman tries and fails to rescue a drowning baby is attributed to a fear of miscarriage, or losing the baby. Such alarming dreams may be-come quite common to an expectant mother who is concerned about pregnancy and childbirth. As joyful as pregnancy is, it can understandably make a woman nervous.

An expectant mother should share her dreams with her spouse, a close friend, a relative, or her doctor, to dispel any worry that the dreams themselves may create. In the second trimester, for exam-ple, a woman may dream about misplacing, dropping, or forget-ting about a baby. The dream may spring from her concern about whether she will be a capable mother. Sometimes a pregnant pa-tient will reluctantly tell me that she dreamed about a birth-defec-tive baby, and she is worried. She thinks that the dream is a sign that something is going to be wrong with her child. Dreams are not omens; they are merely mirrors of a woman's own anxieties. Since anxieties may increase during pregnancy, dreams may seem more vivid than usual. A woman should talk about her dreams and not let them scare her.

In the last trimester, dreams may become especially unsettling because a woman may be nervously anticipating the pain of labor and childbirth. If she does not reveal her nervousness, it may show up in her dreams. A woman may see herself all alone, in

* New York: William Morrow/Quill, 1985.

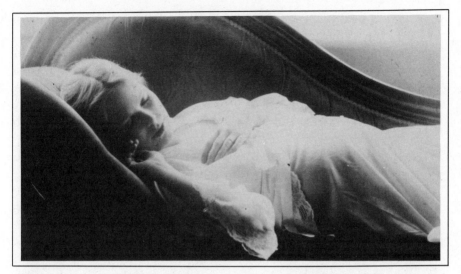

Figure 12-1. *Dreams during pregnancy. A woman's dream world becomes much more vivid—a reflection of her emotional changes—during pregnancy.* Reproduced by permission of H. Armstrong Roberts.

oceans, lakes, or ponds, trying to stay alive. Dreams during pregnancy release anxiety that she has tried to suppress. A woman's emotions are shifting and intensifying as she moves closer to childbirth, and her dreams are healthy outlets for her feelings.

WILL A WOMAN'S MOODS AFFECT HER BABY?

A pregnant woman's moods may swing from tranquil to impatient, from sad to glad, in a matter of minutes. This switch is normal and expected. Her physical discomfort, her hormonal fluctuation, and her psychological concerns may at times make her susceptible to unpredictable behavior. One woman told me that she cried during television commercials for cat food and she was worried that she was becoming emotionally unhinged. Another patient said that she was looking forward to having a baby, but sometimes she wished she weren't pregnant. She fretted that during her "down" spells, her negativity would be felt by her baby. Both women had a sense of being out of control.

During pregnancy, a woman may not be as emotionally stable as she was before, but her natural-for-her-condition mood swings are not going to damage her unborn baby. Researchers have never uncovered any evidence that emotional ups and downs adversely affect a healthy pregnancy. The effects of severe stress, however, are quite different.

Some stress is normal for daily living. Most of us cope with stressful events all the time. The photocopier at work breaks down, or you miss a deadline, or the bus is late, but you manage. A life crisis that occurs while a woman is pregnant, however, may create *severe stress* and physical effects that touch the fetus. A job loss, an illness, or a death in the family happening during pregnancy, when sensitivity is heightened, can be deleterious to both mother and baby.

A pregnant woman under severe stress may experience an increased heart rate. Her uterus may begin to contract, and if stress is prolonged, the contractions can reduce the oxygen supply to the fetus. A developing baby will not receive the nourishment it needs to grow properly. Newborns who are the products of stress-filled uterine environments may have low birth weights. They may suffer mental deficiencies and be growth retarded throughout their lifetime.

In a crisis, stress management is a must. A woman who feels overwhelmed by the events of her life should ask her obstetrician or midwife about ways to reduce her stress. The relaxation techniques taught in natural childbirth classes can often be used to diffuse stressful situations. Exercise, meditation, consultation with a trained therapist, and biofeedback are all methods of stress reduction. A woman can also combat the effects of stress with a well-balanced diet supplemented by two prenatal vitamins and B-complex containing 100 milligrams of B_1 daily. Nutritional awareness becomes more necessary in times of stress, when the body's store of vitamins and minerals is naturally depleted. Under stress, a pregnant woman should reach out for help—for herself and for her baby.

LEARNING IN THE WOMB

As far as we know, a fetus will not be affected by a woman's daily moods, but researchers are discovering that unborn babies do react to external stimuli. Dr. Anthony DeCasper, a psychologist at the University of North Carolina, reports that a fetus can hear a mother's stomach noises, her heartbeat, and her voice. In his studies of fetal learning, he has asked expectant mothers to read *The Cat in the Hat* by Dr. Seuss to their unborn children twice a day for the last six and a half weeks of pregnancy. After birth, the newborns sucked on nipples during readings of *The Cat in the Hat* by their mothers, but they did not respond to readings of other poems.

Studies on fetal rats conducted by researchers at Oregon State University also support the existence of prenatal conditioning. A

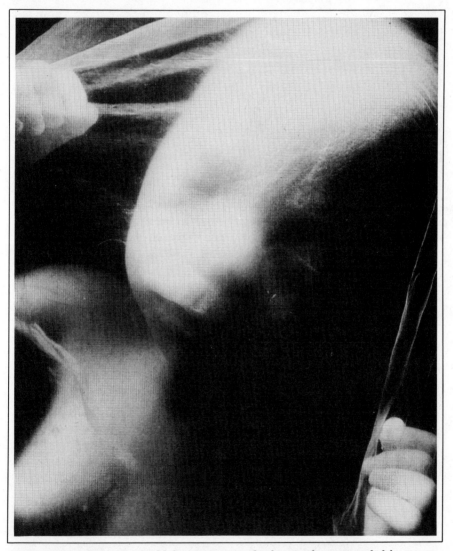

Figure 12-2. *A four-month-old fetus, seen inside the womb, surrounded by its protective amniotic fluid and the transparent amnion (fetal membranes). A fetus at this time is fully developed and can easily be affected by external stimuli.*

certain substance injected into the amniotic sac brought on a minor fetal illness. After birth, rats who were exposed to the substance in the womb recoiled from it, whereas unexposed newborn rats consumed it. The rats who had been exposed as fetuses seemed to remember the smell of the substance well enough to reject it before taking a taste!

Since researchers are showing that a fetus can differentiate sensory stimuli, an expectant mother might now and then talk lovingly to her unborn baby, and she might occasionally play peaceful music. In utero learning is a new and exciting discovery that I advise every pregnant woman to explore.

QUESTIONS ABOUT DREAMS AND EMOTIONS

Do You Think the Baby Can Feel My Ambivalence?

My husband and I always said that someday we would start a family, but "someday" always seemed far in the future. We had friends who had infertility problems and they took a long time to become parents. Everyone told us that making a baby was not that easy. One month I took out my diaphragm sort of as a trial run. I never thought I'd get pregnant but now I'm in my fifth month. Sometimes I still think it wasn't the "right" time to do this. Of course I want the baby, but I wonder how it will change my life. Do I really want this child? I go back and forth all the time, and at this stage, I thought I would feel more positive. What's wrong with me? Do you think the baby can feel my ambivalence?

G.C.
Winona, Minnesota

Ambivalence in pregnancy is normal. There really is no "right" time to have a baby, and many women wonder if they should have waited to conceive. Ms. C. is in her fifth month, when she is just beginning to show. Soon she will experience "quickening," which is the start of fetal movement. As the baby becomes more of a person to her, her ambivalence is likely to disappear and be replaced by an attachment to the baby. She will be curious to see what her child is going to look like.

No strong scientific evidence links an expectant mother's everyday emotions to fetal distress. (A severely stressed pregnant woman, however, must be mindful of constricting the blood supply to her unborn baby.) Nevertheless, *The Secret Life of the Unborn Child,** by Thomas Verney, M.D., with John Kelly, confronts the question of whether a fetus is affected by a mother's habits and emotions. The authors carefully review the research that has been conducted internationally, and they report that an Austrian study headed by Dr. Gerhard Rottmann of the University of Salzburg did find a connection between an expectant mother's feelings and the psychological and physical conditions displayed by her child.

Dr. Rottmann divided 141 pregnant women into four groups: ideal mothers, ambivalent mothers, cool mothers, and catastrophic mothers. Ideal mothers had the most trouble free pregnancies and the healthiest offspring, whereas catastrophic mothers endured problem pregnancies and delivered low-birth-weight babies and emotionally disturbed infants. Ambivalent mothers appeared to have children with behavioral and gastrointestinal problems that were not experienced by the newborns of the ideal mothers, and the offspring of cool mothers seemed to be lethargic. The findings are fascinating, but the connection between a mother's emotions and her unborn baby's development remains controversial.

U.S. researchers are reluctant to conclude that there is a definite link between an expectant mother's emotions and the wellbeing of her baby. Emotions are difficult to categorize. Unless extreme stress exists, a woman's emotional state is not considered to be a strong influence on fetal development.

The ambivalence that Ms. C. describes is quite common. It often arises because a woman is confused about her future role as a mother. Yet women who have had Ms. C.'s misgivings early in pregnancy regularly give birth to healthy babies—and they become competent mothers. When they hold their babies in their arms, these women forget that the past held any ambivalence at all.

I Dreamed I Delivered a Baby Monster.

I've had a few nightmares in connection with my pregnancy, but the worst one happened last night. I dreamed that I gave birth in the hospi-

---

*New York: Summit Books, 1981; New York: Delta, 1982.

tal, and I went to the nursery to see my baby. The nurse held up a baby monster wrapped in a blanket. Its face was grotesque. Now I'm afraid that something is wrong with my baby. Maybe I'm going to have a child with birth defects. Sometimes dreams are predictions. I'm afraid this one might come true. Have you ever heard of this happening?

C.K.
Salt Lake City, Utah

Dreams are outlets for anxieties that we do not resolve during waking hours. Whether a woman is pregnant or not, her dreams will be unpleasant more frequently than they will be happy. That's the nature of dreams. They are the mind's way of working out problems while we sleep.

During pregnancy, a woman may be more anxious than usual because, among other things, she may be worried about the health of her unborn child, her future as a mother, and how her marriage may change with the new baby. These concerns often reveal themselves in dreams, which change from trimester to trimester. Ms. K.'s nightmares are not unusual. Her deep concern for the health of her baby seems to have shown itself in the dream she describes. Her worry is natural, but only a small percentage of newborns arrive in the world less than perfect. Of course we have all heard stories of dreams that came true, but most dreams disappear with the dawn. A dream is not a prophecy.

Ms. K.'s dream is merely releasing her anxiety. She should share the dream with her husband and discuss her feelings about her baby's health. If she can alleviate her worry while she is awake, her sleep may be more peaceful.

I Was Relieved When I Saw the Baby Move on the Ultrasound Screen.

I've been worried about whether the baby was doing all right, but I didn't know the extent of my anxiety until a sonogram changed my outlook. As soon as I saw the TV screen with the ultrasound picture of the baby, I felt wonderful. There he was (we could tell it was a he!) in perfect condition. Modern technology is psychologically more helpful than most people realize.

E.C.
Portland, Oregon

As mentioned in Chapter 10, ultrasonography seems to be stimulating intrauterine bonding. An expectant mother who undergoes ultrasound testing has a chance to see and develop an attachment to her baby. Usually maternal bonding takes place after childbirth, but nature's way may be subject to change.

Anthony E. Reading, Ph.D., assistant professor in the department of psychiatry and biobehavioral sciences at the University of California in Los Angeles, and Lawrence D. Platt, M.D., associate professor in the department of obstetrics and gynecology at the University of Southern California, recently evaluated the impact of fetal testing on maternal anxiety. They concur with Ms. C.'s feelings. In their study, women who were allowed to look at ultrasound screen images relaxed considerably and felt more positive about their babies than did women who were denied viewings.

Since studies have shown ultrasonography to be a safe technique, perhaps it could be used more routinely when women have serious anxiety about their pregnancies. My own observation has been that any woman who has been suffering emotionally because she has had a strange sense that something was wrong with her baby has been greatly relieved after an ultrasound screening. Thanks to ultrasonography, worry gives way to optimism.

I Have a Lack of Sexual Desire.

My husband is especially turned on by my pregnant body. He wants to make love all the time, but I'm reluctant. I had a miscarriage last year, and I'm afraid of losing this baby. I'm in my fourth month. I know that once you pass the first trimester, sex is less risky, but I still don't want to have intercourse. My lack of desire is a real strain on our marriage. What should I do?

H.M.
Englewood, New Jersey

The safety of intercourse and orgasm are discussed in Chapter 6. Ms. M. may be having a high-risk pregnancy, since she previously miscarried. Her doctor may have advised her not to have intercourse in the first trimester, but she does not mention his recommendation in her letter. If she were my patient, I would suggest that she postpone intercourse until the second trimester, when the fetus is less likely to be disturbed by uterine contractions brought on by orgasm. Every woman should check with her doctor about the safety of intercourse and orgasm in her particular case. In a problem-free pregnancy, intercourse is safe in the first trimester.

Now that she has passed the danger point, Ms. M. might try relaxation techniques such as meditation or yoga to overcome her inhibition about lovemaking. An expectant father often feels alienated from the baby that he has helped create, and he needs empathy from his partner. Ms. M.'s husband is reaching out to her and their unborn child.

Ms. M. might ease her way back to intercourse by first exploring other ways of lovemaking. Touching, kissing, holding, and oral stimulation of the genitals may please and excite her. She and her husband should find a mutually comfortable position. When a man's body presses against a pregnant woman's heavy abdomen and sensitive breasts, lovemaking can come to a halt. Ms. M. might try sexual relations in side-to-side or sitting positions with her husband.

Sometimes a husband is afraid to approach his pregnant wife sexually because he has conflicts of his own about hurting the baby. When a baby moves during intercourse, a man may withdraw physically and emotionally from a woman. The fact that there is "something alive in there" may inhibit him. Mr. M., on the contrary, wants to be close to his wife.

Mutual caring and sharing, adjusting to each other's physical and emotional needs—this is the foundation of the pregnancy experience. Lovemaking creates a unique bond between two people. During pregnancy, this bond is more important than ever. Ms. M. will be making a more tranquil uterine environment for her baby if she enjoys the emotions that sexual intimacy generates. She and her husband are partners, but they are also *lovers* who need each other's support.

MEN HAVE FEELINGS TOO!

When he learns that he is an expectant father, a man often becomes anxious immediately. He worries about providing financially for his new dependent, and he contemplates the type of father he will be. Yet while a woman has visible signs of the change she is going through, outwardly he remains the same. That is, unless he is one of the approximately 10 to 30 percent of men who display symptoms of the *couvade syndrome*.

From the French verb *couver,* which means "to brood or to hatch," the couvade syndrome was initially observed in South American tribesmen. The Chaorati men there mimicked labor and delivery as they performed ritual dances while their children were being born. Afterward, these new fathers rested for several days in their hammocks. Today men who gain weight and become nauseated, fatigued, and generally out of sorts during their wives' pregnancies are known as *couvade fathers.* These men long to share the nine months of pregnancy intimately with their wives.

Many men feel removed from the development of their children, and they want to know what their wives feel physically. Emotionally there may be some worry that a new baby will take its mother's full attention. An understandable amount of jealousy may present itself to a man, but this is normal.

A pregnant woman needs her husband's love and support, but he also needs hers. I advise expectant mothers in my care to set aside time to be with their husbands, to talk to them, to elicit their concerns and their joys. Pregnancy is a time of transformation for all involved. Yet if trepidation is shared along with love, a wonderful togetherness will evolve. A baby will be born into a communicative and caring family.

SHARE YOUR FEELINGS

An expectant mother will experience a gamut of emotions as she wrestles with life-changing issues during her pregnancy. She is not alone. All pregnant women have many highs and lows in common. In early pregnancy, the satisfaction of having conceived a child is often mixed with concern over the possibility of miscarriage. The middle months can generate a new sense of attachment as a woman feels the baby move, but at the same time, she may be preoccupied with thoughts about her future role as a parent. She may wonder about how her relationship with her husband will change. As the third trimester progresses, curiosity about what the baby will look like grows along with trepidation over the prospect of labor and childbirth. These diverse emotions may be somewhat suppressed during the day, but they cannot be hidden from nighttime dreams.

As explained in Eileen Stukane's book *The Dream Worlds of Pregnancy,* since an expectant mother is often physically uncomfortable at night, she has frequent awakenings and better recall of her increasingly vivid dreams. I recommend this book as an aid to understanding these dreams. This volume contains myriad true-life night visions, explained and analyzed. (Some of them may be similar to yours!) I find it enlightening that the dreams described often reveal images of women swimming in calm or stormy seas, in lakes, ponds, or oceans; like their unborn babies, women are in watery environments. Dream images can sometimes be a little scary, but a woman should not be frightened. She has a support team—her childbirth educator, her doctor, her husband, her family and friends—ready to comfort and guide her.

If a woman is nervous about childbirth, early in pregnancy, she might enroll in a childbirth education course. She will find the birth process explained and demystified by a trained educator. In addition, pregnancy exercise classes can bring her closer to other expectant mothers with whom she might share her feelings. Her husband and family are available to talk to her, to hear her thoughts, and to discuss the dreams she has during sleep. And, of course, she should take her obstetrician or midwife into her confidence. Her doctor, the person who will help bring her child into the world, should be her partner throughout her pregnancy. If he seems too busy to talk to her during a visit, she should write a letter to him and ask for counsel to overcome her anxieties.

A pregnant woman need not be alone with her thoughts and concerns. The emotional seesaw created by pregnancy is ridden by many expectant mothers. By sharing her sensations and feelings with those close to her at this time, she will find warmth and a willingness to make her pregnancy a memorable, pleasurable passage.

CHAPTER 13

Is Your Pregnancy in Trouble? How to Recognize Emergencies and Handle the Unexpected

Sometimes a pregnant woman may feel a twinge here or an ache there, but these discomforts are usually without consequence. Often she does not even remember to tell her doctor about them during her monthly visits. Sometimes, though, a twinge or an ache may be a sign of a pregnancy in trouble. A headache, spotting, or cramps may be symptoms a woman dismisses because she does not want to bother her doctor, yet these symptoms occasionally presage serious difficulty. I urge expectant mothers to write down physical occurrences that take place between visits, whether or not they call me at the time. With these notations, they will remember to inform or question me during our meetings. The best way to keep one step ahead of an emergency, however, is to act immediately and contact the doctor whenever a suspicious condition surfaces.

Since a woman should not be expected to judge the severity of her situation, I tell my patients, "Call me if you feel anything out of the ordinary. Better to be safe than sorry." Their replies are often the same: "You're so busy; I don't want to bother you," or "I don't want to rush to the phone with every little thing," or "Is there any way to tell the difference between 'nothing' and a serious problem?"

No good doctor grows annoyed about receiving distress calls that turn out to be nothing. On the other hand, a competent physician would be dismayed if a woman failed to reach him with a concern that evolved into a complication later. Then, by the time he is called, he has lost his chance to make a difference.

If a woman has the smallest doubt about a condition that arises during her pregnancy, she should notify her doctor. In the meantime, she can be attuned to certain warning signs. Symptoms such as dizziness, abdominal pain, the already mentioned headache, spotting, cramps, and other conditions that will be described in this chapter are red-alert warnings that something may be wrong. Awareness of these signals can protect a pregnancy.

Today pregnancies are categorized as "low-risk" or "high-risk" at the start. A woman in a low-risk pregnancy is in good health, under thirty-five, and has conceived easily. Her personal health history is free of genetic disorders and conditions that might bring on complications. A low-risk pregnancy is almost always trouble free. A high-risk pregnancy may mean that a woman has prevailing medical problems or that for other reasons complications may be anticipated. This type of pregnancy must be monitored more closely than a low-risk one. A woman who has conceived in her teens or when she is thirty-five or older is considered high-risk because a very young or relatively old expectant mother may encounter special physical problems. A woman who has had difficulty in a previous pregnancy, miscarried, delivered by cesarean section, or given birth to a stillborn baby is also a high-risk case.

An expectant mother may appear to be fine. She may be in her first pregnancy and at an optimum age, but she qualifies for high-risk attention if her health history indicates diabetes, fibroid tumors, high blood pressure, heart problems, endometriosis, tuberculosis, asthma, thyroid disorders, debilitating allergies, or pelvic abnormalities. These are just a sampling of high-risk causes. A woman who is carrying a multiple birth such as twins or triplets, a woman who has been exposed to drugs, radiation, or infections early in pregnancy—both are at high risk. Many diverse women populate this category. A perinatologist, an obstetrician who specializes in high-risk pregnancies, devotes himself to caring for these mothers-to-be.

When she is having a high-risk pregnancy, a woman becomes more sensitive to warning signs than she would in a low-risk condition. Yet *all* expectant mothers, no matter what their category, should be cognizant of biological threats to themselves and their unborn babies. Unforeseen internal happenings may lead to high blood pressure, toxemia, or a viral infection, and suddenly a low-risk expectant mother becomes high-risk. A poorly located placenta or premature labor may transform a routine pregnancy into a guarded one. Often warning signs lead to nothing, but the concerned expectant mother nonetheless takes heed. With her doctor's and her own knowledge and awareness, a high-risk pregnant woman can be smoothly brought to term and a low-risk woman who has become high-risk can be returned to low-risk once more.

THE HIGH-RISK DIFFERENCE

For a perinatologist, a visit from a thirty-nine-year-old pregnant woman is an everyday event. He is accustomed to dealing with expectant mothers who need special care because they are "high risk." His office is equipped with the latest instruments for monitoring and protecting pregnancy, and he keeps up with modern methods of treating exceptional cases. He is the physician a high-risk expectant mother should choose as her medical partner. Who qualifies as a high-risk expectant mother?

As mentioned, women in their teens and women over thirty-five become high-risk expectant mothers. A family history of a genetic disorder such as sickle cell anemia, thalassemia, or Tay-Sachs disease creates a high-risk situation. Women who have had obstetrical problems that might include miscarriage, stillbirth, premature birth, or cesarean section are also placed in this category. A high-risk pregnant woman might have a prevailing condition such as diabetes, chronic urinary tract infection, severe anemia, heart disease, asthma, or a pelvic abnormality. The presence of a sexually transmitted disease, Rh blood disease with abnormal blood, fibroid

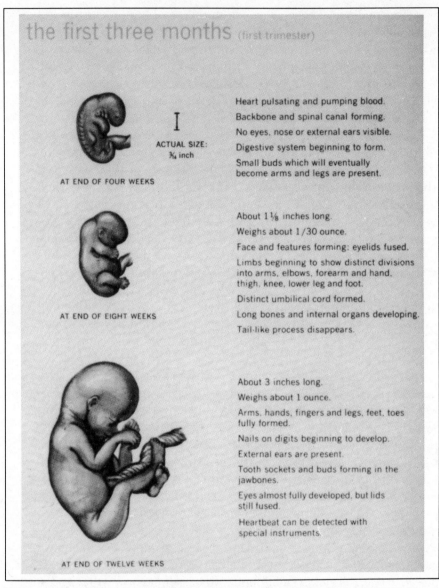

the first three months (first trimester)

ACTUAL SIZE:
¾ inch

AT END OF FOUR WEEKS

Heart pulsating and pumping blood.
Backbone and spinal canal forming.
No eyes, nose or external ears visible.
Digestive system beginning to form.
Small buds which will eventually
become arms and legs are present.

AT END OF EIGHT WEEKS

About 1⅛ inches long.
Weighs about 1/30 ounce.
Face and features forming: eyelids fused.
Limbs beginning to show distinct divisions
into arms, elbows, forearm and hand,
thigh, knee, lower leg and foot.
Distinct umbilical cord formed.
Long bones and internal organs developing.
Tail-like process disappears.

AT END OF TWELVE WEEKS

About 3 inches long.
Weighs about 1 ounce.
Arms, hands, fingers and legs, feet, toes
fully formed.
Nails on digits beginning to develop.
External ears are present.
Tooth sockets and buds forming in the
jawbones.
Eyes almost fully developed, but lids
still fused.
Heartbeat can be detected with
special instruments.

Figure 13-1. *An illustration of fetal development during the first trimester. A normal growth associated with a healthy pregnancy can be monitored through ultrasound.* Reproduced by permission of the Carnation Company.

tumors, or an ovarian cyst may lead to a high-risk classification. Sometimes a woman is labeled high-risk if she is from a low-income family and has not received proper nourishment before conceiving. If a woman conceives more than one baby, has a baby in the breech position, experiences premature rupture of the membrane, or passes her due date, she also becomes high-risk.

Trouble in pregnancy may appear anywhere along the nine-month course or not at all. A high-risk expectant mother must watch for the same warning signs as other pregnant women while knowing that sometimes she may be more susceptible to the underlying causes of her symptoms. Yet knowledge can reassure. As each warning sign is described and questions about possible problems are answered in this chapter, the high-risk expectant mother's sense of security can grow. If she understands her condition and is under the care of a perinatologist, her pregnancy can be a trouble-free, healthy experience.

WARNING SIGNS

Most pregnancies progress smoothly, but potential problems always line the road to childbirth. An ectopic (outside the womb) conception or a miscarriage can occur early in pregnancy, while later on, premature labor or toxemia (which can lead to seizure) can threaten the outcome of delivery. Along the way, a doctor also watches for conditions such as a low-lying placenta or abruptio placentae, which is a placenta that begins to separate from the womb. Although babies are conceived and born every day, pregnancy remains somewhat unpredictable.

A pregnant woman may be able to safeguard her health and her baby's, however, once she knows how to handle unexpected events. Nature offers warning signs that tell us it is time to be cautious. Sometimes these signs, which take the form of physical symptoms such as a sudden pain, a burning headache, or a fainting spell, are just passing events, but nevertheless, they cannot be lightly regarded. Spotting, cramping, swelling of the joints, headache, excessive nausea and vomiting, fever, extreme fatigue, dizziness—any one or a combination of these symptoms may portend a serious complication.

Emergency situations throughout pregnancy, from the possibility of a miscarriage to the chance of premature birth, are described in this chapter with their appropriate warning signs. If a symptom is hardly noticeable, you may not have to contact your doctor right away. If you "feel something" in the middle of the night, you may be able to wait until morning. Always call your doctor within twenty-four hours, though, to prevent the unexpected from growing into an outright crisis. This is the moment to remember that you and your physician are working toward a wonderful, mutual goal—your child.

WHAT DOES BLEEDING DURING PREGNANCY MEAN?

Whenever a woman experiences any sign of blood during pregnancy, she should lie on her left side and elevate her legs. In this protective position, she creates a healing inner environment because a greater amount of blood flows to the fetus. Her spotting or staining may soon subside, but no matter what happens, she must talk to her doctor about the incident.

Sometimes bleeding starts and stops on its own, and pregnancy proceeds uneventfully. When it is nature's warning sign, bleeding may mean different things at various points in pregnancy:

In Early Pregnancy

Before a woman even realizes that she is pregnant, she might notice a slight staining or spotting and think that her menstrual period has begun. When her pregnancy test is positive, she might wonder why the blood appeared at all. She probably experienced *implantation bleeding,* which can occur when a fertilized egg implants itself into the placenta on the wall of the womb.

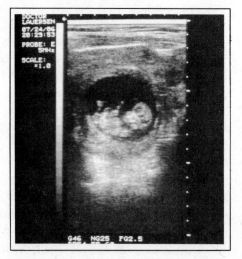

Figure 13-2. *Bleeding during pregnancy does not necessarily mean that you will lose the baby. If a woman bleeds at any time during pregnancy, an ultrasound image should immediately be obtained to determine fetal size, any abnormalities, as well as the location of the placenta. The above ultrasound image was taken when an expectant mother began to bleed at eleven weeks. The sonogram shows a normal fetus, head to the right. The fetus is lying on the placenta, which indicates that the placenta was low. This mother was given natural progesterone to relax her uterus and stop the bleeding. She went on to deliver her healthy child.*

At other times during the first twelve weeks of pregnancy, the appearance of blood may signal an *impending miscarriage*. The bleeding alone may not be so serious, however, if there are no accompanying cramps or pain. The various types of miscarriage (see pp. 281–83) are usually signaled by the combined symptoms of bleeding and cramping.

A woman may notice a slight staining without cramping, which usually indicates a *threatened abortion* or *miscarriage*. In many instances of threatened abortion, the bleeding stops and the pregnancy proceeds normally. If the staining increases and becomes very heavy, and cramping begins, then a pregnancy may be in trouble. The pain of miscarriage comes from uterine contractions and the untimely widening of the cervix. The placenta is beginning to break away from the womb. A miscarriage, or *spontaneous abortion,* as it is medically named, occurs in 15 to 20 percent of all pregnancies. Often the cause is "blighted ovum syndrome," which means that the fertilized egg or ovum was defective. A conception with a blighted ovum creates an embryo that cannot develop normally, and it disintegrates. A woman passes a fluid-filled sac that no longer contains an embryo or a fetus. In this way, miscarriage ends an imperfect pregnancy.

A blighted ovum might be caused by a defective union of an egg and sperm, or by a chromosomal abnormality that ends the pregnancy early. Some chromosomal abnormalities do not affect the life of an embryo until it is well into the first trimester. These abnormalities ultimately lead to miscarriage, which is one of the reasons it is commonly said that miscarriage is nature's way of cleansing the body because something was wrong with the baby.

Miscarriage can also be caused by a hormonal imbalance during pregnancy. Progesterone, the pregnancy hormone, is produced at a level too low to prevent the uterine contractions that expel the conception. Although miscarriage is highly stressful, it is the body's method of going back to good health.

Vaginal bleeding accompanied by pain may also indicate an *ectopic pregnancy*, which is a potentially life threatening condition. An ectopic pregnancy is one that develops outside the womb, in the fallopian tube, on an ovary, or within the abdomen. Most often, an ectopic pregnancy is situated in one of the fallopian tubes, hence the term tubal pregnancy. As an undetected ectopic pregnancy grows, it begins to strain the tube, which is not an expanding organ. In a tube, an embryo that is six to eight weeks old will often be large enough to cause severe abdominal pain and vaginal bleeding, although bleeding does not accompany every case of ectopic pregnancy.

A mother who has pain and bleeding may think that she is miscarrying, but if her pain is located more on one side than another, an ectopic pregnancy may be rupturing her tube. If a pregnancy bursts a fallopian tube, internal bleeding can become uncontrollable and fatal. The combined presence of bleeding and pain during pregnancy should immediately send a woman to her doctor.

When vaginal bleeding occurs without pain, it may mean that a woman has an infection or lesions, or possibly a polyp has grown on her cervix or in her vagina. A uterine abnormality, such as fibroid tumors, may also be responsible for bleeding early in pregnancy. In addition, a rare condition, a *hydatidiform mole* or *molar pregnancy*, which happens when the placenta begins to form cysts that overtake the womb and eventually abort spontaneously, cannot be ruled out. An expectant mother must be alert to bleeding as a sign of trouble. By responding to this warning with a call to her doctor, she increases her chances of protecting her conception.

Later in Pregnancy

Placenta previa starts at the beginning of pregnancy, when the fertilized egg wrongly implants itself in the lower portion of the uterus. Then, as the placenta grows, it either partially or completely covers the cervix, the mouth of the womb. Symptoms for this condition, which is often referred to as a low-lying placenta, appear anywhere from the third month to the end of pregnancy. Placenta previa causes bleeding, which often begins as spotting and may stop, only to recur a few weeks or months later as much heavier bleeding. If this "second bleed" is not properly cared for, it may lead to a third bleeding episode days or weeks later. Then a woman will require hospitalization to save her unborn baby and possibly her own life.

With placenta previa, the placenta never leaves the wall of the uterus. However, another condition that causes bleeding, *abruptio placentae*, is precisely due to the separation of the placenta from the womb. This separation may happen anywhere from the sixth month to the end of pregnancy. A woman may feel that her womb is sore and tender, and she may notice sporadic bleeding. This is a mild case of the condition. Abruptio placentae in a more severe form can cause relentlessly long, extremely painful contractions that cut off the fetal blood supply. In this instance, an immediate cesarean section must be performed for the baby's and the mother's survival.

Bleeding may also be caused by premature labor. If the labor is advanced and the cervix has begun to dilate, a woman may pass clots of blood or have a steady flow.

Anytime during pregnancy, a warning sign might appear. Occasionally a pregnant woman who is just too active for her condition may see spotting or bleeding if she maintains a too-tight schedule of appointments and continues her physical activities. Her body sends her this warning sign to slow down. An accidental fall or an emotional trauma might also bring on an interval of bleeding. Sexual intercourse may cause some blood to appear afterward, because vessels may have been broken as the uterus was pushed. Pain-free bleeding during pregnancy usually means that the problem is minor and quick to disappear. But whether or not a woman is hurting while she is spotting, she should tell her doctor what has happened. Everything may be fine, but she has been given a sign to pay special attention to her pregnancy.

HOW AND WHY DOES MISCARRIAGE TAKE PLACE?

For a perfect pregnancy to take place, many biological factors must be precisely coordinated, but sometimes something is out of sync. A fertilized egg does not develop properly, or a hormonal imbalance occurs, or the cause is hidden, and a pregnancy ends in miscarriage, medically termed *spontaneous abortion*. Approximately 15 to 20 percent of all pregnancies miscarry, but before a pregnancy absolutely terminates, a woman may experience different events. These events characterize various stages, or "types," of miscarriage:

Threatened abortion. This term is used to describe vaginal bleeding that varies from very light to heavy and appears at any time during the first 24 weeks of pregnancy. This bleeding may be accompanied by cramps or backaches. If these pains intensify, miscarriage may be inevitable, but if a doctor examines a woman early, before great pain develops, the pregnancy might be saved. An internal examination will reveal an open or closed cervix. An open cervix means that dilatation has already begun and the product of conception will probably be expelled within twenty-four hours. A closed cervix, however, means that a spontaneous abortion is only threatened, and the pregnancy may possibly be saved. A doctor should perform ultrasonography to determine the fetal environment, and he should also obtain blood to be tested for its level of human chorionic gonadotropin (HCG), the hormonal indication of pregnancy. If all tests show a healthy pregnancy, by resting in bed with her feet elevated, and with possible treatment with natural progesterone until the bleeding stops, a woman may prevent a miscarriage.

Inevitable abortion. When a pregnant woman notices a discharge of fluid along with the bleeding and pain, a miscarriage is imminent. When a doctor examines a woman who has bleeding and pain and sees an open cervix and a gush of fluid, he should tell her that the membrane has ruptured. A miscarriage will take place within twenty-four hours during an inevitable abortion. At this point, the pregnancy cannot be saved.

Incomplete abortion. This means that a miscarriage has occurred, but some fetal tissue and part of the placenta remain in the uterus. If any product of conception is left behind, vaginal bleeding may become incredibly heavy, and the uterus will not be able to contract as it usually does to stop the flow of blood. Hemorrhaging can become so severe that a woman goes into shock. A dilatation and curettage (D&C), a procedure in which the cervix is widened (dilated) and the tissue remaining in the womb is gently scraped or suctioned away, must be performed immediately.

Complete abortion. When the placenta has completely separated from the uterine wall and all the gestational tissue is expelled from the womb, a miscarriage is complete. The pain stops, the bleeding slows, and the uterus begins to contract and return to its normal size. With a complete abortion, a D&C is not always necessary.

Missed abortion. A missed abortion means that fetal death took place before the twentieth week of pregnancy, but the conception did not miscarry. Bleeding and pain, the usual warning signs, did not appear, and the cervix remained closed. A pregnant woman's first hints of a missed abortion may be that her breasts stop enlarging, she no longer gains weight, and the unborn baby stops moving. A pregnancy test and ultrasonography are used to diagnose a missed abortion, which definitely requires a D&C. If a fetus dies after the twentieth week, this death is called *fetal demise*, and labor is induced with prostaglandin vaginal suppositories.

Habitual abortion. This occurs in only 0.5 percent of all pregnancies; habitual abortion is the term used when a woman has three or more spontaneous abortions. If repeated miscarriages occur, a woman should be carefully evaluated and properly treated so that future pregnancies can succeed.

At the first sign of a bleeding problem, without waiting to see if she has any pain, an expectant mother should notify her doctor. Her action may stop a threatened abortion from becoming inevitable.

THE CAUSES OF MISCARRIAGE

A miscarriage is always difficult to endure. For an expectant mother, the loss of her pregnancy seems unfair and inexplicable. There are, however, a number of medical reasons a pregnancy does not progress to term.

The majority of miscarriages occur during the first twelve weeks of pregnancy because the embryo is not healthy enough to develop beyond the initial trimester. In many reported miscarriages, a defective sperm or a defective egg (ovum) has resulted in a "blighted ovum," a poor conception that cannot grow properly. This blighted ovum disintegrates, and a woman passes a fluid-filled sac that no longer contains an embryo.

An embryo that has a chromosomal or structural abnormality might also abort spontaneously within the first three months. In one study, researchers reported that 60 to 70 percent of the gestational tissue analyzed after miscarriage was chromosomally abnormal. Under these circumstances, spontaneous abortion may be nature's way of preventing the birth of a baby that would have had severe congenital malformations and an extremely hard life.

At times, however, miscarriages can be traced to the internal environment rather than to the conception itself. A damaged fallopian tube may hinder the movement of a fertilized egg. Scar tissue, fibroid tumors, or endometriotic cysts in the uterus may prevent an embryo from implanting itself properly in the placenta. A stronger possibility is that hormonal imbalance or, more precisely, an inadequate progesterone level has led to a woman's miscarriage.

Chromosomal abnormality and hormonal imbalance are the two main reasons for miscarriage. After an egg is released from an ovary during ovulation, it leaves behind its outer casing, the corpus luteum, producer of the pregnancy hormone progesterone. If the corpus luteum does not create a high level of progesterone after ovulation, the uterine wall will not relax enough to hold the implanted egg securely. A low level of progesterone will cause the uterus to manufacture prostaglandins, contraction-causing hormonelike substances. Prostaglandins will instigate cramping, and the fertilized egg will be shed as miscarriage ensues. If natural progesterone is administered in the early stages of pregnancy, often the hormonal balance can be corrected and the conception saved.

A number of other situations, such as pregnancy when a woman has a condition such as endometriosis or hypertension or an illness such as diabetes, may also contribute to miscarriage. Although miscarriage is emotionally wrenching, a woman who has miscarried once has gained insight into her physical vulnerabilities. During her next conception, she and her doctor should take steps to create nine months of good health, and a healthy baby.

QUESTIONS ABOUT BLEEDING DURING PREGNANCY: MISCARRIAGE, ECTOPIC PREGNANCY, MOLAR PREGNANCY, PLACENTA PREVIA, AND ABRUPTIO PLACENTAE

I Had My Period While I Was Pregnant. Does That Mean I'm at Risk?

I was pregnant with my son and I didn't know it. I went to the doctor because I was nauseated at work and I was afraid I was getting an ulcer. He told me that I was three months pregnant. I had had my period for three months! When you have bleeding during pregnancy, I now know that the pregnancy is touch-and-go. I'd like to get pregnant again, but I'm wondering if I have to expect the same situation. Am I liable to have another risky pregnancy?

M.B.
West End, North Carolina

Many women notice some bleeding close to the time that they are expecting their period, and they do not consider pregnancy possible. When they later learn that they are pregnant, they are understandably amazed. Thinking back, however, they usually say that their period was lighter than normal. What they mistakenly thought was their period was actually implantation bleeding.

One of Ms. B.'s staining episodes was probably due to the implantation bleeding that occurs when the fertilized egg attaches itself to the placenta. The edge of the implantation site, where the embryo meets the placenta, may shed a small amount of blood. A couple of weeks after the conception is secured, the placenta, the rich vascular lining in the womb that nourishes the growing fetus, begins to produce the female hormone progesterone, the maintainer of pregnancy. The placenta takes over progesterone production from the corpus luteum, the body of tissue from which the ovulated egg escaped. The corpus luteum, which the egg leaves behind on the ovary, manufactures progesterone until it disintegrates, approximately two weeks after ovulation. At this time, the placenta begins its progesterone production, but the level of progesterone it creates may be low.

When progesterone is inadequate, prostaglandins, contraction-causing hormonelike substances that are also produced by the placenta, increase. The level of prostaglandins goes up when progesterone is down. Cramping and bleeding may ensue, and a woman like Ms. B. may feel that she is experiencing a menstrual period. The fact is that a threatened abortion is at hand, which may or may not lead to a miscarriage. Sometimes a pregnant woman may have painless spotting near the time of the month that she usually has her menstrual flow, because her body is adjusting to new hormonal levels and is not completely synchronized to the changes. Nevertheless, bleeding should always be brought to a doctor's attention.

Ms. B.'s bleeding may not have been a sign of a serious problem, but on the other hand, she may have had a low progesterone level that might have cost her her baby. She was fortunate to carry safely to term. In future pregnancies, she should consider herself at high risk since she had a prior bleeding problem, and she should seek the care of a perinatologist. Ms. B. may not relive her episodic bleeding, but she should be alert to a recurrence. Recognized early, a bleeding problem can often be corrected.

In a future pregnancy, Ms. B. should be examined by her doctor on a weekly basis. Since she has a history of bleeding, he might take a blood test for the level of beta-subunit HCG (human chorionic gonadotropin) during her first visit. HCG is a hormone produced by the placenta and the brain during pregnancy. A steady rise of beta-subunit HCG indicates a healthy, growing placenta. After several weeks of testing, the HCG level should show whether Ms. B.'s pregnancy is progressing normally.

If the beta-subunit HCG remains level or low for Ms. B, or for any woman during pregnancy, she may be approaching miscarriage or may be having an ectopic pregnancy. A woman may also be staining at the time the test is taken. A sonogram should be obtained to determine whether there is a "pregnancy ring" created by the fetal sac. If there is no pregnancy ring, Ms. B. may be experiencing an ectopic pregnancy. If there is no embryo within the ring, a "blighted ovum" might have been created by a disintegrated conception, and a miscarriage may be developing

A doctor can also measure the level of progesterone with a blood test. If test results show that progesterone is below the level needed to maintain pregnancy, natural progesterone in the form of an injection or a vaginal suppository may be administered on a daily or weekly basis. Natural progesterone should not be confused with synthetic progesterone—progestins or progestogens. The safety of synthetic progesterone during pregnancy has been questioned by researchers. On the other hand, natural progesterone is the same progesterone that is produced by the placenta. This hormone is metabolized by the body and has no adverse effects on the fetus. Pregnancy can often be saved with treatments of natural progesterone. Women like Ms. B—expectant mothers with bleeding problems or histories of miscarriage—are now having healthy pregnancies with the help of natural progesterone, which doctors administer as soon as conception is confirmed.

Of course, as soon as a woman notices staining, she should rest in bed. By lying on her left side and elevating her feet, she is allowing an unobstructed blood supply to flow directly to the fetus. Often, in this position, a woman protects her pregnancy and the bleeding stops. It should always be remembered that bleeding without pain, without cramps, is usually less serious than bleeding accompanied by pain.

Can a Miscarriage Be Prevented Once You Start to Stain?

I just found out that I am pregnant, and since I'm thirty-six, I'm very worried about the chance of miscarriage. Suppose I start to stain in the first trimester. Can a miscarriage be prevented or is it already too late?
P.R.
Omaha, Nebraska

Bleeding during pregnancy is a warning sign a woman should heed, even if she has no accompanying pain. As mentioned earlier, spotting or staining in the first trimester may forewarn a woman of several conditions, including miscarriage, ectopic pregnancy, molar pregnancy, or even a vaginal infection. If Ms. R. sees that she is staining, she must consult her physician. He will determine the reason for her bleeding, and yes, if the bleeding is caused by a threatened abortion, he may be able to prevent it.

Sometimes, early in pregnancy, women begin to stain after vigorous sexual intercourse (see Chapter 6), strenuous exercise, or simply because they are expected to fulfill demanding daily schedules. Initially just how much trouble a woman's pregnancy may be in can be judged by a doctor in a *three-step evaluation* that includes an internal examination; a sonogram, which offers a look inside a woman's womb; and a blood test for the level of the beta-subunit of HCG (human chorionic gonadotropin). As already mentioned, HCG is a hormone normally produced by the brain. During pregnancy, HCG is also manufactured by the placenta, and placental HCG contains the beta-subunit that is used to measure the progress of pregnancy. (The beta-subunit is not produced in the brain—the brain's HCG contains mostly alpha-subunit.) Researchers have determined a "normal level" of beta-subunit HCG that can be used as a guide for determining the status of pregnancies.

An internal examination will reveal a closed or an open cervix. If a woman's cervix is closed, her bleeding is probably a sign of a threatened miscarriage, and it is not too late to try to save her pregnancy. (Bleeding with a closed cervix could also be a sign of an ectopic pregnancy, and then, of course, the pregnancy cannot be saved.) A sonogram will help pinpoint the cause of the bleeding, because a doctor will study the ultrasound image and be able to tell whether the pregnancy is progressing normally. The blood test for beta-subunit HCG will give even more precise information about the health of a woman's pregnancy. If the beta-subunit is normal for the length of her gestation, then the pregnancy may be saved. If the beta-subunit HCG is lower than normal, there may be nothing that can be done to prevent a miscarriage from occurring, since the conceptus may already have begun to disintegrate. The level of beta-subunit HCG can also provide insight into other conditions. If two blood tests show that the level is steady or only slightly increasing, either a threatened miscarriage or an ectopic pregnancy may be the cause. A high beta-subunit HCG might signal a multiple birth or a molar pregnancy.

Once he has the results of the internal examination, the sonogram, and the blood test for beta-subunit HCG, an obstetrician may make a tentative diagnosis. Usually this evaluation offers an early indication of a problem, but a doctor may have to wait days or weeks for test results that positively identify the condition. Meanwhile, a woman should immediately begin bed rest, which she should continue until bleeding stops and her doctor permits her to resume normal activity. She should lie on her left side with her feet elevated. This position directs the richest blood supply to the fetus.

After he has an insight into a woman's pregnancy, a doctor may decide to assess her condition further by taking a blood test for her progesterone level. It may be that in her body, progesterone, the female hormone that relaxes the uterus and maintains pregnancy, is low. This situation can be corrected, and a pregnancy saved, by administering natural progesterone, often for several weeks. This hormone, in its natural state, has not been found to affect a fetus adversely. (See the following question and answer about the safety of progesterone.)

I never tire of reminding my patients that any sign of blood during pregnancy must be taken seriously. One woman told me that during pregnancy, one night after intercourse, she began to bleed. She telephoned her doctor and he said that if she did not have noticeable pain, she was probably fine and she could go back to sleep. This woman was so worried, however, that she went to the emergency room of her local hospital. The obstetrician on duty told her that her pregnancy was in trouble and she should lie on her left side with her feet elevated. He took blood for further testing. As it turned out, she needed natural progesterone to prevent miscarriage, and she went on to have a healthy baby. I tell this story to my patients as an example of a vigilant expectant mother whose concern saved her child. Sometimes a woman does not need medication; she just has to slow down, refrain from intercourse for a while, and lie in the protective position to stop her bleeding. Even these precautions might be forgotten, however, unless she consults her physician at the first spot of blood.

NATURAL PROGESTERONE: IS IT SAFE TO USE DURING PREGNANCY?

Many women who are worried about miscarriage are also concerned about the natural progesterone their doctors might administer by injection or with suppositories. Certain hormones that were given to "support" pregnancy in the decades of the forties, fifties, and sixties were later found to cause serious problems in offspring. For example, in the seventies, researchers discovered that DES (diethylstilbestrol), a synthetic estrogen that pregnant women took to prevent miscarriage, could lead to rare cervical and vaginal types of cancer in the daughters and infertility problems in both sexes of offspring of these mothers.

Synthetically manufactured progesterone also came under scrutiny. A study of 50,282 mother/child pairs conducted by the Drug Epidemiology Unit of the Boston Collaborative Perinatal Project (CPP) led the FDA to warn doctors about possible harmful fetal effects of the hormone and to recommend limited use. The CPP study linked synthetic progesterone to cardiovascular birth defects, problems in the central nervous system, and masculinization of the female genitals. The CPP researchers themselves were cautious about making strong assertions because so many variables in their study were uncontrollable. Still, the evidence did offer cause for concern, and the FDA responded.

Right up until the present, researchers have continued to evaluate the effects of progesterone on the fetus, and all subsequent studies have negated the early findings and have been unable to detect an association between synthetic progesterone and congenital malformations. Several leading researchers in this country and abroad have concurred that the relationship between synthetic progesterone and birth defects is tenuous at best. The latest study from a research group in Israel once again concludes that there is no increase in harmful effects to unborn babies exposed to synthetic progesterone.

Natural progesterone has not been involved in the controversy, since studies continually prove it safe. This natural hormone has been used extensively, and internationally, to prevent miscarriage. The only effect, if any, of natural progesterone use has been demonstrated by some studies conducted in the United States and England, which showed the IQ of children whose mothers had used the hormone to be higher than that of children whose mothers had not been given progesterone. Natural progesterone is a safe choice; however, no drug or hormone should be administered to a pregnant woman without careful consideration. If a woman's pregnancy is in trouble—if she is at risk of losing her baby, and progesterone might prevent this devastating occurrence—she should discuss with her doctor the possibility of using natural progesterone as a treatment.

I've Had Two Miscarriages. Will I Ever Be Able to Have a Healthy Baby?

I've lost two pregnancies so far. I never get beyond the eighth week, and it's emotionally killing me. I want to have a baby but I'm afraid it will never happen. Can you tell me if there is anything I should be doing to have a healthier pregnancy?

P.V.
Maywood, Illinois

It is not uncommon for a woman to experience one miscarriage before she carries to term and gives birth to a healthy baby. Usually one miscarriage does not cause concern. A doctor performs the three-step evaluation described in the section Can Miscarriage Be Prevented Once You Start to Stain?, and he determines whether the miscarriage was caused by a "blighted ovum," a chromosomal abnormality, or a hormonal imbalance. During his examination, he will also look for any miscarriage-causing uterine abnormality that may be created by fibroid tumors or endometriosis. In addition, after a woman's first miscarriage, a doctor may want to take a blood test for thyroid function. The thyroid hormones stimulate the brain hormones that influence ovulation, the course of the menstrual cycle, and the maintenance of pregnancy. If a thyroid test shows hormonal levels to be low, daily thyroid medication may be prescribed to help enhance conception and support pregnancy. A doctor might also suggest that a woman who has had one miscarriage take prenatal vitamins and follow a healthy regimen of exercise and nutritionally balanced meals. Another recommendation might be the use of natural progesterone to help maintain a subsequent pregnancy.

Ms. V. has suffered two miscarriages, however, and her doctor should have already treated her as just described. In addition, her husband should undergo an analysis of his sperm to determine whether the miscarriage could be caused by an abnormality of the sperm or an infection from chlamydia or T-mycoplasma. After two or more miscarriages, investigation is needed to find out if there is a serious underlying cause. A woman and her husband should consult a genetic counselor (see Chapter 10). A blood test for chromosomal analysis of a couple's genes can identify genetic problems. Sometimes both partners' chromosomes are perfectly normal, but occasionally a slight abnormality can be detected. Once a prospective father, the husband of one of my patients, learned that he had a minor chromosomal abnormality that would cause half of his wife's pregnancies to end in miscarriage. Knowing that her chances were going to be fifty-fifty all the time, my patient had a comforting sense of awareness. She never gave up trying to conceive and finally, happily, she gave birth to a son.

If no genetic factors are discovered through genetic counseling, a doctor usually continues testing by taking the already mentioned blood test for thyroid function and a biopsy of the uterine lining, the endometrium, to investigate ovulation and analyze hormonal status. He should also suggest a hysterosalpingogram, an X ray of the uterus and tubes, to check for abnormalities such as Asherman's syndrome, which is the presence of internal scar tissue and adhesions that hinder success in pregnancy. A hysterosalpingogram also helps identify fibroid tumors as the source of miscarriage. (See the question and answer in the next section.)

Ms. V.'s two miscarriages were early in pregnancy. A woman who has a second-trimester miscarriage might have an *incompetent cervix,* a condition that can be caused by a congenital abnormality and has also been linked to repeated therapeutic abortions. A cervix that is widened and stretched for more than one abortion can become weakened. During pregnancy, this weakened cervix can dilate prematurely and the fetus can be expelled. An incompetent cervix, once it is revealed through a hysterosalpingogram, can be reinforced through surgery. Using the Shirodkar procedure, a doctor stitches and tightens the cervix after the twelfth week of pregnancy. Once the cervix is sutured, a woman must rest in bed as frequently as possible and avoid strenuous activity and sexual intercourse for the rest of her pregnancy.

A new theory about the cause of habitual abortion or repeated miscarriage comes from Dr. John McIntyre of Southern Illinois University and his research colleagues in England. These physicians have shown that miscarriage may be related to the immune system. The sperm, the fertilized egg, and the fetus are foreign bodies, and a woman's immune system would normally develop antibodies to combat them. The placenta, however, produces a blocking factor that stops an expectant mother's immune system from rejecting this "foreign" matter. When parents' tissues are too much alike, though, the blocker is not created.

By injecting genetically mixed cells from several donors into a

291

prospective mother, Dr. McIntyre and his team have "tricked" a woman's body into making the missing blocker. Ten women in the United States and twenty-four women in Europe, all of whom had habitually aborted their pregnancies, gave birth to healthy babies after treatment. Dr. McIntyre's research is still in its early stages, however, and his procedure is not widely available. Meanwhile, the future looks hopeful for other breakthroughs in the area of miscarriage.

A study conducted by Dr. Alan E. Beer, professor and chairman of the department of obstetrics and gynecology at the University of Michigan Medical School, reported that repeated miscarriage often could be caused by an incompatibility between the parents' cell types. Dr. Beer and his associates have started immuno-therapy—multiple vaccinations of lymphocytes (white blood cells) pooled from prospective fathers' and outside donors' blood-streams. The mixed lymphocytes are injected into a woman who has a history of miscarriage before she becomes pregnant again. This technique is not generally available, but research is continuing under the guidance of Dr. Beer, and one day the treatment may be in doctors' offices.

Today, in fact, the testing and treating of women who have repeated miscarriages is being conducted at several centers. Researchers are exploring the effects of injecting these women with a pool of white blood cells from donors' blood, fathers' blood, or a mixture of the two. Dr. Susan Cowchock, professor of medicine, obstetrics/gynecology at Jefferson Medical College in Philadelphia, has successfully treated a large number of women with histories of repeated miscarriage, and in a recent study, she reports that after injections with white blood cells, 80 percent of such women have conquered the problem and delivered full-term babies.

Drs. D. Ware Branch and James R. Scott at the University of Utah Medical Center in Salt Lake City have treated women with mixed donor lymphocyte (white blood cell) transfusion with good results. The doctors were also successful with another treatment: 50 percent of thirty-one women who had had more than one miscarriage successfully gave birth to healthy babies after taking 40 milligrams of prednisone and 81 milligrams of aspirin every day. The medication was started on the day conception was confirmed, and ended when antibody tests were completed. Many physicians will be somewhat hesitant about recommending a steroid such as prednisone during pregnancy. There have been promising results in the fight against recurring miscarriage with the use of baby aspirin taken daily, without a steroid. This baby aspirin may be a simple solution for some women who have had repeated miscarriages.

The following centers are treating women who suffer repeated miscarriages with white blood cell injections:

Allan A. Beer, M.D., Dept. of Ob/Gyn, University of Michigan School of Medicine, Ann Arbor, Michigan

Susan Cowchock, M.D., Dept. of Medicine, Jefferson Medical College, Philadelphia, Pennsylvania

Marie A. Lubs, Ph.D., Mailman Center for Child Development, University of Miami, Miami, Florida

John A. McIntyre, Ph.D., Dept. of Ob/Gyn, Southern Illinois University School of Medicine, Springfield, Illinois

J. Scott, M.D., Dept. of Ob/Gyn, University of Utah, Salt Lake City, Utah

The following physicians are presently testing women who have had repeated miscarriages for the anticardiolipin antibody and antibodies to nuclear antigens, which may be the source of the problem:

D. Ware Branch, M.D., University of Utah, Salt Lake City, Utah

Susan Cowchock, M.D., Jefferson Medical College, Philadelphia, Pennsylvania

Michael Lockshin, M.D., New York Hospital for Special Surgery, New York, New York

Donald Meier, M.D., University of Connecticut, Farmingham, Connecticut

Researchers continue to search for the causes of miscarriage in order to bring more women to motherhood. Ms. V. should do everything she can to learn why her miscarriages occurred, and then, depending upon the reason, follow her doctor's advice about future pregnancy. Once the source of a miscarriage is discovered, steps can be taken to overcome the problem. Although Ms. V.'s pregnancies miscarried, the fact that she is fertile and quite capable of conceiving is a positive sign. Once she conceives again, she will be ready to battle the forces that have stood in the path of her childbirth.

Will My Fibroids Grow and Make Me Lose the Baby?

A friend of mine lost her baby in the fourth month, after years of trying to conceive. Apparently she had fibroids, which grew along with the baby and caused her to miscarry. Her regular doctor had never found her fibroids, although the obstetrician said they must already have been in her uterus when she got pregnant. Right now I'm trying to have a second child, and I'm very worried. During my last checkup, my doctor found a cluster of tiny fibroids peppering the inside of my uterus. Of course, now I'm terribly afraid that if I do get pregnant, the fibroids will grow, just as my friend's did, and I will lose the baby. Is it possible to have them removed before I go ahead with this second pregnancy? Will my fibroids grow and make me lose the baby?

N.S.

Rockport, Massachusetts

Fibroid tumors are benign growths of the womb. They are located in three areas: *subserous* fibroids are outside the uterus; *intramural* fibroids are in the muscle layer, and *submucosal* fibroids are within the uterine cavity. Intramural and submucosal fibroid tumors are the most hazardous to pregnancy. These tumors change the shape of the uterus, and they are made of fibrous tissue, which lacks an abundant blood supply. If a placenta grows in the area of a fibroid tumor and a fertilized egg implants itself in that spot, the developing fetus will not receive a blood supply great enough for growth, and bleeding and miscarriage may occur. Fibroid tumors will begin to grow due to the high estrogen and progesterone levels of pregnancy. This growth will make a woman's uterus enlarge abnormally, and this expansion could in turn trigger late miscarriage or premature labor and birth. A woman with fibroid tumors must be especially cautious during pregnancy. If she has any sign of cramping or premature labor, she should be seen immediately by her doctor and treated with either natural progesterone or Yutopar (ritodrine), a medication used to halt premature labor. Sometimes women who conceive with fibroids have bleeding during pregnancy but they are able to carry to term if they are properly cared for by their doctors. Bed rest is essential.

Ms. S. should have a pelvic sonogram and a hysterosalpingo-gram, an X ray of her uterus, to determine the precise size and placement of her fibroid tumors. The hormonal changes in a woman's body during pregnancy do stimulate the growth of the tumors. If Ms. S.'s fibroid tumors are intramural or submucosal, they may become large enough to obstruct her pregnancy. Her doctor's judgment is important, and if he is a knowledgeable physician, he is very likely to recommend a *myomectomy*—surgery for the removal of the fibroid tumors only—before Ms. S. becomes pregnant. Ms. S. should be very aware that some doctors suggest a hysterectomy—surgical removal of the womb—when fibroid tumors are present. If a hysterectomy is her doctor's recommendation, she should certainly seek a second opinion. I have seen many women enjoy healthy, normal pregnancies after their fibroid tumors have been removed during myomectomies.

My Miscarriage Has Left Me Grief Stricken.

Everyone was so happy for me when I told them I was pregnant. I miscarried in my ninth week, however, and no one seemed to know what to say to me. A few days after my miscarriage, my friends didn't even mention it. I lost a child, but they acted as if nothing happened. It has been two months since my miscarriage, and I still feel grief stricken. My husband doesn't want to talk about it, and I'm very disturbed. Will this sadness ever go away?

L.D.
Tannersville, New York

Miscarriage is a physical and emotional loss combined, and it can have a lingering effect on a woman. What Ms. D.'s family and friends don't realize is that she needs their support now more than ever. She is really in a mourning period, and if she can talk about her feelings, she will be able to shorten her grieving time. By not wanting to recognize the miscarriage they both lived through, her husband is adding to her distress.

Many women have found that the sadness of miscarriage is only lessened after they confide their sorrow. Pregnancy-loss support groups are now being organized by hospitals as outpatient programs, by churches and synagogues, and by local women's clubs. One organization, SHARE (Source of Help in Airing and Resolving Experience), is a nationwide network of self-help groups for families that have experienced miscarriage, stillbirth, or neonatal death. A local telephone directory may have a number for SHARE.

Ms. D. will find strength by talking to other women who have overcome their pregnancy losses. She might ask her doctor and clergyman if they are aware of a support group in her community, and she should urge her husband to attend a meeting with her. If a spouse is supportive and comforting in the aftermath of miscarriage, a woman's sadness diminishes sooner. Ms. D. should share her grief with others, for it is only after she feels strong again that she will be able to plan a future pregnancy. Most women who have had one miscarriage go on to conceive and give birth to healthy babies.

Why Aren't More Women Aware of the Symptoms of Ectopic Pregnancy?

I had a friend who lost one tube and an ovary after an ectopic pregnancy, so when I became pregnant, I was very aware of my body. I felt that I had a pain on my left side toward the end of my first trimester. I was going to tell the obstetrician about it on my next visit, but then I began to stain. I knew I was in trouble. I called the doctor and he told me to come to his office right away. He examined me, used the ultrasound, and sent me right to the hospital for surgery. My tube was saved, but I know if I had waited until the last minute, as my friend did, I might have lost some of my organs. Why aren't more women aware of the symptoms of ectopic pregnancy?

S.R.
Sunnyvale, California

One in approximately one hundred pregnancies takes place outside the womb and is called an ectopic pregnancy. A fertilized egg does not enter the uterus but, instead, it implants itself in one of the fallopian tubes, or on an ovary, or somewhere in the abdomen. Without being attached to the placenta, it is just about impossible for a pregnancy to progress to term. There have been cases of abdominal pregnancies that have almost come to term, at great risk to the life of the mother, but these are extremely rare conceptions.

The incidence of ectopic pregnancy has risen in recent years to become a major health hazard. The increase of pelvic infections

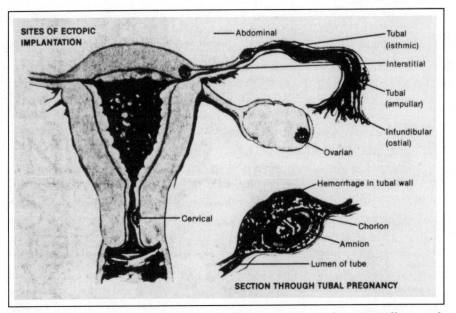

Figure 13-3. *A cross-section of the uterus, fallopian tube, and ovary is illustrated. Note the indications of sites where an ectopic pregnancy may occur.* Reproduced by permission of The Female Patient, from the article, "Ectopic Pregnancy," by Sally Faith Dorfman, M.D., M.S.H.S.A., February 1986.

and endometriosis seems to be a major reason for the rise. The majority of the time, a woman has a tubal pregnancy. A blockage or irritation in the tube obstructs the egg's passage into the uterus. This obstruction may come from a previous infection, which could have been IUD related or caused by pelvic inflammatory disease (PID), a sexually transmitted disease such as chlamydia, or endometriosis. Since a fallopian tube is not an expanding organ, as a conceptus grows, it strains the tube and causes pain. The placenta, which establishes itself in the tube, begins to break away from the wall of the tube, because there is an inadequate blood supply available. Then bleeding begins. As blood leaves the fimbriated end of the tube and seeps into the abdominal cavity, pain intensifies. Since in an ectopic pregnancy, a woman's hormonal level is lower than normal for pregnancy, light vaginal bleeding may begin. (It is important to remember, however, that vaginal bleeding does not always appear.) A woman who does not reach her doctor at the first signs of ectopic pregnancy, as Ms. R. did, might then experience labor pains that can become so severe she cannot move. At this point, the fallopian tube may burst and lead to internal hemorrhaging that can be fatal. *An ectopic pregnancy is a life-threatening condition.*

All pregnant women should be alert to the possibility of ectopic pregnancy, but women who have had pelvic infections, sexually transmitted diseases, or endometriosis should know that they are at especially high risk. Expectant mothers who are at high risk for ectopic pregnancy should ask their doctors to perform ultrasonography early in pregnancy to see if the intrauterine pregnancy ring from the fetal sac is visible in the womb. The pregnancy ring is missing when an ectopic pregnancy exists. Also, a doctor should take a weekly blood test for beta-subunit HCG. The beta-subunit HCG, which normally rises throughout pregnancy, will increase to a certain level and remain steady if an ectopic pregnancy has occurred. If a doctor feels that an ectopic pregnancy may be a reality, he may admit a woman to the hospital for a D&C and a possible *laparoscopy,* a surgical procedure that will enable him to view the fallopian tubes through a *laparoscope,* a surgical instrument like a periscope. If no gestational tissue is found after the D&C, the pregnancy is then known to be outside the uterus, and that is when a laparoscopy must be performed. If the laparoscopy reveals a tubal pregnancy, then an exploratory laparotomy is needed to remove the product of conception.

Every woman, however, should be keenly aware of the symptoms of ectopic pregnancy if she believes she is pregnant. The most common symptoms are abdominal pain, often localized on one side or the other, cramping, and occasionally vaginal bleeding. If a woman has these symptoms, an important self-diagnostic test would be to push down on her stomach. If she feels pain, she is likely to be having an ectopic pregnancy. If she pushes and releases and does not feel any pain, the chances are that her symptoms are due to miscarriage rather than ectopic pregnancy. During an ectopic pregnancy, in addition to the abdominal pain and bleeding, a woman may also feel shoulder pain. This pain results from the fact that the diaphragm nerves, which are connected to the shoulder, are being irritated.

Timing is essential when treating an ectopic pregnancy. Ms. R. was able to visit her doctor and enter the hospital in an immediate, but nonemergency, situation. Her physician could then perform careful surgery in which he could remove the pregnancy but save the tube. Such microsurgery is delicate, because the tube has to be severed in such a way that it is capable of *reanastomosis,* or joining together again. In an emergency, when a woman's tube is about to burst or has burst, she is bleeding internally and there is no time for delicate, precise surgical techniques. Then a woman's life is in danger and every step is designed to stop internal bleeding and promote her survival. Protecting her tube is low on the priority list when a woman is on the verge of bleeding to death due to a burst fallopian tube.

Ms. R., however, is in another high-risk category now. Once a woman has had one ectopic pregnancy, her chance of having a second tubal pregnancy is about 25 percent, and that percentage increases if her tube was badly damaged the first time. Ms. R. should have a hysterosalpingogram, an X ray of her uterus and tubes, to find out whether her tubes are in relatively good condition. A woman who has Rh-negative blood should always be given an injection of rhogam within three days after an ectopic pregnancy (see Chapter 10). Once a woman who has had a tubal pregnancy has conceived again, she should be monitored with ultrasound and weekly blood tests for beta-subunit HCG until a doctor can safely say that her pregnancy is healthy. Having survived one ectopic pregnancy, she would not want to run the risk of allowing a subsequent conception to reach an emergency state. All expectant mothers might follow Ms. R.'s lead and be very aware of their bodies.

How Could an Ectopic Pregnancy Have Existed Without My Knowing It? Why Didn't I Have Any Symptoms?

I had to have emergency surgery for an ectopic pregnancy and I was completely alarmed. I had had no symptoms until the pain arrived that practically paralyzed me. Beforehand, I hadn't spotted, and I didn't have abdominal pain. I had only had a slight backache, which I thought was normal for expectancy. How could an ectopic pregnancy have existed without my knowing it? Why didn't I have any symptoms?

C.L.

Boulder, Colorado

Ms. L.'s situation is not common. Most women do have some symptoms of ectopic pregnancy. Usually spotting alerts a woman to trouble, and subsequently abdominal pain develops. Rare is the occasion when a woman is unaware of having an ectopic pregnancy, but it can occur. What is more likely is that a woman will not have a warning sign of vaginal bleeding, but she feels the pain.

The symptoms of ectopic pregnancy include abdominal pain or cramping, a swollen abdomen, dizziness, blurred vision, fainting, shoulder or neck pain, and mild to severe vaginal bleeding. A woman may have one or two of these symptoms or all of them, but rarely does she lack any physical sign. Also, obstetricians are on the lookout for ectopic pregnancy, and a woman's doctor will usually perform an ultrasonography or ask a woman if she feels any unusual abdominal pressure early in pregnancy.

Perhaps Ms. L. had a symptom or two of ectopic pregnancy that she attributed to something else. Once in a while, backache can signal ectopic pregnancy, and this might have been her signal. At any rate, in Ms. L.'s case, apparently her tube expanded rapidly and caused a rupture and a painful internal hemorrhage. Often pain can go on for several days before there is a chance of rupture.

Ms. L. had an unusual experience, but her story emphasizes how important it is that a woman be attuned to her body during pregnancy.

I Had a Molar Pregnancy. Can I Still Have a Baby Someday?

I suspected that something was wrong with my pregnancy from the start. I looked about eight months pregnant at three months. I was staining and vomiting into the fourth month, but I could hear the fetal heartbeat and that consoled me. My doctor thought that the placenta might be in the wrong position, but he did not do a sonogram. I remained nervous. I went to another doctor for a second opinion two weeks later. At that point, the fetal heartbeat had stopped and a sonogram showed a round mass where a molar pregnancy had consumed the placenta. The fetus was not alive but was still there, which my new doctor told me was rare to see. He performed an abortion and for months afterward monitored my blood, because apparently if there are leftover cells from a molar pregnancy, they may become cancerous. My blood showed no signs of a cancerous condition, and now, almost a year later, he tells me that I am ready to become pregnant again. I am quite skeptical of relying on one doctor, however, and I want another opinion. What do you think? Can I still have a baby someday?

W.E.
South Burlington, Vermont

A *hydatidiform mole* or *molar pregnancy* is a rare occurrence—about 1 in every 1500 to 2000 pregnancies in the United

States—and it is most frequently seen among Asian women. In the South Pacific and Mexico, molar pregnancies have also been reported frequently. Usually a molar pregnancy starts out normally but for an inexplicable reason, the placental tissue begins to change. The placenta that has been nourishing the fetus gradually transforms into small cysts (moles), which overtake the womb and usually destroy the fetus in the first few months of pregnancy. These cysts, if viewed in a cross section, look like bunches of grapes crowded together and filling the uterine cavity. Since the cysts are hollow, the cross section shows many small openings. Usually once a molar pregnancy starts, it transforms the entire contents of the womb, but occasionally a partial molar pregnancy will take place and a fetus will survive. A normal vaginal delivery might even occur.

A woman will have continual staining as a molar pregnancy damages the placenta to the point of miscarriage. Bleeding will become quite heavy, and a D&C must always be performed. No molar tissue should be left behind. A woman who has a bleeding problem during pregnancy, as Ms. E. did, should insist that her doctor take weekly blood tests for her beta-subunit HCG level and do a sonogram to examine her pregnancy. A higher-than-normal level of beta-subunit HCG indicates that a woman might be experiencing either a molar pregnancy or a multiple birth, meaning that she could be having twins or triplets. A sonogram will certainly reveal the facts.

Ms. E.'s second doctor diagnosed her molar pregnancy and correctly performed a suction abortion. If her first physician had been more aware of modern techniques, he might have discovered her condition sooner. A molar pregnancy should be detected as early as possible so that a suction abortion and a D&C can be carried out before the cysts have greatly proliferated. If a fetus is surviving within a molar pregnancy and a woman is only bleeding lightly, a doctor should advise her to rest. A woman and her doctor, of course, would want to aim for a healthy childbirth, but such an occasion is rare with a molar pregnancy. Yet unborn babies have been known to survive this uterine environment, and there is sometimes a chance.

The benign cells that create a molar pregnancy can, in rare instances, develop into a form of cancer called *choriocarcinoma.* That is why the swift removal of a molar pregnancy is a must. A woman who has had a molar pregnancy must be observed for at least a year in case this cancer appears. The beta-subunit HCG dramatically increases during a molar pregnancy, and it only drops little by little over time after the pregnancy ends. A monthly blood test indicates whether the beta-subunit HCG is falling. Some of the tissue that caused the molar pregnancy may remain, and a diminishing beta-subunit HCG means that the tissue is disappearing and, with it, the possibility of choriocarcinoma. If the beta-subunit HCG rises, then the cells may be becoming malignant, and a woman probably should consult an oncologist.

Since pregnancy causes beta-subunit HCG to rise, a woman should not become pregnant for the year following a molar pregnancy because a physician will not be able to obtain an accurate reading from the blood test. The birth control pill, which does not interfere with the HCG level, offers the safest form of contraception at this time. If the beta-subunit HCG stays low for a year, then a woman can consider her body to be a safe haven for her unborn baby.

Ms. E. appears to have gone through a year with a low beta-subunit HCG, and her doctor's recommendation is appropriate. A molar pregnancy can sometimes cause an abnormally shaped uterus because it creates an unnatural enlargement of the womb. Adhesions of the uterus can also occasionally form after a D&C. Ms. E.'s doctor should examine her, and if her organs are healthy, he can safely advise her to embark on her next pregnancy. If she does not conceive after trying for six or seven months, the doctor should order a hysterosalpingogram, an X ray of her uterus, to determine whether any intrauterine adhesions could be inhibiting a pregnancy. The chance of a recurring molar pregnancy is practically nil; in fact, I have seen a number of healthy, robust babies born to women who have previously experienced the sadness and fear of molar pregnancies. They, too, had had some reluctance to conceive again, but once they became pregnant, they never looked back.

The Bleeding I Had from Placenta Previa Has Stopped. Why Can't I Go Back to Work?

I had no problems with my first pregnancy. My daughter, a healthy three-year-old today, inspired me to have a second child even though I am juggling an executive career. I'm thirty years old and I've always considered myself healthy, so I did not expect to have any problems. Then one day during my fourth month, I was walking out of a restau-

rant after a business lunch and I felt a trickle down my leg. I charged into the rest room, looked, and saw that an amazing amount of blood was flowing from my vagina. It was a frightening experience. My luncheon companion rushed me to the nearest hospital, and I was diagnosed as having placenta previa. My obstetrician later agreed with the emergency room doctor's recommendation that I stop work and rest in bed for the remainder of my pregnancy. A month has gone by and I have never had any more bleeding. I can't envision myself spending four more months in bed! Isn't this treatment superconservative? Why can't I go back to work?

M.Y.
New York, New York

Ms. Y. must continue to be cautious. The condition she has, placenta previa, occurs when a fertilized egg does not implant itself in the upper portion of the uterus, where it should be. The fertilized egg instead drops to the lower half of the womb and implants itself there. Implantation in this area causes a placenta to grow over all or part of the cervix, the mouth of the womb. In a *complete* or *central placenta previa,* the placenta entirely covers the cervical canal, and a baby must be delivered by cesarean section. When the placenta only partly obstructs the internal opening of the cervix, the *os,* then it is called either a *marginal* or *partial placenta previa,* or a *low-lying placenta.* In this latter situation, as the placenta grows with the unborn baby, it can move upward and away from the cervix. Then, by the time the baby is ready to be born, there may be no placenta previa at all.

The incidence of placenta previa is rare—approximately six out of every thousand pregnancies. Partial placenta previa is more difficult to calculate and probably more frequent. Women in their first pregnancies are not likely to experience placenta previa, but in subsequent conceptions, when their wombs are larger, fertilized eggs are more likely to fall. Placenta previa might also occur when a congenital malformation or fibroid tumors have expanded a womb.

Ms. Y. is in her second pregnancy, and her expanded uterus has probably contributed to her condition. She writes that she is "juggling an executive career," however, and I wonder if she may be a smoker. *Research indicates that placenta previa increases 25 percent among moderate smokers and 92 percent among heavy smokers.* Nothing can be done to stop placenta previa once it starts, but there's a chance it can be prevented if a woman who smokes quits before she conceives. Statistics show that placenta previa and abruptio placentae are responsible for at least one-half of the excessive fetal and neonatal deaths associated with maternal smoking during pregnancy. I repeatedly remind my smoking patients to stop. For me, nothing is more tragic than to see an expectant mother light up a cigarette.

Ms. Y. says that she has always considered herself to be healthy, so I do hope that she is a nonsmoker. She, unfortunately, suffered the first sign of placenta previa—painless bleeding—while she was in a public place. She may have lost as much as a cup of blood. When the uterus expands and the placental blood vessels in the area of the cervix begin to enlarge and become more fragile, one of them might erupt. The placenta will begin to bleed without causing pain or cramping. Usually this happens in the fourth or fifth month, and it is called the first bleed. *While suffering placenta previa, a woman may experience three episodes of bleeding.*

This first, painless bleeding is Ms. Y.'s warning to slow down. A doctor might have performed ultrasonography on her earlier in her pregnancy and known that her placenta was improperly positioned, but since she did not have a first-trimester sonogram, the bleeding now means that she must rest in bed and refrain from sexual intercourse and physical activity. If she becomes active right now, she may rupture more blood vessels, bleed heavily, and lose the baby.

Every woman's pregnancy is unique and every case of placenta previa is different. If she rests on her left side, Ms. Y. can direct a rich blood supply to the fetus. If she has partial placenta previa, she may even be able to give birth vaginally when the time comes. Sometimes a woman has a bleeding episode, as Ms. Y. did, and weeks or months go by when she might think that the problem is resolved, but then a "second bleeding interval" occurs. This second-trimester second bleed is often more severe than the first, and a woman may need hospitalization for blood transfusions and intravenous infusion. A woman may be sent home to rest after the bleeding has stopped, but her doctor must keep in close contact with her. A third bleed may follow near term.

A third bleeding episode from placenta previa is the heaviest, and to prevent severe internal hemorrhaging or the loss of the fetus, a woman must once again receive the emergency care that saved her during her second bleed. Usually a woman has to be delivered immediately by cesarean section during a third bleed, but even at this stage, bleeding may stop spontaneously. It is the goal of every doctor to see that a woman carries her unborn baby as close as possible to term, and if an emergency delivery can be postponed, he will delay.

A complete placenta previa leaves no option other than a cesarean; however, if the situation is nonemergency, a doctor will perform an amniocentesis to ascertain the L/H ratio, the measure of the baby's lung maturation. He will wait until the baby has reached optimum development before scheduling the C-section. With partial placenta previa, which is, I hope, Ms. Y.'s condition, rest is needed to keep pregnancy progressing. With rest, by the time childbirth is at hand, the condition may have disappeared. Placenta previa requires great patience from an expectant mother, but her reward is a beautiful, healthy baby.

What Is Placental Separation?

I am recently pregnant and, of course, I'm reading everything. I want to know more about something called placental separation, because it happened to my sister in her last pregnancy. When she was in her seventh month, one day she got a stabbing pain in her abdomen. My brother-in-law had to rush home from work and take her to the hospital. She had to have an emergency cesarean because the doctors said that she had placental separation. The baby was only two pounds but he survived and is eighteen months old now. What is placental separation? Is it hereditary? Could it happen to me too?

K.E.
Glen Arm, Maryland

Placental separation, also called *abruptio placentae,* means that part or all of a normally placed placenta has become detached from the uterine wall. This is a complication of late pregnancy. Sometimes placental separation occurs during labor; sometimes it brings on premature labor; and sometimes, as in Ms. E.'s sister's case, it leads to an emergency C-section. The severity of abruptio placentae depends upon how much of the placenta separates and when—how far along is the pregnancy when the separation takes place? Does the complication arise in the seventh month, before the baby achieves its greatest growth, or in the ninth month, when the fetus is just about ready to arrive as a newborn? Minor separations probably occur more often than we realize, but complete separations are quite rare. Less than one out of every five hundred pregnant women are likely to experience abruptio placentae. The odds are that Ms. E.'s pregnancy will be a healthy one, free of her sister's problem. As far as we know, abruptio placentae is not hereditary, but its origins are hard to pin down.

Often doctors do not know why abruptio placentae takes place, but about 25 percent of the cases are linked to high-risk conditions such as chronic hypertension and preeclampsia/toxemia. A poor diet is another suspected cause. When a woman is malnourished, her placenta may be fragile and more susceptible to separation. A fall or a jolt in an automobile may also tear the placenta away from the womb. Researchers tracking down reasons for abruptio placentae have discovered an astonishing connection to smoking. One study reported that the risk of abruption increases 24 percent for moderate smokers and 68 percent for heavy smokers. Investigators at the Pennsylvania State University College of Medicine found that mothers who stopped smoking had a 23 percent lower frequency of abruptio placentae than women who continued to smoke during pregnancy. (If Ms. E. smokes, she increases her chances of having abruptio placentae.) There has also been a connection made between a folic-acid deficiency, one of the B vitamins, and abruptio placentae, which is yet another reason for pregnant women to take extra vitamins and eat nutritiously (see Chapter 5).

The warning signs of abruptio placentae run the gamut from mild to severe, depending upon the extent of the condition. A slight separation may cause little or no abdominal pain or bleeding, while a major placental detachment can bring on internal hemorrhaging and a plaguing pain like an unrelenting "charley horse" of the womb. If a placenta separates in the center of the uterus, blood may collect in the space between the placenta and the uterine wall and not escape until the separation is complete. This internal collection of blood creates an extremely painful condition. Light vaginal bleeding as a symptom of abruptio placentae probably means that the separation is near the cervix.

A doctor will perform ultrasonography to confirm suspected abruptio placentae. If he sees that the bleeding behind the placenta is barely distinguishable and the fetal heart rate is good, a woman may be able to be brought to term for a vaginal delivery. Bed rest can be the cure, as long as she lies on her left side with her feet elevated. Sometimes a doctor also administers Yutopar (ritodrine), a medication that inhibits premature labor.

In a more advanced condition, blood becomes encased in the separated area between the placenta and uterine wall and irritates the uterus, which goes into painful spasms. As a result of this spasmodic activity, the placenta pulls away even more, and the fetus begins to lose its life-sustaining supply of oxygen and nutrients. Extensive placental separation may trigger premature labor or lead to an emergency C-section even if there is no labor. The baby's life is certainly threatened if the separation is grave, as it must have been for Ms. E.'s sister. An expectant mother is also at risk in this situation.

A woman who develops any degree of vaginal bleeding and/or abdominal pain during pregnancy must contact her doctor. There are so many possibilities. Perhaps she is just exerting herself a little too much. On the other hand, she may be facing a miscarriage, an ectopic pregnancy, placenta previa, or abruptio placentae. Spotting and staining may be "nothing," or something quite serious. Does she have accompanying pain? Is her uterus tender to the touch? She cannot know her condition by herself. This is when the partnership between her and her doctor really emerges.

HOW TO RECOGNIZE OTHER SIGNS OF TROUBLE

Premature Labor

A nationwide effort is being made to inform expectant mothers about the subtle early warning signs of premature labor. Each year over 300,000 babies—1 in 14—are born between the twentieth and thirty-seventh weeks of pregnancy. They are "preemies" who are fighting for their lives. (Birth before the twentieth week is considered a miscarriage; after the twentieth week, premature.) Two-thirds of the over 45,000 infants who die each year in the United States are premature. Thousands of premature infants survive today, but many have serious handicaps or chronically poor health. Now, however, doctors are optimistic about techniques that help women detect premature labor in time to bring their babies to term with proper treatment, which may include medication.

Dr. Robert K. Creasy, chairman of obstetrics and gynecology at the University of Texas Health Science Center at Houston Medical School, founded the groundbreaking Premature Birth Prevention Program (PBPP) when he was chief of obstetrics and gynecology at the University of California–San Francisco (UCSF). Funded by the March of Dimes, the program is similar to one originally created by a group of French physicians in Paris. Premature births at UCSF hospital were halved with this program, which teaches women to monitor their bodies for early warning signs. In the past, many pregnant women have attributed ill-timed contractions to false labor. They did not want to think that something might be wrong. The Preterm Birth Prevention Program, which has been established at a number of medical centers across the country, encourages women to be sensitive and brave about the information they receive from their bodies. Before describing the step-by-step method of discovering early warning signs as presented by the PBPP, you should know whether you are a woman who has a greater-than-average chance of experiencing premature labor. Certain factors put a woman at higher risk.

ARE YOU AT RISK FOR PREMATURE LABOR?

No doctor can tell you with certainty whether you will experience premature labor, because the medical establishment still does not fully understand what triggers this event. Apparently the fetus receives some stimulation that puts it under stress, and this stressfulness causes the fetus to send hormonal signals, which bring on contractions, to the placenta. It is almost as if the fetus feels the need to escape from an environment that is no longer peaceful, safe, and secure.

A pregnant woman may suffer a shocking emotional crisis, and premature labor may ensue. A psychological jolt changes a woman's susceptibility. If an expectant mother is aware of the factors that may influence her uterine environment, she may be more alert to the possibility of premature labor. The factors that appear to increase her chances of premature labor are:

- a past history of premature labor and delivery
- carrying twins, triplets, or more
- a weakened "incompetent" cervix
- infections in the urinary tract or cervical area
- abnormalities in the uterus, such as fibroid tumors
- a history of more than one therapeutic abortion
- being under eighteen or over forty

- being overweight to the point of obesity or being malnourished and underweight (weighing less than 100 pounds before pregnancy)
- a fever with a high temperature
- previous uterine surgery
- high blood pressure
- kidney infection or liver or heart ailments
- severe anemia during pregnancy
- strenuous physical exertion
- extraordinary emotional stress
- heavy cigarette smoking
- heavy alcohol or drug use during pregnancy
- being a DES daughter

A woman who finds herself in the high-risk category for premature labor should probably be cautious about her pregnancy. She should avoid excessive exercise, lifting heavy objects, and sexual intercourse from the fifth month (see Chapter 6). She should also relax and try to remain as stress free as possible. Whenever possible, she should rest on her left side with her feet elevated. In this position, she will be directing a rich, nourishing blood flow to the fetus and making the uterine environment much safer.

How Can I Tell the Difference Between False Labor and Real Premature Labor?

I am worried because I have a high-pressure job in public relations. The clients the agency signs up are demanding, and my boss will not tolerate anything less than quick thinking and on-the-spot decisions. I am in my first trimester and I am concerned because I am going to be under great stress throughout this pregnancy. I've read that stress can lead to premature labor, and I want to be able to recognize it if it happens. How can I tell the difference between false labor and real premature labor if I'm in the situation? Can you give me some tips?

L.F.

Denver, Colorado

False labor contractions, called *Braxton-Hicks contractions,* are irregularly spaced and are not accompanied by cervical dilatation. Still, it is often very difficult for a woman to assess the timing of her contractions and be able to identify labor as true or false. If she thinks she is experiencing some form of labor, she should call her doctor immediately. She should also have the phone number for the labor unit of her hospital handy, just in case the doctor is unavailable in this emergency.

That being said, there *are* ways to recognize early warning signs for premature labor and to differentiate it from Braxton-Hicks contractions.

The first noticeable signs of premature labor may be mistaken for backache or constipation. Before a symptom ever surfaces, however, a woman may be able to discover a sign. Due to her high-pressure job, Ms. F. might be at risk for premature labor and she might be wise to follow the technique for detecting *silent contractions,* taught at the Preterm Birth Prevention Program. This technique, described here, is helping to bring babies to term:

It is suggested that during the time from the twentieth to the thirty-seventh week, an expectant mother at risk should conduct this screening twice a day, for half an hour: Lie down and place the fingertips of each hand lightly on the abdomen, just over the uterus. Most of the time, just the action of lying down will cause the uterus to contract. A woman will feel her uterus tighten, or harden, into a contraction. When the contraction passes, she can feel the uterus relax, or soften, again. As the half-hour passes and a woman becomes accustomed to the way her uterus responds, she can recognize contractions that she would not normally know were occurring. If she is resting yet still contracting every ten minutes or so, even painlessly, she is experiencing a *crucial early warning sign* of premature labor, and she should notify her doctor immediately.

A woman who has staining anytime during the fifth to ninth month should consider herself at risk for premature labor. Stomachache, backache, or rectal pressure should not be dismissed by a woman who is aware of the chance of premature labor during her last trimester. To help women detect warning signs that are not silent, the Preterm Birth Prevention Program offers a pamphlet that includes symptoms and how to proceed if you have these symptoms. Here, adapted from the pamphlet *Recognizing Premature Labor* by Marie Herron, R.N., of San Francisco's PBPP,* are the "Warning Signs of Premature Labor:

---

* The Regents of the University of California, University of California (San Francisco: 1983).

SYMPTOMS
- uterine contractions that occur every 10 minutes or more often without pain
- constant or intermittent menstrual-type cramps in the lower abdomen, directly above the pubic bone
- intermittent pelvic pressure, which feels as if the baby is pushing down
- abdominal cramping with or without diarrhea
- low, dull backache felt as a tight band around the base of the spine above the buttocks
- any change or increase in vaginal discharge, especially if it becomes mucuslike, watery, or tinged with blood

IF YOU HAVE ANY OF THESE SYMPTOMS
- Lie down tilted toward your side, with a pillow supporting your back. An hour's rest may slow or stop the symptoms.
- Do not lie flat on your back; this may cause more frequent contractions.
- Do not turn completely on your side; you may not be able to feel the contractions.
- Time contractions for 1 hour, from the beginning of one contraction to beginning of the next.
- Call your doctor or go to the hospital if you have contractions every 10 minutes or more often (more than five contractions in 1 hour), or if any of the other symptoms persist.

The real difference between false labor and true premature labor is the rhythm of the contractions. Continual rhythmic contractions, at timed intervals, are signals of actual labor. If they happen to Ms. F., she should call her doctor immediately. If he suspects premature labor, he will probably ask her to come to his office or go to the hospital to be examined. The obstetrician or a hospital physician will look for cervical changes that she cannot see and will evaluate uterine activity with a fetal monitor. These changes, such as a shortening of the cervix or the onset of cervical dilatation, dictate the type of treatment she should have.

Cervical changes and regular labor contractions mean that uterine activity has started and, therefore, a doctor may begin an intravenous infusion of a uterine relaxant such a Yutopar (ritodrine), the only FDA-approved medication for slowing premature labor. (Treatment for premature labor is described more extensively beginning on p. 313.) If no cervical changes are seen, an expectant mother may be advised to remain in the hospital for observation and then sent home to rest. Of course, once labor has progressed too far, it is impossible to stop premature birth, and the result can be devastating. A baby may not survive due to its premature arrival, or it may have to stay for several months in a neonatal intensive care nursery and even so, may suffer neurological impairment. So knowledge of early warning signs is imperative. By getting the jump on premature labor, expectant mothers and their doctors give unborn babies more time to grow in the womb, where they are receiving the important foundations of life.

NEW HOME MONITORING DEVICE FOR DETECTING
PREMATURE LABOR

Premature labor has become such a prevalent complication during pregnancy that it has stirred many types of research. The neurological disorders and infant mortality resulting from prematurity have emphasized the need for prevention. A number of companies have tried to create ways to detect premature labor through technology, and right now the TERM GUARD System from the Tokos Medical Corporation in California seems quite helpful and promising. TERM GUARD consists of a small monitoring device incorporated into a belt. A woman who is at high risk for premature birth, whether she is at the stage of observation or treatment, places the belt around her abdomen two or three times a day. The monitor responds to labor contractions and send signals that can be transmitted by telephone to one of the monitoring centers staffed with nurses. If signals warn of premature labor, a woman can immediately be admitted to the hospital, where, hopefully, labor can be stopped before progressing to an inevitable birth.

I have used this system on expectant mothers who have been in early premature labor that was confirmed by examination. I have preferred to treat these women at home with Yutopar (ritodrine) tablets and bed rest rather than place them in the hospital. Women who have been treated in the hospital, however, can also use TERM GUARD for at-home monitoring afterward. Medical insurance is presently paying for this system. For further information, a woman can contact Director of Patient Services, Tokos

Medical Corporation, 1821 East Dyer Road, Santa Ana, CA 92705, or call: (800) 248–6567, or (800) 258–6567 (in California).

I Was Treated for Premature Labor and My Doctor Saved My Baby.

I was six months pregnant when I thought I felt some cramping, but it went away. I told my obstetrician, who insisted that I come for an immediate office visit. I didn't think it was all that important, but he did. When he examined me, he said that my cervix had begun to change and that it looked like I might be in trouble. This happened on a Monday morning, after a weekend of running around to antique fairs in the country and having more frequent sex with my husband than I do during the week. The doctor told me that my two days of excessive activity may have instigated premature labor, but he felt it could be stopped without putting me in the hospital. He gave me a prescription for Yutopar [ritodrine] tablets and told me to take one every four hours. He also asked me to stop work and stay in bed. I stayed on the Yutopar for two months, and the labor never came back. I was able to have natural childbirth after nine months of pregnancy. I'm writing you this letter because I've heard you talk about horror stories in gynecology and obstetrics and I want people to know that it's not always that way. I know that some doctors do not take a pregnant woman's cramping complaints seriously, but mine did. I would like to know, though, if there are any long-term side effects from Yutopar.

M.T.
Greenwich, Connecticut

Ms. T. was fortunate that her labor could be halted safely by her doctor. She was obviously at the stage that she could be helped by taking oral doses of Yutopar (ritodrine), one of a group of relatively new drugs called *beta-mimetics.* These medications stimulate the womb's beta cells, which then relax the uterine muscles and slow contractions.

If Ms. T.'s labor had been *less advanced,* she might have been advised to rest in bed without a uterine relaxant such as Yutopar. Bed rest has been the traditional way to lessen premature contractions, because a horizontal position shifts the full weight of the baby from the cervix and allows oxygen-rich blood to reach the fetus in greater supply. If an expectant mother lies on her left side to relieve the pressure on the vena cava, the large vein in the back

313

of the abdomen, a better flow of blood moves through the vessel. In this position, the fetus is more thoroughly nourished, and premature labor may be stopped without medication.

If Ms. T.'s labor had been *more advanced,* she would have been admitted to the hospital immediately for intensive monitoring of her own and her unborn baby's vital signs. It might have been necessary to administer Yutopar (ritodrine) intravenously for twelve hours and to prescribe Yutopar tablets afterward. In some instances, however, labor has progressed so far that the cervix is dilated more than five centimeters, and the course of nature cannot be changed. A doctor has no choice other than to deliver a premature infant. Childbirth must also proceed when an expectant mother goes into premature labor and is seriously ill, and/or when the fetus is in great distress. Delaying childbirth in these cases might jeopardize the life of mother or child.

Normally doctors want women to be able to detect premature labor to give them time to do whatever is humanly possible to prevent an unscheduled birth. When a baby does not have a full nine months in the womb, key organ systems do not develop properly. A common problem afflicting premature newborns, for example, is respiratory distress syndrome (RDS), also known as hyaline membrane disease. A baby with RDS is born with immature lungs that lack a sufficient supply of *pulmonary surfactant,* a substance that lubricates the lungs' tiny air sacs, helps them inflate, and keeps them from collapsing with each breath. Other serious problems of prematurity may include *intraventricular hemorrhage* (bleeding within a part of the brain) and *retrolental fibroplasia,* which may cause blindness. Technology has provided premature intensive care units with special isolettes, equipment, and drugs, but nothing can match the environment in the womb, nature's ideal intensive care unit. Everything that can be done should be done to keep an unborn baby in the womb until it has fully matured.

Today if a doctor sees that a woman is in premature labor but she has not dilated more than about four centimeters, her membranes are intact, and she has no complications such as high blood pressure, bleeding, maternal diabetes, intrauterine infections, hyperthyroidism, or preeclampsia, he knows that he has a greater than 80 percent chance of stopping labor with Yutopar (ritodrine). Once he decides to go ahead with the drug, a woman is admitted to the hospital, where she receives ritodrine intravenously. Often, within ten to twenty minutes, the uterus relaxes and the cramping stops. The doctor may continue intravenous treatment for as long as twelve hours, enough time for the hormones responsible for the premature contractions to be excreted.

After her intravenous infusion ends, a woman is started on oral ritodrine—two 10-milligram tablets every two hours. This dosage may be lowered later. A woman remains in the hospital for another day or two of observation while she is on the oral ritodrine, and then she is sent home with doctor's orders to continue the medication until the thirty-sixth or thirty-eighth week of gestation. At that point in pregnancy, a baby should be out of danger. Years ago, beta-mimetics did not exist in the treatment of premature labor, and Ms. T. is lucky that her pregnancy occurred at a time when Yutopar is available. Since her premature labor was mild, her doctor was able to treat her with ritodrine tablets, and he avoided intravenous treatment.

THE SAFETY OF YUTOPAR (RITODRINE)
Ms. T. is certainly wise to inquire about the long-term effects of ritodrine. For the mother, some side effects may occur while she is taking the drug, but no long-term effects are known. Since beta-mimetic drugs stimulate heart rate, they are not given to women with high blood pressure or cardiac problems. (Expectant mothers who do take ritodrine should have their heart rate carefully monitored during intravenous treatment.) Most women tolerate ritodrine very well, however, if the drug is properly administered. Some side effects that have been reported during intravenous treatment, and to a lesser degree with oral doses, include palpitations, headaches, or occasional nausea. None of these symptoms has been considered severe.

The short- and long-term looks at ritodrine's safety for the fetus are also good. In the short term, the drug increases the baby's heart rate and blood sugar, but these are minor, nonworrisome side effects. As for the longer term, ritodrine was studied over an extended period in Europe and the United States with completely positive results. I participated in the United States study, in which the newborns of mothers who had taken ritodrine during pregnancy were followed for nine years, along with a control group of newborns whose mothers did not use the drug. Both groups of newborns were born on corresponding days and years. Birth weight and other biological factors were also coordinated. Over nine years of observation, the two groups have shown no notable differences in mind or body. Physicians believe that ritodrine is a drug that can be administered safely, a drug that can gain precious time for a developing girl or boy who desperately needs it.

A NOTE ABOUT STEROIDS

In the past, in order to help the maturation of an unborn baby's lungs, corticosteroids (steroids) were often given to women who had experienced premature labor before the thirty-second week. Since it is now believed that steroids may impair a child's immune system or lead to other abnormalities later in life, today these hormones are only recommended in particular instances. A pregnant woman treated with ritodrine usually does not need corticosteroids, since the ritodrine itself aids the development of the baby's lungs.

Prematurely Ruptured Membranes

What Happens When Your Water Breaks Prematurely?

I know that when your baby is due and your water breaks, you're supposed to deliver within twenty-four hours, but what happens when your water breaks prematurely? If you have no contractions, is labor induced so early in pregnancy?

A.G.
Macon, Georgia

When an expectant mother leaks amniotic fluid between her twentieth and thirty-seventh weeks, her "water has broken" prematurely. Often this leakage comes as a complete surprise, and even doctors have been baffled about the cause of what is technically called premature rupture of the membranes. It may be that, at times, stress or excessive exercise may bring on unnoticed contractions that cause the cervix to open slightly. Then sexual intercourse may introduce bacteria that pass through the cervix and infect the membranes. Once they are weakened by infection, the membranes may rupture. Sometimes multiple birth or an incompetent cervix leads to the rupture too.

I regularly advise my patients to slow down, exercise in moderation, and eat nutritiously to combat such complications. Studies have shown that zinc may be especially helpful in strengthening the membranes, and I recommend a zinc supplement of 50 to 100 milligrams daily. (See Chapter 5 for information on nutritious eating; zinc and iron supplements should not be taken together.)

A pregnant woman who feels that her water has broken prematurely should call her doctor as soon as it happens and go to the hospital. Testing will confirm whether the liquid she felt is amniotic fluid and not urine or vaginal discharge. If she has no labor, the membranes can sometimes seal themselves if she is placed on complete bed rest in a sterile hospital environment. In this way, everyone can buy time for the fetus.

While a woman is resting, her temperature must be checked several times a day, her heart rate must be monitored, and blood counts must be taken daily to make sure that her white blood cells aren't rising. An increase in the white-blood-cell count indicates infection, which can be dangerous to the baby. If an infection or fever develops, labor has to be induced before the fetus is affected.

If premature rupture of the membranes occurs *with labor,* it is not recommended that a doctor attempt to stop the contractions. In this instance, concern over infection is much greater, and a premature delivery is allowed to proceed. If the membranes rupture closer to term, a woman usually goes into labor within twenty-four hours. This is a blessing, since the risk of infection is reduced with the rapid onset of labor. A doctor will induce labor himself if it does not occur spontaneously in late-pregnancy ruptures. A newborn should have little trouble surviving birth after the thirty-fifth week.

MULTIPLE BIRTH

It takes a little extra care and caution to have more than one baby at a time, but many women deliver twins, or more, quite successfully. In fact, I have often heard my patients exclaim, when they have learned the news of their twins, "Thank God, now I only have to be pregnant once!"

The chance that a woman will naturally conceive twins has dropped in recent years. In the fifties, twins occurred in 1 out of every 80 pregnancies, but lately the incidence has been 1 out of 100 pregnancies. Conceiving triplets, quadruplets, or other multiple births is quite unlikely under normal circumstances. Today, though, the increased use of fertility drugs has changed the frequency of multiple births—more are occurring than ever before.

News stories about women having five, six, and seven offspring after using a fertility drug have sent shivers up many female spines. What the newspapers do not report, though, is information about mothers who gave birth to one or two beautiful babies thanks to fertility treatment. It cannot be denied that fertility drugs do increase the incidence of multiple birth: 7 out of 100 pregnancies are twins; 5 out of 1000 are triplets; 3 out of 1000 are quadruplets; quintuplets occur in slightly more than 1 percent of every 1000 pregnancies. Most physicians, however, are able to control the number of eggs that are fertilized by carefully monitoring their patients with ultrasound and by taking blood tests that check hormone levels.

How Does a Multiple Birth Change Prenatal Care?

Women in their thirties are more likely to conceive twins than are women of other ages. And among the races, black women are more likely to bear twins than are Caucasians, who are more likely to have twins than are Asians. It used to be that expectant mothers could tell they were carrying twins long before their doctors could confirm their suspicions. Medicine was slow to verify female intuition until recent years. Today, with the aid of ultrasound, an obstetrician can detect a multiple birth in the first two months. This early detection is important, because now a woman can start taking special care of herself quite soon after conception.

A one-baby pregnancy is 40 weeks long, but for a multiple birth, gestation is shorter. Twins are normally born in 37 weeks, triplets in 35 weeks, and quadruplets in 34 weeks. So much changes during multiple birth. While gestation is shorter, the chance of premature labor is higher. Multiple birth is one of the leading causes of prematurity. It all adds up to the fact that a woman who is expecting more than one baby must treat herself delicately during pregnancy.

Studies from Scandinavian countries have shown that women carrying twins had a much higher incidence of premature birth if they *continued working* after the fifth month, when compared to women who *quit working* after the fifth month and rested. As a result, Scandinavian doctors now recommend that women in multiple-birth pregnancies take time off from the fifth month on. This belief in extra rest for multiple birth is shared by doctors around the world. At the start, even if a woman can only take an extra hour's nap, she should.

The faster a woman learns the news of a multiple birth, the sooner she can begin to take it easy. After the fifth month, I prefer that my pregnant patients take the Scandinavian approach: quit work, stay home and rest. Right from the start, I advise these expectant mothers to avoid lifting heavy objects and to refrain from sexual intercourse and exercise workouts. I recommend taking two prenatal vitamins a day as well as extra iron and vitamin B. (See Chapter 5.) The pressure on the stomach created by more than one baby makes eating large meals practically impossible. An expectant mother should eat about six small daily meals, which include fresh fruit and vegetables, lean meat, fish, poultry, and dairy products. (See Chapter 5).

A woman who has conceived more than one baby should also be prepared to see her doctor more frequently than the "normal" expectant mother. Visits are scheduled for every two weeks rather than every three to four weeks, so that an obstetrician can more closely monitor the growth of the fetuses. Sometimes one baby receives more nourishment than another and grows faster, creating a situation called twin transfusion syndrome. When a woman is pregnant with more than one baby, she is also more prone to problems such as water retention, heartburn, morning sickness, insomnia, hemorrhoids, and toxemia, which can be life threatening (see p. 327). Those added visits to the doctor are for her health as much as for the well-being of the babies.

With a multiple birth, a doctor also looks for cervical changes when he examines an expectant mother. A cervix that is dilating (widening) or effacing (thinning out) before term is signaling possible premature labor. There is such a great chance of premature labor and delivery with multiple birth that a woman and her doctor must remain vigilant. (See information on Premature Labor in the preceding section.) If a woman carrying twins or more ever experiences contractions, she should call her doctor immediately. (See How Can I Tell the Difference Between False Labor and Real Premature Labor? in the preceding section.)

As with all pregnancies, the goal is to bring the unborn to term. Since multiple birth increases the possibility of having a premature delivery, an expectant mother and her doctor must be alert to all warnings. Premature labor can often be slowed and pregnancy prolonged by Yutopar (ritodrine) tablets, which an expectant mother can take at home. In the most risky third trimester, a pregnant woman should lie down as much as possible. A few weeks before her due date, she should have complete bed rest.

The need for the special care that protects all pregnancies doubles and triples with more than one in the womb.

How Are Twins Born?

As already mentioned, twin gestations, which are about 37 weeks long, are shorter than normal pregnancies. Each twin is smaller than a baby that has been growing in the womb by itself, and each arrives in the world according to its position. About 50 percent of the time, both twins are in the vertex (head down) position in the womb, but with about 40 percent of twins, one is head down while the other is breech. Both twins are in a breech position about 10 percent of the time. There are rare instances when a twin is transverse in the womb, and in this situation, a cesarean section is the safest delivery. Whenever vaginal birth seems safe, however, physicians encourage and assist expectant mothers in the natural childbirth of their twins.

For a woman carrying twins, the chance of cesarean section being necessary is greater than for a woman with a singleton, and women who are pregnant with triplets, quadruplets, or more are more likely to have cesareans than all other expectant mothers. On the other hand, when twins have been carefully monitored with ultrasound throughout the length of pregnancy and they have grown to term without complications, are both the same size, and are in the vertex position, an expectant mother should be able to have a trouble-free vaginal delivery. Sometimes a twin in the vertex position arrives vaginally, but the second twin is in a breech position and cannot easily be turned or guided by the doctor. Then a C-section is called for.

Many doctors are concerned about attempting vaginal delivery of a breech twin, because the shorter gestation of twins makes their heads somewhat more fragile. Physicians worry about harming such a delicate newborn. So although many studies have shown that a vaginal breech birth can be undertaken successfully, the prevalent feeling is that with a breech twin, a cesarean is safer. Doctors are also aware of the high incidence of prematurity with twins.

No matter what their position, all multiple-birth babies are more likely to be born prematurely than are singularly conceived infants. If a woman expecting twins experiences premature labor that cannot be slowed (see the discussion of treatment of premature labor, p. 313), a cesarean is, once again, the safest, healthiest way to deliver her babies.

Everything about the birth of twins depends upon the individual details of an expectant mother's pregnancy, however. She and her doctor must weigh her particular pros and cons, and together they must choose the *safest* childbirth for her babies.

I've Just Learned That I'm Carrying Twins. Will Pregnancy Be Much Harder for Me?

I'm thirty-four years old and I'm pregnant for the first time. I'm in my second month, and the doctor has just told me that I'm going to have twins. I'm not surprised, because both my husband and I have family histories of twins. The thing is that my doctor has scared me a bit because he makes it seem as if I'm going to suffer a lot more during pregnancy. Is he right? Will pregnancy be much harder for me?

R.V.
Elyria, Ohio

First I would like to congratulate Ms. V. on the conception of her twins. Yes, she does have to be somewhat more cautious during pregnancy, but her added caution will bring added joy once the babies are there in her arms. Meanwhile, she should not be anxious. With the screening techniques and knowledge available to today's obstetricians and pregnant women, a multiple-birth pregnancy can be cared for in ways that make it almost trouble free. (See How Does a Multiple Birth Change Prenatal Care?)

The fact is, though, that two fetuses do make all the normal discomforts and concerns a little more pronounced. Ms. V. might have more intense morning sickness and heartburn, since her two unborn babies are driving up the acidity in her system. In early pregnancy, the chance of miscarriage may be more on her mind because twins increase the probability that something may go wrong. That does not mean, however, that she should dwell on the possibility of double trouble. The greater likelihood is that she will enjoy nine uncomplicated months. Her awareness, however, should be heightened. Only she can really make sure that she rests and takes life easy right now.

As pregnancy progresses, the two babies will put quite a bit of pressure on her vascular system, and that pressure could result in varicose veins or hemorrhoids. She should wear support hose and elevate her legs as much as possible. Fibrous foods are a must in her diet.

The main fact that Ms. V. should know is that everything about twin gestation points to the need for more rest. The two babies are putting stress on her body, causing more fatigue, and if she does not rest from the fifth month on, she may be tempting fate unnecessarily. Rest can create an inner environment that is less likely to produce toxemia, premature rupture of the membrane, premature labor, or premature birth, which can be associated with twins. Ms. V. does not have to suffer more during her pregnancy, but she does have to rest more. She should take a leave of absence from any job she may have once she enters her fifth month, and she should spend her days resting in bed. A twin pregnancy is definitely an occasion to lie down as often as possible. Bed rest—lying on her left side with her feet elevated—from the fifth month on can reduce the chance of complications. Scandinavian studies have emphasized the need for bed rest from the fifth month of a multiple-birth pregnancy, and I have followed this recommendation with my own patients. Just as the Scandinavian studies have pointed out, my multiple-birth patients have had healthier pregnancies when they have been less active and have rested more.

How Does Diabetes Affect Pregnancy?

A woman who suffers from diabetes mellitus has a good chance of having a healthy baby in this modern age of medicine. Today innovative techniques are overcoming the problems of the past. The congenital abnormalities found in the offspring of diabetic mothers and the growth of overly large babies who often could not survive are occurring less often with careful management. A woman who has a history of diabetes, particularly juvenile-onset diabetes, should seek the advice of a genetic counselor before becoming pregnant. Genetic counseling can help her understand her own specific options.

The disease must be kept under control during pregnancy, and with careful supervision by a perinatologist (a high-risk obstetrician) and a specialist in diabetes, the chances for a healthy pregnancy are excellent. Before conception, well-managed insulin administration, a specially balanced diet, and vitamin supplements give a diabetic woman the best preparation for expectant motherhood.

Gestational Diabetes

A person becomes diabetic when the pancreas does not produce the amount of insulin her body needs to metabolize sugar. Sugar then builds in the blood, and the body's metabolism of proteins, fats, and other nutrients changes. The high blood sugar levels and altered metabolism of a pregnant woman may lead to serious congenital abnormalities in newborns that are so large their lives are in danger, stillbirth, and fetal demise. A woman who was diabetic before pregnancy is controlling the disease with diet and synthetic insulin and no doubt knows that her health requires careful monitoring after conception. *A woman who was not diabetic before pregnancy may become so, however.* Pregnancy-induced *gestational diabetes* may develop as a pregnancy progresses. The onset of gestational diabetes is usually discovered when excessive sugar appears in an expectant mother's urine test during a routine examination. It seems, though, that certain women are more prone to the condition.

Gestational diabetes is more prevalent in pregnant women who have a family history of diabetes, who have given birth to a large (over nine-pound) baby, or who have suffered inexplicable stillbirth or miscarriage. These women are usually over twenty-five and are likely to be overweight, hypertensive, and susceptible to moniliasis, a common vaginal yeast infection.

A woman hears of the *possibility* of gestational diabetes after a urine test shows an abnormally high level of sugar. Confirmation follows a glucose tolerance test: First, she enjoys three days of unrestricted diet and exercise. Then she fasts for at least eight hours overnight. The morning after her fast, the doctor measures her blood sugar (glucose) level, and immediately after, she drinks a specified amount of "sugar water." Her blood sugar is then measured at thirty minutes and one, two, three, and perhaps up to five hours. These readings indicate whether gestational diabetes truly exists.

If the test confirms gestational diabetes, an expectant mother is placed on a special diet and is scheduled to visit her physician for frequent urine and blood tests to monitor her blood sugar levels. She may also learn how to monitor her blood sugar herself. (See p. 325.) Usually gestational diabetes can be controlled by diet, but occasionally blood sugar jumps so high that a woman must be given insulin injections for the rest of her pregnancy. The important fact to remember is that diabetes in all forms can be controlled during pregnancy, and a healthy, normal-size baby can arrive, to the joy of its parents.

If You Become Diabetic

Many women have nervously asked me this question. They have read about the possibility of developing diabetes during pregnancy and they are worried that they may suddenly suffer this condition. Gestational diabetes seems to appear in about 3 to 12 percent of all pregnancies, but I would not be surprised if this percentage was falling. Lately physicians are so alert to the problem that screening for sugar levels in urine is conducted quite carefully throughout the trimesters. A woman who is gaining much more than the recommended weight (see Chapter 5) for her point in pregnancy is considered suspect, and so is a woman who has suffered a previous stillbirth or miscarriage that cannot be explained.

Before pregnancy, all women are strongly encouraged to develop healthy eating habits and to follow diets that provide vitamins and minerals in a balance of carbohydrates, protein, and fats. A nutritious diet plan before conception, besides being good preparation for pregnancy, seems to combat the onset of gestational diabetes. (A woman who is previously diabetic probably has eaten a sugar-free, healthy diet and taken insulin injections all along, so she should be quite fortified for pregnancy.)

The second and third trimesters are when the stress of pregnancy makes the body most susceptible to the possibility of diabetes. If a urine analysis reveals high blood sugar and gestational diabetes is confirmed after a glucose tolerance test, you will be placed on a sugar-free diet. Essentially, both before and during pregnancy, a woman should be on a low-sugar, balanced diet, but once a prediabetic or diabetic situation occurs, her diet should be watched even more carefully. The diet for insulin-dependent diabetic women includes between 2200 and 2400 daily calories in a combination of 45 percent carbohydrates, 25 percent protein, and 30 percent fat. Gestational diabetes calls for a similar eating program, which either a perinatologist or a specialist in diabetes recommends. If a diabetic condition is not controlled, an abnormal metabolism may increase the acidity in a woman's body and create a condition called *ketoacidosis*, which acidifies the fetal environment. In an acidic environment, fetal growth is impaired and sudden fetal death can occur. Obviously blood sugar must be kept at healthy levels during pregnancy.

Doctors require diabetic expectant mothers to come in for frequent urine and blood checks to monitor blood sugar levels. In addition, more control of the disease now comes from a new medical advance that has made at-home monitoring possible. A diabetic woman may be taught by her doctor, a diabetologist, or by a specially staffed unit of the hospital to use a machine called a Dextrometer to test her own blood sugar level several times daily. A specially designed instrument pricks her finger, and she places a drop of blood on a chemically treated paper strip called a Dextrostix. The Dextrostix is then inserted into the Dextrometer, which reflects a blood sugar reading.

If, in spite of careful dieting and monitoring, blood sugar cannot be maintained at a healthy level during pregnancy, a woman may be hospitalized for insulin therapy. Insulin injections help change the uterine environment so that a fetus may grow into a healthy baby. I assure my pregnant patients that they should not be nervous about receiving insulin but, instead, they should be comforted by the fact that the potentially damaging effects of diabetes are being suppressed.

A diabetic woman may be safely followed to term as long as her blood sugar levels remain normal. If they do, then she can anticipate the experience of a natural, vaginal childbirth.

I Know That My Diabetes Increases the Risk of Birth Defects. What Can I Do to Have a Healthy Baby?

I am a pregnant diabetic in my first trimester. I know that my diabetes increases the risk of birth defects in my baby and I am aware of the care I need. My doctor has told me that I will probably have to be hospitalized in my last trimester so that my insulin intake can be monitored. Still, I am worried. I wonder whether my doctor knows all the latest advances. In your opinion, what can I do to have a healthy baby?

F.C.
Scotch Plains, New Jersey

Ms. C., like most diabetic women, is informed about her condition and knows she must be watched carefully and protected against complications during pregnancy. She should be under the care of a perinatologist and a diabetologist throughout her pregnancy. My hope is that she prepared for pregnancy by following a strict, well-balanced, sugar-free diet and has received careful insulin management, and that she is feeling exceptionally strong now. A healthy

325

prepregnancy diet, with insulin control of diabetes, can help reduce congenital abnormalities.

In the past, diabetes has been a deadly condition during pregnancy. A decade ago, it was estimated that maternal diabetes caused 15 to 20 percent of either stillborn or newborn deaths. Birth defects brought on by a malfunctioning metabolism created by diabetes included heart problems, damaged kidneys and lungs, cleft lip, and cleft palate. These diabetes-related congenital abnormalities would still be occurring in great number if modern monitoring had not been able to keep watch over the blood sugar levels that affect the fetal environment. The use of the Dextrometer (see preceding section) for at-home monitoring has been a tremendous aid to physicians and diabetic mothers. This personal monitoring, coupled with screening by ultrasound and urine and blood analyses, can keep a steady check on your blood sugar and alert you to potential trouble. Ms. C.'s doctor has informed her that she will be hospitalized for insulin intake in her last trimester. Every diabetic individual is different. Her physician has made his recommendation based upon her specific health history. (Hospitalization is common, because it is often difficult to control the diabetes at home.)

Ms. C. must remember, however, that the first trimester is also important. This is the time when the fetus's major body organs and biological systems are taking shape. She might be interested in investigating a battery-operated insulin pump that has been provided to pregnant women through certain Boston hospitals (Boston Hospital for Women and New England Deaconess Hospital). The pump, which can be worn on a belt, injects a controlled amount of insulin through a needle implanted under a woman's abdominal skin. The insulin is released at mealtimes during the crucial first trimester. As long as Ms. C. and her doctor are watchful, however, and her blood sugar levels are carefully monitored, her diet is strictly followed, and her insulin intake is properly adjusted, everything is being done to bring her a healthy baby.

Will Diabetes Continue After Pregnancy?

A woman who has had gestational diabetes should have a glucose tolerance test several months after childbirth to make sure that her body has returned to good health. Her blood sugar level should drop to normal. It has been found, however, that some women still have glucose intolerance years later. Exceptionally overweight women who develop gestational diabetes are especially likely to exhibit a future diabetic condition. Once a woman has had gestational diabetes, she must be highly aware during subsequent pregnancies. The condition, once it has been experienced, may return with the next pregnancy.

TOXEMIA: A DANGEROUS, MYSTERIOUS COMPLICATION

"I thought we were just doing something people do every day—having a baby," said a husband whose wife had survived toxemia in her first pregnancy, although they had lost their unborn baby. "It never occurred to me that we would be in danger, but I almost lost my wife too." The onset of toxemia can jeopardize the survival of both mother and baby. It is a condition that is seriously regarded by obstetricians who regularly check expectant mothers for its symptoms—water retention, high blood pressure, and proteinuria (protein in the urine).

Literally, the word *toxemia* comes from the Greek *toxikon,* meaning "poison," and *haima,* meaning blood. Toxemia was thought to come from a toxin in a pregnant woman's blood. The truth is that doctors still do not know definitely how toxemia develops, although theories abound. Researchers have hypothesized that toxemia may be related to an abnormal blood-clotting factor caused by an increased release of the hormone renin from the kidney, to an allergic reaction between mother and baby, to poor nutrition, or, according to the latest thought, to a defect in the immune system.

It is confusing when physicians refer to toxemia because often they use the words *toxemia, preeclampsia,* and *eclampsia* synonymously. Preeclampsia is the milder form of toxemia, in which a woman experiences water retention, high blood pressure, and proteinuria, but she does not suffer seizures. Eclampsia is the more advanced stage, in which elevated blood pressure and severe kidney damage may lead to nerve impairment and convulsions. Since early detection and treatment of toxemia have made it possible to control preeclampsia, severe full-fledged eclampsia is rarely seen today in the United States.

Toxemia may occur as early as the fifth month, but it is more likely to develop closer to a woman's due date, after her thirty-seventh week. It is usually seen in first pregnancies and is most prevalent among women who already have high blood pressure, a kidney disorder, or diabetes. Women who are malnourished, overweight, carrying twins, or under eighteen or over thirty-five are also more likely to suffer toxemia.

The first sign may be a rapid weight gain due to a rise in body fluid. As a result of water retention, swelling, also called *edema,* becomes apparent around the joints of the hands and feet. It used to be thought that eating salt led to water retention and toxemia, and a salt-free diet was recommended. Today salt consumption is not considered the culprit in causing toxemia, but following a low-salt diet is still advisable. Water retention frequently diminishes if salt is reduced and a woman also rests. If it is not brought under control by bed rest, the added fluid stresses the body and causes the kidney to secrete a hormone called renin, which, in turn, increases blood pressure. Once blood pressure is elevated, a vicious cycle begins in which kidney damage (which is recognized by proteinuria) can occur and water may be retained all the more. Usually the *complete triad of symptoms*—edema shows up first, followed by elevated blood pressure, and then proteinuria—must appear before a doctor will say that a woman has toxemia. In the past, "water retention" and "toxemia" were terms used almost interchangeably by physicians. That's not so today. Many pregnant women do not have toxemia but they nevertheless retain water and suffer edema. Today's toxemia means that the triad of symptoms is present and must be treated. If it is not attended to, preeclampsia,with its rising blood pressure, may lead to brisker reflex action and, eventually, to an eclamptic convulsion similar to a grand mal epileptic seizure. Should this seizure recur, it can bring on coma, brain damage, and death of a mother or baby or both. Fortunately toxemia is usually detected in time to stop its frightening progress.

How Is Toxemia Treated?

Whenever a doctor has a suspicion that toxemia may be occurring in a pregnant patient, he will suggest that she eat a low-salt diet and rest in bed. If she lies on her left side with her feet elevated, she will be easing the pressure on her kidneys, directing a rich blood supply to the fetus, and, hopefully, alleviating the problem. If the triad of symptoms exists and a doctor also discovers that a woman's reflexes show hyperreflexia (brisk tendon reflexes), he may hospitalize her to control the situation. Physicians want to prevent preeclampsia from moving into the more serious stage of seizure, called eclampsia. In a hospital, a woman will be monitored for weight changes and blood pressure levels. She may also receive a mild sedative, such as phenobarbital, to relax her body. Toxemia can usually be controlled in this way, but if the condition should continue, and if it seems that eclampsia is imminent because the reflexes are brisk, then other measures must be taken. A doctor will immediately begin intravenous infusion of magnesium sulfate, which is the most successful drug for the control of seizure disorder. If the threatened eclampsia is thwarted, then a physician must decide whether the baby is mature enough to deliver. Childbirth and removal of the placenta are the only ways to finally cure this potentially life-threatening condition.

If toxemia occurs when the fetus is premature, antiseizure and antihypertensive medication can be administered, which, along with rest, should gain growing time for the fetus. If the condition is unstoppable, however, a doctor may have to deliver an infant prematurely by cesarean section. When toxemia takes place closer to term, a physician may perform amniocentesis to determine the L/S ratio, which indicates whether a baby's lungs have matured to the point that childbirth is safe. When a safe birth is assured, labor will be induced or a cesarean section will be performed. Remember, toxemia only disappears once the newborn and the placenta are no longer in a woman's body.

If a woman has advanced toxemia—eclampsia—anytime during pregnancy, then she will be given magnesium sulfate intravenously. A strong anticonvulsant, magnesium sulfate reduces muscle tremors and depresses the central nervous system. Eclampsia can thus be stabilized until the baby can be delivered. If the condition cannot be completely controlled, then labor will be induced or a cesarean section performed. (Usually the magnesium sulfate will be excreted by the mother before it significantly enters the fetal environment.) With all the latest awareness about toxemia, expectant mothers should feel comforted. The condition rarely goes unnoticed, and when it is detected, all efforts are made to prevent it from evolving into eclampsia.

And before eclampsia occurs, a woman will have warning signs. She will experience water retention, headache, abdominal cramping, and, sometimes, double vision. Anytime a woman encounters these symptoms, she should immediately contact her doctor. A pregnant woman and her obstetrician are sharing a nine-month partnership, and once she alerts him to her symptoms, he will act quickly to cure the problem. Together they will combat a potentially dangerous condition.

I Thought My Pregnancy Was Normal. Why Did My Labor Turn into Toxemia?

I had a normal pregnancy, gained just the right amount of weight, and I felt pretty secure as I got closer to my due date. Then, in my last trimester, one day became particularly scary. I woke up with a headache and unbearable gas pain, and I vomited. I was also very swollen. It seemed as if I had blown up overnight. I called the doctor and told him that I didn't think I was having signs of labor but something was happening. He told me to go to the hospital right away. There he found that I had gained seven pounds very suddenly, that my blood pressure was high and my reflexes were rapid. He told me that I had toxemia, actually preeclampsia. I was put on intravenous magnesium sulfate, and my blood pressure dropped. My condition seemed to be brought under control, but a few hours later, labor started. My blood pressure went up and the doctor said that the toxemia had worsened. He gave me intravenous blood pressure medication, but I wasn't dilating fast enough. He said that we couldn't wait any longer, that the toxemia could be dangerous to the baby and to me, and he had to do a cesarean. The baby and I are both healthy, but I still don't really understand what happened. Why did my labor turn into toxemia?

L.V.

Greensboro, North Carolina

Sometimes toxemia can appear in the seventh month or earlier, but if it shows up that soon, an expectant mother is usually a woman who has had hypertension or kidney problems before pregnancy. More often, toxemia appears closer to term and the symptoms, like Ms. V.'s, start with headache and bloatedness. Gas pain and vomiting, which she also described, mean that the toxemia is more progressed. When a doctor finds high blood pressure and brisk reflexes along with these symptoms, then he has reason to diagnose toxemia. If the urine contains protein, then she has a full-blown preeclamptic condition.

Although the cause of toxemia is still not understood, doctors are aware of certain predisposing factors. One theory is that when a woman is carrying a very large baby, or twins, her uterus is overexpanded and stretched to capacity. When a womb is so severely stressed, which happens most often in a first pregnancy, the fetus may not be receiving an adequate blood supply. Then a continuing internal reaction occurs, but researchers still have not been able to pin down exactly how this vicious cycle begins. Nonetheless, a signal of the inadequate blood supply goes from the placenta to the kidneys. This signal can almost be thought of as a call for help from the fetus. The only way the kidneys can respond to this cry for help is to secrete renin, a hormone that increases blood pressure.

Elevated blood pressure will send more blood and oxygen to the baby via the placenta. Although this increased blood flow might initially help the fetus, it will begin to have a deleterious effect on the mother. She will start to retain water and may eventually develop kidney damage. The first sign of this damage appears when protein is discovered in her urine. Then a woman has preeclampsia.

Due to this vicious cycle, a woman's blood pressure gets higher and higher, her body becomes more and more swollen, and at the same time, her nerves are affected. The point at which the nerves enter into the muscles—the neuromuscular junction—is altered by the internal changes, and reflex actions are quickened. If the body chemistry is not brought back into balance, seizure can ensue.

Ms. V.'s condition was controlled, but when she went into labor, toxemia returned. Labor can stress the body to such a degree that the kidneys once again overproduce renin, the hormone that causes blood pressure to rise. If blood pressure gets very high, a woman may experience a more severe form of preeclampsia and her life may be in danger. She could have a stroke. A doctor will try to bring down a woman's blood pressure with magnesium sulfate in combination with blood pressure medication such as Apresoline (hydralozine hydrochloride). (Diuretics, which might be harmful to the mother or the baby, are no longer recommended.) If he cannot lower the pressure within a reasonable time, and if labor is not progressing satisfactorily, he will have to perform a cesarean. A physician must end the preeclampsia/eclampsia, and the only real cure is delivery of the baby and the placenta. Once the baby is born and the placenta is gone, a woman's body readjusts itself. Blood pressure returns to normal, and only in rare cases is there lingering kidney damage and chronic hypertension.

After childbirth, Ms. V. should have been observed carefully for twenty-four hours. The risk of returning toxemia and seizure lasts for twenty-four hours postpartum. A woman who has experienced severe toxemia should receive intravenous magnesium sulfate during that twenty-four-hour period, and her blood pressure and reflexes should be checked frequently. A woman in Ms. V.'s situation should report symptoms such as headache and burning urine to a doctor or nurse immediately. These are early signs of returning toxemia. *Postpartum preeclampsia* is not seen that often, but you must nevertheless be monitored.

A woman who has had toxemia should not allow the experience to prevent her from having another baby. Toxemia arises more often in first pregnancies, and a woman who has had it once is not likely to suffer through it again. She and her doctor should be on the alert for symptoms, however, if she becomes pregnant again. Her blood pressure should be regularly checked in future pregnancies, and she should try to spot warning signs such as headache and bloatedness. Above all, a woman who has had toxemia should eat a healthy, well-balanced, low-salt diet and rest as often as possible after she conceives again. Good nutrition is the best defense against toxemia.

INFECTIONS DURING PREGNANCY

During pregnancy, an important, curious alteration occurs in a woman's immune system. You would think that nature would strengthen an expectant mother against all forms of illness, but studies are showing that a pregnant woman has more resistance to bacteria than to viruses, which sometimes cross the placenta and affect the fetus.

The rubella (German measles) virus, for example, may produce a slight fever and body rash that disappear in a few days, but in an unborn baby, rubella can cause brain damage, deafness, and blindness. Fortunately, as explained in chapters 1 and 10, a rubella vaccine *before pregnancy* prevents a woman from catching German measles, but what about other illnesses? Colds and respiratory problems are common during pregnancy. Are these serious? Women have asked about influenza, hepatitis, varicella (chicken pox), herpes, cytomegalovirus, venereal warts, and AIDS—all viral infections. Questions about chlamydia, urinary problems, and surgery during pregnancy are also on their minds.

Expectant mothers and their newborn babies are usually strong, healthy, and beautiful. Pregnancy should be enjoyed, and I answer these questions to lift lingering shadows of concern and brighten this experience.

What if You Get the Flu?

When a pregnant woman feels a cold or the flu coming on, she should immediately slow down and rest. Often the sniffles that appear in pregnancy are nothing more than annoying. Usually I recommend the time-honored way to strengthen a woman's immunity when a respiratory ailment strikes. I advise her to rest, take extra vitamin C, and drink plenty of fluids, such as fruit juices, chicken soup, and hot tea with honey. It is also important to stay warm when the flu is trying to overtake your body.

The flu can often run its course rather uneventfully, but there is always a chance that it will bring on a high fever. If a pregnant woman's temperature goes over 101 degrees, the chance of premature birth increases, and that is why the flu causes concern. A viral flu does not respond to antibiotics, but I prescribe antibiotics to protect a woman against the rising risk of a bacterial infection. Untreated bacteria can cause a sore throat, bronchitis, and pneumonia.

So if the conservative treatment of rest, vitamin C, extra fluids, and warmth does not seem to be controlling flulike symptoms, if a woman is still tired, achy, and feverish, I will prescribe antibiotics to protect her against a rising temperature and a bacterial attack. Penicillin and ampicillin are safe to use during pregnancy because they do not harm the fetus. (See Chapter 9.) I must emphasize, however, that a doctor must be informed as soon as an expectant mother feels herself coming down with the flu. Sometimes my patients, thinking that they "only" have a cold, don't call me, and before I can treat them, they are already burning with a high fever. *A high fever is just what you want to avoid,* so let your doctor know about your colds and flus. (If you are only at the point of *planning* to conceive, you might want to get this year's flu shot. Then you can relax when a new virus invades.)

NOTE: *Toxoplasmosis,* a disease transmitted by a parasite that can be found in raw meat and the fecal waste of cats, cattle, sheep, and pigs, causes symptoms similar to a mild flu. As explained in chapters 1 and 10, a woman can have a blood test for toxoplasmosis, and if she does not have antibodies for the disease, she must be particularly careful during pregnancy. A domestic cat is not likely to harbor the parasite because such a pet usually eats commercially prepared cat food and does not hunt in the wild. Some cats do play outdoors, however, and for safety's sake, I recommend that a pregnant woman avoid contact with kitty litter. (She should also eat properly cooked red meat and pork.)

All these words about toxoplasmosis are a warning to take flu symptoms seriously. It may be a good idea to have another blood test to see whether there is any change in the antibodies for toxoplasmosis if you develop the flu. While toxoplasmosis will bring only slight discomfort to an expectant mother, there is a 40 percent chance that it will reach the fetus and cause blindness, deafness, or mental retardation. Should toxoplasmosis occur during pregnancy, a woman must seek genetic counseling. For more information about toxoplasmosis, you can request a copy of *Cat Owner's Guidelines* to protect both pregnant women and pets from toxoplasmosis, a brochure available from the National Institute of Allergy and Infectious Diseases. Copies are available from Toxoplasmosis/HL, NIAID Information Office, Building 31, Room 7a32, Bethesda, Md. 20205, or by calling (301) 496–5717.

What Should I Do About My Exposure to German Measles?

I'm a pregnant fifth-grade teacher in a school system that has recently experienced an outbreak of German measles. I have a few students who are out sick and I'm worried. I haven't been vaccinated and I'm in my sixth month. Am I still in danger? Should I quit work? What should I do about my exposure?

S.C.
Orange, New Jersey

Ms. C. does not mention whether she has had a blood test to determine the presence of rubella (German measles) antibodies. If she has these antibodies, she is already immune to the virus. On the other hand, if she does not have the antibodies, and she was not vaccinated, then she is certainly susceptible. As explained in chapters 1 and 10, if a woman does not receive a rubella vaccine at least three months before pregnancy, then she should do everything she can to avoid exposure. A vaccine is a live injected virus that might reach the fetus and cause brain damage, deafness, and blindness. Rubella vaccine cannot be given during pregnancy.

The fetus is most vulnerable to rubella in the first trimester, when cells are developing rapidly and major organs are forming. Ms. C. is at the end of her second trimester, so the risk of fetal harm is not as great, but it still exists. The incubation period for rubella ranges from fourteen to twenty-one days. A number of Ms. C.'s students have already become sick, so I would advise her to take a leave of absence for a month. After that, the outbreak should have subsided.

Every pregnant woman should be wary of situations in which she may be exposed to rubella. I am very cautious about this disease. Even when a woman's antibodies indicate that she has already had rubella, I still advise her to avoid contact with anyone who may be infected, because from time to time, the virus changes subtly. Since we have learned more about the effects of rubella, I warn women to be self-protective—don't visit anyone who may be sick, especially families with exposed children, and during flu season, always eat properly and get plenty of rest to keep resistance high.

HEPATITIS IN PREGNANCY

As a fetus grows, its weight may press against an expectant mother's gall bladder and create a buildup of bile in her liver. She may feel nauseated, become jaundiced (yellowed), and think she has hepatitis, but her self-diagnosis may be hasty. Liver disease, gallbladder and gallstone conditions, and infectious mononucleosis have all been mistaken for hepatitis during pregnancy. The symptoms of hepatitis include jaundice, tremendous fatigue, decreased appetite, nausea, vomiting, and itching, but a group of blood tests must always be taken to confirm the condition.

An inflammation of the liver, hepatitis occurs when bile, which is normally destroyed, circulates in the blood. The visible sign is jaundice, or a yellowing of the skin and the whites of the eyes, which is produced by the extra bile in the blood, known as bilirubin. Hepatitis is usually brought on by one of three viruses: hepatitis A virus, hepatitis B virus, and non-A-and-B virus. The type A and type B viruses are the more common.

Hepatitis A, formerly known as *infectious hepatitis,* is transmitted through food and oral/anal contact. Hepatitis B was considered *serum hepatitis,* since it was only thought to be contracted through diseased blood transfusions or through the use of contaminated needles among the drug addicted. Hospital personnel who may have accidentally pricked themselves with needles used on hepatitis patients have also been frequent victims of the disease. Today it is known that all the viruses can be transmitted both orally and by injection, and the distinctions no longer apply. No matter which virus causes the disease, the term *viral hepatitis* is used. It is important to identify the different viruses, however, for the purpose of prevention.

A pregnant woman who has recently been exposed to hepatitis A might receive gamma globulin preventatively to boost her immunity. The incubation period of the type A virus is about two to seven weeks, so a woman should be treated as soon as she discovers her exposure. The injection should not harm her pregnancy.

There is a vaccine against hepatitis B, called Heptavax B, but it should be taken *before pregnancy* by health care personnel, nurses and doctors, and women who know they are at high risk of exposure. Two vaccine injections are given one month apart, and a booster is administered six months later. An expectant mother who is exposed to hepatitis B during pregnancy should not be vaccinated, but she should be cared for by a perinatologist.

If blood tests confirm viral hepatitis, no matter which type, an expectant mother will need a nutritionally balanced diet and bed rest. She will usually be admitted to the hospital for observation and monitoring while she rests, and she will be placed in isolation until she recovers. The hepatitis virus rarely passes through the placenta to the fetus, and this disease is not considered dangerous to pregnancy. If a woman contracts an extremely severe case of hepatitis in her last trimester, she may face an increased risk of premature birth, but again, this hardly ever happens.

Most of the time, a woman with hepatitis is more of a threat to the people treating her. She is highly contagious, and doctors and nurses will take precautions during her stay in the hospital. Constant bed rest and a well-balanced diet should return a pregnant woman to good health without having any effect on her pregnancy. Occasionally a patient will tell me that she has heard that a pregnant woman who gets hepatitis must have her pregnancy interrupted. This is not true. A pregnant woman who gets hepatitis can have a normal pregnancy and childbirth, but after childbirth, she should be placed in isolation, and her baby should be followed by a neonatologist.

A newborn who has been exposed to the hepatitis virus usually will receive an injection of gamma globulin immediately after birth to build immunity. If the virus is type B, the hepatitis B vaccine will probably also be administered. A woman who has had hepatitis during pregnancy may be able to transmit the virus in her breast milk if she is still contagious. Breast-feeding may not always be advisable.

I Had Hepatitis During Pregnancy. Can I Breast-feed My Baby?

I have heard conflicting opinions from people about whether it is safe for me to breast-feed my baby. I had hepatitis during pregnancy, and my doctor says I can breast-feed, but friends say that he's wrong. I want to give my baby a good start on life by breast-feeding him, but I'm worried.

V.P.
Sacramento, California

The hepatitis virus can be transmitted through breast milk, so if a woman is still contagious after childbirth, she should not breast-feed her baby. In general, a woman who has had hepatitis during pregnancy is told to be cautious about intimate contact.

Ms. P. should be given a blood test to see if she is still contagious. If she is completely disease free, her doctor might permit her to breast-feed, but if any doubt about her condition lingers, she should be advised against breast-feeding.

I Had Hepatitis 25 Years Ago. Do I Have to Worry About Contaminating My Baby?

When I was eight years old, I got hepatitis from eating raw oysters. I'm now thirty-three, and I have been checked many times over the last twenty-five years. Although my blood tests have always been negative, when I mentioned my former hepatitis to the nurse after I delivered my baby, she became very worried. She said that my daughter had to be put in isolation. Although my doctor said there was no danger, the nurse insisted. Was the isolation really necessary? Do I have to worry about contaminating my baby?

V.G.
West Portsmouth, Ohio

With today's concern about viral infections, particularly AIDS, hospital personnel have become quite cautious. Since years ago researchers did not identify hepatitis by type, the nurse had no way of knowing whether Ms. G. had the more dangerous serum hepatitis, type B, when she explained her health history. The nurse wanted to take an extra precaution.

Ms. G. has had repeated blood tests over the years and she has established that she is no longer contagious. It is most likely that the raw oysters gave her the less serious type A virus, which only lives a few months. Ms. G. should have had a blood test a few months before her due date to confirm her "negative" status just in case the hospital staff had any questions. After childbirth, she and her baby had blood tests that showed their good health. Her baby was needlessly isolated.

When a woman has had hepatitis many years before conception, and a blood test during pregnancy indicates that she is free of the disease, most doctors recommend that she not mention the disease to the hospital staff. Staff caution, though it is understandable, can cause a separation of mother and child at a time when bonding is important.

OTHER CONCERNS

Is Chicken Pox Dangerous During Pregnancy?

I'm having an argument with my sister. She says that both German measles and chicken pox can cause birth defects in babies. I say that only German measles is a problem. Who is right? Is chicken pox dangerous during pregnancy?

L.R.
Fall River, Massachusetts

When a child has chicken pox, medically termed *varicella*, it is an unpleasant, usually mild illness. It lasts about two weeks, during which time the child has a slight fever and itchy, red bumps, like large mosquito bites, on her or his skin. Eventually the sores go away and the memory of chicken pox fades. Not so for an adult! When an adult contracts varicella, she or he can become seriously ill with pneumonia. It is not an easily dismissed sickness.

Since varicella can severely strike an adult, it is an illness that can threaten a healthy pregnancy. Ms. R.'s sister is right—both German measles and chicken pox can cause birth defects. The effects of chicken pox were discovered in 1947, when a newborn's growth and motor retardation problems were traced to chicken pox during the mother's first trimester.

The chance of birth defects resulting from chicken pox is small but nonetheless real, especially if varicella appears early in pregnancy. Chicken pox in the first sixteen weeks of gestation may damage fetal development. There is a greater chance that the fetus will be unaffected, but physicians cannot in good conscience advise a woman to continue her pregnancy under such doubtful circumstances. It is less likely that the fetus will be affected if chicken pox occurs later in pregnancy; however, just before or during delivery, the virus could reach the newborn.

The chicken pox (varicella) virus appears related to the shingles (herpes zoster) virus, and treatment for a newborn who has been exposed to chicken pox or shingles is the same. After birth, an injection with zoster immune globulin (ZIG) or varicella-zoster immune globulin (VZIG) can be given to a newborn to prevent varicella. The new herpes medication Zovirax (acyclovir) might also be given intravenously to the newborn to increase protection. The best prevention, of course, is to stay away from anyone who might have varicella while you are pregnant.

My Baby Got Herpes. Should I Have Had a Cesarean?

I have a history of herpes, and I had two outbreaks early in my pregnancy. The doctor said not to worry. I did have an outbreak two months before my due date, but when the time came to deliver, there was no sign of the disease. During labor, it was difficult to hear the baby's heart rate and the doctor inserted an internal electrode. I gave birth vaginally, and shortly after, the baby developed a herpes sore right on the spot where the electrode had been placed. Should I have had a cesarean?

C.S.
West Hollywood, California

The symptoms of herpes simplex virus and its effects upon pregnancy are discussed in Chapter 10. As mentioned in that chapter, estimates are that as many as 25 million Americans may be suffering from this sexually transmitted disease, which surfaces in oral, genital, and anal areas. Ms. S. is referring to genital herpes, which is usually caused by the herpes simplex virus type 2 (HSV–2). With this virus, a woman will experience an overall fatigue followed by a vaginal itch. Then one or a cluster of blisters will appear in or around her vagina. These tender, painful blisters will burst and become oozing sores that may take up to three weeks to heal.

Recently researchers have discussed herpes as one possible cause of miscarriage, but generally, outbreaks early in pregnancy are not considered harmful to the fetus. Worry about herpes usually focuses on childbirth. The main concern is that herpes will affect a newborn who may be exposed to the sores and the virus while passing through the birth canal. A newborn does not have a fully developed immune system. In the past, it has been found that about 50 to 100 percent of the infants who are contaminated by the herpes virus die, and the ones who live may suffer severe handicaps, such as blindness and permanent damage to the nervous system. When, like Ms. S., an expectant mother has herpes outbreaks during pregnancy, periodic vaginal cultures must be taken to see whether the virus is alive in the birth canal.

Ms. S. writes that she had a herpes outbreak two months before her due date and that she did not appear to have an active virus before delivery. She does not specify whether her doctor took a vaginal culture, which he should have, two to three weeks before the expected birth of her baby. Usually a cesarean is a must only if the vaginal culture is positive or if a fresh herpes sore is visible just prior to delivery.

The placement of an internal electrode on the baby's head to monitor a heart rate that cannot be picked up externally is quite common. It is a safe way to determine the heart rate, and no complications would be expected from this procedure. Ms. S. must have had vaginal shedding of the virus, which entered the opening in the scalp of her baby. Since there was a live virus in the birth canal, the baby might have been contaminated even without the involvement of the electrode. The issue here is not the electrode but her doctor's awareness of her viral condition. A positive vaginal culture could have warned him of the live herpes virus. After birth, the newborn should have been isolated and placed under the care of a neonatologist, who would have administered intravenous acyclovir, a preventive herpes medication.

Physicians today monitor herpes carefully near the time of

childbirth. By being watchful, newborn exposure has been cut to a minimum. With the practice of extensive monitoring of the active herpes virus in the last few weeks of pregnancy, childbirth problems can almost be eliminated. A woman who has had herpes at some point in her life need no longer worry about her ability to carry a healthy child. If Ms. S. had had a vaginal culture a couple of weeks before the birth of her baby, the culture most likely would have been positive and a C-section would have been performed.

Cytomegalovirus

Many expectant mothers are likely to ask, "Why do I have to know about cytomegalovirus?" when I mention the multisyllabic word, which is also more simply known as CMV. The parasite that causes CMV can be inactive in a person's body, and although estimates are that 80 percent of adults in the United States harbor the parasite, few are likely to be aware of it. Only when stress or some unknown factor lowers immunity is cytomegalovirus triggered, but even then, the infection may go unrecognized.

A number of doctors and clinics routinely take blood tests to screen for CMV in pregnant women. On the other hand, many physicians do not feel that a screening is valuable, since so many people have the virus. If a woman has cytomegalovirus antibodies, then she has been exposed to the disease; and if her resistance is weakened, the virus may manifest itself. Should CMV become activated, especially in the first trimester, the virus may cross the placenta and damage fetal development. (If your blood test indicates a high CMV titer and your doctor feels you should have your pregnancy interrupted, do not make this decision until you contact the Centers for Disease Control [CDC] in Atlanta. Physicians are sometimes confused about the significance of the CMV titer, but the Information Office of the CDC can explain the titer level accurately.) If the virus is active during childbirth, a newborn may become infected during its passage through the birth canal. CMV can also be transmitted through breast milk.

Roughly 1 in 100 newborns is affected in utero by CMV and shows signs of brain impairment, hearing disorder, blindness, or other birth defects. The CMV virus is a serious concern to physicians, because there is still no vaccine or treatment for the disease (although several vaccines are on the horizon). At the moment,

341

prevention is key. Cytomegalovirus will have more difficulty taking hold in the body of an expectant mother who is in good health, eats a well-balanced diet, exercises moderately, and rests often. Her immune system will be stronger. Good health is one of the best defenses against CMV.

What Happens if My Chlamydia Recurs Before the Baby Is Born?

When my doctor discovered that I had chlamydia, my husband and I took tetracycline and I conceived a month later. Now I'm in my fourth month and I understand that even when chlamydia is cured, it can come back. What happens if my chlamydia recurs before the baby is born? My doctor seems vague on the details.

L.S.
Newport, Arkansas

Chlamydia trachomatis used to be considered a virus, but researchers found that it is a sexually transmitted bacterialike organism that is responsible for what is now the most widespread sexually transmitted disease in this country. An estimated 4.6 million Americans will contract chlamydia this year, and since it provides no symptoms or only mild symptoms, most of these people will not even know they are sick. (NOTE: Women who have used IUDs may be particularly susceptible.)

Ms. S. is lucky to have had her chlamydia detected, and she is also fortunate that it did not cause her permanent infertility. Chlamydia invades healthy tissue—usually the cervix and the urethra in women, and the urethra in men. Physicians now know that nongonococcal urethritis (NGU), sometimes called nonspecific urethritis (NSU), can often be traced to chlamydia. The organism flourishes in the ulcerated lesions of an inflamed cervix or an irritated urethra. An infected cervix or urethra may not hurt, and a woman may be completely unaware of her infection. Some clues to chlamydia may be an uncomfortable though not debilitating burning during urination, a vaginal discharge, and sensitivity in the lower abdomen. These symptoms can be so mild, however, that they go unnoticed, and chlamydia spreads to other reproductive organs. This spread can cause pelvic inflammatory disease (PID), tubal damage, and eventual infertility or ectopic pregnancy.

Testing vaginal cultures for chlamydia used to be slow, unreliable, and expensive, but cheaper, faster, more accurate tests such as Chlamydiazyme and MicroTrak have greatly improved detection. Ms. S., I assume, benefited from one of these newer testing methods, and her physician then prescribed ten to fourteen days of tetracycline. Since chlamydia is sexually transmitted, both a husband and wife must take the course of medicine together.

Chlamydia worries obstetricians because this infection can affect the fetus. A recent study at the University of Maryland School of Medicine indicated that pregnant women with chlamydia may be three times more likely to give birth prematurely. Chlamydia has also been linked to premature rupture of the membranes, low birth weight, stillbirth, and sudden infant death syndrome. And a newborn that is exposed to chlamydia while passing through the birth canal may suffer eye infections, pneumonia, or ear infections.

Ms. S. should definitely be tested for a chlamydia recurrence. In a study conducted at Jefferson Medical College in Philadelphia, pregnant women who had chlamydia at 36 weeks gestation were treated with erythromycin, and later they gave birth to healthy babies. Tetracycline should not be taken during pregnancy, but fortunately erythromycin, which does not harm the fetus, also combats chlamydia. I suggest that Ms. S. be tested two to three weeks before her due date, and if the culture is positive, she should be treated with erythromycin.

About T-mycoplasma, Also Called Mycoplasma Hominis

Sometimes, when a woman has had repeated miscarriages, her husband's sperm may be infected with either chlamydia or T-mycoplasma, another newly discovered microorganism. A sperm analysis should be done and antibiotics taken by both partners if a man is infected. Like chlamydia, during pregnancy, T-mycoplasma can recur and affect the fetus. A woman who has been exposed to T-mycoplasma should be cultured at 36 weeks and, if necessary, treated.

Do I Have to Be on the Alert for a Urinary Tract Infection?

I am in my second month and I have never urinated so much in my life. I know a pregnant woman has to urinate more than normal, but I have a history of cystitis and I'm a little concerned. Do I have to be on the alert for a urinary tract infection?

C.P.
Wisner, Louisiana

Here is how the urinary tract works to remove wastes from the body: The *kidneys* filter the blood and separate the liquid waste, the urine, which is then transported through long tubes called the *ureters,* to the *bladder.* Urine collects in the bladder until it is voided through the *urethra,* a tube that carries the flow from the bladder out through an opening between the vagina and the clitoris.

During pregnancy, changes occur in the urinary tract. The ureters dilate, and the bladder increases in capacity but decreases in tone. Due to these changes, an expectant mother becomes more susceptible to the bacteria that can produce urinary tract infections. Since a woman does have to urinate more frequently in the first and third trimesters, she might quite naturally confuse this normal consequence of pregnancy with the onset of infection.

In rare cases, women with no symptoms may have a urinary tract infection called *asymptomatic bacteriuria,* but usually there are some signs. *Cystitis,* a bladder or lower tract infection, creates an urgency to urinate frequently, pain or burning on urination, and sometimes blood may even appear in the urine. A fever may occur, and the infection may spread to the upper tract, the kidneys, where it brings on a more serious condition called *pyelonephritis.*

In the first prenatal visit, a doctor performs a urine analysis, and one of the things he looks for is bacteria that may be causing infection. This check will let an expectant mother know if she has asymptomatic bacteriuria. (Follow-up checks are usually done for women who are more susceptible to urinary tract infections—women with histories of cystitis, or women who have sickle cell anemia or diabetes.) At any time in pregnancy, if an expectant mother has symptoms, a urine analysis will detect infection and treatment can begin before the bacteria travel to the upper tract. A urinary tract infection can be treated safely with ampicillin, Negram, or Macrodantin, which will not harm the fetus. Sulfa medications, which are usually recommended for urinary tract infections, should not be taken. Sulfa drugs may lead to jaundice in the newborn.

Most pregnant women try to strengthen their resistance during expectancy, and they are often able to prevent a bacterial invasion. Ms. P. will have a little more of a battle against infection, however, because women who have a history of cystitis and women with sickle cell anemia or diabetes are more vulnerable. Ms. P., and all other highly susceptible women, should have a monthly urine analysis to monitor her condition. Since urinary tract infection has been associated with premature birth, it should not be allowed to take hold.

Do I Have to Worry About AIDS?

Recently a man who worked in my office died of AIDS. My husband is freaked out because I'm pregnant. He thinks that maybe the baby could get birth defects from AIDS, and maybe now I've been exposed. Do I really have to worry about AIDS? How contagious is it?

B.E.

Yonkers, New York

AIDS—acquired immune deficiency syndrome—is carried by a virus that is transmitted in body fluid. Basically, AIDS is considered a blood-borne disease that weakens the body's immune system so that associated cancers occur. Ms. E. should not be overly concerned because there is no indication that AIDS can be contracted in the workplace. The disease has been found to be transmitted primarily through intimate sexual contact and intravenous drug use. Although AIDS seems to be spread through heterosexual contact in Africa, in the rest of the world, it is transmitted mainly by homosexual contact.

As of this writing, the Centers for Disease Control in Atlanta have reported twenty thousand cases of AIDS. Homosexuals comprise 73 percent of the total, and of those, 11 percent are also intravenous drug users. An added 17 percent are intravenous drug users, and the remaining 10 percent are hemophiliacs and small miscellaneous groupings. Hospital personnel, for example, sometimes accidentally prick themselves with used needles and expose themselves to AIDS.

Ms. E. should calm her husband's fears. As long as she has not had sexual relations with her co-worker, she should not be worried about AIDS. Studies have shown that the possibility of a woman getting AIDS from a man during sex is somewhat higher than for a man getting AIDS from a woman, but even so, AIDS does not spread immediately upon contact. I have known several cases in which husbands have died of AIDS, and years later, their wives and children were still unaffected. Although the babies of women who have had AIDS throughout pregnancy may have problems, it is not likely that a woman like Ms. E., who merely worked with an infected man, harbors the virus. Ms. E. should not dwell on AIDS as a problem, but she should continue to follow a healthy regimen and to practice good hygiene until childbirth.

The conquering of AIDS is a priority among researchers, and there is a strong possibility that a vaccine will be developed within the next few years.

I Had Venereal Warts in the First Trimester, but They Disappeared. Do I Still Need a Cesarean?

I had venereal warts in the first trimester of this pregnancy. They disappeared and I thought everything was all right, but a friend told me that you have to have a cesarean whether they're there or not. I'm going to Lamaze classes now and I want to know if I'm wasting my time. Do I still need a cesarean?

M.T.
Coconut Grove, Florida

Venereal warts (*Condylomata acuminata*) are sexually transmitted growths that appear in the genital areas of men and women. Caused by different viruses, warts may take the form of lesions that come and go, or they may be clustered growths that defy exact description. They may be large or small, long or round, pink or gray or white. Although venereal warts are more widespread than ever before, it is difficult to know who is susceptible. Some women who have been exposed by their husbands for years have never developed one wart.

These protrusions used to be considered painless nuisances, but lately, they have come to be regarded much more seriously. Studies have indicated that there may be a link between warts found on the cervix and cervical cancer. Warts have also been linked to cancers of the lower genital tract. We now know, too, that a certain type of flat wart on the cervix seems to be creating abnormal Pap smears. In the event of an abnormal Pap test, a physician should examine a woman with a special viewing instrument called a *colposcope* to see whether a flat wart is present. A biopsy may be needed.

Warts often spread, and there is a danger that during pregnancy, they may grow to block the birth canal. There is also a danger that even if warts are not obstructive, they may be harmful during childbirth. Physicians have discovered that when a newborn has passed through a birth canal in which an active wart virus is thriving, the baby may be contaminated. The virus, aspirated by the baby, may attack the vocal cords. Venereal warts on the vocal cords of infants are extremely serious, and microlaryngeal surgery is the only way to remove them. Even then the warts may grow back.

Ms. T. is fortunate that her warts disappeared, but has she had any recent growths? Any woman who has had an outbreak of venereal warts should be scrupulous about examining her vaginal area for unusual protrusions. If there are no visible warts a few weeks before her due date, Ms. T. should have a Pap test to determine whether any active wart virus exists. Naturally her doctor should regularly examine her for a reappearance of warts. If neither she nor her doctor notices a venereal wart and if a Pap test indicates no abnormality, then Ms. T. might be able to deliver vaginally. Some physicians feel, however, that the risk of exposing the newborn is too great, and if a wart has appeared at any point in pregnancy, they will recommend a cesarean birth. With a cesarean, the newborn completely avoids the birth canal, which is a possible site of contamination.

Every woman should be aware that treating warts during pregnancy is hazardous. Podophyllin, an acidic wart-killing medication, should not be used. Other remedial methods such as electrocautery (burning), laser surgery, or cryosurgery (a freezing technique), may bring on heavy bleeding because the vaginal area has an enriched blood supply at this time. The hope is that if warts appear at all, they will disappear just as quickly.

I Have Asthma. Will My Baby Get Enough Oxygen?

I have periodic, I believe stress-related, asthmatic attacks, and usually I can control them with medication. I'm concerned, however, that if I have an attack now that I'm pregnant, either the baby won't get enough oxygen or the medicine will harm the fetus. Will my baby be all right?

F.O.
Theodore, Alabama

Ms. O. should be under the care of both an obstetrician and a pulmonary specialist during pregnancy. Women with severe asthma may become worse during pregnancy, while mild asthmatics may not be affected. It is difficult from her letter to judge Ms. O.'s condition. She may have an uneventful pregnancy and then experience intense asthma during labor and delivery.

There are a number of pregnancy-safe nasal sprays that dilate the bronchial tubes and relieve asthma. Tedral is such a spray. It contains beta-mimetics, the drug at the root of ritodrine, the medication that slows premature labor. Tedral can relieve Ms. O., and her unborn baby will be fine. If, however, an attack does not subside, Ms. O. may have to be hospitalized in order to receive intravenous theophylline. Her physicians will do everything they can to prevent *status asthmaticus*, a prolonged state of asthma. An injection of corticosteroids may even be given in an emergency. Even though steroids are best avoided during pregnancy, when a life-threatening situation exists, a physician may take drastic action.

What About Surgery During Pregnancy?

Expectant mothers often feel clumsy during pregnancy. The extra weight is unwieldy, and their bodies in general seem alien. Accidents may happen and bones may break. Sometimes surgery is required to set a leg or an arm. Other conditions may arise too—appendicitis, for instance, or gallbladder problems. A woman may need surgery now as in any other time of her life, and an operation, even an abdominal one, can be performed safely.

An X ray should be avoided if possible, but if a limb is broken, then a woman's abdomen should be shielded with a lead apron during X ray of the injured bones. Ultrasound and an evaluation of the fetal heart rate can determine damage to the placenta and fetus. Ultrasonography is also the preferred diagnostic tool for pelvic pain. When combined with blood tests, ultrasound can often indicate whether surgery is needed immediately. If necessary, surgery can be conducted quite successfully by today's skilled physicians.

The safety of anesthesia. A pregnant woman who needs an operation should meet her anesthesiologist before surgery to discuss her anesthesia. Certain kinds of anesthesia will not affect the fetus and are considered safe to use. An expectant mother should learn what procedure her anesthesiologist intends to follow so that she may be assured by her obstetrician that she is embarking upon a safe course. An anesthesiologist will usually administer oxygen along with the anesthetic to his pregnant patient. This extra oxygen is a precaution to make sure that the fetus is never in short supply.

A perinatologist should attend the surgery of an expectant mother to safeguard her pregnancy. If surgery is performed in the last half of pregnancy, a perinatologist will watch for signs of premature labor in the recovery period. If there are any signs, Yutopar (ritodrine) can be administered until the crisis is over. (See Premature Labor in this chapter.) It is truly amazing how resilient the human body is. Pregnant women have even undergone open-heart surgery and afterward given birth to beautiful babies.

Can I Have a Breast Lump Biopsied During Pregnancy?

I have a lump on my breast that is worrying both me and my doctor. He did an ultrasound and told me that he may recommend a biopsy. I am in my sixth month. Shouldn't I wait until after the baby is born?

N.N.

Ypsilanti, Michigan

The milk glands enlarge during pregnancy, and a woman may feel unusual lumps in her breasts. A lump that is located on the side of the breast toward the armpit is more suspicious than most. Ms. N.'s physician was correct to examine her breast lump with ultrasound so that she was not exposed to X ray. I am sure that Ms. N. would like to postpone a biopsy, but waiting is not wise when the issue may be a life-threatening disease such as cancer.

Ms. N. should have a second opinion, however, before she agrees to the biopsy. It may also be necessary to have a mammogram and, of course, her abdomen should be shielded with a lead apron for this procedure.

Should she undergo the biopsy, she should consult with the anesthesiologist beforehand to make sure that a safe, preferably local anesthetic is going to be used. A perinatologist should attend the surgery. If the lump is benign, then her pregnancy can continue normally. If a malignancy is found, then she must seek the care of an oncologist. Both a biopsy of the breast and a mastectomy can be performed during pregnancy.

349

Would a Second Opinion Be Beneficial?

I was approximately twelve weeks pregnant and my doctor recommended immediate surgery to remove a large ovarian cyst. I sought a second opinion from a doctor at a large medical center. He told me that he had patients with cysts as large or larger go through normal pregnancies. Often the cyst dissolved. I never did go back to the first doctor. The second doctor did an ultrasound in February and he did not detect the cyst. Finally in June I gave birth to a healthy 7-pound 2-ounce boy. He was born vaginally with no problems. My first doctor told me it would be impossible for the baby to pass through the birth canal. I am so thankful that I sought a second opinion.

F.M.
Camden, New Jersey

Pregnancy is an exciting, positive experience, and this chapter is meant to keep it that way. A problem may occur at any point in this nine-month event. Warning signs can be subtle, but with this chapter as your guide, they can be recognized.

Once symptoms are spotted, their underlying causes can be treated. Expectant mothers get advice from many sources—friends, family, physicians, and scores of books. Sometimes all the information only creates confusion. This chapter is meant to sweep away the swirling facts and replace them with understanding.

CHAPTER 14

Having the Baby: A Safe and Happy Childbirth

GETTING READY FOR THE BIRTH

At first, the focus during pregnancy is on the milestones—overcoming the first-trimester threat of miscarriage, hearing the baby's heartbeat, getting the results of amniocentesis if you're over thirty-five, feeling the baby move—but soon thoughts turn toward the culmination of this experience: the birth itself. With the third trimester, a woman's due date seems suddenly upon her. She and her partner must actively begin to choose a childbirth method. So many questions start arising that couples sometimes wake up during the night just to talk. Mutual support is important right now, between a woman and her mate as well as between a woman and her doctor.

During these decision-making days, a woman should write down questions about labor and childbirth and have frequent discussions with her doctor. She is learning to be an obstetrical expert herself. She is considering different childbirth methods and classes, her feelings about medication during delivery, the possibility of a cesarean section, her partner's role—and in all these matters, her doctor can be a wonderful counselor and confidant.

Advice on how to choose a doctor or a midwife is offered in Chapter 4, and, of course, when you select a physician, you are also deciding *where* you will give birth. A woman should feel good about her birthing environment. She should know exactly where she will be and who will be with her. She should visit the premises and ask about emergency procedures and equipment.

My aim is to help expectant mothers have their many questions answered before labor begins. And yes, the moment will come for you when you feel completely informed, secure in your choices, and ready to give birth. Right now you may have doubts about your future, but I assure you that long before your due date, you will be joyously filled with anticipation and prepared as never before.

CHOOSING WHERE TO GIVE BIRTH

Is a Birthing Center Just As Safe As a Hospital?

A friend of mine recently gave birth attended by a midwife in a birthing center. Her experience was quite positive. She wants me to have my baby in the same place, but I've decided against it. I'm going to a large university hospital because I'm afraid that if I'm in a birthing center, I may not get the right care if something goes wrong. My friend says that I'm being excessively nervous. Is she right? Is a birthing center just as safe as a hospital?

L.B.
Chicago, Illinois

Certified nurse-midwives in reputable birthing centers across the country are skilled in assisting *low-risk* pregnancy women deliver their babies. The key here is *low-risk*—a pregnancy that has no complications and leads to a trouble-free childbirth. Sometimes, however, a low-risk pregnancy can become high-risk during labor and delivery, when unforeseen events change the situation. For example, a placental separation can occur in what may have seemed an untroubled childbirth. Then internal bleeding may threaten the life of the unborn baby. This crisis may require medication or a cesarean section, and a birthing center can do neither. A birthing center is not able to handle emergencies that require medication or surgery, and the health of the mother or her baby may be in jeopardy.

On the positive side, however, the less clinical atmosphere of a birthing center, where the focus is on childbirth as a family event, is certainly desirable. The birthing environment can set the tone for a newborn's arrival. Bonding can develop naturally at a center, whereas a hospital delivery room can sometimes be a cold place for mother and baby to meet.

Ideally, I would like to see the worlds of the birthing center and the hospital combined to create a warm birthing room in a hospital, with highly trained doctors and nurses and technologically advanced equipment. Some hospitals already offer this alternative. The atmosphere is more informal, but if a mother needs medication, a forceps delivery, a cesarean, or the baby is born with a problem that requires immediate attention for its survival, the hospital staff can swing into action. The big drawback to a birthing center is that if a crisis develops, a mother and/or baby must be rushed to a hospital, and in transit, crucial time—sometimes the moments that can mean life or death—is lost.

I believe that Ms. B. is wise to choose a hospital setting for her childbirth, but she should be sure that the hospital birthing environment pleases her. She should tour the hospital facilities and work out the particulars with her doctor right now. If she wants her partner present during labor and delivery, she should make sure that no problems will be encountered. Some couples also want to be together during a cesarean birth. Will this be allowed? Ms. B. and her doctor should reach a mutual understanding about such variables as the use of medication, the need for an episiotomy, and the possibility of a forceps or a cesarean delivery long before she begins labor. When the moment of childbirth arrives, Ms. B. should feel certain that she and her obstetrician are of one mind, and that she and her mate are pleased with the surroundings. If she has any doubts before delivery, she may want to take some time to choose a different doctor who is affiliated with a hospital more to her liking.

PREPARATION FOR CHILDBIRTH

The Road to Natural Childbirth

In the 1920s, the now-famous British physician Dr. Grantly Dick-Read revolutionized perceptions of childbirth with his astonishing book *Childbirth Without Fear.** Dr. Dick-Read, who is now regarded as a pioneer of today's natural childbirth methods, set forth the idea that fear of giving birth produced tension, which increased muscular pain. He advocated lifting the fear by creating a slowly paced, supported labor. His patients were never left alone. They were taught breathing techniques that helped them relax, and they were never medicated. The Dick-Read method aimed to reduce fear with conscious relaxation and thereby to decrease tension and pain. His approach did not mean painless childbirth, however, and over time, other methods were devised to help women handle the hurt.

The desire to have natural, drug-free childbirth did not grow in popularity in the United States, however, until the 1960s, when women became more health conscious and wanted greater control over their bodies. This was a perfect time for the popularity of psychoprophylaxis—which in the United States developed as the *Lamaze method*—to spread from Europe. The psychoprophylactic approach actually had its origins in the Soviet Union in the 1940s. Using Pavlov's "conditioned reflex" discovery and Dick-Read's belief that women who feared childbirth would suffer more pain, Soviet physicians attempted to "decondition" expectant mothers. Psychoprophylactic relaxation techniques, which included complex breathing exercises, were taught witht the aim of changing conditioning and lessening pain. The approach found a proponent in a French physician named Dr. Fernand Lamaze, and in 1959, his views were presented in this country.

An American trained in France, Marjorie Karmel, wrote *Thank You, Dr. Lamaze* in 1959 and forever altered the feelings of American women.† A year later, the American Society for Psychoprophylaxis in Obstetrics (ASPO) was born, and childbirth educators had a professional organization. The Lamaze method proliferated in classes around the country. (Elisabeth Bing, R.P.T., a distinguished force behind the popularity of the Lamaze

* New York: Harper & Row, 1978.
† Philadelphia: J. B. Lippincott Company, 1959.

method, wrote the classic *Six Practical Lessons for an Easier Childbirth,** available in paperback.)

The Lamaze method of childbirth education is undertaken in the third trimester, when a woman and her partner, who becomes her labor coach, learn relaxation and breathing exercises that will be synchronized with uterine contractions. The labor coach, who is usually the husband, offers emotional and physical support during labor and helps a woman accomplish the exercises. The Lamaze method does not prohibit medication, and if a woman is in great discomfort, she may have some form of analgesia or anesthesia.

On the other hand, the *Bradley technique,* developed in the 1960s by a California doctor, Dr. Robert Bradley, takes a stronger stand against medication. The Bradley method employs natural breathing by the woman and creates husband-and-wife teamwork. Bradley teachers are certified by the American Academy of Husband-Coached Childbirth. With this approach, the husband is trained to coach his wife through labor and delivery by using special tactics learned in class. The Bradley technique views the childbirth experience holistically—from the moment of conception through pregnancy, labor, delivery, and baby care. Dr. Bradley influenced innovations such as immediate breast-feeding of the newborn and permitting the baby to remain with its mother after birth rather than be isolated in a hospital nursery.

Many childbirth educators now offer classes and counseling early in pregnancy, on through the postpartum time. With modern childbirth education, women can discover the best care for their babies, from conception to the early months of life outside the womb.

Which Method Is Better—Lamaze or Bradley?

Prepared childbirth aims to eliminate fear and tension during labor through education. A drug-free delivery is the desired goal. Relaxation and breathing techniques, which require your full concentration during labor, are the basis of Lamaze. If you choose the Bradley method, instead of learning intricate breathing patterns, you will be breathing naturally and following instructions from your husband, who will be trained to distract you from the pain. A Bradley-trained husband leads his wife away from the pain

* New York: Bantam Books, 1982.

by constantly directing her to focus on different areas of her body. With either technique, you will be actively involved in childbirth, but the more popular Lamaze method gives greater control to the mother. Lamaze also permits a woman to request medication if she is in great distress, whereas Bradley instructors do not want their mothers to use any medication.

The method you choose may depend upon what is available in your community. Natural childbirth with the Bradley technique is more prevalent in the western United States. Lamaze educators are located across the country.

When you are trained in prepared childbirth, you are less tense and need no or little medication, but labor and delivery are never pain free. I believe that if the pain is extremely difficult to bear, a small amount of Demerol painkiller, given at the right time, under careful supervision, might help you deliver more easily. If the drug is given no less than a few hours before childbirth, it should be eliminated from your bloodstream and will not affect your newborn. If birth takes place within two hours of a Demerol injection, a mother and/or her newborn should be given a Demerol neutralizer such as Narcan.

The Leboyer Birthing Method

While women were demanding greater participation in childbirth, a French physician, Dr. Frederick Leboyer, asked a startling question: Why not think less of your own feelings and more about your baby's? In 1975, Dr. Leboyer's book *Birth Without Violence* presented the concept of gentle birth—a baby arrives in the world without immediately feeling a cold steel scale, being held upside down, or being quickly cut from the umbilical cord. Instead, a baby enters a dimly lit, hushed environment where he feels his mother's touch.

After years of personal psychoanalysis in which he relived his own birth experience, Dr. Leboyer came to believe in early infant awareness. He was able to reinforce his belief with the work of behaviorist Konrad Lorenz, the man who put forth the theory of imprinting. By observing the actions of young animals, Lorenz proved that learning begins exceptionally early in life. Dr. Leboyer became armed with knowledge about newborns, but it was only after a visit to India that he was able to put his insights to practical use.

In India, Dr. Leboyer witnessed unhurried births. East Indian hospitals did not have the activity and noise of Western institutions, and Dr. Leboyer decided to recreate these tranquil environments. He proposed a childbirth method that allowed a baby to be born in a quiet, dimly lit room. Once in its new world, the baby rests on its mother's stomach, umbilical cord intact, for about five minutes, while everyone present speaks in hushed tones. The Leboyer technique slows the pace of delivery room activity and focuses on the baby's needs. As the baby begins to adapt to its new surroundings, the umbilical cord stops pulsating, is severed, and the infant is held in a warm bath. Soft lights, whispered words, and gentle touches replace the glare, the cries, and the abrupt movements of other types of childbirth.

Can I Use the Bradley Technique with the Leboyer Method?

I've read about different methods of childbirth and talked to my friends, and I've decided that I'd like to combine them. I want to use the Bradley technique with the Leboyer method. Is this possible?

E.R.

West Islip, New York

Both the Lamaze and Bradley classes for natural childbirth are valuable experiences for expectant parents. Not only do these programs educate couples about labor and delivery, but they also bring men and women together to share mutual concerns. Still, although both methods are good, an expectant mother is usually limited to one that is offered close to her home.

Ms. R. lives in New York, and in her area, the Bradley technique is not as prevalent as Lamaze. If she knows of Bradley classes in her community, and if she prefers this husband-coached approach, then she certainly should enroll. I encourage her, however, to consult with her doctor beforehand. Before entering a natural childbirth course, an expectant mother should make sure that she is having a low-risk pregnancy and that the technique she has chosen is safe for her.

Sometimes prepared childbirth classes can create the illusion that all deliveries will be smooth. Ms. R. should remember that no matter how carefully she may plan the steps of her childbirth, an unforeseen complication may alter events. If medical intervention is needed, she should be ready to shift her attention. An ability to adapt is essential at this time.

As for a Bradley/Leboyer combination birth, I see no problem. While Bradley helps the mother, Leboyer is for the infant. Ms. R. may have a practical problem, however, because few hospitals precisely follow Leboyer's recommendations. In their birthing rooms or regular delivery rooms, many institutions have adopted certain of Leboyer's suggestions: dim lights, low voices, an immediate mother/baby bonding after birth; but a relatively small number of hospitals will immerse the baby in a warm bath. The value of this part of the Leboyer technique has been debated, and Ms. R. may have difficulty locating a facility in which the staff agrees to carry out Leboyer to the letter. On the other hand, most doctors and nursing staffs work hard to support an expectant mother during childbirth, and I am sure that Ms. R. will be able to arrange a satisfying delivery.

Ms. R. should be aware that after birth, the baby may be examined immediately by the doctor if he has any concerns. She may have to postpone the moment when she holds her infant. Of course, you always hope that a baby's arrival will be trouble free, but everyone must be prepared for the unexpected.

I Had Premature Labor a Month Ago. Will Childbirth Classes Be Dangerous for Me?

I overcame premature labor at the beginning of my seventh month. Now I'm approaching the eighth month and my doctor feels that I will go very close to term. He says it's safe for me to take natural childbirth classes, but my mother is against it. She says that I shouldn't strain or push myself because I could go back into labor. Will childbirth classes be dangerous for me?

L.V.
Berkeley, California

All high- and low-risk expectant mothers can benefit from prepared childbirth classes. These are educational experiences. Ms. V. will meet other expectant mothers, join in discussions, see films, read books, and learn how to conquer any fears she may have about childbirth. She can also develop an understanding of cesarean birth.

Ms. V. should inform her childbirth educator about her premature labor and about any medication she may still be taking for this condition. When the breathing and pushing exercises begin,

Ms. V. should become a conservative participant. She can learn the breathing pattern, but vigorous pushing may be too great a strain on her pregnancy. In this case, Mother is right! Ms. V. may stimulate early labor if she stresses the fetal environment, which right now needs tranquillity.

KEEPING TRACK OF THE BABY IN THE LAST TRIMESTER

Why Is a Record of the Baby's Movements So Important?

My baby is four months old, and I've just had my first moment to spare. I was telling a pregnant friend about keeping track of the baby's movements in the last trimester, and I suddenly realized that I didn't understand why I did that. I wrote down the baby's movements on my calendar, brought it to my doctor visits, and everything was fine. Still I don't know what the doctor was looking for when he checked my notations. Why is a record of the baby's movements so important?

H.W.
Hibernia, New Jersey

Since fetal movement varies so much from pregnancy to pregnancy, until 1971, doctors did not consider a woman's reports of her baby's activity to be a significant judgment of fetal health. In 1971, this thinking changed. At Hadassah University Hospital in Jerusalem, Dr. Eliahu Sadovsky encountered a diabetic pregnant woman who complained about diminished fetal movement three days before she was scheduled for a cesarean. Doctors could still hear the baby's heartbeat, and they urged her to wait until the scheduled day for delivery. The day before the scheduled delivery, she felt no movement. She went back to the doctors, who showed no sign of alarm because they could still hear the heart rate. But by the next day, when the baby was due to be born, a heartbeat was no longer audible and the infant was dead. This experience prompted Dr. Sadovsky to devise a program for monitoring fetal movement. Today his technique has saved the lives of countless newborns.

Beginning at the twenty-seventh week, a woman should lie on her left or right side with her hand on her abdomen and concentrate. A woman in a *low-risk* pregnancy should count fetal movements twice a day for twenty to thirty minutes. The best times for counting are when she awakens and before she goes to sleep at night. Five or six movements during each counting period is a reassuring sign. A woman in the *high-risk* category should count movements three times a day—early in the morning, mid- or late afternoon, and before retiring. If she counts five to six movements in each thirty-minute period, she does not have to extend her counting time. If she notices less than three movements in a half-hour, however, she should continue counting for an hour or more. If *any* expectant mother, low or high risk, counts fewer than ten movements in a twelve-hour period, no movements in the morning, or fewer than three movements in eight hours, or if she becomes concerned for any reason, she should contact her obstetrician. He should send her to the hospital for testing.

Ms. W. was actually helping to monitor her baby's health when she noted daily movements. My guess is that she probably detected a familiar pattern in the activity, but her baby's movements are not likely to match those of her friend's baby. Dr. Sadovsky measured the average daily movements in 127 pregnant women who had healthy deliveries, and he found an amazing range. The number of daily movements rose from about 200 in the twentieth week to over 500 in the thirty-second week. Afterward, movements dropped to about 280 a day. Movements on the whole fluctuated from 200 to 700 a day.

In the womb, the unborn baby goes through wakefulness and sleep, and a woman should not worry if she notices a time of internal quiet. If an expectant mother eats, or drinks a glass of orange juice, perhaps, the rise in her blood sugar should stimulate the fetus to move. When a woman lies down after snacking or goes to bed early following dinner, her baby's movements can become accelerated. An expectant mother usually comes to recognize her unborn baby's internal rhythm, and she can often tell whether the fetus seems intermittently or regularly busy. Sometimes women have worried that something might be wrong with their baby when fetal movement seems too great. Dr. William F. Rayburn conducted a study at Ohio State University in which he asked 931 pregnant women to chart fetal movement. Of these, 47 women recorded signs of excess fetal activity. Dr. Rayburn followed their offspring and reported that at birth, they showed good Apgar scores and from three to eighteen months later were growing normally. He concluded that excessive fetal activity was not a worrisome sign.

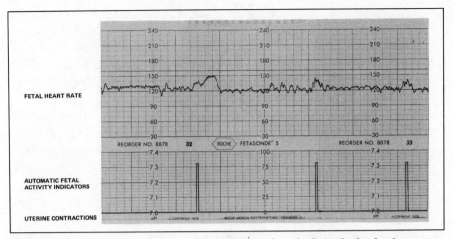

Figure 14-1. *Nonstress test. This test is performed with the aid of a fetal monitor. The top graph shows fetal heart rate, and the vertical bar on the lower portion indicates fetal movement. No uterine contractions are seen. This test is termed "reactive" since the fetal heart rate accelerates during each movement, indicating that the fetus is doing well.*

On the other hand, if a woman notices diminished activity and eating does not rouse the fetus, she should inform her doctor. As a rule, a woman should follow the Sadovsky recommendations and call her doctor whenever she feels unusual movement—either too much or too little. Sometimes smoking mothers conceive fetuses that breathe less in the womb and are, therefore, less active. A drop in fetal motion can also signal imminent labor. Over and over, women have reported that they felt the fetus slow down, and a day later labor began. Slowing down, however, should not be confused with stopping. Even when a fetus slows down before labor, it will still become active after a woman eats or drinks.

Whenever a woman is in doubt about her baby's activity, she must trust her questioning mind and call her doctor. Her insights should lead to an evaluation of her baby's health, as will be described, and may save the infant's life.

If Movement Is Questionable, How Is the Baby Tested?

Nonstress testing (NST) is a type of external fetal monitoring that a physician can turn to in times of uncertainty over the fetal movement and other high-risk problems, such as passing your due date. What is called Doppler ultrasound nonstress testing is used mostly in high-risk pregnancies, but it is available to all expectant mothers. It can be performed in a doctor's office or in the hospital. During nonstress testing, an obstetrician places a transducer over a woman's abdomen. This device picks up the fetal heart rate so that it can be recorded on special monitoring paper. The heart rate is correlated with fetal movement either automatically or with the help of the mother, who presses a button each time she feels the baby move. The heart rate should increase with the baby's movement; if it does not, then the baby may not be receiving enough oxygen or the nervous system may not be functioning well. The lack of increasing heart rate is a warning sign that could mean the baby is in jeopardy. Then a woman should undergo further testing.

In the hospital, a woman may have the *oxytocin challenge test* (OCT), in which she is given an intravenous infusion of Pitocin, a synthetic form of the labor-inducing hormone oxytocin, and the fetal heart rate is recorded on a fetal monitor. If the unborn baby's heart rate remains stable even after good labor has been induced, which means at least three contractions within a ten-minute interval, the OCT will be diagnosed as "negative" or "good." Then a woman may be sent home to wait for labor or asked to return for another test within twenty-four or forty-eight hours. If the fetal heart rate decreases during the test, however, the OCT is termed "positive" or "bad." The baby may be in danger, and in this case, labor should be induced or a cesarean section performed. Whatever the results of nonstress testing or the oxytocin challenge test, an expectant mother's sensitivity toward her baby's movements is essential. Every pregnant woman who keeps a record of fetal activity is protecting the life of her unborn child.

LABOR

How Do You Tell the Difference Between True and False Labor?

A few days ago, I went to the hospital to give birth to my third child. I thought I knew the ins and outs of pregnancy by the third time around, but when the doctor examined me and said that my cervix was closed, I knew I was not in labor yet. How could I have made such a mistake? When I went home, I was terribly embarrassed, as my two children looked at me in anticipation and asked, "Where's the baby?" Where did I go wrong? How can you tell the difference between true and false labor?

M.J.
Salem, Massachusetts

As described in Chapter 12, painless *Braxton-Hicks,* or false labor, contractions occur now and then throughout pregnancy, but they appear with greatest frequency toward the end. The increase in these irregularly spaced contractions can be confusing even to an experienced woman, as Ms. J. points out, until a doctor examines her cervix. Cervical dilatation, a widening of the cervix, never takes place during Braxton-Hicks contractions.

Usually a woman who has gone through natural childbirth classes has learned about false labor, but, as in Ms. J.'s case, the actual experience can be another story. False labor contractions are usually mild, although on rare occasions, they can seem quite powerful. Ultimately they have no pattern. They can come regularly for five or ten minutes for an hour or two, but if you lie down on your left side and feel for fetal movement, the contractions can disappear. True labor never goes away when you relax. If you begin to experience contractions that last for a minute or longer but are somewhat irregular in pattern, they are usually false labor contractions, even if they are painful. True labor always builds. It begins with short contractions that build to greater and greater intensity. A time-honored test of true labor is drinking an alcoholic beverage. If an expectant mother sits down and drinks a glass of wine or a cocktail, false labor can disappear in a few minutes. True labor is not affected by the alcohol. By the way, one drink at this point in pregnancy will not harm the baby.

Braxton-Hicks contractions have a function in that they exercise the uterine muscles and increase the circulation of maternal blood to the placenta. They prepare the body for the onset of the real thing. True labor contractions may be irregular at first and only thirty seconds long every fifteen or twenty minutes, but they will build slowly and grow closer and longer in duration. A true labor contraction should last a full minute, and a woman should feel peaceful relaxation between her true contractions. And no matter whether a woman rests or moves around, a true labor contraction will not stop.

Whenever a woman is concerned about the onset of labor, she

should call her doctor. During pregnancy, a mucous plug develops in the cervix to protect against infection. A woman may lose this plug in the form of a "bloody show," or her bag of waters may break while she is trying to evaluate her labor. In either event—and both are covered in more detail in this chapter—a woman must contact her physician immediately. True labor may still be a day or two away, but it may be happening right then and there.

What Triggers True Labor?

An expectant mother's due date is estimated at 280 days from her last menstrual period, but actually, she can expect to give birth anywhere from 38 to 42 weeks after her last period. The length of pregnancy is really up to her baby, for the baby itself chooses its moment of arrival.

As the fetus grows, it begins to fill its internal home. In a healthy pregnancy, at about 280 days, the fetus has no more room and the placenta is unable to nourish its guest. As animal studies have shown, this is when true labor seems to be triggered. The fetus, stressed by its environment, releases cortisone from its hypothalamus and adrenal glands. Then a complex hormonal interplay takes place. The level of the hormone progesterone falls at this time, as the placenta's vital blood supply declines. The cortisone stimulates the placenta to release estrogen, and estrogen, in turn, causes an increase in a hormonal substance called *prostaglandins*. Until now, the progesterone produced by the placenta has been maintaining the pregnancy, fending off any contractions. With its progesterone guard down, the uterus becomes more and more sensitive to a contraction-causing hormone called *oxytocin,* which is being released by the baby's and the mother's pituitary glands at this time. The combination of prostaglandins and oxytocin (synthetically manufactured under the name Pitocin) starts true labor.

The rise of prostaglandins and the spurts of oxytocin create true labor contractions. Soon the unborn baby is pushing on the mother's cervix. The sensitive cervix responds and sends a signal to the mother's pituitary, which releases even more oxytocin than the baby's pituitary. The escalating hormones escalate contractions. As oxytocin from both the baby and the mother increases, the prostaglandins build in the placenta and the uterus, and the onset of labor is complete. Now it is only a matter of time before a mother will embrace her child.

Are More Babies Born During a Full Moon?

This is one of those questions that divide scientists into camps. Those on the pro side contend that human beings have biological high and low tides governed by the moon and that the full moon, of course, affects behavior. Crime rates rise during a full moon, and more babies are born. One of those on the con side is George Abell, a respected astronomer who conducted a study of almost twelve thousand births in a five-year period at UCLA Hospital. He reported no correlation between number of births and phases of the moon. I have not, however, encountered an obstetrical doctor or nurse who agrees with him.

When the barometric pressure is low just before a full moon, or in bad weather—during hurricanes, snowstorms, or rainy days—labor floors are filled with women giving birth. On high-pressure days, the floors are fairly empty. Perhaps the low barometric pressure shifts the amniotic fluid and instigates labor. Around the time of the full moon, I can almost count on being in the hospital around the clock. And the feeling that more babies are born at night than in the day is not my imagination. Studies at the University of Minnesota have confirmed that twice as many women go into labor at midnight than at noon.

Understanding Labor

Before moving on to more questions about contractions, how they progress, and what events such as the breaking of the bag of waters mean, there are certain terms that are helpful for an expectant mother to know. These terms—engagement, cervical dilatation, cervical effacement, and station (of the presenting part)—describe different activities of labor, and understanding them will give a woman a better sense of what is going on in her body. She will also be able to communicate with her doctor more easily and to grasp what he means when he tells her, for example, that the baby is at zero station. From engagement to dilatation, the baby is getting closer and closer to birth. Here is what is happening:

Engagement. When a doctor says that the baby is *engaged,* he means that the baby has dropped; its head has entered into the woman's pelvis. This shift of the baby's weight is also called *lightening,* because a woman can feel a certain lifting of the pressure she has come to associate with her pregnancy. For a first-born, this engagement may happen two to four weeks before a woman goes into active labor. In later pregnancies, engagement may be postponed until labor is under way.

In a sense, engagement is the first step toward childbirth. The fetal head slips inside the pelvis and begins to maneuver into the bony birth canal. This *descent* is aided by uterine contractions, Braxton-Hicks contractions in a first-time mother, or true labor in a woman who is already a mother. Since the pelvic bones are tilted, the baby must go through a series of twists and turns to make its way into the outside world. Following engagement and descent, these movements are labeled *flexion, internal rotation, extension, external rotation,* and *expulsion,* to help doctors identify the baby's progress.

Ninety-five percent of the time, the baby moves into a *vertex,* meaning *head-down,* position in the pelvis. This vertex pose can be at a number of angles. In 40 pecent of births, the baby is facing the mother's right side, while 25 percent of babies face her left side. Another 25 percent are looking toward the mother's back, and 10 percent look toward the mother's front. When a baby faces the front of a woman's body, its skull presses on her spine and causes pressure on her lower back. This posterior position may lead to "back labor," which is described later on.

Four percent of babies that are not in the vertex position may be in a *breech presentation,* which usually means that the buttocks are where the head should be. Sometimes the uterus can be relaxed and the baby turned, but a breech may result in a cesarean section. If the baby is not in a vertical position in the womb but in a *transverse lie*—positioned from side to side with neither head nor buttocks in the birth canal—a cesarean will be needed. A transverse lie, however, only occurs in 1 percent of all births, and sometimes the contractions of labor correct the position and the baby shifts into a vertex pose in the pelvis.

When a fetus is properly engaged and descent begins, a doctor checks the downward movement by judging the station of the baby's presenting part, which, in a vertex position, is the head.

Cervical dilatation. When contractions cause discomfort, a widening, or dilatation, of the cervix has begun. Labor pulls the uterus downward and pushes the baby's head deeper and deeper into the pelvis. The baby turns and presses against the cervix, which, having *effaced,* or thinned, is primed to be opened, or dilated. As contractions grow closer and effacement gets nearer and nearer to completion, the cervix dilates more and more rapidly. The traditional rule of thumb is that when a woman is in active labor, she will dilate approximately 1 centimeter per hour. This time-honored theory is matched by modern research, which indicates that the average active labor lasts approximately fourteen hours—twelve hours for the first stage and two hours for the second, "pushing" stage. The cervical dilatation is initially slow, but toward the end, it grows faster. (See Friedman Curve.) Once a cervix is 100 percent effaced and 5 centimeters dilated, in two or three hours of strong labor, the cervix could be fully dilated—

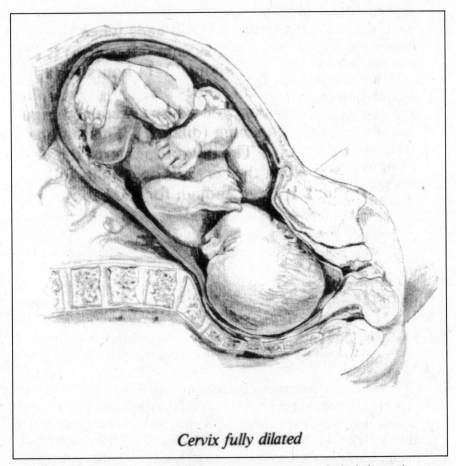

Cervix fully dilated

Figure 14-2. *The cervix is fully dilated (10 centimeters) with the baby in the vertex (head-down) position. The cervix is fully effaced and seen only as a thin membrane surrounding the baby's head.* Reproduced by permission of Stuart Pharmaceuticals, from their booklet, "Prenatal and Postnatal Care."

opened to 10 centimeters or about 4 inches, wide enough to accommodate the baby's head.

The opening of the cervix may be slow at first, when the contractions are fifteen or twenty minutes apart and the cervix is only 20 percent effaced. A woman may ask her doctor how dilated she is, and he will usually give her the answer in centimeters. Some doctors measure with their fingers—for instance, two fingers dilated means 3 centimeters—but since the size and shape of a person's hand varies, a centimeter reading is most accurate. If she is 30 percent effaced and 5 centimeters dilated, labor will take a while. As mentioned before, if a doctor says that a woman is 100 percent effaced and 5 centimeters dilated, and contractions are good, she could give birth within a few hours. In addition, by knowing the baby's plus or minus station, a woman has a more complete picture.

In her prepared childbirth class, a woman will learn that she should not try to "push" the baby until she is fully 10 centimeters dilated. Complete effacement and total dilatation mean that stage two of labor, which includes childbirth, is ready to commence. While she is still in stage one, when her cervix is dilating from 5 to 8 centimeters, it is difficult for a woman to relax, but it is dangerous to push before dilatation is complete. Early pushing may force the cervix down with the baby's head. This action can weaken the muscles around the bladder and cause serious bladder problems as well as a prolapse (dropped) uterus later in life.

Cervical effacement. During pregnancy, the cervix forms a protective barrier between the vagina and the opening of the uterus. The cervix stays firmly closed and remains about 1½ inches thick, preventing the invasion of bacteria. As hormonal changes begin and labor draws closer, however, the cervix transforms: it becomes *effaced,* which means that it gets softer and shorter, and, finally, it almost disappears. This effacement can start well before true labor begins.

Cervical effacement is a gradual process. Sometimes the cervix will begin to dilate before it is fully effaced, but usually dilatation does not go full speed ahead until effacement is complete. Slight dilatation of 1, 2, 3, or 4 centimeters can occur before full effacement, but once the cervix is completely effaced—thinned out to a delicate tissue that can part and slip back around the baby's head—dilatation and labor usually move quite quickly.

Effacement can begin painlessly, days or weeks before a baby is

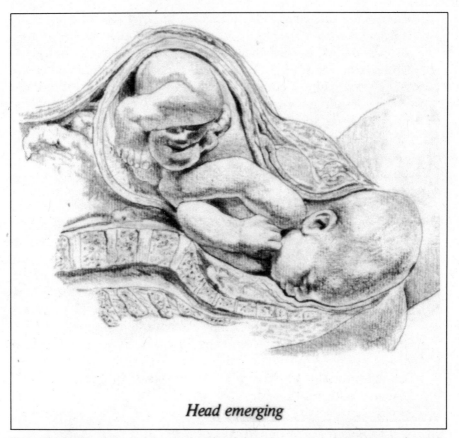

Head emerging

Figure 14-3. *The fetus is in a vertex (head-down) position; gestation is plus 2–3, and the top of the baby's head can now be seen through the birth canal.* Reproduced by permission of Stuart Pharmaceuticals, from their booklet, "Prenatal and Postnatal Care."

born. It continues to the end of the first stage of labor; in fact, complete effacement usually signals the end of stage one of the three stages of labor. A woman can have a progress report of how close she is to childbirth by finding out how effaced she is. A "long" cervix has not yet effaced and effective labor has still not begun. If a woman learns, however, that she is 20 to 30 percent effaced, then her cervix is beginning to soften and shorten in preparation for childbirth. A 50 percent effacement means that the cervix is probably half the length it was during pregnancy. A cervix that is 100 percent effaced is gossamer thin, and if dilatation has not already started, it will surely begin soon. Effacement is always painless. It is dilatation, the significant stretching and widening of the cervix, that brings on the first sign of pain.

Station (of the presenting part). The station of the presenting part—usually the baby's head—is a measure of how far down the baby has moved into the pelvic area. Through vaginal and rectal examinations, the docor can gauge the baby's progress. When the widest part of the baby's head is at the narrowest part of the pelvis, the area of the ischial spine, then the baby is said to be at *zero station.* Before it reaches zero station, when it is higher in the pelvis, it is at a *minus station.* A baby may be at minus one or minus two centimeters, and if it does not reach zero station, it may be too big to fit through the pelvis. Then a cesarean birth may be inevitable. What usually happens, however, is that a baby moves from a minus station, to zero station, to a *plus station.*

When the widest part of the baby's head passes through zero to a plus station, it means that a vaginal birth is almost assured. At plus one, the baby is one-third of the way between the base of the spine and the bottom, bony part of the pelvis. Plus two is two-thirds of the way down, and plus three means that the head has traveled through the birth canal, reached the perineum, and the baby's birth is imminent. An expectant mother can have a good idea of her progress during labor if she knows the baby's station. She will be fully informed if she also asks, "How effaced am I? How dilated?"

How Will I Know if My Water Breaks or if I'm Just Leaking Urine?

My best friend was sure she was in labor when she felt a trickle running down her leg. She went to the doctor's office after he told her that it sounded as if her water broke, but then he sent her home. Apparently she was only leaking urine. She did not give birth until four days later. I was astonished that she didn't know the difference between her bag of waters and urine, and now that I'm pregnant, I wonder if I'll be able to tell one from the other. Is there some sort of sign I can look for? How will I know if my water breaks or if I'm just leaking urine?

N.T.

Hampton, Virginia

When the bag of waters breaks, or, more technically, when the fetal membranes rupture, a woman may notice a sudden gush or a slow trickle of fluid from her vagina. The fetal membranes encase the amniotic fluid and create the amniotic sac. In 10 to 20 percent of pregnancies, the sac spontaneously ruptures either before or in the beginning of labor, and the amniotic fluid escapes. A woman feels an uncontrollable gush of the one to two pints of fluid, or she experiences a long-lasting liquid trickle.

In contrast, the flow of urine is less copious, and it stops fairly soon after it starts. In late pregnancy, the baby's head can press against a woman's bladder and cause a urine leakage. After a nap or a night's sleep, a woman may find wet bed sheets, or she may release such a buildup of urine in the toilet that she wonders if her water has broken. Sometimes patients have described such incidents to me and they have sounded like women with ruptured fetal membranes. When they arrive in my office, I see that many of these patients were only leaking urine.

Still, a woman should not be in doubt. If during her third trimester Ms. T. thinks that her bag of waters has broken, she should contact her doctor and explain exactly what has happened. Her doctor will ask her to visit either the hospital or his office so that the fluid may be tested. Using a sterile speculum and cotton swab, a physician will take a sample of the fluid near a woman's cervix. He will test the pH level of his sample using a Nitrazine test strip, a litmus-type paper. Amniotic fluid is highly alkaline, has a high pH, and will cause the paper to turn blue. If the paper remains yellow, or unstained, the fluid has a neutral or low pH and is probably urine. If a woman has recurring "false alarms" in which she perceives ruptured membranes but is only leaking urine, a doctor may give her a strip of Nitrazine paper for at-home testing. In this way, she can identify the fluid immediately.

The fetal membranes may break anytime during the third trimester, and as mentioned earlier, 10 to 20 percent of women will have this experience before active labor. For most expectant mothers, the painless rupture of the membranes happens in the labor room. A woman who feels that her bag of waters has broken early, however, should immediately look to see whether the released amniotic fluid is clear or brownish.

If the fluid is clear and she is not yet feeling the regular contractions of labor, she should lie on her left side and assess the fetal movement. She should also check her temperature, drink plenty of fluid, and alert her doctor to her progress. It might take some time before labor begins, but 50 percent of women who experience a rupture of the fetal membranes *before labor* are in labor within twelve hours. Eighty to 85 percent are in labor within twenty-four hours. Prostaglandins (explained in What Triggers True Labor?) stimulate the hormone oxytocin, which escalates labor. When the membranes rupture, there is a sudden release of prostaglandins from the amniotic fluid, and a labor-promoting reaction begins. A woman who is already in labor when the membranes break will have stronger labor within fifteen to thirty minutes.

If the fluid is brown-stained when the membranes break, the fetus may be in distress. If the baby is lying on its umbilical cord, then its blood supply and oxygen level drop. When the oxygen to the baby is low, its sensitive sphincter muscle is less able to control the fetal stool. The stool then enters into the amniotic fluid, making it brown or meconium-stained.

Meconium-stained amniotic fluid is a warning sign of possible trouble in the womb. The fetus may be in jeopardy. A woman who experiences this situation must immediately call her doctor and enter the hospital for further testing as a high-risk patient. She will then be extensively monitored. If the meconium-stained amniotic fluid is thick, indicating more severe fetal jeopardy, a cesarean section may be needed. At childbirth, doctors are put on alert and a pediatrician stands by, because the throat, pharynx, and larynx of the newborn must be cleared of the stained amniotic fluid by suction before it enters the baby's lungs. This meconium fluid can irritate and inflame the fragile newborn's lungs and may lead to serious pneumonia, which the baby may not be able to survive.

Once the fetal membranes rupture, the chance of fetal infection rises. Usually labor begins naturally within twelve to twenty-four hours after the membranes break, but sometimes labor just doesn't seem to happen and doctors worry about the possible onset of infection. If a woman is within two weeks before or after her due date, and if she has no apparent infection or complication, some doctors do permit up to a forty-eight-hour wait for natural birth. If labor does not start spontaneously, an intravenous infusion with Pitocin (synthetic oxytocin) must be given to induce labor. Most doctors, because they fear infection, do not like to wait more than twelve to sixteen hours before they induce or stimulate labor. If there is any sign of infection or fever in the mother, or if more than forty-eight hours have passed since the membranes ruptured, then the newborn should be observed and treated with antibiotics in an intensive-care nursery after birth.

Sometimes the bag of waters breaks but a woman has no sign of labor, and thinking that she should wait until she feels contractions, she lets hours or days go by before she calls the doctor. In the interim, an infection has a chance to take hold. A woman should be alert to her body and her baby's movements, and she should constantly inform her doctor of any changes. More important than whether she feels her fetal membranes rupture or senses a greater-than-normal leakage of urine is her awareness of the baby kicking and moving in her womb. No matter what else is happening, she should always first be assured of fetal activity.

What Is a Bloody Show?

The term "bloody show" can be confusing. Sometimes, toward the end of pregnancy, as the cervix effaces and becomes much more pliable, it also becomes much more fragile. After a doctor's examination, a woman may return to her office or home and notice a slight staining. Some women call this a bloody show, but it is really just a reaction from the transforming cervix.

A woman might also hear the phrase "bloody show" used in reference to the release of the *mucous plug* that is expelled from the cervix as it effaces. The mucous plug is fixed in the middle of the cervix to protect the fetal membrane. As the cervix softens and stretches, either in preparation for or during labor, the mucous plug loosens and eventually falls out. A woman will notice a thick, blood-stained discharge that is the mucous plug and call it a bloody show.

A myth handed down from mother to daughter is that when you see the mucous plug, labor is imminent. This is not true. The plug can be passed during a period of cervical change or during false labor, and true labor might still be days away. What does seem to happen, however, is that when a woman is in the beginning of labor and she sees the plug, labor speeds up. After the plug is expelled, labor becomes more active and often the bag of waters breaks.

The expulsion of the mucous plug, however, is not what physicians are describing when they talk about a bloody show. What doctors and nurses call a bloody show usually occurs toward the end of labor, when the cervix stretches from 5 to 10 centimeters. At this point the bloody show indicates that a woman is well into labor and almost fully dilated. Childbirth is at hand.

How Will I Know When to Call the Doctor?

I'm so nervous that I'll misjudge my labor pains and not call the doctor in time. I have nightmares about giving birth in the car during a traffic jam. How will I know when to call the doctor?

E.W.

Los Angeles, California

Most women seem to go into labor at night, when the possibility of being trapped in traffic is minimal, but the chance of a daytime delivery is still very real. When Ms. W., or any expectant mother, feels the regularly spaced contractions of true labor, she should lie down on her side, breathe easily, and put her hand on her abdomen to check fetal movement. Generally it is a good idea to stay home in the early phase of true labor. By resting at home, a woman avoids the possibility of having to return from the hospital because childbirth is many hours away. A woman usually feels more comfortable at home; the same number of hours pass more quickly there than in the hospital.

Usually there is plenty of time to call the doctor and get to the hospital before strong labor begins. For a first pregnancy, a woman can expect an average of ten to twelve hours of labor. In subsequent pregnancies, the average labor is five to six hours. Every pregnancy is unique, however, and a woman must assess her condition. If her first pregnancy's labor was slow, then future pregnancies are also likely to have slow labors. If in her first pregnancy labor was fast, then future pregnancies will probably have speedy labors. Normally a woman and her doctor work out a plan well in advance. A doctor will tell his patient how he can be reached, what numbers to call for his office and answering service, and he might even provide you with a number for the hospital. When true labor begins, a doctor usually wants to be alerted so he can keep track of your progress. A doctor in a group practice also might want to be notified early so that he, the person who has overseen your pregnancy, and not an associate can try to be in attendance for the birth.

If a physician is not in his office and a message is left with a secretary or an answering service, you must remember to say that you are pregnant and in labor and not merely leave a message asking the doctor to call you back. If the bag of waters has broken or the mucous plug has been expelled, then a doctor should also be contacted early on. (See the two preceding sections.) If the amniotic fluid that has been released is brown (meconium-stained), a woman is in a high-risk situation, and if she cannot reach her doctor, she should tell the answering service that she is going to the hospital to be checked by the doctors there. If the fluid is clear, then she should still plan on going to the hospital, but the urgency is lifted. When the fetal membranes rupture and labor has not yet begun, contractions normally start within twelve to twenty-four hours. When a woman is already experiencing contractions and the membranes break, labor will intensify in thirty to forty-five minutes.

I tell my pregnant patients that if they have released the mucous plug or if their waters have broken through, whatever their color, they should call me right away. If they do not hear from me in ten minutes, they should leave word with my office or service that they have gone to the hospital and I can meet them there. *The emergencies during labor are diminished fetal movement, a gushing of fluid that is not clear, any bleeding, and intense close contractions.* If Ms. W. experiences any of these symptoms, she should contact her physician immediately, and if he is unavailable, she should leave a message that she is en route to the hospital. Her bag should be packed ahead of time. (See What Should I Bring to the Hospital?)

Although there have been a couple of close calls, none of my patients has ever given birth in a car. Women share a keen sense of timing about their labor and delivery, and every expectant mother can feel fairly certain that she will enter the hospital well ahead of the birth of her baby. A practice drive to the hospital is always recommended so that you know exactly how long the trip is from the office and from home. If Ms. W. remains concerned about traffic, she might find consolation in realizing that if childbirth seems to be right around the corner, she can request a police escort, and as long as safety is assured, she probably can travel above the speed limit without being fined. The greater likelihood, however, is that an uneventful trip will bring her to the hospital, and she will pace herself through labor as the baby takes its time in arriving.

Should I Eat Before I Go to the Hospital?

I've heard conflicting opinions about whether you should or shouldn't eat before going to the hospital. When one friend of mine went into labor, her doctor told her to eat a meal, and when she got to the hospi-

tal, she was given an enema to clean her out. The nurse said she shouldn't have eaten. Yet I thought you had to keep your strength up during labor. Should I eat before I go to the hospital?

M.M.

Longview, Washington

Sometimes women are wrongly advised to eat before they go to the hospital to give birth. When strong labor occurs, a woman *should not* consume solid food. At the end of gestation, food takes a long time to digest, and when a woman reaches the "pushing" phase of labor, undigested food could make her sick. Also, there is a real possibility that a birthing woman, whether she is anesthetized or not, could vomit undigested food, aspirate it, and die. Obviously Ms. M. is asking a lifesaving question.

A light snack at the onset of labor when contractions are far apart is all right, but when a woman goes into strong labor, she benefits from drinking fluids for nourishment and hydration. Water and fruit juice, for example, will maintain her body balance and alleviate her discomfort. Most women drink ice water and suck on ice cubes, and they are strong enough to give birth successfully.

What Should I Bring to the Hospital?

I always ask an expectant mother to remember that she is not going to the hospital because she is sick. Her hospital stay is due to a joyous occasion—the birth of her baby—and she should pack with her comfort and happiness in mind.

Labor may be long, so I suggest that a woman include lollipops or hard candies that will moisten her mouth and feel soothing. She should also pack massage cream and rubber balls to bring relief during back labor; these are for her partner to use. By the way, the labor coach may become hungry and have no opportunity to visit the hospital cafeteria, so sandwiches or snack foods are good ideas. Drinks such as mineral water or juice quench the thirst of both expectant parents, and when considering liquids, remember *a bottle of champagne.* You should ask the nurse to refrigerate the bottle when you arrive. Then, when you greet your newborn, it's time to pop the cork!

Another item you might welcome during labor is a big pillow. A hospital may not supply an expectant mother with more than one or two pillows, and it is often convenient for her to have an extra pillow to put between her legs during labor. The pillow may become soiled, however. Since gowns may also become stained during labor and delivery, it is preferable for a woman to wear a hospital gown at this time and to change into her own nightgown later on. Some women bring nursing gowns, since they plan on breast-feeding. Other things to pack are: a robe, slippers, several nightgowns, a nursing brassiere, toiletries, makeup, a mirror, shampoo—whatever will make you feel at home. I have seen new mothers enjoying their favorite tapes on cassette players they brought from home; other women like to use their own sheets and pillowcases, if the hospital permits.

In addition to a mother's suitcase, a smaller bag can be packed for the baby. A receiving blanket, diapers, and seasonal clothing will be needed, and you might also include a few books on child care and breast-feeding. The hospital stay is one of the few times a new mother can relax and read and know that she has no responsibilities.

WARNING: Besides knowing what to pack, an expectant mother should also know what to leave behind. Hospitals are large institutions with many people coming and going, and thievery often occurs. A new mother can be victimized because after childbirth, she is usually too tired to worry about taking care of her possessions. Do not bring valuables such as watches, jewelry, and money to the hospital, and if you plan on photographing or videotaping the birth, keep an eye on your camera. A special tip to photographing parents: test your camera before your baby's birth day. I have seen too many excited mothers and fathers with brand-new cameras they never used before—inevitably, something goes wrong. Practice beforehand, so you can capture the moment that will only happen once!

What Will Happen When I Get to the Hospital?

I've heard that you're put through the mill when you're in labor. Friends tell me about electronic monitoring, enemas, shaving, and being given IVs in the hospital, just to have a baby. I'm wondering if a birthing center would be better. At a center, they aren't supposed to do any of those things, are they? You know hospitals inside out, and maybe you can tell me the truth. What will happen when I get to the hospital and I'm in labor?

C.P.
Stratford, Pennsylvania

It's important for an expectant mother to tour the hospital where she plans to give birth and to ask questions about hospital policies. During such a tour, most women can get a feeling for the hospital and an understanding of the staff's approach to labor and delivery. Many hospitals have adopted quite an enlightened view about childbirth. The staffs are supportive, birthing rooms are available, and few of the traditional practices such as enemas and complete shaving are used. Ms. P. should visit the hospital, talk to her doctor, and decide whether the environment in which she will give birth suits her needs. She may be encouraged by the changes that have taken place in recent times.

Generally when a woman enters the hospital, either her doctor or the physician on call examines her and determines her cervical effacement, cervical dilatation, and the station of the presenting part. (See Understanding Labor.) A woman can get a good sense of how her labor is progressing by asking: "How effaced am I?" "How dilated?" and "What is the baby's station?" If, for example, she is 100 percent effaced, at least 5 centimeters dilated, and the baby is in a plus station, then childbirth is near. If, on the other hand, her cervix is long and closed and the baby is posterior, then she has a long way to go.

I recommend that a *fetal monitor* be used immediately to be sure that the baby's heart rate is normal. This monitoring can be carried out noninvasively. A small device (a Doppler transducer) is placed on the mother's abdomen to record the fetal heartbeat. If a woman is in early labor, she may be monitored intermittently for ten to twenty minutes. She may then be allowed to walk around for fifteen- or twenty-minute intervals and again be monitored for five to ten minutes in between. Fetal monitoring does restrict mobility, but today a number of European hospitals are using a portable telemetric monitor that permits movement. So far, this device is unavailable in the United States, but it may arrive on our shores and change the monitoring procedure.

Many doctors, myself included, will *not* recommend an enema for a woman who is progressing normally in labor, with no sign of toxemia or other complications. If a woman is constipated, feels full or uncomfortable, then an enema could be given, but this is hardly "routine." In the past, a different view was held. Doctors always gave women enemas and completely shaved their pubic area. Over the years, however, research has shown that neither of these procedures is particularly beneficial. Still, some hospitals and doctors are caught in tradition and ritualistically carry out these measures. Ms. P. must ask her doctor and inquire during her hospital tour whether an enema and shaving are common practices during childbirth.

It was once thought that shaving reduced the possibility of bacteria being introduced during delivery. Some years ago, that myth was exploded. Dr. William Sweeney headed a study at the New York Hospital–Cornell Medical Center that showed no difference in the rate of infection between shaved and unshaved women. After that, doctors no longer routinely ordered a complete shaving. What is often helpful, though, is a "mini prep," a minimal shaving of a small area between the vagina and the anus. Should an episiotomy be needed, this preparatory shaving is a precaution against infection.

The regular use of an intravenous (IV) infusion is also a thing of the past. IVs were given when anesthesia was routinely administered to women in labor. The intravenous fluid, usually a solution of dextrose and water, counteracts a possible lowering of blood pressure under anesthesia, which could affect the baby. In years gone by, an IV was also given to prevent dehydration during labor, but today women are asked to drink fluids before entering the hospital. An IV is given only when a complication such as fetal distress or dehydration arises, or when labor is prolonged. When labor is moving along nicely, a woman should not need an IV.

Ms. P. should know her doctor's feelings about all the procedures she questions. Also, if she wants a birthing room in the hospital, she must make arrangements now, before her baby is born. The hospital tour, as mentioned, will offer a comprehensive look at the staff and the facilities she will be encountering, and in the end, Ms. P. may be pleasantly surprised.

Will I Be Able to Wear My Contact Lenses During Labor?

I never remove my lenses. I wear them all day, while jogging, and sometimes I even leave them in at night. I would like to wear them while

379

I'm giving birth so I can see what is happening. Will I be able to wear my contact lenses during labor?

J.B.
Woodmere, New York

Ms. B. should consult her doctor about her particular situation. Most of the time, doctors recommend that contact lenses not be worn during labor because so much happens as a woman nears delivery. In the excitement and the "pushing," the lenses might become dislodged and lost. Her eyes may also become irritated due to the physical activity. In order to avoid such problems, physicians suggest that you use your eyeglasses for childbirth. There is not much to see during the initial hours of labor, and really Ms. B. will only need her glasses for the second stage of labor, when the baby actually arrives. Until then, it may be wise to let her eyes go naked.

WHAT WILL LABOR BE LIKE?

Every expectant mother wants to know what awaits her in the labor room, what labor will be like. There are three stages of labor, and she will definitely experience all of them, but just how she will look back on her labor depends upon the size and position of her baby, her pelvic structure, and certain biological events: how quickly her cervix effaces and dilates, how rapidly her contractions peak and fall. No two labors are the same, and a woman should be careful not to rely on anyone else's account of what it feels like to give birth. If an expectant mother were in my office right now, I would tell her: "No one can predict how your labor will progress, but it will be unique and special for you." That said, a pregnant woman should be prepared for childbirth and fully understand the three stages of labor.

The First Stage of Labor

The first stage of labor has three phases—latent, accelerated, and transitional. This stage, with all its phases, begins with the onset of true labor and lasts until a woman's cervix has reached its full dilatation of 10 centimeters. How long will that take? The latent phase, during which the cervix dilates 2 or 3 centimeters, can last up to eight hours. In the accelerated phase, the cervix dilates

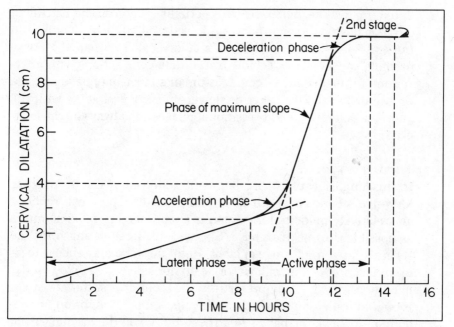

Figure 14-4. *The Friedman Curve. The cervical dilatation is plotted in relation to time in a woman giving birth for the first time. During the latent phase (the first eight to nine hours of labor), the cervix will only dilate slowly, but will begin to dilate more rapidly in the active phase, which only lasts a few hours. The active phase is the time when a woman usually experiences the greatest pain.*

more rapidly and can reach 7 or 8 centimeters in two to three hours. Finally, during the transitional phase, the cervix stretches to its full 10 centimeters in an hour or two. A first-time expectant mother may experience twelve to fourteen hours of labor before her baby is born. All the time, her contractions will grow closer and closer until they last for sixty to ninety seconds, with only one- to two-minute breaks in between. (If siblings are born only a few years apart, each labor will go faster than the one before. If children are spaced five to seven or more years apart, labor will again be slow and reminiscent of the first time around.)

Of course, the twelve-to-fourteen-hour range for a first-born is an average estimate of labor. Several years ago, Dr. Emanuel Friedman of Boston studied and plotted the labor patterns of a large number of women. He created the *Friedman curve*, which charts the cervix as dilating slowly, up to 3 centimeters, for eight or nine hours, and then quickly, reaching 10 centimeters in two or three additional hours. This curve allows twelve hours for the first stage of labor and at least two more hours for the second, "pushing," stage, when the baby actually emerges. The Friedman curve is posted on labor floors and used as a guide by doctors and nurses. Sometimes, if a woman's labor is slower than the curve predicts, a doctor may decide to stimulate contractions with intravenous infusions of oxytocin. A woman's labor may have average timing or be slightly faster or slower, but the first stage with the latent, accelerated, and transitional phases will always be the longest.

THE LATENT PHASE

In this long, slow phase of labor, contractions may last for thirty to forty-five seconds every three or four minutes. These contractions are relatively mild, and a woman is encouraged to relax as much as possible during this phase. She will need her strength for the second, "pushing," stage of labor. Right now she may choose to sit up in bed propped by pillows, or lie on her side with a pillow under her knees, or she may prefer to walk around to stimulate labor. Now and then a nurse will probably put a fetal monitor on her abdomen to check the baby's heartbeat, but when the monitor is not in place, a woman is free to stand, sit, or move about. She should not tax herself unduly, however.

The latent phase is the beginning of one of life's stunning events. A woman must conserve her energy and breathe deeply to relax her muscles. In this phase, she is like an athlete in the warm-up stage. The cervix slowly dilates until it opens to 5 centimeters. As many as eight hours may pass. Once the cervix has opened this far, the accelerated phase then begins. I encourage a woman to stay home as long as possible in the latent phase. She will be more comfortable at home, and her shortened time in the hospital will make labor seem less arduous. She should, however, be in contact with her doctor during her at-home labor so that together they can decide upon the best time for her to enter the hospital.

THE ACCELERATED PHASE

Now the cervix begins a rapid dilatation from 5 to 8 centimeters in about two hours. Contractions in this phase last for forty-five to sixty seconds and occur about two to four minutes apart. In this phase, the discomfort builds. A woman may feel as if she has to urinate constantly due to pressure on her bladder. She may become hot or cold, and her labor coach should be ready to respond with ice water or a blanket, depending upon her need. If muscle spasms occur at this time, she should concentrate on the pain-control techniques she learned in her natural childbirth classes. Deep inhalations and exhalations between contractions help to relax the body and ease the effects of the increasingly powerful inner grip that seizes her abdomen. In about two hours, the cervix stretches about 8 centimeters, and a woman enters the most active phase of labor. When she thinks that she may not have the stamina to continue, she must dip into the well of her strength.

THE TRANSITIONAL PHASE
In this phase, labor contractions last longer than the intervals between them. At their full intensity now, contractions linger for sixty to ninety seconds, separated by short thirty- to ninety-second intervals. The rhythm of the latent and accelerated phases may end as contractions peak and fall without any regular pattern. Now it is more difficult to "breathe through" a contraction. A woman must work with one contraction at a time and relax completely in the few seconds she has between each one. Contractions will build like unpredictable waves that grow and grow and finally crash upon the shore. A woman may become disoriented in this phase, and a labor coach must be prepared. He must help her to remember her breathing and guide her through the cresting and falling of each contraction.

As the cervix opens wider and wider, a woman's pain intensifies. At this point, the cervix stretches to capacity—10 centimeters—and she is in her greatest period of discomfort. Fortunately, at about thirty to forty-five minutes long, the transitional is the shortest phase. A woman may feel the urge to push to stop the pain, but until she is fully dilated, pushing can be harmful to her organs. She must wait until the doctor tells her that it is time. He will instruct her: "All right, now start pushing." If she bears down too soon, she may have to live with long-term bladder problems. When she is fully dilated and ready to push, she will feel a new set of sensations and a strong desire to "push away" the pain.

The Second, "Pushing," Stage of Labor

What a woman is actually doing in this second stage is *pushing the baby out of the birth canal*. She is giving her child its first taste of independence. She is saying in effect, "You are part of me, but you are also a separate, truly individual human being!" If a woman is giving birth for the first time, this stage may take two or more hours, but in subsequent pregnancies, the pushing may only last for five to thirty minutes. Sometimes a woman sees her newborn after only two or three pushes. Throughout the first stage, a woman's cervix effaces and dilates, and her baby manuevers itself through her bony pelvis and down into the birth canal. Just how much final pushing she will have to do depends upon the power of her contractions, the size of her baby, and its position. She cannot control any of these factors, but she is completely in charge of the amount of force she puts into her pushing.

Childbirth classes will prepare her, but she will need support and encouragement from her coach. This is the moment of greatest excitement, but she must be alert while she is thrilled. A woman should breathe deeply before each contraction. Then she must exhale slowly and push down long and steadily as her coach slowly counts, sometimes from one to ten. The focus is low, toward the rectum, and a woman bears down as if she is attempting to move her bowels. The nurse instructs her to pull her legs up and out to the side, to widen her pelvis. A woman might hold her legs apart herself, and at the same time, her coach can grasp the soles of her feet. Then she can push toward his hands and have better leverage. This may sound awkward, but it is actually quite comfortable.

A labor coach must make sure that a woman is satisfied with her pose, and if she is not, then he must help her move until she finds the "right" place on the bed. This second stage actually becomes an awesome experience that, even though it embodies the birth itself, is less painful than the transitional phase of the first stage. When women talk about the pain of giving birth, they are really describing the way they felt at the end of the first stage of labor. The birth itself is less taxing than earlier contractions, and it is joyous, not only because you can finally cradle your baby, but because birth means that the hardest part of labor is over.

The Third Stage of Labor

The baby is a presence in the room, a live, breathing human being, but a mother is not through with labor until she delivers the placenta. The third stage is considered the time from the birth of the baby to the expulsion of the placenta from the womb. Usually this takes from ten to fifteen minutes, but there is no set rule. The placenta may spontaneously emerge in a few minutes or have to be coaxed from a woman's body for up to thirty minutes.

The umbilical cord can be clamped and cut immediately after birth or a few minutes later, after it stops pulsating. When a cord is cut depends upon the health of the baby. Often the doctor asks the father to cut the cord, and it is a memorable sight. At this moment, the father is strongly participating in the birth of his daughter or son. The initial metal clamp is removed and a plastic clamp is clipped low on the cord. Then the cord is cut a few inches from the navel. A doctor examines the cord to make sure that it embodies two arteries and one vein. A blood sample is then taken from the cord to be analyzed for count, type, and overall status of the baby.

After the cord is clamped and cut, the placenta has no more function, and it should naturally and spontaneously expel itself. The uterine muscles begin to contract, the blood supply to the placenta is reduced, and the middle part of the placenta begins to pull away from the uterine wall. Separation of the outer edges of the placenta follows, so that the afterbirth is practically inside out when it leaves the woman's body. The uterus contracts, and the placenta spasms as it dislodges.

While the womb is contracting to expel the placenta, the doctor places his hand on a woman's abdomen and massages her with small circular movements. This uterine massage stimulates a release of any prostaglandins that may help the contractions along. As the separation of the placenta begins, a slight bleeding occurs. When the doctor sees this staining, he may ask a woman to push while he massages. He may also gently pull the umbilical cord to help the removal of the placenta. If a woman starts to breast-feed her baby during this stage, oxytocin will be released, which will intensify contractions and hasten expulsion.

Sometimes, however, the placenta is strongly attached to the uterus because a woman has adhesions from a previous D&C or an abortion, or she has scar tissue from an IUD or a previous birth. Occasionally the placenta becomes slightly inflamed and does not loosen properly. In any of these instances, a doctor may have to remove the placenta either manually or with instruments. If even a small piece of placenta is left behind, a woman can develop serious postpartum bleeding. The doctor will explore the uterine cavity after the delivery of the placenta to be sure that there are no remaining fragments.

Labor is not over until the placenta is delivered. Then the uterus begins to cleanse itself. Fluid and blood will drain from the vagina in varying degrees for several weeks as the womb contracts to return to its normal size. The doctor may ask the labor coach to continue intermittent abdominal massage for an hour or two after the placenta has been delivered. Sometimes Pitocin (synthetic oxytocin) is administered to help the uterine contractions. A woman should expect to remain in the labor and delivery area for two or three hours following childbirth. Doctors and nurses usually want time for observation to be sure that a woman has no postpartum problems.

The Father's Role in Labor

Before I had my baby last month, I did not know what a wonderful help my husband John would be. My labor moved very slowly and the doctor ruptured my membranes. Then the pain grew very strong, especially in my back. My spirits were going down, but then John started talking to me, and he just coached me through it all. He rubbed my back and spoke encouraging words. He breathed with me. I don't know what I would have done without him. When it came time to push, he supported me all the way. He got so excited when he saw the baby's head and all her hair! I don't think we have ever been closer or more in love. Any man who does not think he is important during childbirth is wrong.

L.W.
Fort Worth, Texas

This is a heartwarming letter that shows the value of teamwork during labor and delivery. In fact, studies are revealing that birthing women who have supportive companions in the labor room experience easier, shorter labors and fewer complications than women who go it alone. When an expectant father is a labor coach, he is living through labor and delivery too. As one father wrote to me after his son was born: "When my wife was in labor, in the hands of the medical staff, my responsibilities were limited; therefore, I related to her pain more strongly. I felt it all in my stomach. I guess that's what real 'sympathy pain' is. I was in labor too!"

A father is right there, going through every stage of labor with his wife, but he must not allow himself to succumb to the emotions of the moment. He is on alert, which is why I suggest packing food and drinks for the coach. The actual experience of labor may not unfold exactly as anticipated. In the transition phase, contractions may be so intense that a woman asks for medication, even though she planned on only natural childbirth. A husband-and-wife labor team should discuss the possibility of medication and their combined feelings before they enter the labor room. Then they can speak in one voice when they must make crucial decisions. For example, what if a cesarean is needed? Before labor, they should talk about possible complications and how they want to face them together.

During the transition phase of labor, a woman may become hot or chilled; she may be irritated and angry too. An expectant father/labor coach must be tolerant and supportive now more than ever. If a woman is on a fetal monitor, he can watch the uterine contractions increase and decrease and tell his wife what is happening. I have seen men coach women as they watch the monitored contractions. They report and support: "You're coming down over the top. You're going down. Your contraction is going away. Keep breathing; you're almost there." A labor coach is truly indispensable.

If a woman has back labor, the coach can massage her where she hurts the most. He can be armed with ice cubes, a fan, and a blanket. The coach can also watch the fetal heart rate. Doctors and nurses are in and out of the labor room, but the coach is always there, supervising his wife and his baby. If the fetal heart rate drops below the baseline, he should inform the staff immediately.

Mostly the coach is needed during the second stage of labor, when the mother is pushing. He constantly makes sure that she is in a comfortable position. He might wipe her brow with a moist, cool towel and give her ice cubes if her mouth is parched. She needs encouragement throughout this stage because pushing is hard work. He can breathe with her, count with her, and offer to hold her feet as she pushes against him. During a complication, he can be a source of strength for her. Finally, in the end, the father can cut the cord and bonding can take place between both parents and their newborn. As Ms. W. writes: "Any man who does not think he is important during childbirth is wrong." A labor coach, an expectant father, is essential to a joyous childbirth. As

Ms. W. also writes, marriage benefits too: "I don't think we have ever been closer or more in love." She has said it all.

Is Nipple Stimulation a Natural Way to Make Labor Move Faster?

I want my childbirth to be completely natural but I know that sometimes extenuating circumstances give doctors the right to medicate and operate. Still I want whatever other alternatives are available to me. If my labor does not move at the expected rate, if I don't dilate as fast as the doctors and nurses think I should, can nipple stimulation help? I think there are even other ways to make labor move faster naturally. If I am right, please let me know what they are. Thank you.

S.F.
Binghamton, New York

No two labors are alike. Among other things, the position of the baby, a woman's pelvic structure, and the intensity of her contractions will influence a doctor's decision about how to proceed if labor is moving slowly. There are natural ways to help labor along, but a woman should be aware of whether her labor is being slowed by a complication before she insists on "only natural." If no serious complications exist, she may enhance her contractions with two natural methods: *movement* and *nipple stimulation.*

The habit of having a woman give birth by lying on her back began in the seventeenth century, when King Louis XIV of France wanted to see his mistress have his baby. This supine position won the approval of physicians, who found it convenient for vaginal examination and forceps deliveries. Today, however, many researchers have conducted studies that lead them to conclude that the upright position and movement, such as walking around, ease pain and hasten labor.

If a woman in a low-risk pregnancy is having a slow labor, she may help her progress by walking. Some women do not feel well enough to get up and move around during labor, but if you do, the force of gravity can become an ally. In early labor, as a woman paces up and down, gravity can cause her unborn baby to slip deeper into the birth canal. It then might be possible for the fetal head, pressing against the cervix, to stimulate a hormonal response, for a message to be sent to the mother's brain, and for more oxytocin, the contraction-causing hormone, to be released.

In fact, British researchers compared ambulatory and recumbent women during labor and found that labor was an average of two hours shorter and delivery was generally easier for women who moved about freely.

Should Mrs. F. become high risk in early labor, however—for example, if she faces toxemia or heart problems—she would be advised to remain in bed. Also, if a doctor administers intravenous oxytocin, Pitocin, then walking is usually not allowed in accordance with most hospitals' policies. But during a "normal" labor, a few strolls with the labor coach can be just what a woman needs to coax the baby into the birth canal and move labor along.

Nipple stimulation is, of course, another wonderful way to induce labor naturally. The effect a suckling baby has on the creation of uterine contractions during breast-feeding was recognized as far back as the time of Hippocrates, yet nipple stimulation was not considered a technique for promoting labor contractions. The idea was suggested by Friedrich in an obstetrics textbook published in 1839, but little mention of breast sensitivity as an aid to labor followed. Recently, though, women interested in drug-free labor and childbirth have caused doctors to investigate the effectiveness of nipple stimulation. The result is that this technique is now being practiced more frequently during labor. The belief is that through nerve impulses, nipple stimulation causes a surge of oxytocin to be released by the mother's pituitary. The naturally produced oxytocin then works to intensify contractions in the womb, and a woman never needs the intravenous administration of synthetic oxytocin called Pitocin. Some doctors are beginning to advocate nipple stimulation for a contraction stress test, instead of intravenous oxytocin for the oxytocin challenge test, to evaluate an unborn baby's status prior to labor. (See explanation of nonstress testing and the oxytocin challenge test in the section entitled If Movement Is Questionable, How Is the Baby Tested?)

If labor is not progressing satisfactorily because contractions are weak, nipple stimulation, done either with a breast pump, hot towels, or manual manipulation, may promote labor to such a degree that a natural birth can occur without the need for Pitocin. Even with nipple stimulation, however, good strong contractions may still elude a woman. In some cases, Pitocin may ultimately be given to help her achieve satisfactory labor.

Another natural means of stimulating labor is the rupturing of the fetal membranes. If labor has started slowly and the membranes remain intact, a doctor can break the bag of waters. This rupture releases a high amount of prostaglandins, which encourage uterine contractions to begin in thirty to sixty minutes.

FETAL MONITORING

Electronic Fetal Monitoring: In My Case, I'm Happy It Was Done.

During labor, my baby's heart rate dropped, but my doctor knew it right away because it showed on the fetal monitor. Apparently the baby was lying on the umbilical cord. I was turned on my side, given oxygen, and sure enough, the heart rate returned to normal and I was able to have a natural birth. If we hadn't used the monitor, if the nurse had only checked the heart rate with a stethoscope every fifteen minutes, I don't think the problem would have been caught so fast. My baby might have been brain damaged! I was initially against any unnatural intervention during labor and childbirth, but now I recommend fetal monitoring. In my case, I'm happy it was done. Without it, I might not have had a healthy baby.

S.A.
Encino, California

Monitoring an unborn baby's heartbeat is one of the few ways we have of knowing whether the fetus is doing all right. For more than a century, doctors have been doing this monitoring with a specially designed stethoscope called a *fetoscope*. In fact, obstetricians still use fetoscopes during office examinations of their pregnant patients. Technological advances in the 1960s, however, allowed for the development of the electronic fetal monitor. Due to its accurate recordings of fetal heartbeats and uterine contractions, this modern device was supposed to alleviate worry about fetal well-being and put an expectant mother's mind at ease; instead, it became the focus of controversy.

Many advocates of natural childbirth felt that fetal monitoring printouts were being misread by doctors who then rushed women into unnecessary cesarean sections. Pregnant women also worried that the electronic monitors might harmfully affect their babies and perhaps only fetoscopes should be used. I am pleased to read Ms. A.'s letter because the more women have positive experiences with electronic fetal monitoring, the faster those early misconceptions will fade.

Over the years, fetal monitors have improved, along with the technological knowledge of doctors and nurses. Today, thanks to fetal monitoring, healthier babies are being born and cesarean sections are being avoided. A monitor may be used for nonstress testing (see If Movement Is Questionable, How Is the Baby Tested?) before labor, at any time during labor, and during childbirth. While it is unquestionably agreed that women who are having high-risk pregnancies due to diabetes, heart problems, or other complications should be monitored, there is still an issue over whether low-risk expectant mothers need monitoring. Since a low-risk pregnancy can suddenly become high-risk—for example, when the baby unexpectedly deprives itself of oxygen by lying on the cord—most doctors also want their low-risk patients to have the advantage of monitoring. As Ms. A.'s letter shows, without electronic monitoring, she might not have had a healthy baby. Electronic fetal monitoring may be *external, internal,* or both methods may be used at the same time. Here are how the different monitoring methods work:

External fetal monitoring means that a woman is wearing two belts, each with a transducer, a small sensing device that employs ultrasound waves. One transducer picks up the fetal heart rate and the other registers the mother's contractions. The Doppler ultrasound unit sends the fetal heart rate to the monitoring device, which then prints out the pattern of the beat on a long strip of paper. Uterine contractions are charted in curves on the same paper. External monitoring is noninvasive and safe. The high-frequency ultrasound waves used to transmit the information have not been found to be harmful to mother or baby.

As for mobility, a woman can be monitored early in labor and the belts can be removed while she walks around. She can return from time to time for intermittent monitoring. Less confining fetal monitors that work on telemetry (radio waves) are being developed, but right now they are not widely available. It's probably not too much of a generalization to say that at some point, external fetal monitoring is recommended for almost every woman in labor. The lifesaving component is phenomenal. If there is a drawback to this type of monitoring, it is only that it offers a *generalized* understanding of the baby's heartbeat and condition. The external monitor can lose its accuracy when mother or baby moves. Internal monitoring is far more precise.

Internal fetal monitoring can only take place after the bag of waters has broken or is ruptured by the doctor. With this type of

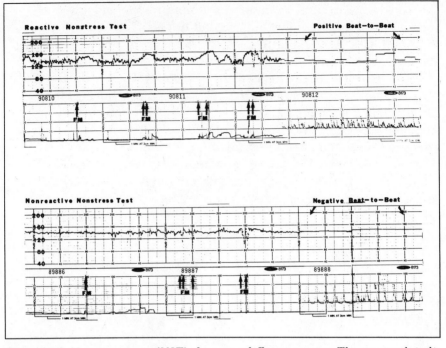

Figure 14-5. *Nonstress tests (NST) from two different women. The top graph indicates a reactive (healthy) NST with good heart rate acceleration after each fetal movement (FM). The beat-to-beat variability, which is another healthy fetal sign, is also good. The bottom graph indicates a nonreactive (problematic) NST that warrants further investigation. The beat-to-beat variability is also negative, indicating some fetal jeopardy.*

monitoring, a tiny sensor, a wire electrode, is inserted through the vagina and placed on the baby's scalp to record its heart rate. At the same time, a thin plastic tube, a catheter, is passed into the mother's uterus to measure her contractions. Movement of the mother or the fetus will not affect the printout of an internal monitor. Each heartbeat is separately recorded, as is the exact timing and strength of each contraction. Internal monitoring is painless. There is a minimal risk of infection to mother and baby, but the baby's scalp is cleansed with an antiseptic solution immediately after birth to reduce the chance of contamination.

Internal monitoring is usually done when a problematic heartbeat pattern shows up on an external monitor, or when an external monitor gives a poor recording. Then a doctor needs a more accurate reading, as the woman may be in a sudden high-risk condition. Certainly if a known high-risk condition exists—if meconium staining of the amniotic fluid has been noticed, for example—there is no question about the use of an internal monitor. In high-risk pregnancies, it is also a good idea for simultaneous external and internal monitoring to be done. A doctor must use every tool he has to deliver a healthy baby.

A nurse or a doctor checks the fetal heart rate pattern by examining a monitor's printout paper, called a *tracing.* A labor coach might want to look at the monitoring strip along with the nurse and doctor. Here's what they might see:

Fetal heart rate acceleration, a sudden, quick increase in the fetal heart rate of 10 to 20 beats, lasting at least 30 seconds, is a healthy sign. The baby is responding to its own movement, a contraction, or an outside stimulus such as a loud noise.

Early deceleration, or an early slowing of the fetal heart rate, is a pattern that shows up as a drop in the heart rate during a contraction but a return to normal at the end of the contraction. This happens about 15 percent of the time and is *nothing to worry about.*

Late deceleration, or delayed slowing of the fetal heart rate, appears as a drop in the heart rate during a contraction and a slow return to normal an interval after the contraction has stopped. If this late deceleration continues with each contraction, there may be a placental problem. The baby may not be receiving adequate oxygen, and its survival may be in jeopardy. Following this type of reading, a doctor should decide to evaluate the baby more thoroughly by taking a fetal blood sampling. This can only be done if the membrane is ruptured and the cervix is dilated at least 3 centimeters. Using a special surgical instrument, he will remove a few drops of blood from the baby's head. This emergency blood sample will be analyzed for its fetal pH values. A low pH level should lead a doctor to deliver the baby immediately, either by forceps, if possible, or by cesarean. I have seen more than one crisis averted and fetal brain damage avoided when a fetal monitor showing late deceleration led to an immediate delivery. On those occasions, I have known that the healthy babies in my arms may not have been so perfect without the help of their fetal monitors.

Variable deceleration, or variable slowing and quickening of the fetal heartbeat, appears as falls in the fetal heart rate that are not synchronized with uterine contractions. This irregular pattern usually means that the umbilical cord is being compressed and the baby is not receiving enough oxygen. Variable deceleration probably occurred in Ms. A.'s case. The situation can be corrected

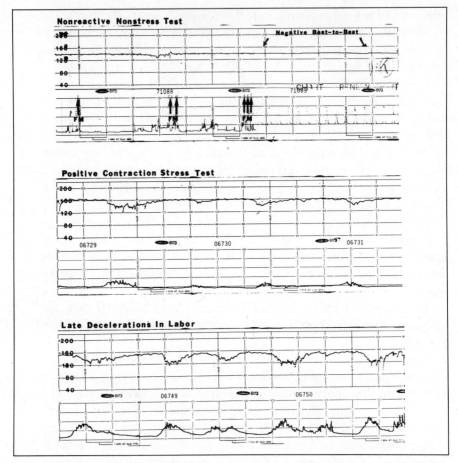

Figure 14-6. *These tracings from fetal monitoring of one pregnant woman indicate fetal jeopardy. The top graph shows a "nonreactive" NST, with no beat-to-beat variability of the fetal heart. This test was followed by a contraction stress test (middle graph). The fetal heart rate is seen to decrease during and immediately after each contraction, which indicates that the baby is in a hostile environment and should be delivered. Labor was induced (bottom graph), and as soon as contractions increased in strength, the late decelerations intensified. A cesarean section was performed and a healthy baby was freed, in time, from its hostile environment.*

by asking a mother to lie on her side, elevating the foot of her labor bed, and giving her oxygen by mask. If the pattern does not change, however, a doctor may have to do a fetal blood sampling and possibly an emergency delivery.

A recent technological advancement is the development of a small electrode to measure the fetal pH level. This electrode is placed inside the scalp electrode that is attached to the fetal monitor. As this pH reading device becomes more frequently used, it will reduce the need for surgical intervention to take fetal blood samples when babies are at risk. In my years of practice, I have seen technology *increase* a woman's chance of having a healthy baby.

What Is Back Labor? Is It Really As Bad As They Say?

A friend of mine says she wouldn't wish back labor on her worst enemy. She had it and she tells me that it lasted forever. No matter how much she shifted and moved around, there seemed to be no way to get her contractions going. Nipple stimulation and rupturing the fetal membranes didn't help. The pain was excruciating, and after she saw the nurse from the day before return for her next day's shift, she agreed to intravenous oxytocin. She had wanted everything "natural," but nothing else could be done. Finally, after twenty-four hours in the hospital, she gave birth to a healthy baby boy. Does this always happen with back labor?

Y.P.
Englewood Cliffs, New Jersey

Usually a baby descends into the birth canal, rotates, faces the mother's back, and is in the best position for birth. About 15 percent of the time, however, the baby faces the mother's front, and with each contraction, the hardest part of its skull presses against her spine. This is the *posterior* position, and it is uncomfortable and painful. If a woman starts having good, strong contractions, the fetus may rotate to the side for an easier birth, but if labor is arduous, then back pain intensifies as the baby stubbornly stays in place. Frequently, when a fetus is posterior, it is a rather large baby that has become fixed—stuck—in the course of its descent into the pelvis.

One way a woman can attempt to find relief is by kneeling or lying on her side. To try and rotate the fetal head, she might also tilt her pelvis back and forth while she rests on her hands and knees. Another alternative is to walk around in an effort to trigger the *Ferguson* reflex, which is the impulse that goes from the cervix to the brain and results in a release of nature's oxytocin, the contraction-causing hormone.

When a woman with back labor has a contraction, her labor

coach must come to her aid. She desperately needs relief. With his fists, the heels of his hands, or by using two rubber balls or tennis balls, he should firmly press against the expectant mother's lower back or the areas of the back where she feels the most pain. The more pressure he can apply, the more relief she will feel. Women have also found relief from either ice packs or heating pads held against the lower back.

Sometimes labor must be stimulated by intravenous oxytocin to assist the baby in its rotation and descent and to lift the pressure from a woman's lumbar spinal area. It is surprising that Ms. P.'s friend found no escape from her back labor in spite of the efforts of doctors and nurses. Movement, nipple stimulation, and a rupturing of the fetal membranes usually yield positive results. After the bag of waters breaks, labor contractions almost always increase in thirty to sixty minutes. Had Ms. P.'s friend been my patient, and had all those methods of labor stimulation failed, I probably would have recommended intravenous oxytocin as well as an epidural anesthesia before twenty-four hours had elapsed. Back labor is a strain on a woman's body, and I would not have wanted to see anyone suffer for so long.

When back labor occurs, a woman and her partner should be attuned to each other and he should strive to give her relief. This is one time when their collaboration is absolutely essential. I hope that Ms. P. does not have to go through a long and painful back labor, but if she does, then she and her partner will have an opportunity to become a closely knit pair who work toward a mutual goal—a joyous childbirth beyond back labor.

Should I Try a Birthing Chair?

Many women are curious to know whether a birthing chair, which allows a vertical delivery, makes childbirth easier. As mentioned before, the idea of having a woman give birth in a supine position was conceived in seventeenth-century France. Until then, most women gave birth while standing, sitting, kneeling, or squatting. This makes sense, because in an upright position, a birthing woman gets help from gravity. On her back, she is sort of pushing uphill.

In the supine, or what is medically termed the *lithotomy* position, the weight of the fetus presses on two main arteries in a woman's back. This pressure can reduce the blood flow to the womb and lessen the supply of oxygen to mother and baby. The mother can become dizzy and nauseated, and the baby can be in distress. It is no wonder that women have sought an alternative to being on their backs on delivery tables. Today two possible alternatives are the birthing chair and the birthing bed.

The most popular type of *birthing chair* is produced by the Century Manufacturing Company in Aurora, Nebraska, and there are hundreds of them in hospitals here and abroad. The chair is made of molded fiberglass on a metal base. It has handles, adjustable knee and footrests, and controls to change the angle of its tilt. The chair can be positioned to give a doctor access to a woman's vaginal area, and when she is sitting up, a mother has a clearer view of the birth. However, the chair is created in one size, and women have said it is not always comfortable and that the rigidity of the fiberglass can be confining. Also, since the chair is made for *delivery only*, a woman has to be brought to it after she completes the first stage of labor, and at this point, a shift can be uncomfortable.

A *birthing bed,* constructed in two sections, permits a woman to remain in the same place for labor and delivery. The head section can be raised vertically, and the foot section can be dropped or removed during birth. Siderails with handles offer support during pushing. Every hospital that has birthing rooms also has birthing beds, which are really far more popular than birthing chairs.

It is important to remember that a birthing chair cannot be used if a woman has epidural anesthesia, because her legs may be too weak to support a seated position. Fetal distress or unexpected complications will also prevent the use of both a birthing chair and a birthing bed. When complications arise, a fully equipped delivery room is safer and more suitable for the birth. A doctor will be better able to care for a woman in a delivery room.

I Was So Proud of Myself for Having an Epidural!

When I started having contractions and went to the hospital, the doctor said I was only 45 percent effaced and 1 centimeter dilated, and he sent me home. That night my water broke, and by early morning, the contractions were three minutes apart and strong. I went back to the hospital. The contractions, which were giving me terrible back pain, remained consistent but I wasn't effacing or dilating anymore. I didn't want Pitocin, but after twelve hours and total exhaustion, I agreed.

Then I was in more pain and took Demerol. It did nothing to the pain—it just made me "high." My dilatation was only 2 centimeters, with 80 percent effacement. All those hours with no result! I was exhausted and I didn't think I could make it. My nurse, Irene, helped a lot by reading the contractions on the monitor and telling me when they peaked and fell. My labor coach let me squeeze her hand so that I could relax my uterus. I listened to classical music. Finally my last labor nurse, Gigi, suggested an epidural. At that point almost twenty-four hours had passed since I entered the hospital. I thought I'd never be able to sit up through the contractions for the twenty minutes it took to administer the anesthetic, but the epidural was wonderful. I finally slept. The relaxation allowed me to dilate. I didn't feel the pain but I felt the pressure of the contractions so I knew when to push. The doctor reached in and turned the baby's head around—it hadn't been pressing on the right place to get the proper movement through my pelvis. I remember feeling the baby finally move down! We were ready to go! First the head, then the shoulder, and pop, another human being—a boy! When it was all over, I was so proud of myself for having the epidural and knowing when enough was enough, when I was hurting my child and myself. I had labor fatigue and felt that I was only moments away from losing consciousness. Maybe the next time I won't need an epidural, but right now, all I can say is, "Thank God I had it."

C.E.
Katonah, New York

Obstetricians and expectant mothers both want to experience trouble-free births. I encourage each woman who attends childbirth classes and who is determined to breathe through the pain when the time comes to keep her spirits high. At the same time, however, I have seen the unexpected overtake a labor room, just as Ms. E. described. She wanted a completely natural labor and childbirth, but her baby was not in the "right" position to stimulate effacement and dilatation, and she suffered excruciating back labor for twenty-four hours. The Pitocin she received created stronger and harder contractions but also intensified the pain of her labor. It can often happen, when pain is overwhelming, that an analgesic such as Demerol has no effect except to make a woman "high." (For the effects of Demerol during pregnancy, see Chapter 9.) Ms. E. was extraordinarily tired because her labor was not progressing. Nothing seemed to help, so in her case, an epidural was the ideal way to change a static situation.

A woman who is suffering for many hours with no progress in cervical effacement or dilatation should not feel that she is less than perfect in childbirth if she accepts an analgesic or anesthetic. Such a woman is keeping herself and her baby in good health, and she is making decisions as a mother who wants the best for her child. Sometimes natural childbirth is not the wisest choice. A woman should know that the hospital where she will give birth has the facilities to administer an epidural properly and perform a cesarean with the same anesthetic if necessary.

Epidural anesthesia is a regional anesthesia that numbs the lower part of the body to pain. This anesthesia does not enter the baby's bloodstream. On the negative side, though, an epidural can lower a mother's blood pressure and prolong labor, because it weakens contractions and a woman cannot feel when to push. Ms. E. writes that she felt the painless pressure of the contractions, however, and did recognize when pushing was needed. Usually a labor coach or nurse can spot contractions on a fetal monitor and tell a woman when the time is right.

Before an epidural, a woman is given a large quantity of intravenous fluid to prevent a drop in blood pressure that could follow the administration of the anesthetic. *An epidural is given as follows:* A woman lies on her side at the edge of the bed or sits up and arches her back like an angry cat. She should bend her neck forward and push her back out to separate her vertebrae. A doctor then washes her back with an antiseptic solution to prevent infection, and he will inject a small amount of novocaine so that a woman will not feel the epidural needle being inserted.

The epidural area is the space within the spinal cord just in front of the membrane that contains the spinal fluid. An epidural needle is inserted between the fourth and fifth lumbar vertebrae, but it does not reach the spinal fluid itself. *An epidural is not a spinal!* Ms. E. writes that the epidural took twenty minutes to administer. In that time, her doctor was probably giving the anesthetic in a small dose at first and building to a higher dose. An initial small dose of anesthetic is given to prevent a rapid drop in blood pressure. After that dose "takes," then another dose can be injected.

Anesthetizing the nerve endings in the epidural area causes a numbing of the uterus. A woman will also feel a slight stinging sensation down her legs. The involuntary muscles and respiratory system will not be affected, however, so a woman can continue

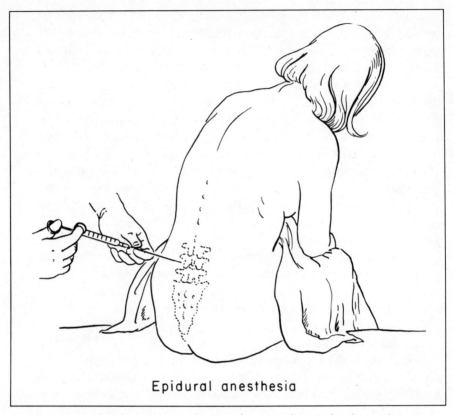

Epidural anesthesia

Figure 14-7. *Epidural anesthesia. During this procedure, a local anesthetic is injected into the epidural space. This type of anesthesia can result in 100-percent pain relief and, when done properly, is safe for mother and baby.*

her breathing exercises. Usually a doctor threads a plastic tube through the epidural needle and tapes the tube to a woman's back so that she may have *continuous epidural anesthesia* when the initial dose wears off. This tube eliminates the need for another round of injections.

An epidural anesthesia is not painful, and if an episiotomy is needed, it can be done without added painkiller. Since an epidural may prolong labor, a doctor must observe a woman's vital signs carefully to be sure her blood pressure does not drop. If labor is slow, intravenous oxytocin will be administered. Sometimes forceps deliveries and cesareans follow epidurals if they cause unduly long labors with no progress. A labor that lasts and lasts can deprive a baby of much-needed oxygen and cause fetal damage. At this point, a baby must be delivered and released from its hostile environment. As Ms. E.'s experience shows, however, an epidural can lead to a happy ending. If she had not had the anesthesia, both she and her baby might have suffered seriously. Every labor and childbirth is different, and a woman should be prepared for the unexpected. When sudden complications appear—such as Ms. E.'s baby being in a posterior position, and her extreme back labor pain—flexible attitudes and balanced thought must govern crucial decisions.

Can I Have Acupuncture During Labor?

I have a friend in San Francisco who gave birth with acupuncture used at a birthing center. She did very well, didn't feel any pain. Could I find a hospital that would give me acupuncture too? Do you think it works?
B.T.
Portland, Oregon

There are many different childbirth techniques to relieve pain. Besides Lamaze and Bradley, in different parts of the United States, women may find such approaches as the *Harris method,* which uses slow breathing and soft touching; the *Gamper method,* which emphasizes the beauty of a woman's body; *underwater birth;* the *Kitzinger psychosexual method,* which regards childbirth as a sexual act; *yoga; shiatsu,* a finger pressure massage; *reflexology,* which also uses pressure to relieve pain; *hypnosis; biofeedback;* and *TENS (transcutaneous electrical nerve stimulation),* which employs electrodes commonly used in physical therapy to relieve pain. Acupuncture may be yet another choice.

Acupuncturists insert a needle in a specific spot on the body, and the placement of the needle is supposed to affect nerves in another specific part of the body. The needles are said to prick but not hurt. Researchers have visited China in the hope of understanding acupuncture better, and their studies have shown that North Americans do not respond well to the technique. Acupuncture does not seem to be as effective a painkiller in the West as it is in the East.

Since acupuncture is not considered a scientifically effective painkiller, Ms. T. might have difficulty locating a professional who would recommend the technique. If she does find such a professional, she may feel perfectly safe in using the method. I suggest, however, that with or without acupuncture, she choose to give

401

birth in a hospital. As I have said many times in this book, you never know when an unexpected complication can arise during childbirth. In a hospital, she will be likely to receive proper care in the event of a sudden crisis.

Can Siblings Be in the Delivery Room?

I want to give birth in a hospital and I would like my six-year-old daughter to be there. I know that birthing centers are more inclined to allow siblings than hospitals are, but I was hoping that I would not be out of line with my request. You know about the policies of hospitals. Can siblings be in the delivery room?

J.S.
Baltimore, Maryland

In hospitals across the country, efforts are being made to create more homelike environments for childbirth. The expectant father,

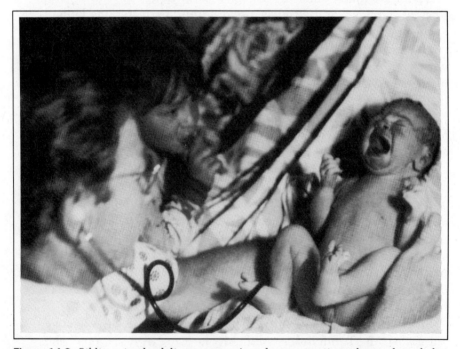

Figure 14-8. *Siblings in the delivery room. As a doctor examines the newborn baby, his brother curiously watches. This controversial issue of sibling participation in childbirth will hopefully be resolved as common practice.* Reproduced by permission of Mariette Pathy Allen. Originally printed in OB/GYN World, October 1985.

of course, is now a "regular" on the delivery team, and the birthing room, where other family members and friends can visit, is becoming more available. The idea of allowing siblings to watch childbirth is a natural extension of the trend toward more family involvement.

There is a small controversy, however. Those who advocate allowing siblings in the delivery room say that when a child sees a brother or sister being born, he grows closer to his sibling. Also, the child gains a greater understanding of reproduction and the life cycle. On the other hand, experts question whether a child might not become confused and frightened when he sees his mother giving birth. The experience might be emotionally overwhelming.

Quite a number of hospitals are adopting a middle-of-the-road approach to sibling involvement. Siblings may not watch the birth, but they see their mothers and newborn brothers and sisters immediately after delivery. Many hospitals offer educational sessions with pictures and films about childbirth, along with tours of labor and delivery rooms and maternity floors, for expectant siblings. Some avant-garde hospital staffs, however, are beginning to initiate programs that permit children in the delivery room at the time of birth.

At the Indiana University Medical Center in Indianapolis, the department of obstetrics and gynecology is working to create an atmosphere that allows sibling involvement in childbirth. In the Indiana program, a child must have a companion, someone other than his father, who knows him and can counsel him during the birth. The companion is the child's support, but the obstetrician is in charge and can ask the child to leave the delivery room if problems arise.

Long before the day of delivery, the parents, the child, and the companion attend sessions to learn what will happen in the delivery room and to talk about childbirth. The parents and the companion are also invited to separate workshops to talk about their concerns as adults. The sibling, in addition, visits the delivery room and the maternity floor before the mother's due date.

Education and preparation are the keys to successful sibling involvement. A child's individual personality is also a factor. A particular three-year-old may be more attentive during classes and more eager to witness childbirth than a certain five-year-old. Ms. S. knows her daughter and has a sense about whether she would benefit from witnessing childbirth. I and many of my colleagues welcome sibling involvement, and as more and more parents request the presence of their other children in the delivery room, there is a good chance that they will become regulars like their fathers. Today more than ever before, Ms. S. may be able to find a hospital that has a place for her daughter in the delivery room.

THE BIRTH

At the end of the first stage of labor, during the transitional phase, a woman may have the urge to push or bear down, but her cervix may not be fully dilated. At this point, a doctor will tell her to pant lightly and save her energy. Only when the cervix has stretched to 10 centimeters wide and dilatation is complete will she be allowed to push. This pushing marks the second stage of labor. As a woman bears down with her diaphragm and abdominal muscles, she is helping the descent of her baby. The baby's head moves forward at the start of each contraction and recedes slightly at the end, when the downward pressure stops. A woman is actually pushing her baby down the birth canal to the opening of her vagina, a distance of about four inches.

Pushing can seem very hard at this point. A woman may feel the pressure of the baby's head against her rectum and have the sensation of being torn apart. Actually that tearing feeling comes from the stretching of the ligaments around the coccyx (the base of the spine). Suddenly, however, the baby will rotate inside the pelvis and drop down. With only one or two more pushes, the baby will be born, and at this time, if a woman is not in a birthing room, she may be moved to a delivery room.

More and more hospitals are creating birthing rooms, where mothers labor and deliver on the same birthing bed and never have to be transferred. A homelike birthing room is preferred, but if a hospital has no birthing rooms available, then a woman will be moved from the labor room to a delivery room. In the delivery room, she will see a fully equipped operating room with the delivery table, anesthesia machine, infant-resuscitation machine, and other needed items. She will be placed on a delivery table that is outfitted with stirrups and grips. The stirrups are designed to support her legs, which are weakened by labor, and if a woman has had an epidural, her legs are limp and numb. Whether a woman is on a birthing bed or a delivery table, her labor coach or nurse should position pillows underneath her lower back or adjust the bed at an angle to elevate her body. The more upright a woman can be, the better she will be able to push, control the birth, and view the delivery.

With the next few contractions, the outline of the baby's head begins to bulge through the perineum, the area between the vagina and the anus. The perineum bulges more and more, until the vulva begins to stretch back and form a circular opening around the top of the baby's head. The baby at this point is facing the mother's back. Most babies make their first appearance head down, facing the floor. As the baby's head becomes more visible, the vulva stretches so far back that it seems as if the perineum completely disappears. What has actually happened is that the perineum has stretched around the baby's head and encircled the small protrusion like a crown. This is why when the baby's head is in view this way it is said to be *crowning*. Now a mother must be disciplined and controlled. She must concentrate on her doctor's instructions and push, pause, and pant as he directs. There is a risk of ripping the vagina and vulva as well as the skin on both sides of the rectum and bladder if a woman pushes too hard.

Each contraction brings forth more of the baby's head. Between contractions, a doctor who is trying to avoid an episiotomy—a small cut between the vagina and the rectum—puts a finger in the lower part of the perineum and massages it gently from side to side in an attempt to stretch the opening for passage of the baby. In a woman who has previously given birth, the vaginal tissues are already stretched and the massage is often all that is needed to avoid tearing. A first-time mother may still require an episiotomy. (See When Is an Episiotomy Needed? Can I Give Birth Without One? in this chapter.)

After the first and second stages of labor, a woman will be surprised by how fast the birth is. With crowning, the doctor rests his left hand on the baby's head. With his right hand, he holds a towel underneath the rectum to prevent contamination from escaping stool. Then he pushes his right hand in and up to feel the baby's chin through the perineum. Once he finds the chin, he slowly lifts it up and brings the baby forward with one hand underneath and the other supporting the top of the baby's head. (If the perineal area looks like it might tear, the doctor may perform an episiotomy now.) The birth of the head is slow and gentle, often between two contractions. A woman may be asked to pant quickly rather than push, as the head emerges.

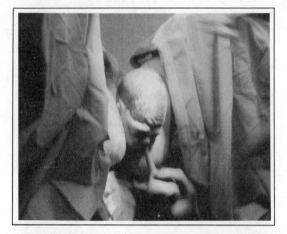

Figure 14-9. *The baby's head has just been delivered, and the baby's mouth is suctioned clean before its first breath to avoid aspiration of mucus into the baby's lungs.* Photo courtesy of Barbara Fila.

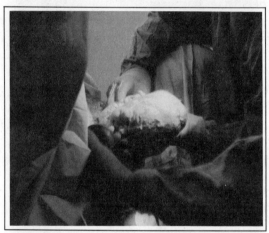

Figure 14-10. *The baby's head is now fully delivered and rotates spontaneously to the left. The mouth is still being suctioned.* Photo courtesy of Barbara Fila.

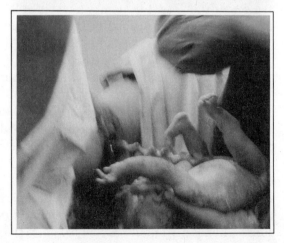

Figure 14-11. *The baby has just been born and is still attached to its mother by the umbilical cord. This newborn is healthy and vigorous.* Photo courtesy of Barbara Fila.

After its appearance, the baby's head rotates to the left or right to align itself with the rest of its body. The doctor opens the baby's mouth and suctions out excess mucus before the baby takes its first breath. Removal of the mucus assures that no meconium or blood-mixed fluid is aspirated into the newborn's lungs. It is awesome at this time to see the baby open its eyes and look around. A dimly lit environment right now is certainly more welcome than the harsh glare of overhead lights.

The doctor locates the umbilical cord next, before the shoulders are born. If the cord is around the baby's neck, he moves it down over the occiput (the back of the baby's head) to prevent it from being compressed by the shoulders. He may have to clamp and cut the cord, but if the baby is not at risk, he continues the delivery and cuts the cord after birth.

The shoulders appear right after the baby turns its head. A woman should put great effort into pushing, since with the next contraction, the upper shoulder will be delivered. The doctor places one hand on each side of the baby's head and pulls the baby downward as the obstetrical nurse puts pressure on the mother's abdomen just above her pubic bone. As the upper, or anterior, shoulder emerges, the doctor lifts the baby upward to deliver the posterior shoulder. The mother continues to push, and once both shoulders are free, the rest of the body easily slips out. (If, for some reason, a mother is unable to deliver the baby naturally, *forceps* may have to be used to aid the birth. See Chapter 14.)

Right after birth, a gush of amniotic fluid mixed with blood appears. This fluid was trapped above the baby in the womb. Then the third stage of labor, the delivery of the placenta, ensues. The doctor focuses on the baby and again suctions the mouth to make sure that no fluid will obstruct its breathing. The umbilical cord is clamped, and after it stops pulsating, the doctor may ask the father to cut it. Now the baby is a separate human being! It's time to pop the cork and toast with champagne! Remember to ask the labor nurse to put the bottle on ice when you arrive for labor so that the entire labor team can join in your celebration.

When a baby is born into a calm, warm environment, there is no reason to expect it to start crying immediately. The days of holding a baby upside down and slapping its behind to make it wail are over. Holding a baby in that position has been found to cause hip dislocation, and it is just not the best way to begin life on earth. Today a mother is allowed skin-to-skin contact with her

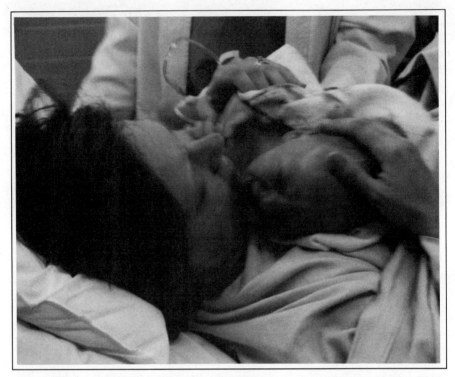

Figure 14-12. *A newborn baby is bonding with its mother immediately after birth.* Photo courtesy of Barbara Fila.

baby immediately after birth if the baby has no problems that need pediatric observation. (See The Apgar Score: What It Means in this chapter.)

A hot blanket is usually put over the baby and the mother for warmth. A mother should massage her baby, rub him up and down his back to stimulate breathing, and cuddle him. She and her child are beginning their new relationship. A father also shares the touch of his child right now, and if a woman is in a birthing room, siblings and other family members may meet the newborn. A new mother will be exhausted but exhilarated as she looks at her infant's eyes and caresses his body. She had been waiting for this moment for nine months, and finally it has arrived!

A Note About Underwater Birth

Advocates of underwater birthing have delivered in tanks, tubs, and even the ocean. Reportedly a thousand underwater births have occurred in the last twenty years, mostly in Russia and France. Controversy surrounds this technique, however, and recently Dr. Keith Russell, past president of both the American College of Obstetricians and Gynecologists and the International Federation of Gynecology and Obstetrics, in a national magazine reminded women that even though a newborn does not have to breathe while it is still attached to the umbilical cord, there is a risk of water entering the bloodstream if the placenta separates while it is still inside the mother. Placental separation is only one complication that may occur, and with an underwater birth, an infant in trouble is not easily accessible to the doctor. I am concerned about the risk of infection and the temperature of the water, which, if it is not the same as the temperature in the womb, may shock the baby. For these reasons, I would discourage my patients from choosing underwater birth.

In the United States, it is very difficult for a woman to find a doctor who will perform underwater birth. Right now this technique is really more of a conversation piece than a reality. And since human beings breathe air, not water, I believe it is nature's way for a baby to be born into the environment that will nourish him and support his survival.

When Is an Episiotomy Needed? Can I Give Birth Without One?

I am afraid of having an episiotomy when I give birth. A friend of mine had three children and she was given an episiotomy for all of them. Later on, she found out that her doctor just gave episiotomies routinely, whether they were needed or not, and she suffered in the end. Intercourse became painful, and the doctor said that scar tissue from the episiotomies was the cause. She had surgery to correct the condition and nothing changed. She is still having painful sex, and now she's talking about divorce. She says that her marriage is wrecked. I don't want to be in her shoes. Please tell me. When is an episiotomy needed? Can I give birth without one?

L.V.
Valhalla, New York

An episiotomy is a small incision through the perineum—the area from the lower portion of the vagina to the anus—that allows the baby to emerge without painfully tearing the mother's vaginal tissue. As mentioned in the previous section, during childbirth, a doctor or a midwife can massage the perineal area to widen the birth canal in an effort to avoid an episiotomy. In fact, even before labor, a woman and her mate can regularly massage the area to make it more elastic. Routine episiotomies, of course, should be questioned, but a straight incision is easier to repair than a jagged tear, and sometimes an episiotomy is the wiser course of action. I have seen women who have *not* had episiotomies suffer nerve injury and vaginal damage that definitely inhibited their sexual activity.

If a woman's perineal muscles are stretching to the point that it appears that the baby cannot be born without tearing her tissue, then an episiotomy should be performed. Most often, the incision is made during the delivery of a first-born. In subsequent pregnancies, vaginal tissue is already stretched.

I sympathize with Ms. V.'s friend, who had an episiotomy with all of her three children. I would not think this incision would have been required each time. And how she has suffered! Often, a woman's painful intercourse after an episiotomy is due to the fact that her physician did not make a skillful incision and a thorough repair.

How an episiotomy is performed: A local anesthesia is given for an episiotomy if a woman has not already received an epidural or general anesthesia. An episiotomy that is made during a contraction is usually painless, however, because the pressure of the baby's head on the fragile perineum creates a natural anesthesia—in this case, an episiotomy can be given without a local. Then a doctor should make a *midline* rather than a *mediolateral* incision.

About 70 percent of all babies are born with the help of episiotomies. Ms. V.'s sexual relations should not be affected if she has an episiotomy that is properly performed. The *midline* cut extends from the bottom of the vagina toward the rectum, whereas the *mediolateal* incision actually goes into the side of the anus. The midline episiotomy is made where there is a greater blood supply and less fatty tissue than in the area of the mediolateral cut, and the midline heals faster. A careful midline episiotomy, if a woman needs it, should not interfere with sexual activity. (Even with a midline, a big baby sometimes can tear a mother's tissue, but a skillful physician can make a perfect repair after delivery.)

My advice to Ms. V. is to massage her perineal area and to be sure she is in the care of a confident, skillful physician. A reputable doctor will not perform an unnecessary episiotomy, especially if Ms. V. does not need one. If she does, however, she should know beforehand that her doctor will make a midline incision. Childbirth requires teamwork. She and her doctor should have the same goals; they are on the same team.

AFTER BIRTH

The Apgar Score: What It Means

At one minute and again at five minutes after birth, a baby's condition is evaluated by what is known as *the Apgar score*. Created by Dr. Virginia Apgar, a reknowned pediatrician at Columbia Presbyterian Hospital in New York, the Apgar score is a standard for ascertaining a newborn's health. Five areas are immediately checked after birth: heart rate, respiratory capacity, muscle tone, reflexes, and skin color. At most, two points are given in each category, so if a baby is in optimum condition, an Apgar score of 9 or 10 is the result.

Sometimes a baby is a little bluish because he is cold after he leaves the womb, and his score is 9 at one minute. Only a really pink baby gets a 10 at the one-minute evaluation. But actually the important Apgar score is the five-minute check. At one minute, a newborn might need oxygen, or if the mother has received Demerol, the baby may need an injection of Narcan to counteract the painkiller. At five minutes, the infant should have adjusted, so this score becomes more meaningful in terms of the child's actual condition. Studies have shown that babies who had a score of 7 or

Apgar Score

Sign	0	1	2
Heart rate	absent	slow (below 100)	Over 100
Respiratory effort	absent	weak cry; hypoventilation	good effort; strong cry
Muscle tone	limp	some flexion of extremities	active motion; extremities well flexed
Reflex irritability (response to stimulation) of skin of feet	no response	some motion (grimace)	crying and active
Color	Blue, pale	body pink; extremities blue	completely pink

above at five minutes have no significant health problems later in life. A score under 7 means that an infant requires observation and medical attention and may have a lingering difficulty.

After the score is given, a helpless infant still needs the watchful eyes of its parents. The first twenty-four hours of life are incredibly important, and any change in the baby's health should be brought to a pediatrician's attention.

Why Do Brand-New Babies Look Funny Sometimes?

Mothers are naturally concerned about their babies' looks, and some women worry because they have seen newborns with skin discolorations or oddly shaped heads, and they do not realize how temporary these conditions are.

At birth, a baby is wet-looking and may be covered with a white, creamy substance called *vernix caseosa,* which protected his skin and acted as a lubricant for delivery. A mother may also notice small white spots called *milia* on the baby's face or red areas from tiny blood vessels on the back of the baby's neck or his nose. These early birthmarks normally fade. The light skin of black, Asian, and Mediterranean babies, on the other hand, darkens several days after birth. Sometimes a baby may be spotted with blood after childbirth, or he might be slightly bluish because he is cold after leaving the womb, but after he is washed and wrapped in a hot blanket, he appears pink and healthy. And a fine, downy hair called *lanugo,* which appears on some babies, will disappear in a few days.

The shape of a baby's head after its journey through the birth canal is probably of most concern to new mothers. Sometimes it can be elongated, and doctors know this as a *banana head.* What happens is that the baby's skull molds to fit into a woman's pelvis, and the occiput, the back of the head, swells as it is pushed by the contracting forces of labor. A banana head will become rounded in a day or two, however, and a mother need not worry.

After birth, a mother should expect to see an antibiotic ophthalmic cream, usually erythromycin, placed on the eyes of her newborn. This medication prevents contamination from the vaginal canal just in case an infection or a disease such as gonorrhea or chlamydia is present. Chlamydia, especially, is known to cause conjunctivitis and serious vision problems if a baby is exposed. In the past, silver nitrate was used on a newborn's eyes, but it was found to be dangerous. A mother should talk to the nurse and ask her about the antibiotic she will apply to her baby's eyes. It is a federal law that an antibiotic ointment or drops be used, and a mother should not be concerned that anything unusual is occurring. A baby also routinely receives an injection of vitamin K to improve his blood coagulation in the first twenty-four hours after birth.

Once an infant has been checked and given an Apgar score, a nurse will take the baby's footprints for identification, and the mother's fingerprints. The footprints prevent any possible mix-up in the nursery. A mother bringing home the wrong baby only happens in the movies! Anyway, a mother should request the prints and keep them with the baby's identification bracelet, as remembrances of this birth-day.

Should I Tip the Nurse?

I had a labor nurse who was just wonderful. She never left my side, and after the baby was born, she stayed on an hour after her shift had ended just to make sure that I was all right. My husband and I felt as if she were part of the family. We even took photos of her with my son right after he arrived. Should I tip the nurse? I'd like to do something for her but I don't know what is proper. Would she be offended if I gave her money? What do you suggest?

M.R.
Mountainside, New Jersey

A high-quality, caring nurse is indispensable. I have seen what a difference a supportive nurse can make during labor, and I always feel that this kind of dedicated person deserves recognition. Ms. R.'s letter is wonderful to receive because it tells me that others feel the way I do. Of course, Ms. R. can thank her nurse for her kindness by giving her a gift. Whether Ms. R. chooses to give money, flowers, candy, or an item related to her or her husband's profession is not as significant as the fact that she is taking the time to acknowledge her nurse's participation in the birth of her son. Any gift is proper and will be gratefully received. The gift is best accompanied by a warm note of appreciation. Your labor and delivery nurse will remember you for a long time and will always welcome a word from you. The hospital administration would also like to know about positive and negative childbirth experiences of their patients. Feedback from new mothers helps to make or break hospital policies.

CHAPTER 15

When Childbirth Takes a Surprising Turn

Most childbirths are joyous events that expectant parents celebrate with a combined sense of relief and excitement. It happens every day of the year. After months of preparation and long hours of labor, the baby finally arrives! Elated, exhausted mothers give birth naturally, without oxytocin to induce contractions or a cesarean section to end the pregnancy.

Yet while the emphasis in childbirth has been on a completely natural approach, sometimes there is a sudden need to change direction. In Chapter 12, the conditions that create a high-risk pregnancy were explained. A woman who is at high risk usually knows ahead of time that she will require special attention and possibly medication or a cesarean when she delivers. However, without forewarning, a low-risk expectant mother can become high risk during delivery. She may experience exceptionally prolonged labor, develop preeclampsia, or bleed unexpectedly; or her baby may develop fetal distress or turn into a breech position. A number of surprising turns may lead her doctor to suggest medication, an epidural anesthesia, oxytocin to induce or stimulate labor, a low-forceps delivery, (see p. 419), or a cesarean section.

In the last two decades, women have strongly advocated natural childbirth and changed delivery procedures across the country. Natural childbirth, of course, is desired by doctors and women alike today, but the question of ensuring a *safe birth* must not be overlooked. A woman who follows a healthy diet (see Chapter 5), exercises moderately, and keeps to an appropriate weight for her month of gestation is more likely to have a successful natural birth than a woman who gains more than the recommended pounds. With too much added weight, a woman can produce a very large baby, and there is a greater chance that she may pass her due date and need oxytocin stimulation as well as a forceps delivery. The baby may also suffer shoulder dystocia. She also increases the likelihood of having a cesarean section in her condition.

Years ago, women complained that oxytocin was administered too freely and cesareans were performed too routinely, that childbirth was arranged more for the convenience of the doctor than the wishes of the mother. Women were right; but now we—doctors and expectant mothers—must be careful not to be so focused on natural childbirth that we hesitate to take the steps needed for safer births. The natural course of childbirth, of course, should not be interrupted when all is going well, but sometimes complications can create occasions for medical procedures. Yet women are still doubtful, and those who have experienced induced labor or a forceps delivery, for example, continue to ask: "Did I really need it?" If intervention is needed during childbirth, this chapter will, I hope, arm you with information to question your doctor's procedures at the time.

When Should Labor Be Induced?

I want to be sure that when I reach my due date, I know what I'm doing. I want to give birth naturally and I don't want to be induced unless it's absolutely necessary. My problem, though, is that I'm not sure what "absolutely necessary" is. When should labor be induced?

L.I.

Dedham, Massachusetts

Pitocin, synthetically produced oxytocin, is a powerful drug used to initiate labor contractions. In the past, it was given to expectant mothers who simply looked as if they were ready to give birth, and at times, the results were disastrous. A woman's uterus could severely spasm from contractions that were too strong for her body, and her baby could seriously suffer.

Today labor is induced only when induction will mean a *safer birth,* and Pitocin is given in minute, controlled amounts with the aid of a device called an *infusion pump.* A mother is constantly checked by fetal monitoring during induction, and the doctor can stop an infusion if the fetal heart rate looks the least bit abnormal. The procedure is safer than ever before, and the occasions for using it are recognized, essential ones: *when there is concern after the rupture of fetal membranes, when a woman has passed her due date and abnormalities appear on a nonstress test or an oxytocin challenge test, when complications such as diabetes or toxemia exist, or when the baby's Rh factor causes a rise in antibodies in the mother's blood.* Other high-risk problems can also create a need for induction, but these are the most common causes.

Rupture of the fetal membranes prematurely is discussed in Chapter 12 and at term in Chapter 13. As mentioned, labor usually begins naturally from twelve to twenty-four hours after the membranes break, and when contractions don't start, doctors worry about the possible onset of infection. When the membranes rupture prematurely, a doctor can perform an amniocentesis to determine the baby's lung maturation, an indication of whether the baby is developed enough to be delivered safely. (Sometimes a doctor will choose to monitor a woman for a few days for any signs of infection and not induce labor right away. This wait gives a premature baby time to grow.)

If a woman is within two weeks before or after her due date, and if she has no apparent infection or complication, some doctors do permit up to a forty-eight-hour wait for natural birth. A number of hospitals, however, have a reduced—twenty-four- rather than forty-eight-hour—policy because they're so concerned about infection. Most doctors do not like to wait more than twelve to sixteen hours before they induce labor. Walking and nipple stimulation, natural methods of labor induction described in Chapter 13, may be tried, and Pitocin chosen as a last resort. A conservative wait-and-see approach may be favorable, in fact, since a study at the University of Texas Health Science Center showed that in cases of premature rupture of the membranes, women whose labor was *not induced* had shorter labors than those whose were—9.7 hours compared to about 11.7 hours. Of course, the time from the rupture to labor was longer for the group whose labor was not induced—22.7 hours as compared to 15.2 hours for the women given Pitocin. When the reason for inducing labor is not rupture of the fetal membranes but one of the other conditions cited earlier, such as toxemia or complications from the Rh factor in a baby's blood, it is important to remove the baby from its hostile environment before any damage occurs.

In Europe and Japan, a prostaglandin gel is administered overnight to trigger mild contractions, prime a woman's cervix, and make induction easier. This gel is not yet approved for use in the United States, but in the future, it may be a big help during induction. At present, the infusion pump replaces the continuous oxytocin (Pitocin) drip and is a tremendous asset. With the pump, a doctor can now control the amount of Pitocin he allows into a woman's bloodstream. The woman remains in bed, with an IV and a fetal monitor attached. The monitor is crucial, because the doctor must check the fetal heart rate constantly during induction. A heart rate deceleration during induced labor would tell him to stop the induction, turn a woman on her side, and administer oxygen by mask.

Done properly, induction begins with a doctor allowing a small amount of Pitocin, perhaps one milliunit, to pass through the infusion pump. The pump offers great control over the powerful drug. The doctor can slowly increase the dosage by one milliunit every fifteen to twenty minutes until good uterine activity is seen on the fetal monitor. Then he can watch the monitor to make sure that all is going well.

The ability to induce labor is a lifesaving measure for babies who are in potentially unhealthy situations in the womb. No reputable doctor would overuse this procedure. A cesarean section may follow induced labor, usually because the condition that created the need for the induced labor may also create the need for the cesarean. Sometimes women have thought that cesarean sections just automatically followed induced labor, but that's not true. Today, with the infusion pump for administering Pitocin, labor can be carefully regulated and a cesarean section may not always be necessary.

417

I Had Been in Labor for 24 Hours When My Doctor Decided to Stimulate the Contractions. Should He Have Waited Longer?

I had a completely normal pregnancy and I went into labor on my due date. However, when I went to my doctor's office, he examined me and said that my cervix was still "posterior" and I should go home and wait. Later that night my cervix hadn't changed and he sent me to the hospital to be monitored. Then, about twenty-four hours after the contractions started, he decided to give me Pitocin to make the labor move along. I wanted everything natural. Should he have waited longer?

M.A.

Hartford, Connecticut

When a labor pattern is prolonged or abnormal, stimulation with Pitocin is a common, helpful practice. I presume that Ms. A.'s doctor was aware and careful and administered the drug with an infusion pump while she was attached to a fetal monitor. This is the proper procedure.

Studies have shown that prolonged or arrested (stopped) labor can be damaging to the fetus. One study headed by Dr. Emanuel A. Friedman at Beth Israel Hospital in Boston compared the IQs of seven-year-old children who had experienced different labors and deliveries: normal labors, prolonged labors, arrested labors, low- and mid-forceps deliveries. Children born after prolonged labors had *slightly lower* IQs, and those born after arrested labors had *significantly lower* IQs, than children born after normal labors. The children born after low-forceps deliveries, by the way, had IQs comparable to the children of normal births, whereas children of mid-forceps deliveries had lower scores.

When labor does not progress satisfactorily—which means that there is not adequate cervical dilatation—Pitocin should be administered. Ms. A.'s doctor did what any competent physician would have done. If a woman is in the second stage of pushing when labor becomes static, a small amount of Pitocin can be given to make the pushing and the birth easier. Pitocin is sometimes called liquid forceps when used in the second stage, since this is the point at which forceps might be called for. A woman should know that labor changes after Pitocin and becomes stronger and more effective. Labor after Pitocin stimulation is often more painful, and she may need relief with medication such as Demerol or an epidural anesthesia. (See Chapter 13.) Neither Pitocin, Demerol, or an epidural anesthesia will adversely affect the fetus when administered properly, and, in fact, these drugs can help bring your baby into the world as a healthier human being.

FORCEPS DELIVERIES

Why Might a Doctor Use Forceps?

In late sixteenth century England, a doctor in the Chamberlen family rushed to a childbirth in his carriage. As he stepped out, he was carrying a large, unidentifiable bundle under his arm. No one knew the contents of his package until the eighteenth century, when "forceps" were revealed to the medical establishment. In the age before cesarean sections were done, an earlier word about forceps might have saved the lives of many mothers and babies. Shrouded in mystery, misconceptions about the use and safety of forceps continue. Some expectant mothers vow to prevent forceps from even being brought into the room when they give birth because they worry about damage to the baby's head and brain. Forceps are used quite safely today, however, and only when a birth will benefit more with them than without them. The type of forceps delivery that caused injury in the past is no longer practiced. Today forceps have a very specific place in obstetrics.

Forceps are like huge salad tongs, with a handle and two spoonlike blades. They are used to help deliver a baby that needs to be turned (rotated) in the birth canal or lifted out. In order to use forceps, a doctor must make sure that the fetal membranes have ruptured, the cervix is 10 centimeters dilated, and the baby's head is "engaged" and in the plus two or plus three station (see Chapter 13). The baby must also be in a vertex, head-down, position.

The three types of forceps deliveries are *low-forceps, mid-forceps,* and *high-forceps.* A *high-forceps* delivery is a thing of the past. This is the type of delivery that gave forceps a bad name. High-forceps deliveries were done before safe cesareans became an alternative. Sometimes a baby's head was not engaged in an old-time high-forceps delivery, and mother and baby both suffered. A woman's birth canal could be traumatized and the baby born with brain damage or die. High-forceps deliveries are never performed today, and even mid-forceps deliveries are rare.

A *mid-forceps* delivery might be called for if a baby's head is en-

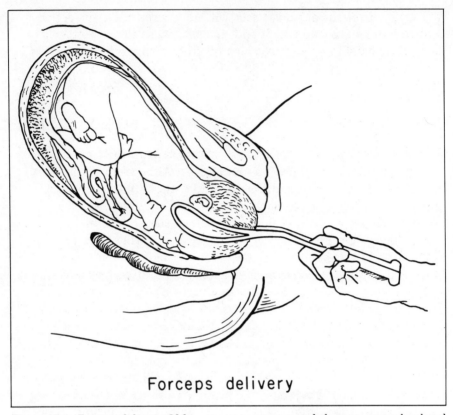

Forceps delivery

Figure 15-1. *Forceps delivery. If forceps are necessary and they are properly placed on the side of a baby's head, they can expedite delivery and safeguard both mother and baby.*

gaged but not properly positioned in the birth canal. Since mid-forceps would mean that the baby has not yet descended to the perineal area, most doctors would only use this type of delivery in an emergency situation. In fact, studies have shown that a cesarean is safer than a mid-forceps delivery time and time again. Most doctors will perform the safer cesarean if the baby does not move or cannot be turned in the birth canal.

Today a *low-forceps* delivery is the one that might be performed if forceps are used at all. If a woman has prolonged labor, or if labor inexplicably stops, or if a sudden drop in the fetal heart rate indicates that a baby's life is in jeopardy, forceps may be applied. Forceps may also be used if a woman has had a painkiller or anesthesia and she is unable to use her abdominal muscles to push properly.

An episiotomy is performed before the forceps are applied, and the anesthesia for the episiotomy numbs the area. A woman will feel pressure but no pain. A forceps delivery is an art that a trained obstetrician has learned. The forceps are placed on each side of the baby's head just above his chin. The baby is at the perineal floor, and with very little pressure, he can be delivered. The forceps are only touching the bony part of the head, and no pressure is placed on the baby's brain. A small mark or redness might show on his face, but it usually disappears within a week after childbirth.

Expectant parents should not be alarmed if a doctor feels that forceps must be used. A low-forceps delivery will not harm an infant and, indeed, should only be performed when needed.

VACUUM EXTRACTION: A SAFE ALTERNATIVE TO FORCEPS?

In the mid-fifties, a procedure called *vacuum extraction* was introduced in Sweden as an alternative to forceps deliveries. The medical establishment is always slow to change, but the vacuum extraction technique has gained some popularity. Magee–Women's Hospital in Pittsburgh credits thousands of deliveries to vacuum extraction.

How vacuum extraction works: Pressure is built inside a vacuum cup by a vacuum pump. The cup fixes firmly on the baby's head. Usually an episiotomy is needed, since a large baby is most often the reason for the extraction. Forceps may cut the vaginal wall when there is a tight fit in the birth canal, but the vacuum cup won't tear the tissue. When the vacuum has been created by the vacuum machine, a doctor will pull on the chain attached to the cup, and the baby will emerge. If too much vacuum pressure is applied, the cup will fall off. The mother pushes at the same time that the doctor is pulling.

If used properly, vacuum extraction is an entirely safe procedure; however, when the baby is high in the birth canal, a cesarean is safer. A vacuum cup should only be used when indicated by a doctor who has experience with the method. There have been incidents of hematoma on the scalp area where cups have been placed. Normally the hematoma and any swelling disappear within twenty-four to forty-eight hours of childbirth, but there is always a small chance that jaundice might develop when the hematoma breaks down. Since the cup falls off when pressure is too great, there seems to be no risk of brain damage.

SHOULDER DYSTOCIA

What if My Baby's Shoulders Are Too Big?

Two years ago, my sister delivered a baby who weighed over nine pounds and had wide shoulders, just like my brother-in-law's. The doctor had a very difficult time delivering the shoulders, and the baby's clavicle was broken. I'm expecting my first child soon and I'm worried that my baby might have the same problem, since my husband is also broad-shouldered. Is there anything I can do to prevent my baby being born with a broken shoulder bone if his shoulders are too big?

R.L.

Morristown, New Jersey

Shoulder dystocia is one of the biggest problems faced by obstetricians, because it is almost impossible to predict or prevent. If you are in good health and you have not gained an excessive amount of weight during your pregnancy and you deliver on or close to your due date, the chances of your delivery being complicated by shoulder dystocia are somewhat lessened. Simply having a large baby, however, does not mean that your baby's shoulders will be large. A study by Dr. Acker and his co-workers at the Harvard Medical School in Boston showed that about half of all deliveries with shoulder dystocia occurred in association with babies weighing *under* 4000 grams (8.5 pounds).

A stronger warning that shoulder dystocia may occur during childbirth is the presence of some abnormal labor patterns: prolonged or arrested labor, labor that appears to require oxytocin stimulation or forceps delivery, failure of the baby to descend. A Dr. O'Leary in Florida reported on one hospital where, after extensive antepartum testing and routine screening for diabetes, cesarean deliveries were performed when any abnormal labor patterns developed that were believed to be the result of a too-large baby. This aggressive technique resulted in a very low rate of shoulder dystocia complications.

Although there is no way that your doctor can accurately foresee whether your baby's shoulders will be broad, it is important that you discuss this potential problem with your obstetrician and have him explain to you how he would anticipate handling such a complication should it occur. Your doctor should be familiar with shoulder dystocia and be aware of the various delivery possibilities. At the same time, however, you need to be aware that shoulder dystocia is a very difficult delivery complication, primarily because it cannot be specifically predicted, and it requires an alert and skillful obstetrician to safely handle the birth.

Once your doctor has determined that your labor is not progressing as it should because your baby's shoulders are too broad, he will probably first ask you to help by pushing very hard. As you push, a doctor or a nurse will help you by pushing down on your abdomen, above the pubis bone, over one of the baby's shoulders, trying to squeeze it in while the doctor pulls on the baby's head in an attempt to rotate your baby, first anteriorly, then like a corkscrew, turning the baby in the pelvis in an attempt to deliver the back shoulder first.

If the pushing-rotating does not work, you may be asked to lift your legs very high and flex them over your stomach to give your baby more space and to help in the delivery of the shoulders. Your doctor may also try to assist your baby by extending the episiotomy. If these techniques do not work because your baby is too large, some doctors advocate breaking the clavicle so that the arms will collapse. Although this is not dangerous for your baby—the clavicle will heal by itself within a few days after birth—it is very difficult to do. More often, the clavicle breaks spontaneously, as in Ms. L.'s sister's case, and thus makes the delivery easier.

When none of the above methods makes your labor progress satisfactorily, particularly if the pushing phase has gone on for too long a time or if the baby is too high to make a forceps delivery safe, your doctor may decide that it is necessary to perform a cesarean. If you have chosen your obstetrician with care and discussed the possible eventuality of having your baby delivered surgically, you can trust that his decision is being made with the primary concern of your health and that of your baby.

BREECH BIRTHS

Does a Breech Presentation Always Mean a Cesarean?

I am thirty-seven weeks pregnant and my doctor just diagnosed that my baby is in the breech position. He said that although he would try to

deliver my baby vaginally, I should be prepared for the possibility of having a cesarean. Can I do anything to help turn the baby around?
L.G.
Sacramento, California

Although some doctors believe that breech presentations can be delivered only by cesarean, Ms. G. is fortunate to have a doctor who is willing to try first to deliver her vaginally. Although the chances for a normal delivery of a breech presentation are slim, particularly for first babies, more and more hospitals are allowing at least a trial labor before recommending surgical delivery.

Sometimes a baby will turn by itself. I have seen one woman at term with her first child in a breech position one day and in the vertex position the next! This is rare, however, since a first baby will usually stay a breech if it is in the breech position during the last few weeks of a pregnancy. On the other hand, in a multiparous woman (one who has delivered several children), it is common for the baby to turn spontaneously at any point up until the last moment—even during labor.

Once your doctor has determined that your baby is in the breech position, there are several things you can do that may help. First there is a simple exercise you can do three to four times a day: kneel on the floor and lower your body so that your chest is over your knees. Put a flat pillow under your head and lay the side of your face on the pillow. Stay in this position for ten to twenty minutes, turning your head from side to side every five minutes to change the position on the nerves. There is no guarantee that this will work, but it may position the baby higher in the pelvic area. You might also drink extra orange juice and lie on your side with your hips higher than your feet. Drinking the orange juice will increase fetal movement, and this may make your baby turn itself around.

When nothing you or your baby do changes the position your baby is in, there is still, in some cases, hope for a vaginal delivery. If you have a good natural progression of the baby into the pelvic area with appropriate cervical dilatation, if your pelvis is adequate (generally the case if you have already delivered at least one baby vaginally), if your labor progresses normally, and if your baby is in the frank breech position (both legs straight up, next to the baby's body), you should have no problem delivering vaginally.

If you go into labor and either your baby is in an incomplete breech position (a foot and a knee next to the baby's bottom) or your baby remains high in the pelvic area, or your baby's head appears to be too large for your pelvis, your doctor may decide that a cesarean is the safest mode of delivery, particularly if this is your first baby. Again, be sure to discuss the possibility of a breech presentation with your obstetrician early in your pregnancy. If your doctor or the hospital with which he is affiliated won't consider trying to deliver a breech vaginally, you may wish to select another doctor.

CESAREAN SECTION

Delivery by cesarean section was a relatively unexpected event in the sixties and seventies, but today the incidence has increased to more than 20 percent nationwide: one out of every five babies is born via cesarean section today. A cesarean section is an operation to deliver a baby through an incision in the mother's abdomen. The earliest historical records of such a procedure date back to 3000 B.C. in Egypt. The term *cesarean* is sometimes thought to be royal in origin, since supposedly Julius Caesar was delivered surgically, but the actual name for this procedure is believed to be derived from a group of laws, *Lex Caesare,* which in Rome in 715 B.C. ordered the surgical removal of any unborn fetus if the mother died.

Until recently, this operation was used only as a last resort. Cesareans could only be performed under general anesthesia, and no good antibiotics were available. The risks of complications and infections were great. This was a dangerous procedure during which many women died. Today, however, improved surgical techniques, particularly the use of epidural anesthesia, and modern antibiotics have made cesarean sections much safer, and the risk of undergoing a cesarean delivery is no greater than that of any other minor surgical procedure such as an appendectomy or a tonsilectomy. So if you truly need to have your baby delivered by cesarean section, you shouldn't worry unnecessarily, as long as you and your partner work closely with your doctor and you are confident that this is the safest mode of delivery for you and your baby.

Why Has the Cesarean Rate Increased So Dramatically?

The rate of cesarean sections has increased from 4.5 percent in 1965 to more than 20 percent today. There are many reasons for

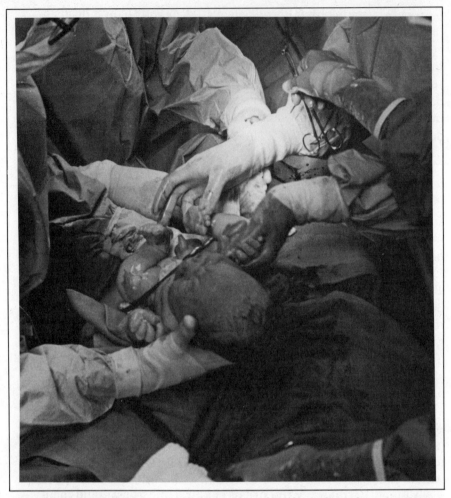

Figure 15-2. *Cesarean birth. A baby boy has just been born through a cesarean section; the umbilical cord has been clamped, and one of the doctors is ready to carry the baby to the pediatrician.*

this increase. Today women often wait until they are older to have their first baby, which subsequently results in many more high-risk pregnancies. For a woman over thirty, national statistics show a cesarean rate of more than 25 percent.

There is also a higher rate of increase in cesarean sections regionally in the East and in the South, perhaps explained by the fact that women in the East and the South have fewer children than women in the West and Midwest, and each birth generally makes the subsequent delivery easier.

Table 8.

Percentage of Cesarean Deliveries by Age of Mother:

1965–1983

			Age of Mother			
	All Ages	**20**	**20–24**	**25–29**	**30–34**	**35**
1983	20.3	15.0	19.0	20.5	24.6	25.4
1982	18.5	13.4	17.6	19.9	20.4	23.6
1981	17.9	13.2	16.0	19.4	21.3	24.4
1980	16.5	14.5	15.8	16.7	18.0	20.6
1979	16.4	13.7	15.6	16.4	19.5	21.1
1975	10.4	8.4	9.0	11.1	13.6	15.0
1970	5.5	3.9	4.9	5.9	7.5	8.3
1965	4.5	3.1	3.5	4.3	6.4	7.9

SOURCE: *National Center for Health Statistics.*

The primary indication (35 percent) for a cesarean today is women who have previously delivered by cesarean section. In 1912, Dr. Edward Cragin of New York City said, "Once a cesarean, always a cesarean." At that time, and in some cases today, that was a valid philosophy. In the past, incisions were not made as well, there were more infections, and, as a result, the uterus was often weaker. Now, however, we know that a normal birth after a cesarean can be perfectly safe if the conditions that necessitated the first cesarean do not recur at the next birth. I have personally delivered numerous babies vaginally after one cesarean delivery had been performed.

The major portion of today's increased rate of cesarean sections is due to advanced medical and technological techniques that enable the doctor to better analyze and diagnose his patients during their pregnancies and more accurately monitor them during labor and delivery. New skills allow the doctor to better protect the health—and lives—of his patients and their babies by intervening early enough to be effective. Twenty-eight percent of cesareans are due to some type of disproportion: either the baby is too large or the progression is too slow; 11 percent are necessitated by breech presentations; and another 7 percent are caused by fetal distress. Other problems such as dysfunctional labor and abnormal heart rate patterns account for the final 19 percent of cesarean sections. Many of these dangers, both to mother and child,

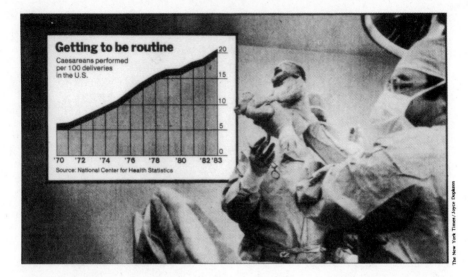

Getting to be routine

Caesareans performed
per 100 deliveries
in the U.S.

20

15

10

5

0

'70   '72   '74   '76   '78   '80   '82 '83

Source: National Center for Health Statistics

The New York Times / Joyce Dopkeen

Figure 15-3. *The cesarean birth rate has risen to 20 percent. Inset into the picture of doctors holding a newborn baby is a graph indicating the dramatic increase in cesareans from 1970 to 1983.* Reproduced by permission. Joyce Dopkeen/NYT Pictures.

were not readily recognizable in the past, and without surgical intervention, many lives were lost or irreparably damaged.

Yet another factor leading to the increase in the rate of cesarean sections are the medical-legal aspects of childbirth. Since the surgery is safe, today many doctors are unwilling to chance a risky forceps delivery when, even though they are practicing superior medicine, they are very apt to be sued if their patients think they could have done better by performing a cesarean.

Although cesarean deliveries are most certainly no longer to be feared and, at times, might even be considered a blessing, I believe a woman should make every effort to select a doctor whom she can trust to try every technique available to allow her to deliver her child naturally. During your antenatal visits with your doctor, you should discuss this issue with your doctor openly and frankly and be sure you and your doctor agree philosophically. You should be certain that if, to deliver your baby safely, a cesarean is needed, your doctor will first consult you and explain why the surgery is indicated. You should also be sure that, given the possibility of a surgical delivery, your doctor is an experienced, competent surgeon. Working as a team with your doctor, your childbirth educator, and your husband, you can develop the assurance and trust that you will need at the moment of delivery.

Table 9.

Reasons for Increase in Cesarean Rate: 1980–1983

Rank	Percent
Total	100.0
1. Previous cesarean delivery	55.3
2. Dystocia	23.7
3. Fetal Distress	13.2
4. Breech presentation	5.3
5. All other	2.5

SOURCE: *National Center for Health Statistics.*

Cesarean Was a Blessing for Me.

I don't understand why anyone complains about having a cesarean. When I had my baby, I had been in labor for almost two days. Although my contractions were strong, apparently they weren't strong enough to dilate my cervix, and because I was only 2 centimeters dilated, hospital policy would not permit me to have an epidural. My baby was in the posterior position and my labor had reached the point that it was so intense that I felt it was impossible to continue. I was exhausted and very disappointed. My doctor was also worried because I was having a "dry" labor—my membranes had broken without me realizing it before I went into labor—and he was concerned about the possibility of infection. Finally the doctor decided to do a cesarean because, in addition to everything else, the monitor showed that the baby was having trouble. For me, his decision was a relief. I recovered quickly and only regret that I had to suffer as long as I did. I don't know why anyone would want any other form of birth.

P.L.
Burlington, Vermont

A cesarean section is still surgery, and although as a surgical procedure, it has been greatly improved and the risk of death to both mother and child significantly lowered, natural childbirth is still the safest way to deliver a baby, causing fewer problems and producing a quicker recovery than a cesarean. On the other hand, as Ms. L.'s letter shows, there are situations in which a cesarean section is clearly indicated. Although a doctor in such a situation would generally try to create more regular uterine contractions by using oxytocin stimulation and thus opt for a vaginal birth, apparently this could not have been done in Ms. L.'s case. She had

429

so-called dry labor, and the umbilical cord could have been pressed during the contractions, producing a dangerous fetal environment and jeopardizing her baby. Certainly in many cases such as Ms. L.'s, indications for performing a cesarean section are appropriate, particularly in view of Dr. Emanuel A. Friedman's previously mentioned study, in which he and his colleagues conducted a seven-year follow-up study comparing the IQs of children born through easy births to those who had prolonged, complicated births. The study concluded that the IQs were nearly 8 points lower in the latter group.

Although Ms. L. does not indicate her age, it is important to note that the greatest increase in the rate of cesarean deliveries is among women over the age of thirty. This is because the tissue becomes less elastic and there is a decrease in the blood supply to the uterus, often creating a more hostile fetal environment.

In any case, whatever your age, I strongly urge you to do all that you can to keep your pregnancy a low-risk one by following sound nutritional programs and avoiding sugar and carbohydrates. If you do gain too much weight, your baby will be larger, perhaps even diabetic, which will make childbirth much more cumbersome and increase your chances of needing a cesarean. You should also, with your doctor's approval, follow some program of exercise to build and strengthen your body, readying it for childbirth.

Reading Ms. L.'s letter, it would appear that the decision to have a cesarean was presented to her by her doctor as a *fait accompli*. I cannot stress enough the value of discussing the potential of a cesarean delivery with your doctor *before* you go into labor. If you have established open communication, you can discuss each phase of your labor with your doctor and better understand and accept his reasoning when he recommends a cesarean. I have found in my own patients, in women who have had long labors and in whom oxytocin stimulation has been used to no avail, that they and their partners accept that although natural childbirth would have been *our* first choice, cesareans are sometimes necessary to avoid jeopardizing the baby.

In addition to determining in advance your doctor's philosophy about vaginal versus surgical deliveries, you should also ascertain how he performs his cesareans. Today a cesarean can easily be performed with a "bikini" incision, and a skillful surgeon can even make the incision under the hairline, so that later on you will hardly see any scars. The incision on the uterus should be tranverse, so that the uterus will heal well, increasing your chances of being able to deliver your next baby naturally. It is also possible for a cesarean to be performed using an epidural anesthesia, so that you can be awake during the birth and can see your newborn immediately. After delivery, I follow the recommendations of the studies done by leading obstetricians that have shown that two to three days of treatment with antibiotics cuts down the rate of infection tremendously as well as shortens the recovery time.

Thus, while no one should seek to have a cesarean, if you have one, there is no need for you to be upset. Modern surgical techniques, used by doctors who understand their patients' needs to participate in their health care decisions, can help you have the healthiest baby possible.

Once a Cesarean, Always a Cesarean—Not Always True!

I had a cesarean section that I never felt was necessary when I delivered my first child. My doctor did not let me be in labor long enough when he decided to do a cesarean. I was too young, however, to fight, and when I became pregnant with my second child, I checked around for a long time before I found a doctor who said he was willing to let me have a trial labor. I couldn't believe how well everything went! The doctor didn't have to intervene at all, and I had a completely natural birth—not even an intravenous! What a relief this was, and I am so pleased that the old saying Once a cesarean, always a cesarean was not true in my case.

P.J.
Oklahoma City, Oklahoma

Until recently, a competent physician would never let a woman deliver naturally after one previous cesarean section. In the past, when performing a cesarean, doctors made a "classical," or upside-down, incision in the uterus, thus weakening the uterus. Cesareans were also generally associated with great morbidity and high infection rates. There was thus a greater chance during a subsequent birth that the uterus would rupture unless the baby was delivered surgically.

Gradually, however, improved techniques led surgeons to use low-flap or low-transverse incisions, and even more gradually, studies began to emerge showing that in many cases, there was no contraindication to allowing patients to have at least a trial labor even if they had previously been delivered via cesarean section.

In 1974, a survey was conducted revealing that 99 percent of women with a previous history of cesarean delivery had repeat cesareans. A growing concern over what seemed to be an alarming increase in the rate of cesarean deliveries, coupled with a twenty-seven-fold increase in maternal morbidity following cesarean sections as compared to vaginal births, led physicians to reinvestigate the possibility of vaginal births after cesareans. In 1982, for example, a study showed that 67 percent of women who previously delivered vaginally and subsequently delivered via cesarean were again able to deliver vaginally, whereas 47 percent of patients who had had no previous vaginal deliveries were still able to deliver vaginally.

If you have had a cesarean and now wish to try to experience natural childbirth, you must be aware that no doctor can guarantee that you will be able to do so. To begin with, whatever problem existed during the first birth that necessitated the cesarean must not exist in the second delivery. It is most important that you find a physician who is open to your trying to deliver naturally. This is becoming easier to do, but much controversy still exists.

Even if your doctor encourages you to try to deliver naturally, you need to understand the potential limitations of your efforts. For example, doctors will not allow oxytocin stimulation, since the stronger contractions could rupture the uterus. If there is any abnormality during labor or delivery, a repeat cesarean will be recommended at once. Also, some physicians are reluctant to use an epidural anesthesia in a repeat birth, because there is a chance that the uterus could rupture and neither the doctor nor the patient would be aware of it. Other doctors believe that there are other means to predict potential rupture of the uterus and thus do allow epidural anesthesia.

Policies of both doctors and hospitals are changing throughout the country, and at this time, even the American College of Obstetricians and Gynecologists has recommended that a trial labor should be allowed after a previous cesarean. The feeling is that this is, first of all, safe and, second, may cut down the increase rate of cesareans performed in this country. All obstetricians have been informed of this recommendation and have been issued guidelines by ACOG to follow in such circumstances.

I have had the great pleasure of delivering many women naturally even after previous cesareans. And I have found that women who do have to have a cesarean are not as upset when I am able to reassure them that one cesarean does not do away with the possibility of experiencing natural childbirth at some point in the future. Regardless of your delivery history, be sure to find a doctor who is willing to treat you the way you deserve.

Can I Choose to Have an Elective Cesarean with My Husband at My Side?

I was an infertility patient for five years and finally conceived with in vitro fertilization. I am thirty-five years old and I have gone through so much to have this child. I am very frightened about my labor and delivery and all the problems that might occur and, because of my age, I know that there is a 25 percent chance that I might have to have a cesarean anyway. I would like to find a doctor who would be willing to perform an elective cesarean section without me even going into labor. I would like to have a cesarean; in fact, several of my friends have had this type of birth and done so well that they've said they wouldn't want to have a baby any other way. My friend's husband was in the labor room when the baby was delivered, and even with a cesarean, they still were able to experience all the bonding and joy of childbirth. This is how I would like my baby born. How can I find a doctor who will support my desires?

T.J.
Boston, Massachusetts

I certainly can understand Ms. J.'s position, her fears and her hopes. Some studies, in fact, have recently emerged indicating that in certain instances, a cesarean delivery using modern techniques—epidural anesthesia and antibiotics—can be a safer mode of delivery than a vaginal birth. If a woman is having a high-risk pregnancy and her delivery is further complicated by her overwhelming fear of the actual childbirth, she may be a candidate for an elective cesarean delivery.

The question of such a delivery, however, is one that must be resolved on a medical-legal basis before such an option is available to the general public. Although I do know of several women who have successfully maintained that having an elective cesarean delivery is their legal right and who have located hospitals and doctors willing to support their beliefs, most physicians prefer to see women enter labor under the most natural conditions possible.

In the past, many doctors would argue with Ms. J. that by having a cesarean, she would miss out on the true wonder and joy of childbirth. Today that is no longer true. By using epidural anesthesia, bonding and breast-feeding are possible immediately after birth. It is clear from Ms. J.'s letter, however, that she has spared no effort to realize her goal of having a baby. I cannot help but feel that if Ms. J. and her obstetrician did, in fact, have a relationship based on trust and understanding, her feelings about giving birth might be different. Surely she is correct in acknowledging the very real possibility that her baby may need to be delivered surgically. But perhaps, if she were equally confident about the availability of the latest equipment and methods to assist her in trying to safely deliver her child naturally, she would be anticipating her due date with less dread.

As to the question of fathers in the delivery room, there are really two issues here. In the first place, fathers need to realize that they are an integral part of the childbirth team so that they want to participate in the delivery of their child. However, just as it is of crucial importance that mothers understand that they are not failures if they are unable to deliver their babies completely naturally, fathers must accept that a lack of ability—or will—to be present at the moment of delivery does not mean they cannot be the world's best father. We are all individuals with different weaknesses and strengths.

Second, you need to be aware of your hospital's policy regarding fathers in the delivery room. More and more hospitals throughout the country now allow fathers to be present at the delivery as long as there are no urgent problems, such as an emergency cesarean section due to fetal distress or other problems when there is not time enough to allow the father to be present. Some hospitals, however, have been slower to develop such policies, primarily due to legal concerns. There have been lawsuits from fathers who fainted in the delivery room, injured themselves, and then blamed the staff the fathers had pressured into allowing them to be present in the first place! Furthermore, in all fairness to hospital administrators, we need to remember that a cesarean section *is* surgery, and most consumers would not insist that they be allowed to participate in, for example, a family member's appendectomy. So before you insist that your husband be allowed to attend a cesarean delivery, you need to consider his true feelings and to understand the legal rationale behind the policies of the hospital with which your obstetrician is affiliated.

I Am Past My Due Date and My Doctor Wants to Induce Labor. Should I Let Him?

I am thirty-two years old and I delivered my first baby completely naturally in the forty-second week of my pregnancy. This, my second pregnancy, has also been totally uneventful, but since I am now two weeks past my due date, my doctor thinks I should be induced. I don't think I agree with him—I'd prefer to let everything happen naturally. What should I do?

N.B.

Dallas, Texas

The proper management of a prolonged pregnancy remains one of the most controversial issues in obstetrics today. In the first place, in spite of all our modern technology, it is still very difficult to establish a woman's exact date of confinement, her true due date. The serious problems that can be associated with postdate pregnancies, however, are well known. Once a woman passes her due date, she increases the risk of perinatal mortality, because her placenta may begin to function less sufficiently, thus jeopardizing her baby.

In one study conducted by Dr. Norman F. Gant at Southwestern Medical School in Dallas, Texas, it was shown that by inducing labor at forty-two rather than forty-three weeks gestation, the perinatal mortality rate was reduced from 19 per 1000 women to none. The rate of cesarean sections, however, was the same (20 percent) as for women who were induced one week later. Several other studies have shown that complications arising from postmaturity increase with a woman's age: the risk factor is greater for women over thirty who have gone past their due date and far higher for women over forty.

As a result of their increased awareness of the potential dangers of postdate pregnancies, obstetricians throughout the country now give special care to all women who are past forty-one weeks of gestation. Ms. B. does not mention why her doctor recommends that labor be induced, but perhaps the doctor performed tests that indicated her baby could be at risk if delivery was delayed.

Generally a woman such as Ms. B. would be given a *nonstress test* twice a week as soon as she had passed her forty-first week of gestation. If these tests reveal any abnormality, an *oxytocin challenge test* (*OCT*) should be added, in which oxytocin is given to create uterine contractions. The baby's heart rate is monitored during the OCT, because if the placenta, due to age, does not supply enough oxygen to the baby, fetal heart rate deceleration will be noted during and after contractions. This would indicate a hostile fetal environment, and the baby should be delivered. During this antenatal testing, the fetal well-being should also be monitored with ultrasound to determine the amount of amniotic fluid. If a decrease in fluid level is observed, the baby is increasingly less protected from umbilical cord compression.

Most institutions today advocate induction of labor after the end of the forty-second week of gestation (42 weeks and 6 days from the first day of the last menstrual period). In addition to all the watchful care your doctor is giving, women in Ms. B.'s situation need to pay particular attention to the *movement* of their babies once they have gone past their due date. Above and beyond any information modern technology can give, still the most important is your own observation of fetal movement. If you feel no movement during this time, try to push the baby gently from side to side to see if you can awaken it. If movement is still not felt, lie down on your left side and drink some orange juice. This should increase your blood sugar content and stimulate the baby to move. If the baby still does not move, call your doctor, who will probably send you to the hospital for monitoring. If the monitoring indicates fetal jeopardy, your doctor will probably elect to deliver your baby either through induction or cesarean section.

Although Ms. B.'s doctor may be reacting too quickly, I cannot emphasize enough how seriously postdate pregnancies must be taken, especially if you are older. Be particularly alert to your baby's movements and communicate any changes or abnormalities to your doctor. Be sure that you are seen by your doctor so that he will be able to monitor the fetal environment.

I Am Having Twins. Can I Have a Natural Birth?

Two months ago, my obstetrician realized that I am carrying twins. I was happy until he began to talk about delivering my babies by cesarean section. I have never been pregnant before, and it is very important to me to experience natural childbirth. Why isn't this possible?

C.W.

Vienna, Virginia

It is completely possible for a woman carrying twins—or sometimes even triplets or quadruplets—to deliver her babies naturally. If both twins are in the vertex position when a woman goes into labor and the cervix opens naturally so that the babies progress into the vagina, there would be no contraindication for a natural birth. Immediately after the first twin is delivered, your doctor will put his hand into the uterus onto the second baby's head, slowly guiding the baby's head down as the baby's progress is monitored. If a woman has previously given birth, it is even easier for her to deliver twins naturally. But even first-time mothers should not rule out the possibility of natural childbirth, especially since twins tend to be born earlier and, therefore, are somewhat smaller than single babies, facilitating a natural delivery.

Just as with single births, it is generally difficult to determine the exact mode of delivery until labor has begun. Ms. W.'s doctor was right to warn her of the possibility of the need for a cesarean, and perhaps, although she did not refer to it in her letter, he did explain to Ms. W. his reasons for believing she would need to deliver surgically. Hopefully Ms. W.'s doctor is not one who automatically chooses to deliver multiple births by cesarean simply to avoid any potential future medical-legal complications.

There are certainly several very valid reasons the safest way to deliver a multiple birth is by cesarean. If your first baby is in the vertex position and the second baby is breech, a skillful obstetrician should be able to deliver you vaginally with no problem, since the cervix and the vagina have already been primed. Unfortunately, too many doctors feel that a cesarean is the automatic answer to a breech presentation. But, on the other hand, if you have never had a baby and your first twin is in the breech position, a cesarean section is probably called for. Surgical delivery is also indicated if both babies are in abnormal positions, such as transverse lie.

If you, like Ms. W., are expecting twins, one of the important concerns you should be sharing with your doctor at an earlier point in your pregnancy than if you were carrying one baby is the question of your delivery. On one hand, it is important that you have a realistic understanding of the potential complications you and your doctor will be facing at the moment of delivery. At the same time, I feel that you need to be sure you have chosen a doctor who is willing to do his best to keep your delivery options as open as possible.

I Have a Heart Murmur and a History of Rheumatic Fever. Can I Have a Natural Birth?

My daughter is three years old, and I've recently begun my second pregnancy. Although I am now a healthy thirty-two-year-old woman, when I was thirteen, I had the one serious illness of my life: a bout with rheumatic fever that left me with a slight heart murmur. For my first pregnancy, I used a midwife group. Because of my medical history, they arranged for me to be seen by a cardiologist. He examined me and said I was fine. My first labor was hard—and over twenty hours long—but I came through it fine, without a single complication! This time I'm using a woman obstetrician and I'm not sure if I like her. She doesn't believe the cardiologist did a thorough job examining me and now she wants me to be seen by an internist. I don't want—and can't afford—all the tests the internist says I need. What can possibly be wrong with me? I've survived twenty hours of hard labor. Isn't my doctor being too careful?

> A.R.
> Lewiston, Maine

Ms. R.'s heart murmur indicates that she has a slight heart valve problem, which, along with minor heart diseases such as a floppy or prolapsed heart valve, is a condition that needs only minimum attention. Most people with these conditions do not lead handicapped lives and only need to be treated with antibiotics before surgery or dental work in order to prevent inflammation of the damaged valves.

Many women are first aware of a heart murmur when they become pregnant, because the blood volume expands and the blood flow increases, making it easier for a physician to diagnose the murmur. If a woman knows she has a heart murmur, she should be seen by a cardiologist even before she conceives for an evaluation of the extent of the heart condition and for advice for treatment during pregnancy. If a woman suffers from a more serious heart problem, she should then be classified as a high-risk patient and be followed by a perinatologist. She should also try to arrange to be delivered at a larger hospital, where a cardiologist and all the most modern equipment will be available to assist her through a safe delivery.

In most cases, however, as long as you and your doctor are aware of your heart condition, you should be able to have a natural delivery, especially if you are in good general health and keep yourself fit throughout your pregnancy. I see no problem with Ms. R.'s pregnancy as long as she maintains her health and keeps her weight down, but she probably should be given antibiotics during and after childbirth.

My Mother Took DES. Will I Have Any Problem Giving Birth?

Since my mother took DES, she has always been very careful to be sure I was regularly examined by skillful, competent physicians. Thank God nothing has ever really been wrong! I had been warned that it might be difficult for me to get pregnant, and the doctors were right—it took a long time. Now I'm finally pregnant, but although I'm very pleased and excited, I'm also worried that I may have problems giving birth. Will I have to have a cesarean?

L.H.
Providence, Rhode Island

Women who have been exposed to DES (diethylstilbestrol) *in utero* have, without doubt, a higher incidence of vaginal and uterine abnormalities, and in some cases, DES exposure has led to cancer. It is believed, however, that if a woman has not developed any malignancy by the age of twenty-one, the chance of cancer occurring is very slim.

Ms. H. is fortunate that she did not develop cancer and that she was able to become pregnant. Several studies show that DES can damage reproductive organs and that there is a higher incidence of miscarriage among DES-exposed women. Women who know they were exposed to DES and who are having difficulty becoming pregnant should, therefore, have a hysterosalpingogram (an X ray of the uterus) to be sure that there is no abnormality of the uterus or the fallopian tubes.

Once a woman such as Ms. H. has become pregnant and suffers no miscarriage, there is no indication that she will be risking any higher incidence of having an abnormal birth. Although Ms. H. should be aware that because her cervix may have undergone some changes, she may deliver prematurely, if her pregnancy progresses normally, she should be able to experience a problem-free natural childbirth.

439

Teenage Pregnancies—Are There Greater Chances of Problems?

My daughter is only seventeen, and, unfortunately, we found out that she is pregnant too late for her to have an abortion. Although she is very much in love with the father of her baby and they are definitely going to marry, we feel that they should wait until they finish their schooling. I hope you can understand that we love our daughter very much and want to do what's best for her, but we are in a dilemma and would like your advice. What should we do to be sure our daughter has a healthy child and avoids as much physical and emotional trauma as possible?

S.C.
Jacksonville, Florida

Each year there are now more than 1 million pregnant teenagers in the United States, and more than half of these women continue their pregnancies and give birth. What most women do not realize, however, is that teenage pregnancies present an even higher risk to both mother and baby than do pregnancies in women over the age of thirty. Doctors regularly see a greater incidence of toxemia, prematurity, and morbidity in teenage pregnancies than among women who have passed their teens.

These dangerous physical complications are to a large extent caused by emotional problems. Unfortunately, teenage girls are generally so frightened when they learn that they are pregnant that they delay confiding in their parents or seeking medical attention until the first, very important months of their pregnancies have gone by. It is during the first trimester of a pregnancy that proper nutrition, supplemented by vitamins, is crucial to healthy fetal development. Far too many teenagers try to hide their pregnancies for as long as possible by not eating. This disregard of the nutritional needs of their babies leads to a much higher rate of congenital fetal malformations, and some young women have actually starved their babies *in utero*!

Of even greater concern to obstetricians managing teenage pregnancies is the fact that many teenagers abuse drugs during the early phases of their pregnancies. Some young mothers do this out of ignorance; others use drugs in an attempt to abort their babies. In any case, fear of anger and rejection by family and friends leads too many pregnant teenagers to cause irreparable harm to their unborn children.

Ms. C.'s daughter is fortunate that her parents are willing to support and stand by her during what could have been a devisive time for the whole family. I advise all parents to follow Ms. C.'s example. Being angry with your daughter once she is already pregnant will accomplish nothing other than to further jeopardize your child's emotional and physical health. Granted, having a pregnant unwed teenager is difficult, but this is a time for a family to pull together and, perhaps with the aid of counseling, make the best of the situation.

Ms. C. should be sure that her daughter is seen and followed by an obstetrician who specializes in high-risk pregnancies. At home, she and her husband need to do as much as possible to provide a supportive, relaxed environment and to reinforce the nutritional recommendations of their daughter's obstetrician. Young girls have a tendency to eat more salt and sugar than more mature women do and thus are more apt to gain too much weight as well as to be more susceptible to toxemia, preeclampsia, high blood pressure, and even seizures.

In addition to the generally poor nutritional habits of most teenagers, a pregnant teenager is also apt to overeat because she is depressed about being pregnant. Again, emotional support can help allay potential physical problems. Overeating can cause stretch marks that will remain as a lifetime reminder of a few months of not feeling loved by one's family and friends. Excessive weight gain can also lead to a baby that is too large to deliver naturally and an otherwise beautiful young woman may have to have a cesarean section that will leave an abdominal scar.

For many pregnant teenagers, their difficulties do not end once they deliver their babies. Although it sounds as if Ms. C.'s daughter's future is under control, many teenage mothers—and their families—find it impossible to care for their babies. People in this situation should remember that there are a great number of couples who are unable to have children of their own and whose lives would be made wonderful if they were able to find a baby to adopt. I have seen many happy resolutions of teenage pregnancies when the mother, loving her baby but realizing that she was not equipped emotionally or financially to do the best possible job of raising a child, gave her baby up for adoption. This can turn a less than ideal situation into one that brings joy to the adoptive couple, to the baby—and to the mother who had her child's best interests at heart.

How Do You Deliver a Baby in an Emergency?

I live more than two hours from the hospital where I plan to deliver my baby, and my husband is, of course, very concerned that we are not going to make it to the hospital in time. This is my third pregnancy, and although my first two babies were delivered very rapidly, I have too much confidence in my doctor to change. I do now know all the signs of labor, and we plan to leave for the hospital as soon as the first sign of labor starts. It is still possible, however, that we won't get to the hospital in time, and especially for my husband's sake, I would like to know what we should do in case of an emergency.

E.B.

Winfield, Kansas

Both Ms. B. and her husband are experiencing one of the most common—yet least likely to happen—concerns of all expectant couples. Should, however, Ms. B. and her husband prove to be one of the rare exceptions and need to deliver their baby before they reach the hospital, it's important for them to realize that the only qualifications anyone needs to deliver a baby under emergency conditions are common sense, patience, and a calm attitude.

If you think your contractions are coming too close to enable you to get to the hospital, have your partner check to see if he can see your baby's head. Assuming the head is visible, he should calmly reassure you while he gathers the following basic materials: clean linens (or even clean newspaper), strips of linen or clean shoelaces for tying the umbilical cord (these may be sterilized by ironing them), a pair of scissors, and, if available, an ear syringe. Ideally these items should all be sterilized, but in an emergency, do the best you can.

Your husband—or whoever will be delivering your baby—should next scrub his hands and arms thoroughly. Then a sterile or clean towel should be placed under your buttocks and another sterile sheet, to receive the baby, should be spread lower on the bed.

You should *not* attempt to speed the delivery of your baby by having your partner pull either the baby or the umbilical cord. Be patient and allow the baby to emerge as naturally as possible. When the head begins to appear in the birth canal, the deliverer should stand to the left of you and place his left hand just beneath the baby's head, cradling it but not interfering with its progress by attempting to turn it in any way. Sometimes the baby's umbilical cord will be wrapped around its neck. In this case, your partner may loosen it, but there is no need to try to untangle it until the delivery is completed.

Your next concern is your baby's possible need for assistance with his first breath, since most babies are born with blood and mucus in their nose and mouth. To clear your baby's air passages, your partner should squeeze the bulb of the ear syringe, gently insert it into the nose or mouth, release the bulb, remove the syringe, and squirt out the contents. He can begin this procedure as soon as your baby's head has completely emerged.

Once your baby is all the way out, your partner will need to tie and cut the umbilical cord. Do not try to do this until the cord has stopped pulsing and is limp and pale. Tie one strip of cloth firmly around the middle of the cord about halfway between the mother and the baby, and tie a second one three inches away from the first. Cut the cord between the two ties.

About fifteen minutes later, you should expect the placenta or afterbirth. Your partner should place the baby on your breast with its face to the nipple. Your baby's suckling will trigger a nerve reflex that will cause the uterus to contract and push out the placenta. As soon as the placenta has been expelled, begin to rub your stomach, on the top of the uterus, in small, circular movements to help it contract and stop the bleeding. Once the bleeding has stopped, it will be safe to proceed to the hospital, where your doctor can examine you.

Keep in mind that it is *most* unlikely that you will need to follow these steps. If, however, you are still very nervous about making it to the hospital in time to deliver your baby, you may wish to consider staying with friends or family nearer the hospital when your due date is approaching.

Chapter 16

You and Your Baby

The moment you've anticipated for nine months has finally arrived. You are a parent! As you hold your newborn baby in your arms, you have your first opportunity to see and touch your own baby, a miraculous creation of your own flesh and blood. You can now cuddle and adore this small, helpless individual and rejoice in your baby's first moments of life outside the womb. Now you and your baby will begin to form a very special relationship, a threefold adjustment that will continue to grow for the rest of your lives: your baby has instantly begun to adapt to the world outside the protected environment that has been its home for the past nine months, you have become a parent, and you, your partner, and your newborn have formed a family. Hopefully, the wonder and joy of these first few moments of life will always be cherished and will serve as a source of strength and commitment as you grow and develop as individuals and as a family.

Your desire, so clear at the moment of birth, to do what's best for your baby may be easier to achieve if you realize that your worries and concerns during this postpartum period are shared by most new parents. Looking ahead and considering some of these problems will ease your transition to your new role as a parent.

How Important Is My Baby's Name?

My husband has always hated his name and he is driving me crazy while we are trying to choose a name for our first baby! I'm due next month and I'm sure our child will be born nameless. Just how important is a baby's name?

W.A.
Sacramento, California

The name you choose for your baby is important, because that name will follow your child throughout his lifetime. We are all, to a certain extent, defined by our names, and studies have linked a child's name to the way a child is viewed by others and views himself. Some psychologists have even compared equally bright children in a classroom and demonstrated that children with "desirable" names are more popular with their peers and earn better grades!

There are many factors that Ms. A. and her husband should consider as they search for a name for their firstborn. Some traditions call for naming a baby after a member of the family who has passed away or for selecting a name beginning with the initial of a deceased family member. While adhering to the customs of your particular family, however, it is still possible for you to select a name that your child will be proud of now and in the future.

Use all available resources as you compile a list of potential names: books of names, names frequently appearing in the media, names of young children in your neighborhood, family names. You should be looking for a strong name that is neither out of fashion nor too trendy. Often a name characterized by classical simplicity will best serve your child throughout his lifetime. And you may wish to consider using the mother's maiden name or a last name from the mother's side of the family as a middle name for your child so that his name represents his heritage from both parents.

However you go about the careful process of choosing a name for your baby, remember that you do not necessarily have to be certain of the name prior to your baby's birth. Many parents, in fact, have several names in mind and prefer to wait until they actually see their baby before settling on a given name. I frequently deliver babies who, even though through amniocentesis their parents have known what sex they would be, do not receive their names until their parents have a chance to begin to get to know them.

Is Bonding Really Necessary?

My cousin swears that he is closer to his second daughter because he was in the delivery room during her birth and had the opportunity to hold the baby and to bond with her immediately after she was delivered. My husband and I have been impressed with his experience and we certainly have intended to make bonding an important part of our child's birth. Recently, however, a friend of mine said that she'd read of some new studies that show that bonding was really not that necessary. Whom should I believe?

J.L.
Madison, Wisconsin

The current controversy over whether bonding has any long-range effects on a baby's development tends to ignore the basic fact that by the very real process of giving birth, you and your partner and your baby have formed a permanent, life-long relationship. Bonding is one of many methods you may use to guide the quality of that very special relationship as it grows and evolves.

Establishing communication between you and your baby should ideally begin long before birth. As soon as you can feel your baby moving, you can gently massage your baby through your abdomen. Many expectant mothers have even found that they can quiet and calm a restless fetus by stroking its head, arms, or legs. Studies have shown, too, that a fetus responds *in utero* to its parents' voices and, after birth, a baby is in fact able to react discriminatingly to the sounds it has heard while in the womb. More than one of my patients has reported that a particular piece of music they played frequently while they were pregnant is now their baby's most effective lullaby.

You will generally have your first opportunity for direct visual and tactile bonding within moments of your baby's emergence into this world. Your baby will be placed on your stomach, facing you, while you and your partner reassuringly stroke and touch your child, warming it, helping to stimulate its breathing, exploring the miracle you have created as you welcome it to life. You should also begin talking to your baby right away, and many new parents' first confirmation that they *are* really and truly parents comes at the very special moment when their baby first responds to the sound of their voice.

In the 1950s, bonding was first popularized in this country by Dr. Marshall Klaus and Dr. John Kennel of Case Western Medical Center in Cleveland. Bonding became an integral part of the whole "new" childbirth philosophy, which advocated childbirth classes leading to natural childbirth and increased father participation throughout the pregnancy. This new movement also focused on the birth experience and child rearing, as well as reemphasizing the values of breast-feeding and generally encouraging prospective parents to become more aware of and educated about parenthood. These trends have certainly helped improve the quality both of available obstetrical care and of the nature of giving birth today.

However, just as mothers who are unable to have a totally natural childbirth should not feel that they have failed, parents who are unable to bond with their children at the moment of birth, either as a result of a cesarean or of some condition that requires their baby to be placed in an intensive care unit, should not be discouraged and believe that their opportunity to establish an early intimacy with their children is lost forever.

Perhaps the most positive contribution produced by the debate about the benefits of bonding is the awareness that it is perhaps the quality and quantity of love, not the timing, that matters in the long run. Ms. L. and her husband should by all means continue to plan to enjoy all aspects of their child's birth, and bonding will certainly enhance their joy as well as their love for their child. If for any reason their bonding needs to be temporarily delayed, however, they should not be discouraged. They—and their baby—will still benefit from all expressions of love whether they be before birth, immediately after delivery, or at any point in their deepening and developing relationship as a family.

As Ms. L.'s friend pointed out, several recent studies have questioned the long-term impact of immediate bonding and have shown that there appears to be no difference between children who had bonded at birth and those who had not. I still encourage all my patients to use those few precious moments after birth to get closer to their child, and I hope that their feeling of joy will stretch throughout their lives together. I believe, however, that it is not merely the bonding you first experience as a family that makes the crucial determination of the quality of your child's future. It is, rather, family love expressed openly, freely, and frequently throughout a lifetime that creates a good, healthy family unit and that will assure that your baby has the best possible chance to realize his full potential as a human being.

Is My Baby Okay?

In spite of the natural childbirth classes we attended and all the literature we read, neither my husband nor I was prepared for the first sight of our child. Even after the nurses cleaned our daughter, her head was still horribly distorted and her face was covered with pimples. Although we loved her at once because she was ours, we were very worried that our baby would be okay.

E.S.
Saratoga, New York

Remember, when a mother goes through labor, a baby goes through labor as well. A baby's initial appearance is a result of the length and nature of the labor and the ease of the baby's passage through the birth canal.

To help protect a baby's skin from the liquid environment in the uterus and to ease the baby's passage through the vagina at birth, babies are covered with a layer of soft, waxy secretions called the *vernix caseosa,* which is the white layer that often covers the baby at birth. A baby's body is also covered with soft, fine, downy *lanugo* hair, which will remain for a few weeks.

Ms. S.'s concern with the appearance of her baby's head is a very normal, but unnecessary, worry. A baby's head is very soft to enable it to pass through the birth canal. During childbirth, there is great pressure on the skull as it is forced to conform to the shape of the pelvic bones. This causes the head to be molded into an asymmetrical shape, sometimes elongated and swollen, occasionally referred to as a *banana head.* Don't panic! The shape of your baby's head at birth has nothing to do with your child's brain or

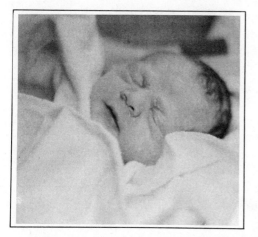

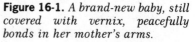
Figure 16-1. *A brand-new baby, still covered with vernix, peacefully bonds in her mother's arms.*

intelligence, and within a few days, your baby's head will be beautiful.

The small white spots—the "pimples" that alarmed Ms. S.—are called *milia* and often appear on an infant's face. They are caused by distended sebaceous cysts and, like most rashes or patches of discolored skin on a newborn, will be gone before you know it. As a matter of fact, only about 5 percent of all birthmarks will last for more than a week or so, and most of these will gradually fade with age.

Should I Breast- or Bottle-Feed My Baby?

My mother had four children and we were all fed from a bottle. We are all healthy and successful and certainly have no problems as a result of not having been breast-fed. I'm expecting my first baby shortly, and my mother is urging me to bottle-feed. She feels that breast-feeding is merely a fad and that my baby will be just as healthy and happy if I use a bottle. I respect my mother's opinions very much, but several of my friends have breast-fed their babies and have been very pleased with the experience. I also can't help believing that it will be better for my baby to be breast-fed. What should I do?

M.T.
Wilmington, Delaware

Breast-feeding is the most natural way to feed a baby and has many advantages for your baby and for you. In the first place, the early milk contains colostrum, which is especially rich in important nutrients for your baby. Your milk also contains protein substances, antibodies, that will help your baby fight bacteria. Breast-feeding also can make your care of your baby easier—and it is certainly more economical than formulas. Furthermore, the experience of breast-feeding is yet another way to give you closer contact and deeper bonding with your child.

If you elect to breast-feed your baby, you should begin either directly after or within a few hours of birth. Position yourself comfortably and rest your baby's cheek against your breast. Your baby instinctively knows how to suck, but you may need to guide your baby to your nipple, making sure his mouth is open wide enough to allow sucking on the areola and not just the nipple. Massage your breast from the outside to the center and gently press the areola to stimulate your milk secretion and its release.

You should not expect "complete" nursing at this point, but the colostrum contained in the few drops your baby will receive will be of great benefit, helping to coat his stomach, build up immunities, and help prevent any bowel and intestinal abnormalities. Your milk will actually "let down," or start flowing, within a few days of childbirth, and until this point, you should not worry that your baby will starve. Nature has cleverly arranged for babies not to need much milk in their first few days of life. Your baby might need additional fluids to hydrate his body and avoid jaundice.

During this period of adjustment to breast-feeding, it is important that you take proper care of yourself and particularly of your breasts. To prepare yourself physically for breast-feeding, it is important that you eat nutritiously, and you will probably need to increase your food intake by 500 to 600 calories a day. Be sure to drink plenty of liquids, and you should continue taking your prenatal vitamins or other vitamins recommended by your doctor. Remember, what you eat, your baby eats as well.

Massaging your breasts, particularly in the shower and after placing a hot towel over them, will help stimulate milk secretion. Knead the breast gently in a circular motion, working from the outside toward the center. You should also be sure your nipples remain clean. Avoid using soap, and be sure your nipples are dry after bathing and after nursing. You do not want your nipples to become dried and cracked. Some nursing mothers have found it helpful to massage with petroleum jelly or baby oil.

I would encourage Ms. T.—as I do all my patients—to try to breast-feed their babies. There are many books, pamphlets, and support groups, such as La Leche League, available to give you all the assistance you need. You should not become discouraged if you and your baby do not instantly mesh as a feeding team. Be patient, and above all, try to remain calm and relaxed. Just as you need to prepare yourself physically to breast-feed, your feelings and emotions must also be oriented to this new experience.

There are some new mothers who cannot breast-feed for various reasons, such as a physical complication with either the mother or the baby. There are other mothers who choose not to breast-feed because they need to return to work as soon as possible or because they simply do not want to breast-feed. Just as you should not feel that you have failed your child in some way if you are unable to have a natural childbirth, you should not be upset or unduly depressed if for any reason you bottle-feed rather than breast-feed your baby. Although I believe Ms. T. should be encouraged to try to breast-feed, ultimately it is Ms. T. who must evaluate all the information she has received and make an individual decision based on what she believes is best for her and her baby.

If you do not breast-feed your infant, you need to collaborate with your pediatrician to choose the best formula for your baby. You also need to deal with the fact that nature intended you to breast-feed, and if you do not, your breasts will become very engorged and painful. To suppress milk let-down, your doctor can prescribe a new drug, Parlodel (bromocryptine). Ice packs and support bras or breast binders may also ease your discomfort if you do not breast-feed.

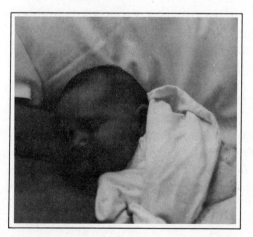

Figure 16-2. *Beth Allison Cohen, one day old, relaxes joyfully with her mother during breast-feeding.* Photo courtesy of her parents, Angela and Richard Cohen.

Is It Normal to Experience After-Birth Pain?

I felt fantastic for the first two days after I delivered my baby. Then my legs began to swell to the point that it was difficult and painful to walk. I also began to be unable to control my urine, and I thought that the pain from my hemorrhoids would kill me. Is it normal to be so miserable and in such pain after birth?

B.A.
Tampa, Florida

Immediately after childbirth, many changes take place in your body. During delivery, you lost a large amount of blood, and while your body heals itself, your body fluids will often shift. It is very common, therefore, for your legs to be swollen for a few days. Ms. A. should watch her salt intake carefully, since salt retains water in the body, and she should keep her feet elevated as much as possible. If her legs remain swollen for more than a week or so, however, she may ask her doctor for a diuretic to rid her body of the excess fluid.

Often as your baby is born—especially if your baby is large—great pressure is applied to your bladder. This, added to the fact that your bladder has been distended for a long time during your pregnancy, causes most postpartum urination problems. As soon as possible after birth, you should begin to do the *Kegel exercise,* which, by contracting the muscles around the vagina, will help your bladder regain its normal size and function. If the bladder problem continues, which happens more often if you are breast-feeding, since your estrogen level will be low, you need to be assured that the condition will resolve itself eventually. You can speed healing by continuing the Kegel exercise.

Ms. A.'s complaint of painful hemorrhoids is also a very common problem after childbirth, but she should be reassured that they will gradually become smaller and may even disappear. To obtain relief, Ms. A. should drink plenty of fluids after birth and be sure that her diet contains a lot of fiber. To help her move her bowels more easily and thus apply less pressure to her hemorrhoids, Colace or Metamucil may be helpful. Many sprays, ointments, or medicated pads may also provide relief, and while she is being sure to keep the area clean, she can gently tuck the hemorrhoid back in herself.

Sitz baths, which can also help alleviate the discomfort of hemorrhoids, are usually recommended to aid the healing of an episiotomy. Immediately after delivery, cold packs are often applied to ease any incision pain, and later, warm, moist heat will make you feel better. Your doctor will also tell you how to keep your episiotomy clean to prevent any infection, and he may prescribe antibiotics as a further precautionary measure.

Many women are also unprepared for bleeding after they give birth, but as the uterus shrinks back to size and heals itself, the lining of the uterus will be expelled. Usually you will bleed for ten to fourteen days, but you may continue for up to three or four weeks. If at any time you experience very heavy bleeding, you should contact your doctor, because this could be a sign of a postpartum hemorrhage, caused by a piece of the placenta having been left in the uterus. In this case, you may need a D&C. Other postpartum symptoms that indicate that you need to consult with your doctor are: a fever; any irritating or foul-smelling vaginal discharge; an inability to urinate or a burning sensation while urinating; a swollen, tender, red area on your leg or a hot, painful, or swollen area on your breast.

Too many women like Ms. A. are prepared by their obstetricians only up to the moment of birth and assume that they will instantly be "like new" once they have delivered. Your obstetrician and your childbirth educator should help prepare you for the discomforts you may face after delivery, and you should also be reassured by knowing that there are methods and medications, such as Motrin (ibuprofen) or Anaprox (naproxen sodium), that can give you excellent relief. Any physical problems you encounter in your postpartum period *will* go away. Be patient as you give your body time to heal itself.

How Should I Care for My Body After I Give Birth?

My girlfriend gained a lot of weight with her first pregnancy and she has never been able to lose it. Even though she is young and has a very pretty face, her body is in such bad shape that she won't even go to the beach. I don't want this to happen to me. How should I care for my body after I give birth to get back to the condition I was in before I became pregnant?

M.F.
Stockton, California

453

The most important thing Ms. F. can do to get her body in good shape after she delivers is not to gain too much weight during her pregnancy. Although she should by no means starve herself and her baby, if she gains an average amount of weight by eating properly and keeps herself in good condition throughout her pregnancy by following a doctor-approved exercise program, she will have fewer problems after she gives birth.

Often women are surprised that after delivery, they still look pregnant. Actually, you usually lose an average of only twelve pounds during delivery! You must also realize that your uterus will take several weeks to shrink back to its normal, unnoticeable size, and it may take even longer for your abdominal muscles to regain their normal elasticity. Your first postpartum look in a mirror, however, should not lead you to begin a strict diet and a rigorous program of exercise. Continue to eat nutritiously, opting for small, frequent meals and avoiding excess salt and sugar for at least six weeks after you give birth. By that time, you will probably have lost twenty to twenty-five pounds. Of course, if you are breast-feeding, you should not try to diet until your baby is weaned, but breast-feeding usually will, in spite of your need for increased calorie intake, help new mothers lose weight more rapidly.

Check with your doctor before you begin any type of exercise after childbirth. His recommendations will be based on the type of delivery you had. If you had a natural, vaginal delivery, the first exercise that will help you is the Kegel exercise, and you may usually begin within a week of giving birth. Contract your vaginal muscles just as you would if you were trying to stop the flow of urination. Hold the contraction for three seconds, then relax for three seconds. Begin with three contractions three times a day and work your way up to twenty contractions three times a day. This will retighten and restrengthen your vaginal muscles as well as improve your urination control. You can also begin simple isometric abdominal exercises at this time, working your way up to more vigorous workouts for your abdomen and buttocks approximately six weeks after delivery.

If you delivered your baby via cesarean section, you should first help speed your healing by taking increased amounts of vitamin C and zinc. Especially because you have had surgery, be sure to check with your doctor before doing any exercises. You will be back in shape much faster if your incision has a chance to heal properly first.

During your body's postpartum recovery time, you should make every effort to get as much rest as possible. Your body's metabolism is changing, your hormones are in a state of flux, and you are undergoing many major physical adaptations. If you work *with* your body by understanding what is happening to it, you will be back to normal before you know it.

Should Our Baby Be Circumcised?

My husband was born in Greece and was never circumcised. If our baby is a boy, he wants our son to look like him and he does not want our baby to be circumcised. All my friends who have little boys, however, have had their sons circumcised and they say that it is much healthier for the baby. Should our baby be circumcised?

P.D.

Newton, Massachusetts

Circumcision is an ancient custom that began over five thousand years ago in Egypt. Ceremonial rites and religious beliefs accounted for most circumcisions up through the beginning of the twentieth century. After World War II, many doctors began to encourage mothers to have their newborn sons circumcised because they felt it would promote cleanliness and thus would be healthier.

Parents gradually came to accept circumcision as a medical given, and today I even find many patients who assume that hospital policy dictates that all new baby boys be circumcised. This is not true. You must give your consent for this surgery, and it should be an *informed* consent.

There is no true medical indication for automatically performing a circumcision on a baby boy. Phimosis, a condition in which the foreskin will not retract over the head of the penis, affects 96 percent of newborn boys, but only 2 percent of these children will not have outgrown this condition by age three. Balanitis is a very painful infection of the penis from which uncircumcised males occasionally suffer. Balanitis occurs when the natural secretion under the foreskin, the smegma, becomes infected. This condition can be prevented by good penile hygiene and cured by antibiotics.

Mr. and Ms. D. should, therefore, read the available literature on circumcision. They may wish to consult Edward Wallerstein's book *Circumcision: An American Health Fallacy*. Then the D.s must decide for themselves. Although I believe that there are no

455

real medical reasons for deciding for or against circumcision, I always advise my patients to consider the psychological aspects when making a decision about circumcision. If you feel that your child is going to be growing up with other little boys who have been circumcised, you may wish to have your son circumcised so that he does not feel different from his peers. The decision is yours. There are no firm medical guidelines.

My First Baby Was Very Jaundiced After Childbirth. Will That Happen Again?

My first baby was born after a very long labor, and my doctor had to use forceps to deliver him. Three days after his birth, my son became very jaundiced. Initially the pediatrician did nothing, but then she advised putting the baby under lights. I was worried because I had read somewhere that the lights weren't safe for babies' eyes. I guess I was unnecessarily upset, because my son is now three years old and perfectly healthy. I am concerned now, however, because I am about to have my second baby and I don't want this child to be jaundiced, especially since it might mean that I will have to go home from the hospital without my baby. Will it happen again?

V.T.

Jacksonville, Florida

Actually jaundice is usually the sign of a healthy child, despite most new mothers' fears to the contrary, and 50 percent of all babies will have slight jaundice. Of those, 10 to 20 percent might need treatment. During a particularly strong or prolonged delivery, hematomas—small collections of blood—can form beneath the baby's skin. After birth, these hematomas break down and blood waste increases so much that the liver cannot metabolize it properly. The ensuing product of the breakdown of the red blood cells is called bilirubin, and when this enters the bloodstream, a yellowish pigment is carried into the mucous membranes of the skin and the whites of the eyes. If a baby can't excrete the bilirubin properly, jaundice can occur, either because the baby has been born prematurely and the liver is not fully developed or because the birth was unusually traumatic.

Babies born to women who gain very little weight during their pregnancies or babies with very low birth weights as a result of their mothers being drug addicts are rarely born with jaundice.

Ms. T. should have been relieved, to a degree, that her baby was slightly jaundiced, because that is generally the sign of a well baby.

There is little you can do during your pregnancy, other than being sure to eat nutritiously and avoiding all alcohol and drugs, to prevent your infant showing signs of jaundice within three or four days after birth. After delivery, be sure your baby has plenty of fluids. This will help dilute the bilirubin and flush it out of your baby. Should your baby be having difficulty excreting the bilirubin, your pediatrician will probably recommend ultraviolet light treatment. Ms. T. was correct to be concerned about her baby's eyes. They should be covered during ultraviolet light treatment, but apart from this precaution, this method of curing jaundice is the safest and most effective for your baby and you shouldn't be concerned if it becomes necessary.

Doctors generally won't release a baby from the hospital until the bilirubin level is under control, because several serious complications can arise. Excessively high levels of bilirubin can cause brain damage. Levels that continue to increase could also indicate other problems, such as an incompatibility between the mother's and baby's blood or perhaps some congenital malformation. That is why doctors are especially alert to jaundice in newborns, and although Ms. T. was quite understandably upset to have to leave her baby in the hospital for a few days, she should understand that her doctors were only concerned with the future health of her baby.

Postpartum Blues—Can It Be Prevented?

I was so depressed after I had my first child that I was actually medicated and under psychiatric care. My friends' and family's reaction to my problem was to try to ignore it and leave me alone. This only made me feel worse. Even my husband couldn't understand what I was going through, and it almost destroyed our marriage. I'm now pregnant again, but I never want to go through another postpartum period as horrible as my first one. Can anything prevent postpartum blues?

J.D.
Augusta, Maine

Eighty-five to ninety percent of women experience some minor mood changes after delivery, and 10 to 12 percent of new mothers like Ms. D. suffer from moderate to severe postpartum depression. It would be desirable if this syndrome could be minimized or eliminated so that women could fully enjoy their newborns. This should be possible if women try to understand the underlying causes of the blues as they learn to cope with their changing emotions.

Postpartum depression is a combination of hormonal, physical, and emotional changes that take place after a woman gives birth. Some studies have linked postpartum mood swings to hormone fluctuations; others have indicated that an abnormal level of thyroid hormones may be responsible. All these studies have presented many valid and interesting results, but no definitive, conclusive findings pinpoint specific medical explanations of how hormones affect emotions. While not ignoring the role hormones play in causing postpartum depression, more recent research has indicated that since 62 percent of all *fathers* experience symptoms of postpartum depression, the underlying causes must be a mixture of physiological and psychological factors.

Planning to avoid the misery of a postpartum period of emotional upheaval should ideally begin before conception. Today it is far easier for couples to plan to have a family at a time when they are financially secure, their careers are stabilized, their marriage is mature, and an emotional support network of family and friends has been established. Granted, it is not always possible to wait for the "right moment" to have a baby—and sometimes waiting too long to start a family results in infertility problems. Obstetricians today, however, are beginning to see fewer couples in the emotional dilemma of adding a baby to a life-style that is already fragile and fraught with seemingly insurmountable difficulties.

Assuming you are having your baby at a time when you and your partner want to have a child, you need to spend part of your pregnancy learning about and planning for the changes that will occur when you deliver your baby. First-time mothers such as Ms. D. are, indeed, more apt to experience postpartum depression. This is common partly because it is very normal to have a strong emotional reaction to a physical event that, through lack of knowledge and understanding, can be frightening.

The first thing you can do to prepare for your postpartum period is to make every effort to keep yourself in good shape throughout your pregnancy. Labor is hard physical work, and you will be better able to handle labor—and to recuperate afterward—if you are in prime physical condition.

The most effective treatment for a woman who has postpartum

depression is emotional support. She might have difficulty sleeping, experience some discomfort in the initial adjustment to breast-feeding, or be generally worried about the child. She may realize that the postpartum period contains some problems as well as joys. Thus she needs support at this particular time from her husband, her doctor, the nurses, and everyone around her. Often, after she has given birth, a woman will find that she is left alone too much of the time. She feels abandoned. Furthermore, she realizes that her needs will now become second to those of her child—she must now be the caregiver rather than the care receiver. She has pain from her stitches, feels tired and worn down and that she will receive no help. This is the time when a mother most needs support and attention.

If you experience some depression within the first few days after your baby's birth, try to fight back! Resume taking two prenatal vitamins daily; increase your intake of vitamin B complex to 100 mg daily and of B_6 to 500 mg daily. Drink plenty of fluids, take showers several times a day, wash your hair, change your clothing, take a walk, get out of the house. Try to work yourself out of the depression.

Should this holistic approach not be sufficient, see your doctor for medical treatment. Sometimes therapeutic prescriptions are necessary; other times, antidepressants are needed. Quite often, the best treatment will be natural progesterone suppositories or injections to help balance your hormones and make you feel better.

Before birth, your partner plays an important part as well. Together you should realistically analyze your current life-style and discuss your priorities. This is not a time to be polite about what is and is not important to your happiness as a human being. You may not resolve any long-standing differences, but hopefully you will understand each other better. You should also very specifically determine what chores are essential to the smooth running of your household and how these tasks will be completed once your baby arrives and you and your partner are no longer in total control of your time.

These prebirth conversations are not cure-alls, but most couples, particularly if their lives have settled into routines, find them helpful preparation for parenting. For example, one of my patients told me that on Saturday mornings, her husband usually did any necessary yard work while she did the grocery shopping. After their baby arrived, she found it very difficult to get to the store with the baby, and to maneuver all the baby's equipment into the car, but she really enjoyed being outside working in the garden while her baby napped in his carriage. Her husband, once he made the trip to the store a few times and was no longer unsure where the various foods were, actually enjoyed the challenge of efficiently and economically shopping for groceries. He even became more involved with planning and preparing meals and developing his previously hidden talent as a chef!

Yet another way for expectant first-time parents to get an idea of the impact a baby will have on their lives is to borrow a baby. Most couples have friends or family with children who would love a day's or, for the adventuresome, a weekend's vacation from their children. There may be no better way to sample the joyful disruption a baby brings to a household!

Planning for your postpartum period should also include establishing a very specific support system with backups. Do not hesitate to alert family and friends that you will be needing help. You will find that this assistance will be more forthcoming if you ask for particular services. For example, don't just tell your mother-in-law that you'll be needing her to help you when you come home from the hospital. Ask her to plan to bring her favorite casserole for dinner on that first night home. Rather than encouraging your best friend to drop in to see your new baby, ask her to come watch the baby while you take a shower or a nap. By being specific, you will get the help you truly need, and the people helping you will feel that they have been of real assistance to you.

Thus, by having a good idea of what you may expect in the first few months after your baby is born and by planning ahead to meet most contingencies, Ms. D. will, like all new mothers, find herself far better able to cope with the real physical changes that will be taking place in her body. Knowing what to expect and preparing flexible solutions to all foreseeable at-home complications will enable most new parents to grow with their babies and to achieve the most delight from this irreplaceable period of adjustment.

What Is the Father's Role in the Postpartum Period?

When my wife became pregnant with our first child, I eagerly participated in what I felt was "our" pregnancy. Throughout the nine months, the labor, and the delivery, we were a team. Then we brought our baby home and I was definitely the odd man out. I had to return to work, and my wife was at home with the baby. Each night when I came home from the office, I felt that during the day their relationship had become even stronger and I was more isolated. I'll admit that I'm no expert diaper changer, and since my wife was breast-feeding, I certainly couldn't assume any mealtime responsibilities, but I'm really sad—and angry—that our "family" no longer seems to include me in any important way.

E.W.
Swarthmore, Pennsylvania

Mr. W.'s situation is, unfortunately, that of too many new fathers. In the past, fathers' roles were very traditional for the most part, and men didn't expect to be an integral part of the childbearing and child-rearing process. Today, however, with the increased emphasis on partner participation in pregnancy and childbirth, men have every right to anticipate an expanded role in all aspects of parenting. Women who deny their partners inclusion in the responsibilities of baby and child care not only restrict their enjoyment of the rewards of raising a child but also unnecessarily complicate their own lives as mothers. In spite of the advances of the women's movement, it often seems that even the most liberated female, once she has a newborn baby in her arms, tends to revert to the most traditional interpretations of the roles of a father and mother.

In all fairness, much of the blame for this situation must be placed on the fathers. They need to foster some of the assertiveness their wives have developed and not sit back and wait for their partners to ask for help. Even if, because of the demands of work, a father's time at home is limited, he should make the most of that time with his baby and insist that he be included in caring for his child. Most apparent possessiveness on the part of a new mother is a result of fear, sometimes subconsciously, that harm will come to her child. Once a father makes it clear that he can—and wants to—learn to care for a baby, most women will relax and enjoy having a willing extra pair of hands to help.

It is at this point of mutual participation in the often overwhelming job of caring for and raising a child that a true family can begin to develop. Shared responsibilities produce shared joys and strengthen the bonds of love that create a healthy and happy family unit.

Motherhood vs. Career

I have always enjoyed going to work and I love my career. I didn't marry until I was in my early thirties and I had never seriously considered the possibility of having children. That was something other women did! Having a baby was, however, important to my husband, and after a few years of marriage, we conceived our first child. I worked up to the day I went into labor and had every intention of returning to work when our baby was six weeks old. As that day approached, though, I realized I was so happy in my new role as a mother and felt so fulfilled caring for our baby that I did not want to go back to work. My firm is pressuring me to know when I will be back, and I'm almost at the point of deciding to give up my career. What should I do?

C.S.
Summit, New Jersey

I hope that within the next ten years, very few women—and men—will be facing Ms. S.'s dilemma. The family unit has evolved dramatically during the past two decades, but for the future prosperity of the next generation, much change remains to be made. Ms. S.'s letter brings to light several problems confronting today's parents, problems that are often incomprehensible to parents of earlier generations.

In the first place, in order to survive in today's economy, both partners usually need to work outside the home. The attitudes and dictates of our society, however, have been slow to give credence to that fact. Yes, it is important that women have been encouraged to pursue careers, but far more often than not, it is an absolute economic necessity for women to work.

At the same time, while recognizing the value of father participation in the childbirth and child rearing experience, we still hear predominantly the question of how a *woman* can successfully juggle motherhood and a career. The true issue needs to become how *parents* can manage to do the best possible for their children, given the economic demands and limitations of today's society.

When faced with a decision such as Ms. S.'s, couples need to be very open and honest with each other as they forthrightly discuss their financial needs, their career goals, and their expectations of family life. Couples need to join the growing movement that shuns labels such as wrong and right applied either to pursuing a career or remaining at home to care for a child. The family unit in our society is in a state of flux. There can no longer be set rules that determine who works and who stays home. It is perhaps in this state of undefined roles that the next generation's most valuable role model of family life will be found. I believe that the flexibility required by the socioeconomic demands of today's society will actually provide parents and their children with previously unequaled opportunities to develop more of their potential and to lead fuller and more fulfilling lives.

Ms. S. and her partner should be encouraged, therefore, to make the decision that best suits them at this point in their lives. They should by no means treat whichever decision they make as irrevocable, however. Perhaps what is best for them now financially and emotionally is for Ms. S. to stay home with their baby. On the other hand, if Ms. S. needs to go back to work for economic reasons, she should not feel guilty. It is the quality, not the quantity of care she gives her child that matters. In a few years, when their child is older, both parents may wish to work. Even later, perhaps Mr. S. will wish to retire early, or to pursue a second career. Only the S.es can make these decisions. It is our hope that similar decisions will become easier for other new parents as businesses realize that the nature of the workplace must evolve and adapt to societal needs.

When Can I Resume Sex After Childbirth?

I am about to deliver my first baby and I was just talking to a friend of mine whose daughter is now one year old. She told me to be sure that I don't have an episiotomy. She had one and said that in addition to the pain right after delivery, she couldn't have sex for a long time after her baby was born. When she was finally allowed to resume sexual relations, it was still very painful, and even today she no longer enjoys sex the way she did before her baby was born. If I do have to have an episiotomy, when will I be able to resume having sex and must it hurt?

L.V.

New Orleans, Louisiana

Most doctors advise their patients to refrain from sexual intercourse for four to six weeks after childbirth. A woman's body needs time to heal properly so that sex will be safe and enjoyable. If a woman has had any form of surgical intervention during her delivery, whether it be an episiotomy or a cesarean section, her incision will need additional time to heal. Although a couple may find this period of abstinence frustrating, intercourse too soon after childbirth can result in ripped stitches or injury to the delicate vaginal area. Refraining from intercourse does not, however, rule out other reassuring expressions of love such as cuddling and hugging.

Many women like Ms. V.'s friend complain that sex after childbirth is initially both painful and not enjoyable. If both partners understand and accept the emotional and physical changes they and their bodies are experiencing, however, they will usually discover that patience is the fastest way to reestablish a mutually satisfying sex life.

Once it is medically safe to resume intercourse, couples should start slowly and gently. Remember that your levels of response are going to be different than they were before childbirth. A woman's hormones may also still be adjusting, especially if she is breast-feeding, and this will affect her sexual response as well as make the vaginal area drier, since the female hormone estrogen will be very low. Using K-Y jelly or Vasoline as a lubricant may be helpful to you the first few times you have intercourse. Many women find it difficult to enjoy sex after childbirth because they are afraid that penetration will cause pain. If this is your case, you may wish to use any of the number of positions that allow the woman to control the entrance of the penis. Other women worry that their partners will not find sex appealing because the vaginal muscles have stretched. Again, the Kegel exercise can restore elasticity and tightness to the vagina within weeks of delivery.

Please be assured that the pleasure of sexual relations after childbirth, both for a woman as well as for a man, will be as great or maybe even greater than before pregnancy. Although some women, particularly breast-feeding mothers, state that they don't have the same sexual drive, especially during the first few post-partum months, in time, sexual fulfillment and enjoyment will be as pleasurable as before birth.

Which Form of Birth Control Should I Use After I Have My Baby?

I am expecting my second child in a few months, and my husband and I do not plan to have any more children. I had pretty well decided that I would have my tubes tied while I was in the hospital. My neighbor, however, told me that her doctor said that isn't a good idea. After a tubal ligation, women often have irregular bleeding patterns and some even develop premenstrual syndrome. Which form of birth control should I use after I have my baby?

L.J.

Concord, New Hampshire

In the past, tubal ligation and tubal sterilization were popular forms of contraception. Many women and their doctors still favor this form of birth control today, particularly if a woman has just delivered her second or third child by cesarean section.

Recent studies, however, confirm the advice Ms. J.'s friend gave her. There are increased indications that after a tubal ligation, the blood supply to the ovaries is decreased. This can lead to severe menstrual irregularities, including PMS, and has prompted many physicians to consider the alternatives to tubal ligation more seriously. Furthermore, as a reflection of today's changing lifestyles, women in their thirties are no longer as certain that they want to be permanently finished with childbearing, and thus tubal ligations are beginning to be less in demand.

Unless there are severe medical problems that would make it safer for a woman not to bear any more children, I recommend that my patients explore all other forms of contraception before requesting tubal ligation. Certainly now that only a few intrauterine devices are available in this country, there are fewer methods to choose from, but there are still plenty of safer—and less permanent—choices than having a tubal ligation. I hope that within a few years IUDs will be even more improved; but in the meantime, I believe women should select a form of birth control that will neither alter their current state of health nor limit their future reproductive options.

As Ms. J. and her partner begin to resume their sexual relationship, I recommend that they use a condom while they readjust to each other and while the vagina has the chance to heal completely. Later, if she is breast-feeding, Ms. J. may wish to try a diaphragm, sponge, or contraceptive jellies. If she is not breast-feeding, she may elect to try one of the new low-estrogen-containing oral contraceptives. Recent studies have indicated that these new birth control pills are much safer than the old ones. There are fewer cardiovascular side effects and, indeed, even apparent benefits, such as reduced menstrual cramps, less endometriosis, and decreased incidence of both ovarian and breast cancer.

Ms. J. should discuss her particular needs and preferences with her doctor so that together they can select the most effective form of birth control for Ms. J. and her husband. If Ms. J. is certain that she and her husband will never want to have another child, however, I would recommend that they consider a vasectomy rather than a tubal ligation.

When Should We Have Our Next Baby?

Our first child is now two years old, and my husband and I definitely want another baby. My mother keeps pushing me to have one now, but I've finally settled into a job I really like, and it's not a good time for my husband to make a career change. My girlfriends say that it's better to space your children three or four years apart, so that each child has the chance to develop his own personality—and also so that you don't end up with more than one child in college at a time. I don't know who's right. When should we have our next baby?

M.F.
Atlanta, Georgia

Few decisions can be more personal than how to space your own family, and although so-called experts can point out the pros and cons of your options, only you can make the final choice. The only absolute medical guideline to follow is that of not becoming pregnant too soon after childbirth. Even a strong, healthy woman who has a completely uneventful pregnancy and an easy natural delivery needs at least a year to rebuild and renourish her body before being in proper condition to conceive a child.

Some people prefer a tightly spaced family with only two years between children. Indeed, many parents who are older when they have their first baby feel they don't have time to wait. There are advantages to having your children close together. Siblings generally enjoy each other's companionship and, especially if resumption of a career is important, diapering days are spread over a shorter period of time.

Longer periods of time between children can also be beneficial. Studies have shown that when children are older at the birth of their brothers or sisters, they can better handle any feelings of competitiveness and there tends to be less sibling rivalry. Other proponents of spacing children over greater periods of time claim that parents can better devote themselves to their children's development if they can concentrate on one child at a time.

No matter what Ms. F. and her husband choose to do, their decisions should be based on their own very unique and individual needs and preferences. They should, however, be cautioned that especially when it comes to planning babies, often the best intentioned and most carefully thought out plans are useless. I have never located a study that indicated how many couples actually conceived when they planned to, but I believe that conception remains one of nature's greatest wonders simply because it remains so often beyond human control.

WHERE TO GO FOR HELP

I hope this book has aided you by answering some of the questions you have about your pregnancy and birth. My goal is to guide you through your childbirth experience with joy by demystifying your perception of creating a child and by calming your concerns as you and your partner prepare yourselves for becoming the parents of the next—better, healthier, and happier—generation.

The previous decade has seen many positive changes in childbirth philosophy and practice. With your increased participation, the field of obstetrics will continue to grow in response to your evolving needs as parents and as individuals. It is also my hope that in the near future, everyone who wants to be a parent will be able to. Daily, new advances are made in the field of infertility, and I continually urge couples who are having difficulty conceiving not to give up. Keep apprised of new methods and techniques, and should it appear at least temporarily impossible for you to conceive, be open to the possibility of adoption. There are many children who need a lifetime of your love to grow and develop.

If you have questions that have not been answered by this book, you may wish to consult the following:

Action for Child Transportation Safety (ACTS)
Child Restraint Committee
P.O. Box 266
Bothell, Washington   98011
An organization devoted to educating parents about child safety in automobiles. Send a self-addressed stamped legal-size envelope and money for the following: *Guide to Dynamically Tested Safety Devices, New and Used;* 15¢. *This Is the Way Baby Rides,* a pamphlet telling what you should know before you buy an infant car seat and listing models found satisfactory in simulated crash tests;

25¢. *Don't Risk Your Child's Life,* a pamphlet telling what you should know before you buy an auto restraint for any child weighing less than 40 pounds, plus satisfactory models; 35¢.

American National Red Cross
17th & D Streets
Washington, D.C.   20006
By addressing inquiries to the Nursing Department, parents can find out about the Red Cross baby care and parent classes in their locality.

American Optometric Association
243 North Lindbergh Boulevard
St. Louis, Missouri   63141
By sending a stamped self-addressed envelope, this organization will send you information on children's vision care and the importance of eye examinations.

American Society for Psychoprophylaxis in Obstetrics (ASPO)
1411 K Street Northwest
Washington, D.C.   20005
This organization sponsors classes in the Lamaze psychoprophylaxis method of prepared childbirth for expectant parents.

Childbirth Without Pain Education League, Inc.
3940 Eleventh Street
Riverside, California   92501
A national organization that teaches the Pavlov-Lamaze method of prepared childbirth. Information available by writing.

C/Sec, Inc.
Cesarean/Support, Education and Concern
15 Maynard Road
Dedham, Massachusetts   02026
This group offers emotional and physical support plus education to parents who have had cesarean births, as well as addresses of cesarean support groups in other states.

International Childbirth Education Association (ICEA)
P.O. Box 20852
Milwaukee, Wisconsin   53220
This organization is dedicated to family-centered maternity care. Membership of both parents and professionals works toward improving the outcome of maternity and infant cre.

La Leche League
9616 Minneapolis Avenue
Franklin Park, Illinois   60131
Everything you want to know about breast-feeding, this organization will tell you. They offer encouragement to new breast-feeding
mothers and a bimonthly newsletter of shared experiences in
child rearing.

Maternity Center Association
48 East 92nd Street
New York, New York   10028
Information on maternity care and prenatal classes is available at
the Center. Total family-centered maternity care for nonrisk deliveries is offered by the Center's midwifery service. Deliveries are in
a homelike atmosphere, and all members of the family may share
in the experience.

National Association for the Advancement of Leboyer's Birth
Without Violence, Inc.
P.O. Box 248455
University of Miami Branch
Coral Gables, Florida   33124
For those parents interested in the Leboyer method of gentle
birthing, write for more information.

National Association for Retarded Citizens
2709 Ave E. East
P.O. Box 6109
Arlington, Texas   76011
An organization devoted to helping parents of retarded citizens
share their special problems and solutions, and raising funds for
better facilities, research, and treatment of the retarded.

National Association of Parents and Professionals for Safe Alternatives in Childbirth (NAPSAC)
P.O. Box 267
Marble Hill, Missouri   63764
This organization is dedicated to assisting parents in finding alternatives in childbirth, both within and outside the hospital. They
have publications with information on childbirth alternatives and
also a directory that can refer parents to appropriate alternative
birth services.

The National Foundation–March of Dimes
1275 Mamaroneck Avenue
White Plains, NY   10605
This organization is devoted to preventing and curing birth defects. They have a fairly extensive public education program, which you can take advantage of by writing for booklets about birth defects and prenatal care.

National Organization of Mothers of Twins Club
5402 Amberwood Lane
Rockville, Maryland   20853
Through this organization, you can learn of local chapters that will put you in touch with other mothers of twins, triplets, etc., with whom you can share problems and solutions.

National Sudden Infant Death Syndrome Foundation
310 S. Michigan Avenue
Chicago, Illinois   60604
Offers solace to parents and up-to-date information on this mysterious killer.

Parents Without Partners
7901 Woodmont Avenue
Bethesda, Maryland   20014
This organization describes itself as "directed toward raising children in a single parent home."

Read Natural Childbirth Foundation, Inc.
1300 S. Eliseo Drive, Suite 102
Greenbrae, California   94904
This group promotes the philosophies of Grantley Dick-Read, M.D., through childbirth classes for expectant parents and offers assistance to anyone wanting to become familiar with the Dick-Read teachings.

U.S. Consumer Product Safety Commission
Washington, D.C.   20207
1-800-492-2937
By calling the toll-free number any time, you can get information on safety standards for cribs, toys, and other accessories for children. Or contact the area office in the closest major city.

Index